discover
THAILAND

CHINA WILLIAMS
MARK BEALES, TIM BEWER, CATHERINE BODRY,
AUSTIN BUSH, BRANDON PRESSER

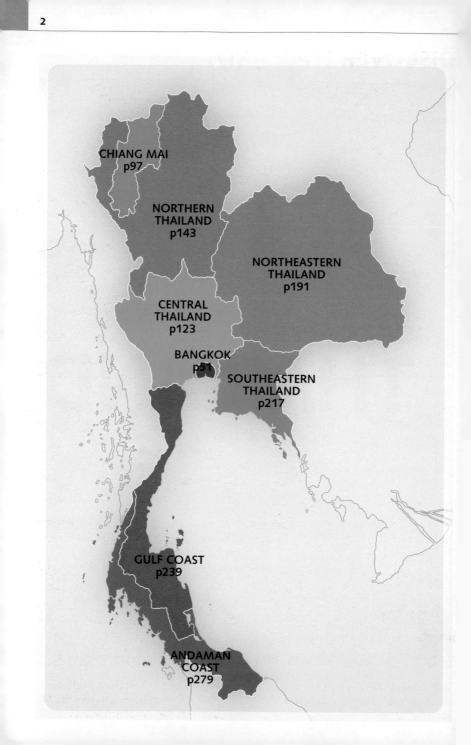

CHIANG MAI
p97

NORTHERN
THAILAND
p143

NORTHEASTERN
THAILAND
p191

CENTRAL
THAILAND
p123

BANGKOK
p51

SOUTHEASTERN
THAILAND
p217

GULF COAST
p239

ANDAMAN
COAST
p279

DISCOVER THAILAND

Bangkok (p51) Thailand's hip and happening city has it all: temples, super-sized shopping and 24/7 entertainment.

Chiang Mai (p97) Provides cultural pursuits, mountain escapes and historic temples.

Central Thailand (p123) With ancient ruins, WWII sites and the rugged western frontier.

Northern Thailand (p143) Historic cities, isolated mountain towns, hill-tribe villages and partying Pai.

Northeastern Thailand (p191) Peppered with Khmer ruins, old-folk ways and sleepy Mekong towns.

Southeastern Thailand (p217) Fishing towns and jungle islands provide weekend getaways from Bangkok.

Gulf Coast (p239) Beaches of all shapes and sizes await, from matronly Hua Hin to youthful Ko Tao.

Andaman Coast (p279) Dramatically punctuated with limestone mountains and cliffs, and home to top-tier beach resorts.

⬊CONTENTS

CHIANG MAI
p97

NORTHERN
THAILAND
p143

NORTHEASTERN
THAILAND
p191

CENTRAL
THAILAND
p123

BANGKOK
p51

SOUTHEASTERN
THAILAND
p217

GULF COAST
p239

ANDAMAN
COAST
p279

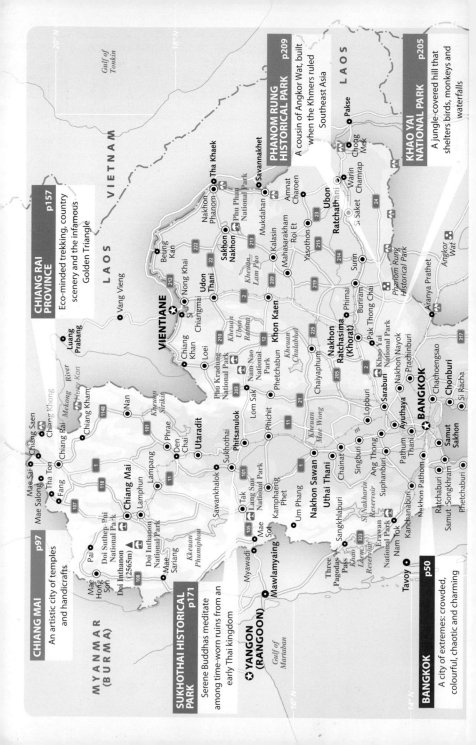

CHIANG MAI p97

An artistic city of temples and handicrafts

CHIANG RAI PROVINCE p157

Eco-minded trekking, country scenery and the infamous Golden Triangle

PHANOM RUNG HISTORICAL PARK p209

A cousin of Angkor Wat, built when the Khmers ruled Southeast Asia

SUKHOTHAI HISTORICAL PARK p171

Serene Buddhas meditate among time-worn ruins from an early Thai kingdom

KHAO YAI NATIONAL PARK p205

A jungle-covered hill that shelters birds, monkeys and waterfalls

BANGKOK p50

A city of extremes: crowded, colourful, chaotic and charming

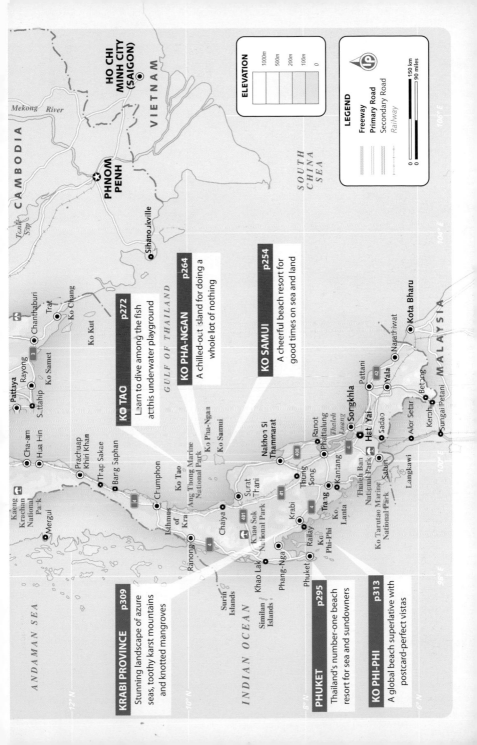

⬊ THIS IS THAILAND

Thailand is lucky. It has the looks, the temperament and the attractions to capture the world's imagination for an exotic escape. It is mysterious and confounding but approachable and inviting. Hospitality is a genuine art, crafted by a culture that takes pride in putting people at ease.

The tranquil southern coastlines, with their picturesque interplay of sand and sea, massage away modern worries like only tropical isles can. And the culture that has been napping under these coconut trees for generations has a knack for fun.

The charismatic culture pulls visitors away from the islands and the exciting city of Bangkok to ancient kingdoms where surviving Buddha figures meditate serenely amongst the wreckage of war and gravity. The trail leads to Chiang Mai, a historic city at the threshold of the northern mountains that fuses Thailand to its ancestral roots in southern China. The tropics become tempered among the mountains where cool-weather flowers flourish and where nationless minority hill tribes eke out a subsistence existence. The interplay of border cultures, the quiet misty mornings and the daily

routines compel visitors to trundle through Chiang Rai and Mae Hong Son Provinces absorbing the landscape through a bus window.

In the northeastern corner of the country, the landscape extends to the horizon in a checkerboard of rice fields. This is Thailand's most traditional region, best viewed during a local festival when the folk beliefs are on full display. The Khmer empire built an ancient highway of remarkable monuments through this rural region, leaving the local people to credit some sort of supernatural force. The Mekong River carves out another thoroughfare that is dotted by riverside towns mimicking its languid character.

'The southern coastlines massage away modern worries like only tropical isles can'

In every corner of the kingdom, Thais concoct a flavourful feast from simple ingredients and demonstrate daily examples of how to be at peace with the world around them. Those who come only for themselves leave with memories of gratitude and generosity imparted by their hosts.

↘ THAILAND'S TOP 25 EXPERIENCES

THAILAND'S TOP 25 EXPERIENCES

1

↘ CHATUCHAK WEEKEND MARKET, BANGKOK

There are markets and then there is Chatuchak Weekend Market (p92), the market that all markets around the world are measured by. You'll find things here that you didn't know you wanted or needed.

Mark Broadhead, Lonely Planet Staff

⬈ DOI SUTHEP, CHIANG MAI

2

We rented a motorbike one day and rode up the mountain to the temple of Wat Phra That Doi Suthep (p112) in Chiang Mai. Joining the chaos of vehicles on the moat road was exhilarating, and experiencing the temple and the views was rewarding.

Robyn Loughnane,
Lonely Planet Staff

3

⬊ NORTHERN THAILAND

One of the best motorcycle rides I've ever taken was the Chiang Mai–Mae Hong Son loop. It's green and lush with amazing vistas. Along the way I stopped in artsy Pai (p184), culturally diverse Mae Hong Son (p180) and sleepy Mae Sariang (p188).

Clay Adler, Traveller, Nepal

1 GREG ELMS; 2 FELIX HUG; 3 AUSTIN BUSH

1 Flower maker, Chatuchak Weekend Market (p92); 2 Dancers at Wat Phra That Doi Suthep (p112), Chiang Mai; 3 Rice fields, Mae Hong Son Province (p180)

⬆ KO PHI-PHI

Rounding the corner of Ko Phi-Phi (p313) on a long-tail boat and gulping in the view of jewel-hued seas, dramatic cliffs and white-sand beaches will take your breath away. There are no cars, no high-rises – but sadly you've got to share it with others.

China Williams, Lonely Planet Author, USA

4

5

⬆ KO PHA-NGAN

Beyond the fracas of its full-moon parties, the island of Ko Pha-Ngan (p264) offers a lot more than just glowsticks and house music. For some serious hush time, hop on a long-tail boat to one of the isolated beaches where bamboo 'n' thatch takes the place of drum 'n' bass.

Rafael Wlodarski, Lonely Planet Author, UK

↘ PHUKET

In **Phuket** (p295) we rented a motorbike and went sightseeing up the coast where it started raining so hard we had to stay overnight. In the morning we returned home and found that the only people out were the prostitutes going home and the monks collecting food charity.

Pablo Movilla Gil, Traveller, Spain

6

4 FELIX HUG; 5 KRAIG LIEB; 6 AUSTIN BUSH

4 Snorkelling (p314), Ko Phi-Phi; 5 Hat Khuat (Bottle Beach; p267), Ko Pha-Ngan; 6 Hat Kamala (p301), Phuket

⬎ KO TAO

Ko Tao (p272) and its coral gardens are famous, but if a scuba tank makes you nervous, go snorkelling in the shallow bays filled with schools of fish that swim in sync so as to look more threatening to predators. Just remember to sunscreen the back of your legs!

China Williams, Lonely Planet Author, USA

7

8

⚓ KO SAMUI

The travellers' grapevine thinks that Ko Samui (p254) is too commercial, but those who take the time will find it just right. There are still huts on the beach, great Thai markets and tangible southern Thai culture, plus yoga by the sea.

⚓ KHAO YAI NATIONAL PARK

9

Khao Yai (p205) may disappoint as a peak, but cavorting monkeys, technicoloured critters, tangled trails, roaring waterfalls and a surround-sound wildlife soundtrack make for a postcard-worthy time. Reports of bloodsucking leeches are true – wear hiking boots and long socks.

Stacey McCarthy, Traveller, USA

7 4CORNERS / TAYLOR RICHARD; 8 AUSTIN BUSH; 9 ANDERS BLOMQVIST

7 Ko Tao (p272); 8 Rocky Resort (p258), Ko Samui; 9 Gibbon, Khao Yai National Park (p205)

THAILAND'S TOP 25 EXPERIENCES

10 ↘ PHANOM RUNG HISTORICAL PARK

It is a dusty ride past rice paddies and sauntering sarong-clad farmers to the far-flung Angkor monument of **Phanom Rung** (p209). Sitting on a hill, this 1000-year-old relic surveys the countryside with imperial authority.

↘ OUTDOOR ACTIVITIES, CHIANG MAI   11

Rafting down a fast-flowing river outside of **Chiang Mai** (p112) was a highlight. The rafts consisted of long bamboo poles tied together. What started out as a leisurely paddle soon became an exhilarating water chute. I caught myself loudly whooping with joy as the adrenalin rush hit me full in the face. Unforgettable!

Paul Starkey, Traveller, UK

↘ AYUTHAYA

Evening boats circum-navigate the canals and rivers that make Ayuthaya (p134) a land-locked island. The major attractions are the riverside temples, but the show-stealers are examples of ordinary life: wooden shacks with satellite dishes, and kids splashing in the water. The boats unload at the evening market, where everyone comes for dinner.

↘ SONGKRAN

Chiang Mai during the Songkran Festival (p46) is the place to be. The whole city is alive and involved in celebrating the new year. Young and old, locals and visitors, everyone gets into the spirit, turning the city into one big and very good-natured water fight. It's definitely not to be missed.

Amanda Phipps, Traveller, China

10 ANDERS BLOMQVIST; 11 JOHN BORTHWICK; 12 NICHOLAS REUSS; 13 BERNARD NAPTHINE

10 Stone relief, Phanom Rung Historical Park (p209); 11 Rafting, Chiang Mai (p112); 12 Ayuthaya (p134); 13 Songkran Festival (p46)

THAILAND'S TOP 25 EXPERIENCES

14

↘ MAE SALONG

An ethnic Chinese village, Mae Salong (p162) feels a lot further away than a bus ride from Chiang Rai. Getting there is an adventure in transport and for some reason waiting and going are always fun in Thailand.

↘ SUKHOTHAI HISTORICAL PARK

Take the time to detour off the Bangkok–Chiang Mai trail to **Sukhothai Historical Park** (p171). The old ruins are rarely crowded and nicely shaded so you can cycle around all day marvelling at the brick temples in various states of decay and work on that perfect shot of a meditating Buddha figure.

15

14 MARGIE POLITZER; 15 MARK KIRBY

14 Akha woman and child, Mae Salong (p162); 15 Sukhothai Historical Park (p171)

⬎ ERAWAN NATIONAL PARK, KANCHANABURI

The waterfall in **Erawan National Park** (p142) involved walking for about an hour up a never-ending cascade past beautiful limestone pools; watching monkeys leap from trees into the water; and getting nibbled by the large fish that swam in the milky-blue pools.

Bruce Evans, Traveller, Australia

16

17

⬐ AO PHANG-NGA

Canoeing in Ao Phang-Nga (p298) and experiencing the caves is one of the most fascinating things to do in Phuket. Incredibly breathtaking.

Holly Casswell, Traveller, Australia

⬐ UBON RATCHATHANI

Ubon Ratchathani (p211) is a delight to visit. Beautiful hand-woven silk and cotton fabrics, friendly, fun-loving people and colourful festivals are some of the attractions. I adored the sweet sticky rice cooked in bamboo –sometimes still warm – sold by street sellers.

Elaine Morgan, Traveller, Australia

18

16 GARY DUBLANKO / ALAMY; 17 AUSTIN BUSH; 18 ROMAN SOUMAR

16 Waterfall, Erawan National Park (p142); 17 Sea kayaks, Ao Phang-Nga (p298); 18 Sunrise on Mae Nam Mun, Ubon Ratchathani (p211)

⬊ RAILAY

Railay (p311) is a rock-climber's paradise. Now I'm not a rock climber but the limestone cliffs, thick jungles and beautiful beaches did it for me. I loved kicking back on oversized cushions, eating spicy fish and sipping Beer Chang while watching those hasty rock climbers scaling immense heights.

Jessica Racklyeft, Lonely Planet Staff

19

20

↘ KO LANTA

Living in a wooden hut on the beach, listening to the waves at night, seeing the sun set over a beautiful beach. Watching the school children piled three or four on a moped whizzing to school. The fishermen browned by long hours at sea. I love this way of life on **Ko Lanta** (p316).

Nadine Jones, Traveller, UK

19 JERRY ALEXANDER; 20 JOHN ELK III

19 Rock climbers, Railay (p312); 20 Beach soccer, Ko Lanta (p316)

21

⬊ MAE HONG SON

Most visitors return south after a stay in Chiang Mai or Chiang Rai, but if you're going between November and January, a stop at Mae Hong Son (p180) is a must. Perched on the hills north of Chiang Mai, this province – lost in the clouds – is the stuff dreams are made of.

oranutt, lonelyplanet.com member

⬊ ELEPHANT NATURE PARK

22

Feed elephants, bathe elephants and walk beside elephants at the Elephant Nature Park (p113). Incomparable experiences and photo opportunities aside, whether visitor or volunteer, your support will help save the lives of elephants abused or decommissioned from logging and tourism industries. It's an experience that, like the elephants, you won't forget.

Debra Herrmann,
Lonely Planet Staff

⬃ OVERNIGHT SLEEPER TRAIN

23

The overnight train (p390) between Bangkok and Chiang Mai is an experience. Tiny aisles are lined with bunks separated by blue curtains that flap in the breeze. A Thai woman patters between carriages, selling orange juice and Beer Chang. Stations with pink flowers and dogs sleeping on the platform zip by, hour after hour.

Poppy Helm, Traveller, UK

24

⬃ ROAD-TRIP THAI-STYLE

My siblings and I ended up on a wacky road trip with a Thai friend. For three days, we drove to various districts picking up family members who all crammed into one car. We never knew where we were going and gave up asking. We finally got to Nong Khai (p214) for the fireball festival (p216).

Deirdre O'Shea, Traveller, USA

21 AUSTIN BUSH; 22 FELIX HUG; 23 DAVID GEE 3 / ALAMY; 24 BILL WASSMAN

21 Wat Phra That Doi Kong Mu (p181), Mae Hong Son; 22 Elephants (p112), Chiang Mai; 23 Overnight sleeper train (p390); 24 Monks, Nong Khai (p214)

⬙ RUSH-HOUR IN BANGKOK

During rush hour in **Bangkok** (p50), I needed to get across town and only the youngest motorcycle taxi driver with the smallest bike would take me. I could hardly fit, and the other drivers cheered as we took off. We tore through traffic, and near misses elicited only half smiles from my driver.

Matthew Baum, Traveller, USA

25

GREG ELMS

Traffic congestion, Bangkok

⤵ THAILAND'S TOP ITINERARIES

JET-SETTERS' GAME PLAN

FIVE DAYS BANGKOK TO CHIANG MAI

Thailand makes an easy 'pop-in' for anyone passing through the eastern half of the globe. Touch down in Bangkok, day-trip to Ayuthaya and jet off to Chiang Mai.

❶ BANGKOK

Introduce yourself to one of Asia's most dynamic capital cities with a two-day crash course. Be dazzled by Wat Phra Kaew (p155), get lost in the cluttered but peaceful temple grounds of Wat Pho (p63), ride the Chao Phraya Express (p95) and drink to the stars from a rooftop bar (p86). The next day, shop till you drop among the hoi polloi at MBK Center (p90), and the high society at Emporium Shopping Centre (p91). Admire more pretty stuff at Jim Thompson's House (p91) and tap into the modern-art scene at the Bangkok Art & Culture Centre (p73). Stay out late at the rollicking bars (p86) and grab a noodle night cap at Soi 38 Night Market (p55).

❷ AYUTHAYA

Balance out conspicuous consumption with culture in the ancient capital of Ayuthaya (p184), an easy day trip from Bangkok. Hire a bicycle, an elephant taxi or a knowledgeable guide for a tour of the Unesco-listed ruins, built during Ayuthaya's heyday as a powerful city-state and a stop on the Asian trade-winds route. Fill your camera with pictures and then take a bus back to Bangkok to beat rush hour.

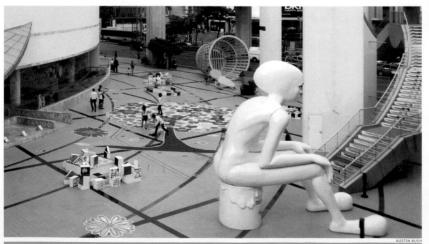

AUSTIN BUSH

Bangkok Art & Culture Centre (p73)

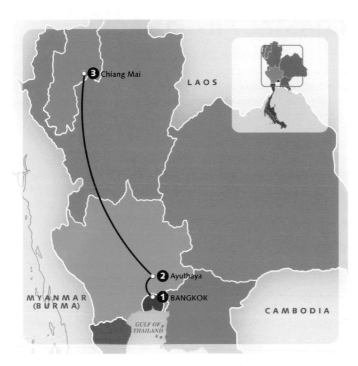

❸ CHIANG MAI

Fly to the laid-back university town of Chiang Mai (p97). Explore the old quarter, filled with the distinctive temple architecture of northern Thailand. Hunt down a bowl of *kôw soy,* the north's signature noodle dish, and hang out with the locals and expats at the Riverside Bar & Restaurant (p119). The next day, make a morning pilgrimage to the cool environs of Doi Suthep (p111) and its sacred hillside temple. If it's a weekend, visit the Saturday Walking Street (p107) and the Sunday Walking Street (p107) for souvenir shopping and people-watching. To return home, save yourself a Bangkok backtrack by booking a direct flight onward from Chiang Mai.

COASTAL PILGRIMAGE

TEN DAYS KO SAMUI TO KRABI

Soak up the sun and the tropical scenery by surveying the beaches and islands of Thailand's famed coasts. Flights from Bangkok to Ko Samui shorten the journey and minibuses burn rubber across the peninsula for travellers going bi-coastal.

❶ KO SAMUI

Arrive in **Ko Samui** (p254) by air and make a beeline for Chaweng, Samui's stunning stretch of sand. Explore the quieter northern beaches, or snorkel and kayak around **Ang Thong Marine National Park** (p277). Stressed-out professionals flock to Samui for a dose of health and wellness in addition to the usual rest-and-recreation routine.

❷ KO TAO

Once you've been cooked and tenderised on Samui, catch an inter-island ferry to **Ko Tao** (p272) for underwater-scouting missions. This little island competes with Thailand's best beaches because of its many near-shore coral gardens and hang-outs for aquatic creatures. Strap on your snorkelling gear and do an island swimming tour with the fish or dive to greater depths for underwater landscapes.

❸ SURAT THANI

A ho-hum southern town, **Surat Thani** (p276) is the mainland way-station for beach-bound transport. Ferries trundle between Surat Thani and the Gulf islands while buses and minivans vacuum up the

Chaweng Beach (p257), Ko Samui

JOHN BORTHWICK

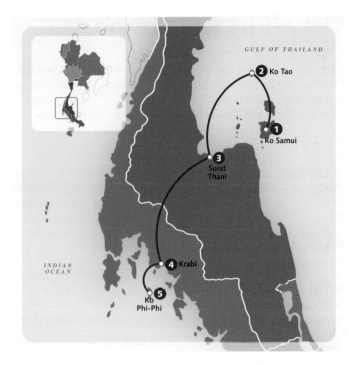

sun-soaked faces bound for the opposite coast. Though not the fast-est option, an overnight ferry to/from Surat Thani is a quintessential journey. **Chumphon** (p253) is an alternate mainland jumping-off point.

❹ KRABI

The Gulf coast is pretty and, more importantly, pretty relaxing, but the Andaman coast – with its stunning karst mountains jutting out of jewel-coloured seas – is beautiful. **Krabi town** (p309) provides ferry service to the offshore islands and beaches. Rock climbers and scenery buffs head to **Railay** (p311), a cramped pinch of sand between bearded limestone towers. There are also sweaty jungle hikes, sea kayaking and cave exploring.

❺ KO PHI-PHI

For beauty connoisseurs, **Ko Phi-Phi** (p313) is the winner with its perfect proportions: hour-glass shaped beach, shallow emerald and jade seas, and dramatic limestone cliffs. There are wreck and pinnacle dives as well as snorkelling tours through uninhabited islands. It is also upmarket enough to give it a semi-precious price tag.

TRAVEL IN THE SLOW LANE

TWO WEEKS LOPBURI TO KHAO LAK

With two weeks, you can explore the country at a slower pace. Break up the Bangkok-to-Chiang Mai trip with stops in Lopburi and Sukhothai. Climb into the high-altitude wilderness northwest of Chiang Mai. Take a breather from the beaches with a jungle layover in Khao Sok National Park before diving into Khao Lak.

❶ LOPBURI

The little town of **Lopburi** (p137) boasts a small collection of time-worn ruins built by ancient kingdoms, including the Khmer and Dvaravati. But it's the troupe of monkeys that live and play in the principal temple that attracts most of the attention. Lopburi sits on the Bangkok–Chiang Mai train line and can be visited en route in a day or overnight.

❷ SUKHOTHAI

The ruins of one of Thailand's first kingdoms reside in a peaceful park setting far enough from the modern city of **Sukhothai** (p171) to feel like a lost treasure.

Rent a bicycle and spend the day among the eternally meditating Buddha figures. For ruins amongst the countryside, do a daytrip to Si Satchanalai-Chaliang Historical Park (p177), outside Sukhothai. If you're travelling north by train, disembark at **Phitsanulok** (p167) which boasts two very Thai superlatives – a famous Buddha and a famous noodle dish. From Phitsanulok bus to Sukhothai before

Young hill-tribe girl, Chiang Mai Province

FELIX HUG

THAILAND'S TOP ITINERARIES

TRAVEL IN THE SLOW LANE

continuing on to Chiang Mai (p97). Alternatively you can bus directly to Sukhothai from Lopburi or Bangkok.

❸ PAI

From Chiang Mai, climb into the forested frontier that Thailand shares with Myanmar (Burma) with a stop in Pai (p184), a mountain retreat for artists, backpackers and urban Thais. Pai does a little bit of everything: partying, mainly; trekking, some; and a lot of hanging out. Remember to bring some cool-weather clothes as the mountains get chilly after dark.

❹ MAE HONG SON

The next stop on the northwest mountain circuit is this provincial capital that attracts cultural enthusiasts turned off by Pai's party scene. Mae Hong Son (p180) displays its Burmese heritage with distinctive temple architecture and signature market meals. It is also a gateway to remote jungle landscapes. From here the road circles back to Chiang Mai where you can transit through Bangkok to the beaches.

❺ KHAO SOK NATIONAL PARK

The southern rainforest refuge of **Khao Sok National Park** (p292) provides the perfect antidote to beach fatigue (if such a thing exists) as it sits midway between the two coasts. The park is filled with rugged limestone mountains criss-crossed by muddy trails and a dam-filled lake best explored by kayak. Your visit might coincide with the flowering of the giant *Rafflesia kerrii*, whose vegetal perfume mimics the smell of putrid flesh in order to attract carrion pollinators. Minivans can be arranged from **Surat Thani** (p276) if you're transiting between the Gulf and Khao Lak.

❻ KHAO LAK

A mainland town on the Andaman coast, **Khao Lak** (p292) is the most convenient gateway to the famous dive sites in the **Surin Islands Marine National Park** (p294) and the **Similan Islands Marine National Park** (p295), two protected areas renowned for their underwater geography and marine species. Dive companies arrange multi-day liveaboard excursions that cut out the commute, giving you more chances to slip below the ocean's surface. From Khao Lak you can bus south to the Andaman's other famous beaches, including **Phuket** (p295), **Railay** (p311) and **Ko Phi-Phi** (p313).

FELIX HUG

Surin Islands Marine National Park (p294)

⬊ PLANNING YOUR TRIP

THAILAND'S BEST

BEACH BUMMING

- **Ko Phi-Phi Don** (p313) Behold the prettiest tropical island you've ever seen.
- **Ko Pha-Ngan** (p264) Master the art of hammock-hanging.
- **Ko Samui** (p254) Devote yourself to great beaches, sleepy fishing villages and seaside yoga.
- **Phuket** (p295) Bullseye for high-energy, international resorts.
- **Ko Samet** (p229) Escape the capital for a beach retreat.

SHOPPING

- **Bangkok** (p90) From markets to malls, you can shop while you sleep.
- **Chiang Mai** (p119) This handicraft centre has homespun and chic.
- **Surin** (p208) Craft villages practise silk weaving and silversmithing.

- **Ko Kret** (p77) See pottery in situ on this river island near Bangkok.
- **Nong Khai** (p214) The riverside market sells souvenirs and grilled fish; people-watching is free.

HISTORY HUNTING

- **Ayuthaya** (p134) Ride an elephant through the tumbledown temples.
- **Phanom Rung Historical Park** (p209) A beacon from the Khmer empire.
- **Sukhothai Historical Park** (p171) A meditative journey through an early Thai kingdom.
- **Phimai** (p203) The closest Khmer ruin to Bangkok for history buffs short on time.
- **Lopburi** (p137) For monkeys and old temples.

Sunglasses stall, Phuket (p295)

AUSTIN BUSH

⬈ EATING & COOKING

- **Bangkok** (p82) A culinary superstar with noodles, haute cuisine and immigrant fare.
- **Chiang Mai** (p113) Learn how to chop and wok through Thai cooking.
- **Hua Hin** (p250) Combine two great Thai specialities – seafood and night markets – into one.
- **Phuket** (p304) Sample southern fare, seafood and fusion.
- **Nakhon Ratchasima** (p202) *Sôm·đam* (papaya salad), *gài yâhng* (grilled chicken) and *kôw nĕe·o* (sticky rice) fuel Thailand's muscles.

⬈ TEMPLE SPOTTING

- **Bangkok** (p63) Glittering temples protect the faith and attract the faithful.
- **Chiang Mai** (p106) Teak and mirror-mosaic temples decorate the old quarter and the sacred mountain.
- **Chiang Rai** (p157) Historic temples compete with the curiously contemporary Wat Rong Khun.
- **Lampang** (p155) View this mini-Chiang Mai by horse-drawn carriage.

⬈ JUNGLE TREKKING

- **Khao Sok National Park** (p292) Trek and paddle through this southern tropical rainforest.
- **Kanchanaburi** (p138) For elephant riding, river-rafting and waterfall-spotting.
- **Mae Hong Son** (p180) A rugged corner straddling geopolitics.
- **Khao Yai National Park** (p205) Monkeys, waterfalls, wilderness – just around the corner from Bangkok.
- **Ko Chang** (p233) Frolic in the ocean and the jungle.

⬈ RIVERS & OCEANS TO EXPLORE

- **Bangkok** (p70) Hire a long-tail to see vestiges of 'Venice of the East'.
- **Ao Phang-Nga** (p298) Paddle through limestone canyons into echo-chamber caves.
- **Surin Islands Marine National Park** (p294) and **Similan Islands Marine National Park** (p295) Snorkel and dive the reefs of these two marine preserves.
- **Ko Tao** (p272) Get dive certified on this turtle-shaped island.
- **Ko Lanta** (p316) Fish – big and small – flock to Lanta's coral.

THINGS YOU NEED TO KNOW

⬈ AT A GLANCE

- **ATMs** Common and convenient for international banking
- **Bargaining** In markets and where prices aren't posted
- **Credit cards** Visa and MasterCard accepted at most hotels and restaurants but not at small family-owned businesses
- **Currency** Baht
- **Language** Thai; English is spoken in tourist areas
- **Tipping** In upmarket hotels and restaurants; 10% gratuity and 7% tax
- **Visas** 30-day arrival visas for most nationalities arriving at airports

⬈ ACCOMMODATION

- **Guesthouses** Thailand's most common option; some are simple rooms in a family's home, while others are small hotels for small budgets. They all tend to have a common lobby and restaurant for socialising.
- **Hotels** Hip and fashionable options abound in Bangkok, Chiang Mai, Ko Samui and Phuket, but the dour and impersonal Thai-Chinese hotels in the provinces often feel a little lonely.

⬈ ADVANCE PLANNING

- **One month before** Start shopping for airline fares, planning an itinerary, booking accommodation and arranging domestic train and plane tickets.

- **One week before** Book your Thai cooking course and dive trip. Start watching the web for Thailand news.
- **One day before** Confirm your flight, find a hearty book for the plane ride and bid adieu to ho-hum home life.

⬈ BE FOREWARNED

- **Check travel advisories** Prior to your trip look for advisory warnings to Thailand on the website of your government's diplomatic mission abroad; see p374.
- **Health** Dengue fever is a concern throughout the country; malaria, in rural areas.
- **Public holidays** Domestic transport can be crowded or booked out during long holidays.

⬈ COSTS

- **1700B or less per day** Midrange hotels or guesthouses, meals at local restaurants or markets, and daily transport hire.
- **3400B to 6800B** Boutique hotels, international restaurants and organised tours.
- **More than 6800B** Top-end hotels, private tour guides and extensive shopping sprees.

⬈ EMERGENCY NUMBERS

- **Fire** (☎ 199)
- **Police/Emergency** (☎ 191)
- **Tourist Police** (☎ 1155; ⊙ 24hr)

⬈ GETTING AROUND

- **Air** Domestic routes from Bangkok are plentiful.
- **Bus** Inter-city buses are convenient, affordable and comfortable but should be booked at bus stations as unscrupulous agents abound.
- **Private transport** Bangkok has metered taxis, elsewhere túk-túk, motorcycle taxis and taxis have negotiable fares; motorcycles and cars are easily rented.
- **Public transport** Bangkok has public buses, an elevated train system (Skytrain) and a subway. Most Thai cities have *sŏrng·tăa·ou* (converted pick-up trucks) that run fixed routes.
- **Train** Slow but scenic travel, popular for the overnight trip between Bangkok and Chiang Mai.

⬈ GETTING THERE & AWAY

- **Air** International flights arrive and depart from Bangkok's Suvarnabhumi International Airport (pronounced *sù·wan·ná·poom*). Some international flights go to Phuket and Chiang Mai without a Bangkok layover.

⬈ TECH STUFF

- The main video format is PAL.
- Thailand uses 220V AC electricity; power outlets feature two-prong round or flat sockets.
- Thailand follows the international metric system.

⬈ TRAVEL SEASONS

- **Best months** November–February
- **Beat the crowds** April–October

BRENT WINEBRENNER

View from the back seat of a túk-túk

↘ WHAT TO BRING

- **Light wash-and-wear clothes** Laundry is cheap in Thailand, so pack light. You can buy most toiletries everywhere.
- **A pullover or jacket** For places that are over-air-conditioned and those fresh mountain mornings.
- **Slip-on shoes or sandals**
- **Other handy items** A small flashlight (torch), waterproof money/passport container (for swimming outings), earplugs and sunscreen (high SPFs are not available outside of big cities).

↘ WHEN TO GO

- Thailand's weather is pleasant during the cool season (November to February) but this is also its busiest tourist time. The shoulder months (October and March) can be a nice compromise.
- The monsoon starts in July and progresses from an afternoon downpour to daylong soakers by September or October. The intensity of the rains varies regionally: the south is the wettest, the northeast is the driest.
- During public holidays and national festivals bus and rail tickets sell out and accommodation can be difficult to book. See the Calendar section (p48) for more information on festivals.

JOHN ELK III

Railay (p311), Krabi Province

GET INSPIRED

BOOKS

- **Bangkok 8** (2004) John Burdett's first and best Bangkok-based cop thriller is an excellent insight into Thai Buddhism.
- **Fieldwork** (2008) Mischa Berlinski concocts a fictional hill-tribe village in northern Thailand, with a complicated cast of anthropologists, missionaries and an aimless journalist.
- **Sightseeing** (2005) This collection of short stories by Rattawut Lapcharoensap gives readers a 'sightseeing' tour into Thai life.
- **The Beach** (1998) The ultimate beach read by Alex Garland follows a backpacker's discovery of secluded island utopia.
- **Very Thai: Everyday Popular Culture** (2004) By Bangkok-based writer Philip Cornwel-Smith, it explains the dashboard shrines, obsessions with uniforms and other common but confounding sights.

FILMS

- **Ruang Rak Noi Nid Mahasan** (Last Life in the Universe; 2003) Renowned Thai director Pen-Ek Ratanaruang unfurls a dark but poignant tale of two lost souls who find little comfort in each other.
- **Fah Talai Jone** (Tears of the Black Tiger; 2000) As pretty as a picture book, Wisit Sasanatieng creates a stylised tribute to Thai action flicks and melodramas in this movie about star-crossed lovers.

- **Ong-Bak: Muay Thai Warrior** (2003) Thailand's martial arts hero, Tony Jaa, gave the bad guys a good pummelling unaided by special effects or wires. The five-minute-plus chase scene makes up for the B-minus plot.
- **Agrarian Utopia** (2009) Director Uruphong Raksasad is a farmer's son who was inspired to depict the hardships of agricultural life in this film-fest darling.

MUSIC

- **Ting Nong Noy** (Modern Dog) The latest album from Thailand's alt-rock gurus.
- **Made in Thailand** (Carabao) The country's classic classic-rock album.
- **Best** (Pumpuang Duangjan) Compilation of the late *lôok tûng* (Thai country) diva's most famous tunes.
- **Boomerang** (Bird Thongchai) One of the most popular albums from the reigning (and ageing) King of Thai pop.

WEBSITES

- **Lonely Planet** (www.lonelyplanet .com) Country-specific information and user-exchange on Thorn Tree forum.
- **Bangkok Post** (www.bangkokpost .com) English-language daily.
- **Agoda.com** (www.agoda.com) Discounted hotel booking site.
- **One Stop Thailand** (www .onestopthailand.com) A one-stop Thailand travel site.

CALENDAR

| JAN | FEB | MAR | APR |

Revellers, Songkran Festival

CLINT LUCAS

☑ FEBRUARY

FLOWER FESTIVAL

Chiang Mai adorns itself with flowers during its signature agricultural fair which includes flower-bedecked parade floats and cultural performances.

☑ APRIL

SONGKRAN   13–15 APR

Thailand's lunar new year begins as a trickle and turns into a deluge. It starts in the temples, where Buddha figures are paraded about and sprinkled with water. Afterwards Thais in Chiang Mai and Bangkok load up their water guns and head out to the streets for battle. Take cover or be prepared to be doused.

ROYAL PLOUGHING CEREMONY

This royally officiated ceremony employs astrology and ancient Brahman rituals to begin the rice-planting season in May. Sacred oxen are hitched to a plough and part the ground of Sanam Luang (p64) in Bangkok.

ROCKET FESTIVAL

In the rural northeast, rice-planting season is heralded by raucous rocket festivals in which bamboo missile launchers (bâng fai) are fired into the sky to encourage the rains and ensure a plentiful growing period. This festival is most fervently celebrated in Yasothon, but Ubon Ratchathani and Nong Khai are more tourist-friendly. Dates vary but most occur near the Buddhist holy day of Visakha Puja (Buddha's birth and enlightenment) in May.

| MAY | JUN | JUL | AUG | SEP | OCT | NOV | DEC |

⬂ JULY

KÔW PAN·SĂH

The start of the annual monsoon coincides with the beginning of *kôw pan·săh* (Buddhist Lent), the period when young men enter the monastery. This is also when monks would retreat from the outside world for a period of meditation. Merit-makers present monks with daily necessities (toiletries, robes etc) for their impending retreat.

CANDLE PARADE

Ubon Ratchathani celebrates the start of *kôw pan·săh* with a parade of huge wax sculptures at its annual **Candle Parade** (p213). Offering candles to monks is a vestigial practice from the days before electric lights, and Ubon's unique interpretation shows off the town's artistic sensibilities. Nong Khai also has a candle parade.

⬂ AUGUST

HM THE QUEEN'S BIRTHDAY   12 AUG

The Queen's Birthday (12 August) is a public holiday and national Mother's Day. The royal avenue of Th Ratchadamnoen Klang is decorated with billboards for the queen and Thais wear blue, the colour associated with the day of the week the queen was born.

⬂ SEPTEMBER–OCTOBER

VEGETARIAN FESTIVAL

A holiday from meat is taken for nine days in adherence with Chinese Buddhist beliefs of mind and body purification. Cities with large Thai-Chinese populations, such as Bangkok and Phuket, are festooned with yellow banners heralding vegetarian

ANDREW WATSON

Dragon dancers, Vegetarian Festival

CALENDAR

vendors. In Phuket the festival gets extreme, with entranced marchers turning themselves into human shish kebabs.

BANGKOK INTERNATIONAL FILM FESTIVAL

Bangkok's annual film festival (www .bangkokfilm.org) spotlights home-grown talent and overseas indies making their way around the globe's silver screens. This stop on the film tour is testament to Thailand's reputation as a creative force. Dates vary.

ÒRK PAN·SĂH

Òrk pan·săh (the end of Buddhist Lent) in late October/early November is a holy day filled with temple visits and merit-making. Many Mekong River towns use the holy day to hold festivals honouring the *naga* (a mythical serpent) believed to reside in the river. To coincide with *òrk pan·săh*, Nakhon Phanom launches giant bamboo rafts festooned with lanterns and devotional offerings, while Phon Phisai has the **Naga Fireballs experience** (p216).

NOVEMBER–DECEMBER

SURIN ELEPHANT ROUND-UP

Held on the third weekend of November in Surin, Thailand's biggest elephant show celebrates the country's emblematic animal. The **Elephant Round-Up** (p194) begins with a colourful parade and culminates in a fruit buffet for the pachyderms. Re-enactments of Thai battles showcase mahouts and elephants wearing royal military garb.

Young spectators, Elephant Round-Up

AUSTIN BUSH

| MAY | JUN | JUL | AUG | SEP | OCT | NOV | DEC |

Loi Krathong Festival
FELIX HUG

◥ DECEMBER

HM THE KING'S BIRTHDAY   5 DEC

This public holiday marks the monarch's birth as well as national Father's Day. Th Ratchadamnoen Klang in Bangkok is decorated with lights and regalia. Everyone wears yellow shirts, the colour associated with the king's birthday. Phuket also holds the King's Cup Regatta during the first week of the month in honour of the monarch.

LOI KRATHONG

Thailand's most beloved festival is celebrated on the first full moon of the 12th lunar month (November or December). The festival thanks the river goddess for providing life to the fields and forests and asks for forgiveness for the polluting ways of humans. Small handmade boats (called *grà·tong*, also spelled *kràthong*) are sent adrift in the waterways. Loi Krathong is a peculiarly Thai festival that probably originated in Sukhothai, where it is celebrated among the historic ruins. In northern Thailand the festival is also called Yi Peng and includes the launching of illuminated lanterns into the sky. Chiang Mai and Mae Hong Son are two picturesque places to celebrate Loi Krathong.

King's birthday poster
TOM COCKREM

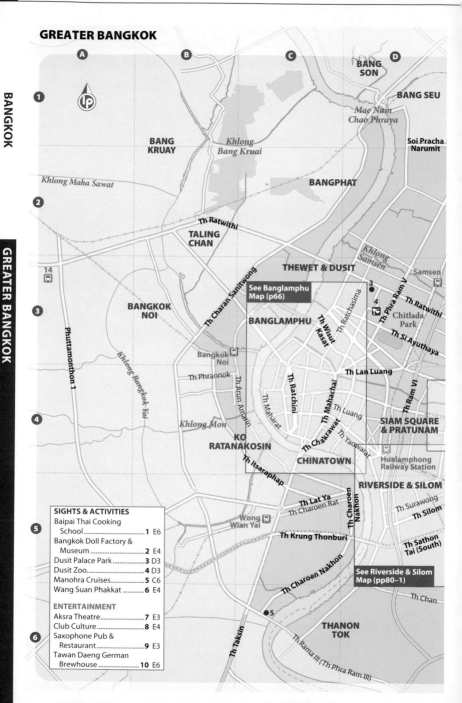

GREATER BANGKOK

SIGHTS & ACTIVITIES
Baipai Thai Cooking
  School **1** E6
Bangkok Doll Factory &
  Museum **2** E4
Dusit Palace Park **3** D3
Dusit Zoo..............................**4** D3
Manohra Cruises...................**5** C6
Wang Suan Phakkat **6** E4

ENTERTAINMENT
Aksra Theatre.......................**7** E3
Club Culture.........................**8** E4
Saxophone Pub &
  Restaurant **9** E3
Tawan Daeng German
  Brewhouse **10** E6

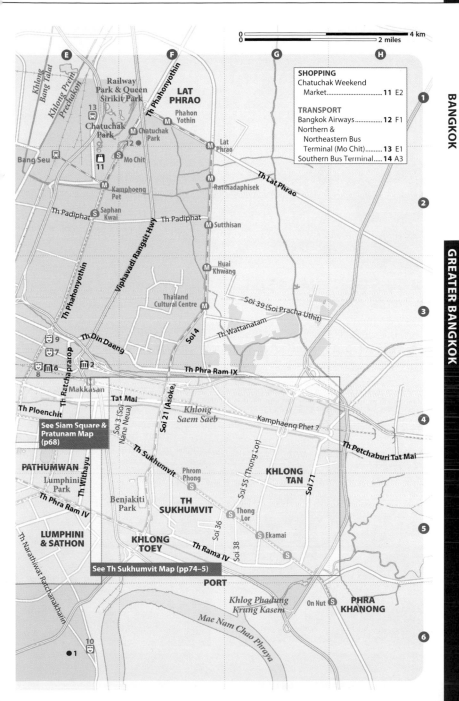

SHOPPING
Chatuchak Weekend
Market.................................. **11** E2

TRANSPORT
Bangkok Airways................ **12** F1
Northern &
Northeastern Bus
Terminal (Mo Chit).......... **13** E1
Southern Bus Terminal..... **14** A3

0 ──────── 4 km
0 ──────── 2 miles

LAT
PHRAO

Railway
Park & Queen
Sirikit Park

Th Phahonyothin

Phahon
Yothin

Chatuchak
Park

Chatuchak
Park

Lat
Phrao

Khlong
Bang Talat

Khlong Prem Prachakon

Bang Seu

Mo Chit

Th Lat Phrao

Kamphoeng
Pet

Ratchadaphisek

Th Padiphat

Saphan
Kwai

Th Padiphat

Sutthisan

Viphavadi Rangsit Hwy

Th Phahonyothin

Huai
Khwang

Thailand
Cultural Centre

Soi 39 (Soi Pracha Uthit)

Th Din Daeng

Soi 4

Th Wattanatam

Th Phra Ram IX

Th Ratchaprarop

Makkasan

Tat Mai

Th Ploenchit

Soi 3 (Soi Nana Neua)

Soi 21 (Asoke)

Khlong
Saem Saeb

Kamphaeng Phet 7

Th Petchaburi Tat Mai

**See Siam Square &
Pratunam Map
(p68)**

Th Sukhumvit

Phrom
Phong

Soi 55 (Thong Lor)

KHLONG
TAN

Soi 71

PATHUMWAN

Th Withayu

Lumphini
Park

Benjakiti
Park

**TH
SUKHUMVIT**

Soi 36

Thong
Lor

Th Phra Ram IV

LUMPHINI
& SATHON

KHLONG
TOEY

Soi 38

Th Rama IV

Ekamai

See Th Sukhumvit Map (pp74–5)

Th Narathiwat Ratchanakharin

PORT

Khlog Phadung
Krung Kasem

On Nut

**PHRA
KHANONG**

Mae Nam Chao Phraya

BANGKOK

BANGKOK HIGHLIGHTS

1 | CULINARY BANGKOK

BY DUANGPORN (BO) SONGVISAVA, CO-OWNER & CHEF, BO.LAN RESTAURANT

Bangkok is just like Paris. All the good ingredients from across the region end up here. In terms of food, the city is very flavourful and acts as a 24-hour dining room. My parents were both great cooks and I studied for a culinary career in Australia, lived and worked in London and ate my way through Europe.

↘ BO'S DON'T MISS LIST

❶ FRESH MARKETS

At my restaurant, seasonal produce dictates the menu. I love to go to **Khlong Toey Market** (p72); it has loads of local vegetables, some of which I've never seen before. I often talk with the vendors to get the know-how of ingredients. **Pak Khlong Market** (p72) is great for its quality of products, always fresh and tempting me to buy.

❷ FINE DINING

Cy'an (p85) is the best Western restaurant in Bangkok. Every component in a particular dish is well thought out and the presentation is always of a very high standard. I learned how to cook Mediterranean food there. Of course I should tell you about my restaurant **Bo.lan** (p85). The restaurant is based on slow-food philosophy: promoting food biodiversity, cooking everything from scratch and safeguarding food heritage. I want Bo.lan to be a gastronomical destination for foodies to explore, experience or simply indulge in Thai food.

Clockwise from top: Night market, Chinatown; Neon lights, Th Sukhumvit; Crispy noodle dish; Fish for sale, Pak Khlong Market (p72); Floating market

❸ *GŎO·AY ĐĔE·O* (NOODLES)

I love noodles and I often eat at the small shops and street stalls that serve noodle soups. There are hundreds of places in Bangkok and everyone has their own recommendations. I like to go to **Rung Ruang** (Soi 26, Th Sukhumvit), which does noodle soups with pork and fish balls. There's also a little **no-name shop** (cnr Th Rama IV & Th Chua Pleang) under the expressway that does pork noodles. At these places, the noodles are cooked properly and the soup broth is great.

❹ NIGHT MARKETS

Night markets are everywhere in Bangkok and are a great way for tourists to explore culinary experiences. I like the night market at Suan Luang on Soi 103, Th Sukhumvit, but that is outside of town. Centrally located ones include **Soi 38 Night Market** (p84).

↘ THINGS YOU NEED TO KNOW

Top Survival Tip Thais use chopsticks to eat noodles but use a spoon to eat rice dishes **Avoid** Thai food in a restaurant context can be overrated; street stalls are better places to get some ideas for Thai food

BANGKOK

BANGKOK HIGHLIGHTS

2 | CHAO PHRAYA RIVER

BY PYLIN (JANE) SANGUANPIYAPAND, OWNER OF SEVEN HOTEL

The Chao Phraya River (or River of Kings) is the bloodline of the Thai people. We use it for trade and travel, for drinking and cooking. We even bathe in it! So if you want to see a charming way of life, come to the river.

↘ JANE'S DON'T MISS LIST

❶ LONG-TAIL BOAT RIDES

I never get tired of the long-tail boat ride through the **Khlong Bangkok Noi** (p70). I cherish every minute of it. I feel the charm of simplicity. Along the way, there are kids playing in the water, granddads checking out the scene from a humble wooden porch, monks cleaning the temple grounds. There are also *mâa káh* (store vendors) selling all kinds of things from their boats, and housewives preparing dinner. I recommend this trip to all of my guests.

❷ WAT ARUN

Wat Arun (Temple of Dawn; p65) sits directly on the river. It wasn't until I came back from 11 years of study in England that I discovered the joy that all things Thai bring to me. Before that I was rather ignorant of my own surroundings. By accompanying my foreign friends to these tourist sites, I understand now why people fall for the charm of Thailand and the Thai people.

Clockwise from top: Thai royal barge procession, Chao Phraya River; Detail from barge; Chao Phraya Express (p95); Wat Arun (p65) overlooking the Chao Phraya River

CLOCKWISE FROM TOP: FRANK CARTER; RICHARD I'ANSON; CAROL WILEY; AUSTIN BUSH

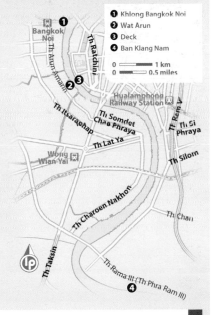

❸ DRINKS BY THE RIVER

Because of my work commitments the closest I usually get to my dream of a simple life is to live in a condo by the river. Every night, I get to watch the show from my very own balcony. Tourists can enjoy the view too from the Amorosa bar at the restaurant **Deck** (p83), which overlooks some of Thailand's most famous temples.

❹ DINNER BESIDE THE RIVER

There are many restaurants beside the river but my favourite is **Ban Klang Nam** (I have even taken the author of this book there). It serves the best Thai seafood in my opinion. Call the head waiter Khun Chai (☎ 08 1581 5848) for a good table.

❶ Khlong Bangkok Noi
❷ Wat Arun
❸ Deck
❹ Ban Klang Nam

0 —————— 1 km
0 —————— 0.5 miles

↘ THINGS YOU NEED TO KNOW

Best Way to See the River Hire a long-tail boat for a tour of the river and canals **Top Tip** Thais like to go to a canal-side temple to release fish as offerings; bring your own bread if you want to feed the freed fish

BANGKOK HIGHLIGHTS

3

➥ EXPLORE KO RATANAKOSIN

The country's most famous and sacred sites are in Ko Ratanakosin, the old royal district. Here you'll find **Wat Phra Kaew** (p65), a glittering and ornate temple that typifies Thai architecture and shelters the revered Emerald Buddha. More subdued **Wat Pho** (p63) is home to the gigantic Reclining Buddha and is the national school for traditional Thai massage.

4

➥ CRUISE THE WATERWAYS

Before the modern era, Bangkok was a city of canals and waterways fed by the Chao Phraya River. Today the river is still one of the busiest thoroughfares in the city and hopping aboard the **Chao Phraya Express** (p95) is a memorable journey to the city's riverside attractions. To plunge deeper into the city's waterways, charter a long-tail boat to explore the canals.

5

⬈ BECOME A SHOPAHOLIC

Bangkok's malls and markets make their overseas counterparts look like country garage sales. Cut your teeth at **MBK** (p90), an indoor mall that has all the energy of a streetside bazaar but without the heat. Then graduate to **Chatuchak Weekend Market** (p92), the mother of all markets that sells everything and the kitchen sink.

6

⬈ TOAST THE STARS

Modern Bangkok is a cascading mountain range of skyscrapers that reaches for the heavens. Atop two of these towers are the rooftop bars **Moon Bar at Vertigo** (p86) and **Sirocco Sky Bar** (p86), where sundowners catch cool evening breezes, admire the twinkling city lights and escape the street-level cacophony.

7

⬈ COOK UP A THAI FEAST

Learn to dice and stir-fry your way through many classic Thai dishes. Bangkok's **cooking schools** (p72) provide an excellent introduction to the cuisine, guided tours of markets and instructions for turning disparate ingredients into edible masterpieces. You also get to eat your handiwork and graduate with your very own recipe book.

3 GREG ELMS; 4 RICHARD I'ANSON; 5 GREG ELMS; 6 AUSTIN BUSH; 7 JERRY ALEXANDER

3 Wat Phra Kaew (p65); 4 Onboard the Chao Phraya Express (p95); 5 T-shirt stall, Chatuchak Weekend Market (p92); 6 Moon Bar at Vertigo (p86); 7 Squid salad

BANGKOK

BANGKOK'S BEST...

⟝ PLACES TO WANDER

- **Chinatown** (p67) Ramble through a maze of old-world commerce.
- **Amulet Market** (p64) Pick through the vendors selling protective talismans.
- **Dusit Palace Park** (p70) Take a stroll through a pretty park filled with other pretty things.
- **Ko Kret** (p77) Putter around this car-free and carefree island.

⟝ PLACES TO BE A CULTURAL VULTURE

- **National Museum** (p64) Get a crash course on Buddhist sculpture.
- **Bangkok Art & Culture Centre** (p73) Peruse the modern art masters.
- **Erawan Shrine** (p69) Make a wish at this wish-granting shrine.
- **Jim Thompson's House** (p91) Admire a homey collection of art and architecture.

⟝ PLACES TO SNACK & SUP

- **Deck** (p83) Enjoy an intimate riverside setting with monumental views.
- **Khrua Aroy Aroy** (p84) A must for the 'curry-ous'.
- **MBK Food Court** (p85) Get a bilingual introduction to street food.
- **Bo.lan** (p85) Dine on haute Thai cuisine.

⟝ PLACES TO BE A NIGHTOWL

- **Center Khao San** (p86) Grab a front-row seat on Khao San's human parade.
- **Diplomat Bar** (p86) Sip among the beautiful people.
- **Brown Sugar** (p87) Settle in for good times and good tunes.
- **Club Culture** (p88) Let the music move you.

LEFT: BRENT WINEBRENNER; RIGHT: GREG ELMS

Left: Streetside stall, Amulet Market (p64); Right: Market vendor, Chinatown (p67)

BANGKOK'S BEST...

THINGS YOU NEED TO KNOW

⇘ VITAL STATISTICS

- **Population** 10 million
- **Best time to visit** November to April

⇘ NEIGHBOURHOODS IN A NUTSHELL

- **Ko Ratanakosin, Banglamphu & Thonburi** Temples, museums and old-fashioned shophouses.
- **Chinatown & Phahurat** An ethnic mercantile district.
- **Silom, Sathon & Riverside** High finance and high-end hotel sphere.
- **Siam Square & Pratunam** Mall mania and youth culture.
- **Sukhumvit** International zone.
- **Central Bangkok** The catch-all for everything else.

⇘ ADVANCE PLANNING

- **One month before** Book accommodation.
- **One week before** Book your Thai cooking course.
- **One day before** Pack your hippest outfits.

⇘ RESOURCES

- **Bangkok Gig Guide** (www.bangkok gigguide.com) Find out who's playing where.
- **Bangkok Information Center** (Map p66; ☎ 0 2225 7612-5; www .bangkoktourist.com; 17/1 Th Phra Athit; ☼ 9am-7pm; river ferry Tha Phra Athit) City tourism office.

- **Tourism Authority of Thailand** (TAT; ☎ 1672; www.tourismthailand.org) Head Office (☎ 0 2250 5500; 1600 Th Petchaburi Tat Mai; ☼ 8.30am-4.30pm; Skytrain City Air Terminal, Metro Phetburi); Banglamphu (Map p66; ☎ 0 2283 1555; cnr Th Ratchadamnoen Nok & Th Chakrapatdipong; ☼ 8.30am-4.30pm)

⇘ EMERGENCY NUMBERS

- **Fire** (☎ 199)
- **Police/Emergency** (☎ 191)
- **Tourist police** (☎ 1155; ☼ 24hr)

⇘ GETTING AROUND

- **Bus** From Siam Square to China-town (bus 73); Siam Square to Banglamphu (bus 15)
- **Metro** From Sukhumvit and Silom to the train station.
- **River ferry** Everything along the river.
- **Skytrain** To/from Sukhumvit, Siam Square, Silom and Chatuchak.
- **Taxi** Plentiful and comfortable; insist on the meter.
- **Túk-túk** Cute but a rip-off.

⇘ BE FOREWARNED

- **Smoking** Banned in indoor bars and restaurants.
- **Street stalls** Don't set up on Monday.
- **Tours** Ignore friendly locals with touring advice.
- **Duty-free goods** Avoid the air-port duty-free shops.
- **Gems** Don't buy unset gems.

BANGKOK

DISCOVER BANGKOK

Formerly the epitome of the steamy Asian metropolis, in recent years Bangkok has gone under the knife and emerged as a rejuvenated starlet, defiantly daring people to guess her age. Her wrinkles haven't totally been erased, but you might not notice them in the ever-expanding and efficient public transportation system, air-conditioned mega-malls and international-standard restaurants. A diverse international community, a burgeoning art scene and a brand-new airport complete the new look, making even frequent visitors wonder what happened to the girl they once knew.

But don't take this to mean that there's no 'real' Bangkok left. The traditional framework that made this city unique is still very much alive and kicking, and can be found a short walk from any Skytrain station or probably just around the corner from your hotel.

Along the way we're sure you'll find that the old personality and the new face culminate in one sexy broad indeed.

BANGKOK IN...

For the best of what this city has to offer, try mixing and matching these suggestions.

One Day
Explore the ancient sites of **Ko Ratanakosin** (p63), followed by an authentic lunch in **Banglamphu** (p82).

After freshening up, get a new perspective on the city with sunset cocktails at one of the **rooftop bars** (p86), followed by dinner downtown such as upmarket Thai at **Bo.lan** (p85) or **Cy'an** (p85).

Three Days
Allow the **Skytrain** (p95) to whisk you to various **shopping** (p90) destinations. Wrap up the daylight hours with a **traditional Thai massage** (p70). Then work off those calories at the dance clubs of **Royal City Avenue** (RCA, p88).

One Week
Now that you're accustomed to the noise, pollution and traffic, you're ready for **Chinatown** (p67). Spend a day at **Chatuchak Weekend Market** (p92) or enrol in a **cooking school** (p72). Fresh air fiends can escape the city at **Ko Kret** (p77), a car-less island north of Bangkok, or charter a **long-tail boat** (p70) to ride through Bangkok's canals.

SIGHTS
KO RATANAKOSIN, BANGLAMPHU & THONBURI

เกาะรัตนโกสินทร์/บางลำภู/ธนบุรี

Welcome to Bangkok's birthplace. The vast city we know today emerged from Ko Ratanakosin, a tiny virtual island ('Ko') made by dredging a canal around Mae Nam Chao Phraya during the late 18th century. Within this area you'll find the glittering temples and palaces that most visitors associate with the city.

Adjacent Banglamphu suffers from an extreme case of split-personality disorder, encompassing both the most characteristically old-school Bangkok part of town as well as Th Khao San, a brash, neon-lit decompression zone for international backpackers.

Directly across the river is Thonburi, which served a brief tenure as the Thai capital after the fall of Ayuthaya. Today the area along the river is easily accessed from Bangkok's ferries, and there are museums and temples here that are historical complements to those in Ko Ratanakosin.

KO RATANAKOSIN
WAT PHO

วัดโพธิ์ (วัดพระเชตุพน)

You'll find significantly fewer tourists here than at Wat Phra Kaew, but **Wat Pho (Wat Phra Chetuphon; Map p66; ☎ 0 2221 9911; Th Sanamchai; admission 50B; ⏰ 8am-5pm; bus 508, 512, river ferry Tha Tien)** is our personal fave among Bangkok's biggest temples.

Almost too big for its shelter, the genuinely impressive **Reclining Buddha**, 46m

CLOCKWISE FROM TOP LEFT: MICK ELMORE; GREG ELMS; AUSTIN BUSH; GREG ELMS

Clockwise from top left: Cookery class, Blue Elephant Thai Cooking School (p72); Skytrain (p95); Massage, Wat Pho Thai Traditional Medical & Massage School (p70); Shoe stall, Chatuchak Weekend Market (p92)

BANGKOK

SIGHTS

DRESS FOR THE OCCASION

Most of Bangkok's biggest tourist attractions are in fact sacred places, and visitors should dress and behave appropriately. Shorts, sleeveless shirts or spaghetti-strap tops, capri pants – anything that reveals more than your arms (not your shoulders) and head – are not allowed. For walking in courtyard areas you are supposed to wear shoes with closed heels and toes, although these rules aren't as zealously enforced. Regardless, footwear should always be removed before entering any main *bòht* (chapel) or *wí·hăhn* (sanctuary). When sitting in front of a Buddha image, tuck your feet behind you to avoid the offensive pose of pointing your feet towards a revered figure.

long and 15m high, illustrates the passing of the Buddha into nibbana (ie the Buddha's death). Mother-of-pearl inlay ornaments the feet, displaying 108 different auspicious *lák·sà·nà* (characteristics of a Buddha).

Wat Pho is also the national headquarters for the teaching and preservation of traditional Thai medicine, including Thai massage, a mandate legislated by Rama III when the tradition was in danger of extinction. The famous massage school has two massage pavilions without air-con located within the temple area and air-con rooms within the training facility outside the temple (p70).

AMULET MARKET

ตลาดพระเครื่องวัดมหาธาตุ

This equal parts bizarre and fascinating **market** (Map p66; Th Maharat; ⏰ 9am-5pm; river ferry Tha Chang) claims both the sidewalks along Th Maharat and Th Phra Chan, as well as a dense network of covered market stalls near Tha Phra Chan. The trade is based around small talismans carefully prized by collectors, monks, taxi drivers and people in dangerous professions.

NATIONAL MUSEUM

พิพิธภัณฑสถานแห่งชาติ

Often touted as Southeast Asia's biggest museum, the **National Museum** (Map p66; ☎ 0 2224 1333; 4 Th Na Phra That; admission 200B; ⏰ 9am-3.30pm Wed-Sun; bus 53, 503, 506, 507, river ferry Tha Chang) is home to an impressive collection of religious sculpture, best appreciated on one of the museum's twice-weekly guided **tours** (⏰ 9.30am Wed & Thu, in English, German, Japanese & French).

SANAM LUANG

สนามหลวง

The royal district's green area is **Sanam Luang** (Royal Field; Map p66; bordered by Th Na Phra That, Th Na Phra Lan, Th Ratchadamnoen Nai, Th Somdet Phra Pin Klao; admission free; ⏰ 6am-8pm; bus 30, 32, 47, 53, river ferry Tha Chang), which introduces itself to most visitors as a dusty impediment to Wat Phra Kaew and other attractions. The park's more appealing attributes are expressed during its duties as a site for the annual Ploughing Ceremony, in which the king officially initiates the rice-growing season.

BANGLAMPHU
WAT SAKET & GOLDEN MOUNT

วัดสระเกศ/ภูเขาทอง

Even if you're *wát-ed* out, you should take a brisk walk to **Wat Saket** (Map p66; ☎ 0 2223 4561; btwn Th Wora Chak & Th Boriphat; admission to Golden Mount 10B; ⏰ 8am-5pm; bus 508, 511, klorng taxi to Tha Phan Fah). Serpentine steps wind through an artificial hill shaded by gnarled trees, some of which are signed

RICHARD CUMMINS

Detail of statue, Grand Palace

➘ WAT PHRA KAEW & GRAND PALACE

วัดพระแก้ว/พระบรมมหาราชวัง

Also known as the Temple of the Emerald Buddha, **Wat Phra Kaew** is the colloquial name of the vast, fairytale compound that also includes the former residence of the Thai monarch, the Grand Palace. Housed in a fantastically decorated *bòht* and guarded by pairs of *yaksha* (mythical giants), the **Emerald Buddha** is the temple's primary attraction. It sits atop an elevated altar, barely visible amid the gilded decorations. Recently restored **Buddhist murals** line the interior walls of the *bòht*, and the **murals of the Ramakian** (the Thai version of the Indian epic the *Ramayana*) line the inside walls of the temple compound.

Except for an anteroom here and there, the buildings of the **Grand Palace** (Phra Borom Maharatchawong) are now put to use by the king only for certain ceremonial occasions, such as Coronation Day (the king mostly resides in Hua Hin).

Things you need to know: Map p66; ☎ 0 2224 1833; admission 350B; ⏲ 8.30am-3.30pm; bus 508, 512, river ferry Tha Chang

in English, and past graves and pictures of wealthy benefactors. At the peak, you'll find a breezy 360-degree view of Bangkok's most photogenic side.

THONBURI

WAT ARUN

วัดอรุณฯ

Striking **Wat Arun** (Map p66; ☎ 0 2891 1149; Th Arun Amarin; admission 20B; ⏲ 9am-5pm; river ferry Tha Thai Wang) commands a martial pose as the third point in the holy trinity (along with Wat Phra Kaew and Wat Pho) of Bangkok's early history. After the fall of Ayuthaya, King Taksin ceremoniously clinched control here on the site of a local shrine (formerly known as Wat Jaeng) and established a royal palace and a temple to house the Emerald Buddha. The temple was renamed after the Indian

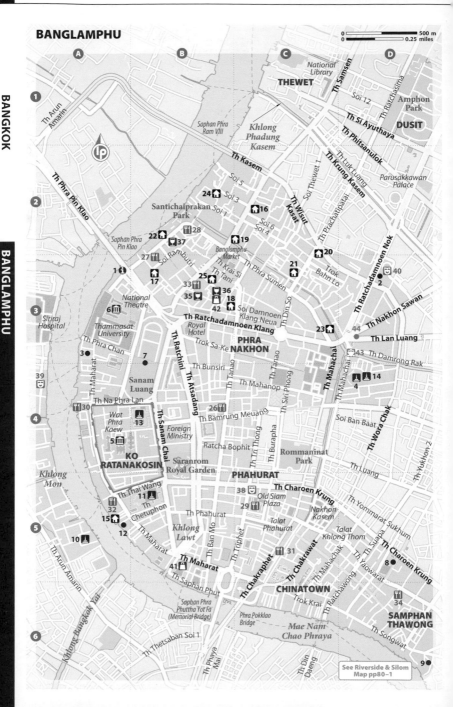

BANGKOK

BANGLAMPHU

god of dawn (Aruna) and in honour of the literal and symbolic founding of a new Ayuthaya.

CHINATOWN & PHAHURAT
เยาวราช(สำเพ็ง)/พาหุรัด

Bangkok's Chinatown (called Yaowarat after its main thoroughfare, Th Yaowarat) is the urban explorer's equivalent of the Amazon Basin.

At the western edge of Chinatown is a small but thriving Indian district, generally called Phahurat. Here, dozens of Indian-owned shops sell all kinds of fabric and clothes.

TALAT MAI
ตลาดใหม่

With nearly two centuries of commerce under its belt, 'New Market' is no longer an entirely accurate name for this **market (Map p66; Trok Itsaranuphap/Soi 16; river ferry Tha Ratchawong, Metro Hualamphong)**. Essentially it's a narrow covered alleyway between tall buildings, but even if you're not in terested in food the hectic atmosphere and exotic sights and smells culminate in something of a surreal sensory experience.

WAT TRAIMIT
วัดไตรมิตร

The attraction at **Wat Traimit (Temple of the Golden Buddha; Map pp80-1; ☎ 0 2225 9775; cnr Th Yaowarat & Th Charoen Krung; admission 20B; ⏰ 9am-5pm; Metro Hualamphong, bus 53)** is undoubtedly the impressive 3m-tall, 5.5-tonne, solid-gold Buddha image, which gleams like, well, gold. Sculpted in the graceful Sukhothai style, the image was 'discovered' some 40 years ago beneath a stucco or plaster exterior, when it fell from a crane while being moved to a new building within the temple compound.

SILOM, SATHON & RIVERSIDE
สีลม/สาธร/ริมแม่น้ำเจ้าพระยา

The business district of Th Silom has only a handful of tourist attractions scattered among the corporate hotels, office towers and wining-and-dining restaurants. As you get closer to the river, the area becomes spiced with the sights and smells of its Indian and Muslim residents. Moving north along Th Charoen Krung, the area adjacent to the river was the international mercantile district during Bangkok's shipping heyday.

BANGKOK

SIGHTS

INFORMATION					
Bangkok Information Center	**1** A3	Baan Chantra	**16** C2	DRINKING	
Tourism Authority of Thailand		Baan Sabai	**17** B3	Buddy Bar	(see 18)
(TAT)	**2** D3	Buddy Boutique Hotel	**18** B3	Center Khao San	**35** B3
		Diamond House	**19** C2	Molly Bar	**36** B3
SIGHTS & ACTIVITIES		Hotel Dé Moc	**20** C2	To-Sit	**37** B2
Amulet Market	**3** A3	Lamphu Tree House	**21** C3		
Golden Mount	**4** D4	Navalai River Resort	**22** B2	ENTERTAINMENT	
Grand Palace	**5** A4	Old Bangkok Inn	**23** C3	Chalermkrung Royal	
National Museum	**6** A3	Penpark Place	**24** B2	Theatre	**38** C5
Sanam Luang	**7** B3	Viengtai Hotel	**25** B3	Patravadi Theatre	**39** A4
Talat Mai	**8** D5			Ratchadamnoen	
Talat Noi	**9** D6	EATING		Stadium	**40** D3
Wat Arun	**10** A5	Chote Chitr	**26** B4		
Wat Pho	**11** B5	Deck	(see 15)	SHOPPING	
Wat Pho Thai Traditional		Hemlock	**27** B3	Pak Khlong Market	**41** B5
Medical and Massage School	**12** A5	Krua Noppharat	**28** B2	Th Khao San Market	**42** B3
Wat Phra Kaew	**13** B4	Old Siam Plaza	**29** C5		
Wat Saket	**14** D4	Rachanawi Samosorn	**30** A4	TRANSPORT	
		Royal India	**31** C5	Tha Phan Fah	
SLEEPING		Rub Aroon	**32** A5	(KlorngTaxis)	**43** D3
Arun Residence	**15** A5	Shoshana	**33** B3	Thai Airways	
		Tang Jai Yuu	**34** D6	International	**44** D3

BANGKOK

SIAM SQUARE & PRATUNAM

SIAM SQUARE & PRATUNAM

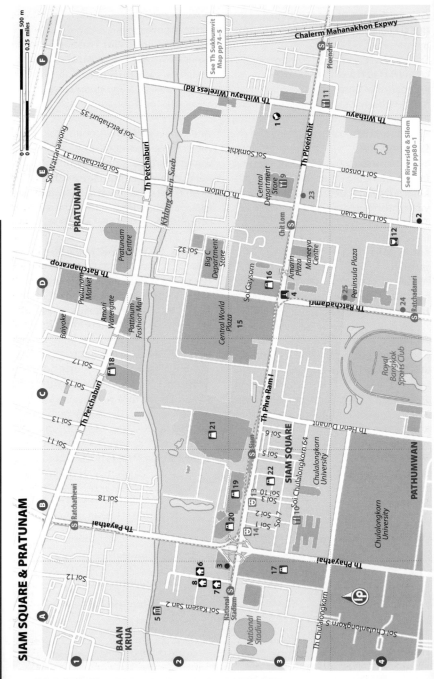

QUEEN SAOVABHA MEMORIAL INSTITUTE (SNAKE FARM)
สถานเสาวภา(สวนงู)

Snake farms tend to gravitate towards carnivalesque rather than humanitarian, except at the **Queen Saovabha Memorial Institute** (Map pp80-1; ☎ 0 2252 0161; cnr Th Phra Ram IV & Th Henri Dunant; adult/child 200/50B; ☼ 9.30am-3.30pm Mon-Fri, to 1pm Sat & Sun; Skytrain Sala Daeng, Metro Silom). Founded in 1923, the snake farm prepares antivenin from venomous snakes – common cobra, king cobra, banded krait, Malayan pit viper, green pit viper and Russell's viper. This is done by milking the snakes' venom, injecting it into horses, and harvesting and purifying the antivenom that they produce.

Daily **milkings** (☼ 11am) and **snake-handling performances** (☼ 2.30pm Mon-Fri) are held on the 2nd floor.

SIAM SQUARE & PRATUNAM
สยามสแควร์/ประตูน้ำ

JIM THOMPSON'S HOUSE
บ้านจิมทอมป์สัน

Jim Thompson's House (Map p68; ☎ 0 2216 7368; www.jimthompsonhouse.com; 6 Soi Kasem San 2; adult/child 100/50B; ☼ 9am-5pm, compulsory tours in English & French every 10min; Skytrain National Stadium, bus 73, 508, klorng taxi to Tha Ratchathewi) is an unlikely but stunning outpost of Thai architecture and Southeast Asian art.

The leafy compound is the former home of the eponymous American silk entrepreneur and art collector. In addition to exquisite Asian art, Thompson also collected parts of various derelict Thai homes in central Thailand and had them reassembled in their current location in 1959.

ERAWAN SHRINE
ศาลพระพรหม

A seamless merging of commerce and religion occurs at all hours of the day at this bustling **shrine** (San Phra Phrom; Map p68; cnr Th Ratchadamri & Th Ploenchit; admission free; ☼ 8am-7pm; Skytrain Chitlom). Claiming a spare corner of the Grand Hyatt Erawan hotel, the four-headed deity Brahma (Phra Phrom) represents the Hindu god of creation and was originally built to ward off bad luck during the construction of the first Erawan Hotel. The shrine was later adopted by the lay community as it gained a reputation for granting wishes.

CENTRAL BANGKOK
ใจกลางกรุงเทพฯ

DUSIT PALACE PARK
วังสวนดุสิต

Following Rama V's first European tour in 1897 (he was the first Thai monarch to visit the continent), he returned home with visions of European castles swimming in his head and set about transforming these styles into a uniquely Thai expres-

INFORMATION			EATING			SHOPPING		
UK Embassy	1	E3	Food Loft	9	E3	Central World Plaza	15	D3
			MBK Food Court	(see 17)		Gaysorn Plaza	16	D3
SIGHTS & ACTIVITIES			New Light Coffee House	10	B3	MBK Center	17	A3
Asian Trails	2	E4	Sanguan Sri	11	F3	Pantip Plaza	18	C1
Bangkok Art & Culture						Siam Center	19	B3
Centre	3	A2	DRINKING			Siam Discovery Center	20	B3
Erawan Shrine	4	D3	Café Trio	12	D4	Siam Paragon	21	C2
Jim Thompson's House	5	A2				Siam Square	22	B3
Siam Ocean World	(see 21)		ENTERTAINMENT					
			EGV Grand	(see 20)		TRANSPORT		
SLEEPING			Lido Cinema	13	B3	Cathay Pacific Airways	23	E3
A-One Inn	6	A2	Paragon Cineplex	(see 21)		China Airlines	(see 25)	
Reno Hotel	7	A2	Scala Cinema	14	B3	Japan Airlines	24	D4
Wendy House	8	A2	SF Cinema City	(see 17)		Northwest Airlines	25	D4

BANGKOK

ACTIVITIES

sion, today's **Dusit Palace Park** (Map pp52-3; ☎ 0 2628 6300; bounded by Th Ratchawithi, Th U-Thong Nai & Th Ratchasima; adult/child 100/50B or free with Grand Palace ticket; ☼ 9.30am-4pm; bus 70, 510). The royal palace, throne hall and minor palaces for extended family were all moved here from Ko Ratanakosin, the ancient royal court. Today the current king has yet another home and this complex now holds a house museum and other cultural collections.

Because this is royal property, visitors should wear long pants (no capri pants) or long skirts and shirts with sleeves.

ACTIVITIES
TRADITIONAL MASSAGE
Ruen-Nuad Massage Studio (Map pp80-1; ☎ 0 2632 2662; Th Convent, Th Silom; 1hr traditional

Traditional Thai massage
GREG ELMS

massage 350B, foot 350B; ☼ 10am-10pm; Skytrain Sala Daeng, Metro Silom) Set in a refurbished wooden house, this charming place successfully avoids both the tackiness and New Agedness that characterise most Bangkok massage joints.

Wat Pho Thai Traditional Medical & Massage School (Map p66; ☎ 0 2221 2974; Soi Pen Phat, Th Sanamchai; 1hr massage 220B; ☼ 8am-10pm; river ferry Tha Tien) The primary training ground for the masseuses who are deployed across the country; there are also massage pavilions inside the temple complex (see p63).

SPAS
Divana Spa (Map pp74-5; ☎ 0 2261 6784; www.divanaspa.com; 7 Soi 25, Th Sukhumvit; spa treatments from 2500B; Skytrain Asoke, Metro Sukhumvit) Retains a unique Thai touch with a private and soothing setting in a garden house.

Oriental Spa (Map pp80-1; ☎ 0 2659 9000, ext 7440; www.mandarinoriental.com/bangkok /spa; 48 Soi 38, Th Charoen Krung; spa package from 1650B) Regarded as among the premier spas in the world, the Oriental Spa also set the standard for Asian-style spa treatment.

RIVER & CANAL TRIPS
Glimpses of Bangkok's past as the 'Venice of the East' are still possible today, even though the motor vehicle has long since become the city's conveyance of choice.

The most obvious way to commute between riverside attractions is the **Chao Phraya Express** (see p95 for details).

For an up-close view of the city's famed canals, numerous long-tail boats are available for charter at Tha Chang, Tha Tian and Tha Phra Athit. Most trips spend an hour along the scenic Nonthaburi canals **Khlong Bangkok Noi** and **Khlong**

Bangkok Yai, with stops at the Royal Barges National Museum and Wat Arun. Longer trips diverge into **Khlong Mon**, between Bangkok Noi and Bangkok Yai, which offers more typical canal scenery, including orchid farms. It usually costs 1000B for the entire boat for one hour, excluding admission and various mooring fees.

For dinner cruises along the Chao Phraya River, see p73.

WALKING TOUR
KO RATANAKOSIN

Remember to dress modestly (long pants and skirts, shirts with sleeves and closed-toed shoes) in order to gain entry to the temples. Also ignore any strangers who approach you offering advice on sightseeing or shopping.

Start at **Tha Chang (1)** and follow Th Na Phra Lan east with a quick diversion to **Silpakorn University (2;** Th Na Phra Lan), Thailand's premier fine-arts university. Continue east to the main gate into **Wat Phra Kaew & Grand Palace (3;** p65), two of Bangkok's most famous attractions.

Backtrack to Th Maharat and turn right. Staying on the west side of the street, the fourth doorway on the left is **Ah Khung (4;** no roman-script sign; ☎ 0 81775 2540; Th Maharat), a vendor of incredibly refreshing bowls of iced *chŏw gŏoay*, grass jelly, your well-deserved first snack stop.

Continue north along Th Maharat, which is a centre of herbal apothecaries and sidewalk amulet sellers. Immediately after passing the cat-laden newsstand (you'll know it when you see it), turn left into **Trok Tha Wang (5)**, a narrow alleyway holding a seemingly hidden classic Bangkok neighbourhood. Returning to Th Mahathat, continue moving north. On your right is **Wat Mahathat (6)**, one of Thailand's most respected Buddhist universities.

KO RATANAKOSIN WALKING TOUR

WALK FACTS

Start Tha Chang
Finish Deck
Distance approximately 5km
Duration three hours

After a block or so, turn left into crowded Trok Mahathat to discover the cramped **Amulet Market (7;** p64).

The emergence of white-and-black uniforms is a clue that you are approaching **Thammasat University (8;** Th Phra

Chan), known for its law and political science departments. The campus was also the site of the bloody October 1976 prodemocracy demonstrations, when Thai students were killed or wounded by the military.

Exiting at Tha Phra Chan, cross Th Maharat and continue east towards **Sanam Luang** (**9**; p64), the 'Royal Field'. Cross Sanam Luang, being sure to get a pic of the royal skyline at Wat Phra Kaew. Cross Th Ratchadamnoen Nai and go south towards the home of Bangkok's city spirit, **Lak Meuang (10)**, which is generally alive with the spectacle of devotion –

Clothing stall, Patpong Night Market (p91)

↘ IF YOU LIKE...

If you like **Talat Mai** (p67), you'll like these fresh markets:

- **Khlong Toey Market** (Map pp74-5; cnr Th Ratchadaphisek & Th Phra Ram IV; ☯ 5-10am; Metro Khlong Toei) is one of the city's largest suppliers of fresh ingredients for the city's restaurants and street stalls.

- **Pak Khlong Market** (Map p66; Th Chakkaphet & Th Atsadang; ☯ 24hr; river ferry Tha Saphan Phut) is a wholesale vegetable market by day but at night transforms into a huge bouquet as the city's largest depot for wholesale flowers.

including burning joss sticks and traditional dancing.

Returning at Th Sanamchai, continue south for 500m and turn right onto Th Chetuphon, where you'll enter **Wat Pho** (**11**; p63), home of the Reclining Buddha and lots of quiet nooks and crannies.

After a restorative drink or snack at **Rub Aroon** (**12**; p83), head to adjacent Tha Tien to catch the cross-river ferry to Khmer-influenced **Wat Arun** (**13**; p65).

Cross back to Bangkok to end your journey with celebratory drinks at the **Deck** (**14**; p83) – if you're there at the right time, you can catch one of Bangkok's premier sunset views.

COURSES
COOKING

Baipai Thai Cooking School (Map pp52-3; ☎ 0 2294-9029; www.baipai.com; 150/12 Soi Naksuwan, Th Nonsee; lessons 1800B; ☯ 9.30am-1.30pm & 1.30-5.30pm Tue-Sun) Housed in an attractive suburban villa, and taught by a small army of staff, Baipai offers two daily lessons of four dishes each.

Blue Elephant Thai Cooking School (Map pp80-1; ☎ 0 2673 9353; www.blue elephant.com; 233 Th Sathon Tai; lessons 2800B; ☯ 8.45am-12.30pm & 1.15-5pm Mon-Sat; Skytrain Surasak) Bangkok's most chi-chi Thai cooking school offers two lessons daily.

Epicurean Kitchen Thai Cooking School (Map pp80-1; ☎ 0 2631 1119; www .thaikitchen.com; 10/2 Th Convent, Th Silom; lessons 2000B; ☯ 9.30am-1pm Mon-Fri; Skytrain Sala Daeng, Metro Silom) This cramped but classy school offers daily lessons that encompass a whopping eight dishes, as well as a one-hour 'short course' of four dishes.

BANGKOK FOR CHILDREN

Housing a colourful selection of traditional Thai dolls, both new and antique,

BANGKOK

COURSES

ART ATTACK

Although Bangkok's hyper-urban environment seems to cater to the inner philistine in all of us, the city has a significant but low-key art scene. Some of the better galleries:

- **Bangkok Art & Culture Centre** (BACC; Map p68; ☎ 0 2214 6630; www.bacc.or .th; cnr Th Phayathai & Th Phra Ram 1; Skytrain Siam) This brand-new state-owned complex combines art and commerce in a multistorey building smack-dab in the centre of Bangkok.
- **Bangkok University Art Gallery** (BUG; Map pp74-5; ☎ 0 2350 3500; http://fab.bu .ac.th/buggallery; 3rd fl, Bldg 9, City Campus, Th Phra Ram IV; ☯ 9.30am-7pm Tues-Sat) This spacious new compound is located at what is currently Thailand's most cutting-edge art school.
- **H Gallery** (Map pp80-1; ☎ 0 1310 4428; www.hgallerybkk.com; 201 Soi 12, Th Sathon; ☯ noon-6pm Wed-Sat; Skytrain Surasak) Leading commercial gallery for emerging Thai abstract painters.

is the **Bangkok Doll Factory & Museum** (Map pp52-3; ☎ 0 2245 3008; 85 Soi Ratchataphan/ Mo Leng; admission free; ☯ 8am-5pm Mon-Sat).

Dusit Zoo (Map pp52-3; ☎ 0 2281 9027; www.zoothailand.org; Th Ratchawithi; adult/ child 100/50B; ☯ 8am-6pm Mon-Thu, to 9pm Fri-Sun; bus 18, 510) covers 19 hectares with caged exhibits of more than 300 mammals, 200 reptiles and 800 birds, including relatively rare indigenous species such as banteng, gaur, serow and some rhinoceros.

A massive underwater world has been re-created at the **Siam Ocean World** (Map p68; ☎ 0 2687 2000; www.siamoceanworld.co.th; basement, Siam Paragon, Th Phra Ram I; adult/child 350/250B; ☯ 10am-7pm; Skytrain Siam) shopping-centre aquarium.

TOURS
DINNER CRUISES

Perfect for romancing couples or subdued families, dinner cruises swim along Mae Nam Chao Phraya basking in the twinkling city lights at night, far away from the heat and noise of town.

Manohra Cruises (Map pp52-3; ☎ 0 2477 0770; www.manohracruises.com; Bangkok Marriott Resort & Spa, Thonburi; cocktail/dinner cruise 900/1990B; ☯ cocktail cruise 6-7pm, dinner cruise 7.30-10pm) Commands a fleet of converted teak rice barges that part the waters with regal flair.

Wan Fah Cruises (Map pp80-1; ☎ 0 2222 8679; www.wanfah.in.th; cruises 1200B; ☯ 7-9pm) Departing from the River City Complex, Wan Fah runs a buxom wooden boat that floats in style with accompanying Thai music and traditional dance.

SLEEPING

Banglamphu and the tourist ghetto of Th Khao San still hold the bulk of Bangkok's budget accommodation, although the downside is that it can be difficult to get to other parts of town.

Both Th Sukhumvit and Th Silom have heaps of midrange options, often within walking distance of the Skytrain or Metro. And the city's most famous hotels are largely found along the riverside near Th Silom.

BANGKOK

TH SUKHUMVIT

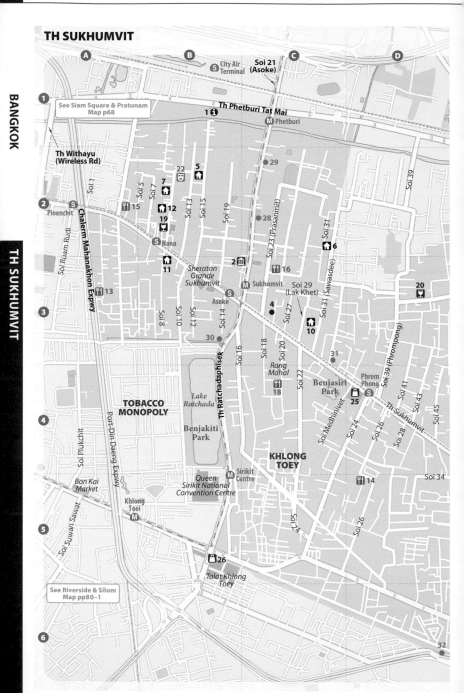

TH SUKHUMVIT

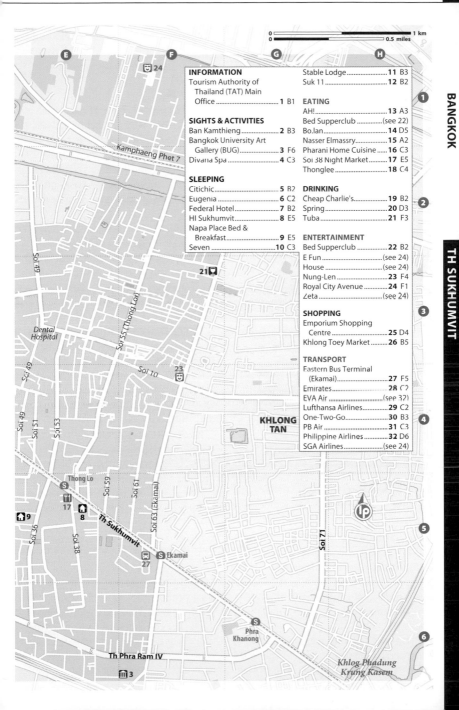

INFORMATION
Tourism Authority of
 Thailand (TAT) Main
 Office **1** B1

SIGHTS & ACTIVITIES
Ban Kamthieng **2** B3
Bangkok University Art
 Gallery (BUG) **3** F6
Divana Spa **4** C3

SLEEPING
Citichic **5** B2
Eugenia **6** C2
Federal Hotel **7** B2
HI Sukhumvit **8** E5
Napa Place Bed &
 Breakfast **9** E5
Seven **10** C3

Stable Lodge **11** B3
Suk 11 ....**12** B2

EATING
AH! **13** A3
Bed Supperclub ....(see **22**)
Bo.lan **14** D5
Nasser Elmassry **15** A2
Pharani Home Cuisine **16** C3
Soi 38 Night Market **17** E5
Thonglee **18** C4

DRINKING
Cheap Charlie's **19** B2
Spring **20** D3
Tuba **21** F3

ENTERTAINMENT
Bed Supperclub **22** B2
E Fun ....(see **24**)
House ....(see **24**)
Nung-Len **23** F4
Royal City Avenue **24** F1
Zeta ....(see **24**)

SHOPPING
Emporium Shopping
 Centre **25** D4
Khlong Toey Market **26** B5

TRANSPORT
Eastern Bus Terminal
 (Ekamai) **27** F5
Emirates **28** C2
EVA Air ....(see **32**)
Lufthansa Airlines **29** C2
One-Two-Go **30** B3
PB Air **31** C3
Philippine Airlines **32** D6
SGA Airlines ....(see **24**)

AUSTIN BUSH

Ban Kamthieng

↘ IF YOU LIKE...

If you like **Jim Thompson's House** (p69), we recommend snooping around these house museums:

- **Ban Kamthieng** (Map pp74-5; ☎ 0 2661 6470; Siam Society, 131 Soi Asoke/21, Th Sukhumvit; adult/child 100/50B; ☺ 9am-5pm Mon-Sat; Skytrain Asoke, Metro Sukhumvit) Be transported to a northern Thai village and a collection of traditional wooden houses.

- **Wang Suan Phakkat** (Lettuce Farm Palace; Map pp52-3; ☎ 0 2245 4934; Th Sri Ayuthaya; admission 100B; ☺ 9am-4pm; Skytrain Phayathai) Five traditional wooden Thai houses display art, antiques and furnishings within a peaceful garden.

KO RATANAKOSIN & BANGLAMPHU

BUDGET

Baan Sabai (Map p66; ☎ 0 2629 1599; baan sabai@hotmail.com; 12 Soi Rongmai; r 190-600B; bus 53, 506, river ferry Tha Phra Athit; ✿ 💻) Truly living up to its name (Comfortable House), this rambling old building holds dozens of plain but comfy rooms, at a variety of prices.

Penpark Place (Map p66; ☎ 0 2281 4733; www.penparkplace.com; 22 Soi 3, Th Samsen; s/d 350/400B; bus 53, 506, river ferry Tha Phra Athit; ✿ 💻) This former factory has been turned

into a good-value budget hotel. There's a communal rooftop area, and plans to add even more rooms in the near future.

MIDRANGE

ourpick **Lamphu Tree House** (Map p66; ☎ 0 2282 0991; www.lamphutreehotel.com; 155 Wanchat Bridge, Th Prachatipatai; r 1200-1800B; klorng taxi to Tha Phah Fah; ✿ 💻 🏊) Rooms are attractive and inviting, and the rooftop bar, pool, internet, restaurant and quiet location ensure that you may never feel the need to leave.

Hotel Dé Moc (Map p66; ☎ 0 2282 2831; www.hoteldemoc.com; 78 Th Prachatipatai; r incl breakfast 1500-1700B; bus 12, 56; ✿ 💻 🏊) The rooms at this classic hotel are large, with high ceilings and generous windows, but the furnishings could certainly use an update.

ourpick **Diamond House** (Map p66; ☎ 0 2629 4008; www.thaidiamondhouse.com; 4 Th Samsen; r 2000-2800B; ste 3600B; bus 30, 53, 506, river ferry Tha Phra Athit; ✿ 💻) Most rooms are loft style, with beds on raised platforms, and are outfitted with stained glass, dark, lush colours and chic furnishings.

Buddy Boutique Hotel (Map p66; ☎ 0 2629 4477; www.buddylodge.com; 265 Th Khao San; r 2000-2600B; bus 53, 506, river ferry Tha Phra Athit; ✿ 💻 🏊) This gigantic complex, which includes a pool, fitness room and, ahem, a branch of McDonald's, is, as far as we're aware, the most expensive place to stay on Th Khao San. Rooms are evocative of a breezy tropical manor house and outfitted with traditional Thai designs.

Viengtai Hotel (Map p66; ☎ 0 2280 5434; www.viengtai.co.th; 42 Th Rambutri; r 2200-3000B; ste 5200B; bus 53, 506, ferry Tha Phra Athit; ✿ 💻 🏊) Long before Th Khao San was 'discovered', this was an ordinary Chinese-style hotel in a quiet neighbourhood. It now sits comfortably in the midrange with reliable but unstylish rooms.

Baan Chantra (Map p66; ☎ 0 2628 6988; www.baanchantra.com; 120 Th Samsen; r incl breakfast 2700-4000B; bus 30, 53, 506, river ferry Tha Phra Athit; ❐ 및) This beautiful converted house is without pretensions, preferring to be comfortable and roomy rather than fashionable and pinched.

TOP END

Navalai River Resort (Map p66; ☎ 0 2280 9955; www.navalai.com; 45/1 Th Phra Athit; r incl breakfast 3000-4500B; bus 53, 506, river ferry Tha Phra Athit; ❐ 및 ☎) There are attractive Thai design touches throughout, but you might end up spending much of your time checking out the views from the rooftop pool.

Old Bangkok Inn (Map p66; ☎ 0 2629 1787; www.oldbangkokinn.com; 609 Th Phra Sumen; r incl breakfast 3190-6590B; bus 2, 82, 511, 512, klorng taxi to Tha Phan Fah; ❐ 및) The 10 rooms in this refurbished antique shophouse are decadent and sumptuous, combining rich colours and heavy wood furnishings.

BANGKOK'S ISLAND GETAWAY

Soothe your nerves with a half-day getaway to **Ko Kret**, a car-free island in the middle of Mae Nam Chao Phraya, at Bangkok's northern edge. Actually an artificial island, the result of dredging a canal in a sharp bend in the river, the island is home to one of Thailand's oldest settlements of Mon people, who were the dominant culture in central Thailand between the 6th and 10th centuries AD. The Mon are also skilled potters, and Ko Kret continues the culture's ancient tradition of hand-thrown earthenware, made from local Ko Kret clay.

The most convenient way to get there is by taxi or bus (33 from Sanam Luang) to Pak Kret, before boarding the cross-river ferry that leaves from Wat Sanam Neua.

BANGKOK

SLEEPING

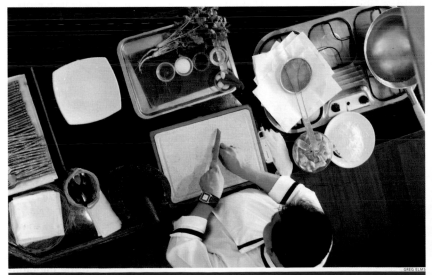

GREG ELMS

Cooking demonstration, Blue Elephant Thai Cooking School (p72) `our pick` **Arun Residence** (Map p66; ☎ 0 2221 9158; www.arunresidence.com; 36-38 Soi Pratu Nok Yung, Th Maharat; r/ste incl breakfast 3500/5500B; river ferry Tha Tien; ✖ ▣) Strategically located across from Wat Arun, this multilevel wooden house on the river boasts much more than just brilliant views.

SILOM, SATHON & RIVERSIDE
BUDGET & MIDRANGE

`our pick` **Lub*d** (Map pp80-1; ☎ 0 2634 7999; www.lubd.com; 4 Th Decho; dm/s/d 520/1280/1800B; Skytrain Chong Nonsi; ✖ ▣) There are four storeys of dorms (including a ladies-only wing) and a few private rooms, both with and without bathrooms.

La Résidence Hotel (Map pp80-1; ☎ 0 2233 3301, www.laresidencebangkok.com; 173/8-9 Th Surawong; s/d 1200-2000B, ste 2700B; Skytrain Chong Nonsi; ✖ ▣) La Résidence is a boutique inn with playfully and individually decorated rooms.

`our pick` **Swan Hotel** (Map pp80-1; ☎ 0 2235 9271; www.swanhotelbkk.com; 31 Soi 36, Th Charoen Krung; s/d 1200-1500B; river ferry Tha Oriental; ✖ ▣ ☎) A recent facelift has it looking better than ever, although the room furnishings are still stuck in the 1970s. The inviting pool area is a bit more timeless, and the entire place is virtually spotless.

Inn Saladaeng (Map pp80-1; ☎ 0 2637 5522; www.theinnsaladaeng.com; 5/12 Soi Sala Daeng; d 1400-1800B; Skytrain Sala Daeng, Metro Silom; ✖ ▣) One of several boutique hotels in the area, the Inn is the newest and most conveniently located.

WHAT TO EXPECT IN BANGKOK

Budget under 1000B
Midrange 1000B to 3000B
Top End over 3000B

Rose Hotel (Map pp80-1; ☎ 0 2266 8268-72; www.rosehotelbkk.com; 118 Th Surawong; r from 1800B; Skytrain Sala Daeng, Metro Silom; ✖ ▣ ☎) Don't let the unremarkable exterior fool you; a recent renovation has the lobby and rooms of this Vietnam War vet looking quite modern.

TOP END

Millennium Hilton (Map pp80-1; ☎ 0 2442 2000; www.bangkok.hilton.com; 123 Th Charoen Nakorn, Thonburi; r 6800-7300B, ste 12,000-26,000B; hotel shuttle boat from River City & Tha Sathon/Central Pier; ✖ ▣ ☎) As soon as you enter the dramatic lobby, it's obvious that this is Bangkok's youngest, most modern riverside hotel. Rooms, all of which boast widescreen river views, follow this theme, and are decked out with funky furniture and Thai-themed photos.

Oriental Hotel (MMap pp80-1; ☎ 0 2659 9000; www.mandarinoriental.com; 48 Soi Oriental/38, Th Charoen Krung; r incl breakfast US$420-600, ste incl breakfast US$600-3000; hotel shuttle boat from Tha Sathon/Central Pier; ✖ ▣ ☎) For the true Bangkok experience, a stay at this grand old riverside hotel is a must. The majority of rooms are located in the modern New Wing, but we prefer the old-world ambience of the Garden and Authors' Wings.

SIAM SQUARE & PRATUNAM

For centrally located accommodation, there's really no better destination than the area surrounding Siam Square.

BUDGET & MIDRANGE

A-One Inn (Map p68; ☎ 0 2215 3029; www .aoneinn.com; 25/13-15 Soi Kasem San 1; d from 650B; Skytrain National Stadium, klorng taxi to Tha Ratchathewi; ✖ ▣) The lobby is a bit messy here, but a peek into the rooms proves that they are well proportioned and good value.

BANGKOK

AUSTIN BUSH

Oriental Hotel

SLEEPING

Wendy House (Map p68; ☎ 0 2214 1149; www.wendyguesthouse.com; 36/2 Soi Kasem San 1; d incl breakfast from 1000B; Skytrain National Stadium, klorng taxi to Tha Ratchathewi; 🖾 💻) The rooms here are small and basic, but well stocked (TV, fridge) for this price range.

Reno Hotel (Map p68; ☎ 0 2215 0026; www .renohotel.co.th; 40 Soi Kasem San 1; d 1280-1650B; Skytrain National Stadium, klorng taxi to Tha Ratchathewi; 🖾 💻 🞱) Only some of the rooms reflect the renovations evident in the lobby and exterior, but the cafe and classic pool of this Vietnam War-era vet still cling to the past.

SUKHUMVIT

There's a bit of everything in Sukhumvit, from the odd backpacker hostel to sex-tourist hovels and five-star luxury.

The former two are largely located between Sois 1 and 4, while the latter doesn't begin to appear until you reach Soi 12 or so.

BUDGET

Suk 11 (Map pp74-5; ☎ 0 2253 5927; www .suk11.com; 1/33 Soi 11, Th Sukhumvit; dm/s/d/ ste 250/500/750/2000B; Skytrain Nana; 🖾 💻) Extremely well run and extremely popular, this guesthouse is an oasis of woods and greenery in the urban jungle that is Th Sukhumvit.

HI-Sukhumvit (Map pp74-5; ☎ 0 2391 9338; www.hisukhumvit.com; 23 Soi 38, Th Sukhumvit; dm 300B, s 550-600B, d 800-850B; Skytrain Thong Lo; 🖾 💻) Located in a quiet residential street a brief walk from the Skytrain, this friendly hostel excels with its neat dorms and accompanying immense bathrooms.

MIDRANGE

Federal Hotel (Map pp74-5; ☎ 0 2253 0175; www .federalbangkok.com; 27 Soi 11, Th Sukhumvit; r 1200-1500B; Skytrain Nana; 🖾 💻 🞱) The upstairs rooms are comfortable and almost contemporary, but the rooms at ground level still scream 1967. The real draws are the frangipani-lined pool and time-warped American-style coffee shop.

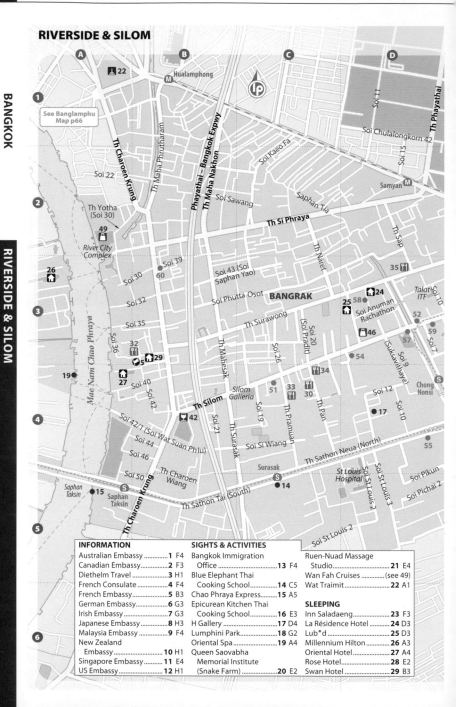

RIVERSIDE & SILOM

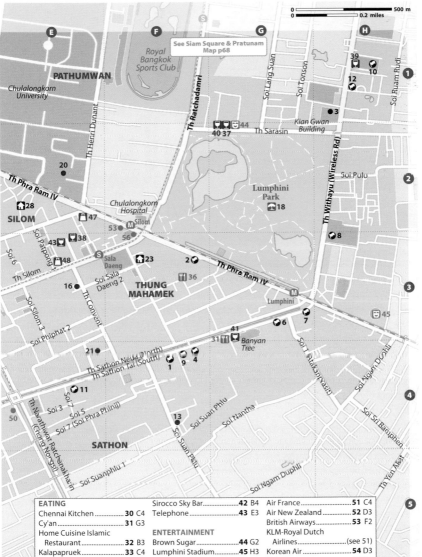

EATING		
Chennai Kitchen	**30**	C4
Cy'an	**31**	G3
Home Cuisine Islamic Restaurant	**32**	B3
Kalapapruek	**33**	C4
Khrua Aroy Aroy	**34**	C4
Scoozi	**35**	D3
Vino di Zanotti	**36**	F3

DRINKING

70s Bar	**37**	G2
Balcony	**38**	E3
Diplomat Bar	**39**	H1
Kluen Saek	**40**	G2
Moon Bar at Vertigo	**41**	G3

Sirocco Sky Bar	**42**	B4
Telephone	**43**	E3

ENTERTAINMENT

Brown Sugar	**44**	G2
Lumphini Stadium	**45**	H3

SHOPPING

House of Chao	**46**	D3
Jim Thompson	**47**	E2
Patpong Night Market	**48**	E3
River City Complex	**49**	A2

TRANSPORT

| Air Canada | **50** | E4 |

Air France	**51**	C4
Air New Zealand	**52**	D3
British Airways	**53**	F2
KLM-Royal Dutch Airlines	(see 51)	
Korean Air	**54**	D3
Nok Air	**55**	D4
Qantas Airways	(see 53)	
Singapore Airlines	**56**	F3
Thai Airways International	**57**	D3
Thai Airways International (Temporary)	**58**	D3
United Airlines	**59**	D3
World Travel Service	**60**	B3

Rub Aroon

AUSTIN BUSH

Stable Lodge (Map pp74-5; ☎ 0 2653 0017; www.stablelodge.com; 39 Soi 8, Th Sukhumvit; r 1500-1700B; Skytrain Nana; 🕮 🖳 🍴) A recent renovation has given a bit of life to the simple rooms here, and the spacious balconies still offer great city views.

Citichic (Map pp74-5; ☎ 0 2342 3888; www .citichichotel.com; 34 Soi 13, Th Sukhumvit; r 2700-3000B; Skytrain Nana; 🕮 🖳 🍴) The name and lobby of this stylish midranger ooze self-confidence. And justifiably so; although they are a bit of a tight squeeze, the rooms here come fully equipped with flat-screen TVs and all other amenities – and all of it done with style.

Napa Place Bed & Breakfast (Map pp74-5; ☎ 0 2661 5525; www.napaplace.com; 11/3 Sap 2, Soi 36, Th Sukhumvit; d 2750-4800B; Skytrain Thong Lo; 🕮 🖳) Seemingly hidden in the confines of a typical Bangkok urban compound is what must be the city's homiest accommodation.

TOP END

Seven (Map pp74-5; ☎ 0 2662 0951; www.sleep atseven.com; 3/15 Soi Sawasdee/31, Th Sukhumvit;

r 3300-6000B; Skytrain Phrom Phong; 🕮 🖳) This tiny hotel somehow manages to be chic and homey, stylish and comfortable, Thai and international all at the same time.

our pick **Eugenia** (Map pp74-5; ☎ 0 2259 9017/19; www.theeugenia.com; 267 Soi Sawasdee/31, Th Sukhumvit; r 5800-7200B; Skytrain Asoke, Metro Sukhumvit; 🕮 🖳 🍴) Decked out in antique furniture and an abundance of animal skins, a stay here is like travelling to Burma c 1936.

EATING

Invariably the safest of Bangkok's infamous carnal pleasures, food is serious business in this city.

KO RATANAKOSIN & BANGLAMPHU
THAI

Chote Chitr (Map p66; ☎ 0 2221 4082; 146 Th Phraeng Phuthon; dishes 30-200B; 🕑 lunch & dinner Mon-Sat; bus 15, klorng taxi to Tha Phan Fah) This third-generation shophouse restaurant boasting just six tables is a true Bangkok foodie landmark. The kitchen can be inconsistent, but when it's on, dishes like *mèe gròrp* (crispy fried noodles) and *yam tòoa ploo* (wing-bean salad) are in a class of their own.

Rub Aroon (Map p66; ☎ 0 2622 2312; 310-312 Th Maharat; dishes 60-95B; ☺ 8am-6pm; river ferry Tha Tien) Strategically located across from Wat Pho, this tastefully restored shophouse is the perfect temple-exploring pit stop.

Krua Noppharat (Map p66; ☎ 0 2281 7578; 130-132 Th Phra Athit; dishes 60-100B; ☺ lunch & dinner Mon-Sat; bus 30, 53, 506, river ferry Tha Phra Athit) Krua Noppharat expends considerably energy where flavour is concerned, and thankfully does not tone down its excellent central- and southern-style Thai fare for foreign diners.

Rachanawi Samosorn (Khun Kung Kitchen; Map p66; ☎ 0 2222 0081; 77 Th Maharat; dishes 70-150B; ☺ 10am-6pm; bus 508, 512, bus 32, 53, river ferry Tha Chang) The restaurant of the Royal Navy Association has one of the few coveted riverfront locations along this stretch of the Chao Phraya. Locals come for the combination of riverfront views and cheap and tasty seafood-based eats.

Hemlock (Map p66; ☎ 0 2282 7507; 56 Th Phra Athit; dishes 60-220B; ☺ 4pm-midnight; bus 30, 53, 506, river ferry Tha Phra Athit) Taking full advantage of its cosy shophouse setting, this white-tablecloth local is an excellent intro to Thai food.

INTERNATIONAL

Shoshana (Map p66; ☎ 0 2282 9948; 88 Th Chakraphong; dishes 30-150B; ☺ 10am-11.30pm; bus 30, 53, 506, river ferry Tha Phra Athit) Although prices have gone up slightly since it began back in 1982, Shoshana still puts together a cheap but tasty Israeli meal.

Deck (Map p66; ☎ 0 2221 9158; Arun Residence, 36-38 Soi Pratu Nok Yung, Th Maharat; dishes 170-690B; ☺ lunch & dinner; river ferry Tha Tien) Deck's claim to fame is its commanding views over Wat Arun, but the restaurant's short but diverse menu, ranging from duck confit to Thai-style pomelo salad, sweetens the pot.

CHINATOWN & PHAHURAT

Old Siam Plaza (Map p66; ground fl, Old Siam Plaza, cnr Th Phahurat & Th Triphet; dishes 15-50B; ☺ lunch; river ferry Tha Saphan Phut) The ground floor of this shopping centre is a candy-land of traditional Thai sweets and snacks, most made right before your eyes.

Royal India (Map p66; ☎ 0 2221 6565; 392/1 Th Chakraphet; dishes 40-130B; ☺ lunch & dinner; river ferry Tha Saphan Phut) Yes, we realise that this legendary hole in the wall has been in every edition of our guide since the beginning, but after all these years it's still the most reliable place to eat in Bangkok's Little India.

Tang Jai Yuu (no roman-script sign; Map p66; ☎ 0 2224 2167; 85-89 Th Yaowaphanit; dishes 120-500B; ☺ lunch & dinner; Metro Hualamphong, river ferry Tha Ratchawong) This longstanding fave is great for a decadent night out, and specialises in Teo Chew and Chinese-Thai specialties with an emphasis on seafood.

WAVING THE YELLOW FLAG

During the annual Vegetarian Festival in September/October, Bangkok's Chinatown becomes a virtual orgy of nonmeat cuisine. The festivities centre on Chinatown's main street, Th Yaowarat, and the Talat Noi area (see Map p66), but food shops and stalls all over the city post yellow flags to announce their meat-free status.

TOM COCKREM

Enjoying a seafood lunch

SILOM, SATHON & RIVERSIDE
THAI
Khrua Aroy Aroy (Map pp80-1; ☎ 0 2635 2365; Th Pan; dishes 30-70B; ☺ 6am-6pm; Skytrain Surasak) Stop by for some of Bangkok's richest curries, as well as a revolving menu of daily specials.

Home Cuisine Islamic Restaurant (Map pp80-1; ☎ 0 2234 7911; 196-198 Soi 36, Th Charoen Krung; dishes 45-130B; ☺ 11am-10pm Mon-Sat, 6-10pm Sun; river ferry Tha Oriental) This bungalow-style restaurant does tasty Thai-Muslim food with an Indian accent.

Kalapapruek (Map pp80-1; ☎ 0 2236 4335; 27 Th Pramuan; dishes 60-120B; ☺ 8am-6pm; Skytrain Surasak) The diverse menu spans regional Thai specialties from just about every region, daily specials and, occasionally, seasonal treats as well.

INTERNATIONAL
Chennai Kitchen (Map pp80-1; ☎ 0 2234 1266; 10 Th Pan; dishes 50-150B; ☺ 10am-3pm; Skytrain Surasak) The arm-length *dosas* (a crispy southern Indian bread) are always a good choice, but if you're feeling indecisive go for the *thali* set that seems to incorporate just about everything in the kitchen.

Scoozi (Map pp80-1; ☎ 0 2234 6999; 174 Th Surawong; dishes 150-350B; ☺ lunch & dinner; Skytrain Chong Nonsi) Now boasting several locations across Bangkok, we still think the wood-fired pizzas taste best at this, the original branch.

SIAM SQUARE & PRATUNAM
Sanguan Sri (Map p68; ☎ 0 2252 7637; 59/1 Th Withayu/Wireless Rd; dishes 60-150B; ☺ 10am-3pm Mon-Sat; Skytrain Ploenchit) There's a limited English-language menu, but simply pointing to the delicious dishes being consumed around you is probably a better strategy.

New Light Coffee House (Map p68; ☎ 0 2251 9592; 426/1-4 Siam Sq; dishes 60-200B; ☺ 8am-11.30pm; Skytrain Siam) Travel back in time to 1960s-era Bangkok at this vintage diner popular with students from nearby Chulalongkorn University.

SUKHUMVIT
THAI
Soi 38 Night Market (Map pp74-5; Soi 38, Th Sukhumvit; dishes 30-60B; ☺ 8pm-3am; Skytrain Thong Lo) After a hard night of clubbing, this gathering of basic Thai-Chinese hawker stalls will look like a shimmering oasis.

Pharani Home Cuisine (Sansab Boat Noodle; Map pp74-5; ☎ 0 2664 4454; Soi Prasanmit/23, Th Sukhumvit; dishes 35-200B; ☺ 10am-10pm; Skytrain Asoke, Metro Sukhumvit) This cosy Thai restaurant dabbles in a bit of everything, from ox-tongue stew to rice fried with shrimp paste, but the real reason to come is for the rich, meaty 'boat noodles' – so called because they used to be sold from boats plying the *klorng* of Ayuthaya.

Thonglee (Map pp74–5; ☎ 0 2258 1983; Soi 20, Th Sukhumvit; dishes 40–70B; ☺ 10am-8pm, closed 3rd Sun of the month; Skytrain Asoke, Metro Sukhumvit) One of the few remaining mom-and-pop Thai places on Sukhumvit, this tiny kitchen offers a few dishes you won't find elsewhere, like *mŏo pàt gà·bì* (pork fried with shrimp paste), and *mèe gròrp* (sweet-and-spicy crispy fried noodles).

ourpick **Bo.lan** (Map pp74–5; ☎ 0 2260 2962; www.bolan.co.th; 42 Soi Rongnarong Phichai Songkhram, Soi 26, Th Sukhumvit; set meal 1500B; ☺ lunch & dinner; Skytrain Phrom Phong) Upmarket Thai is usually more garnish than flavour, but this chic new restaurant, started up by two former chefs of London's Michelin-starred Nahm, is the exception.

INTERNATIONAL

AH! (Map pp74–5; ☎ 0 2252 6069; Atlanta Hotel, 78 Soi Phasak/2, Th Sukhumvit; dishes 60–150B; ☺ breakfast, lunch & dinner; Skytrain Ploenchit) The Atlanta Hotel's delightful vintage diner is one of the few places that excels both in atmosphere and cuisine. Delve back into 1950s-era 'continental' dishes,

such as Hungarian goulash or wiener schnitzel, or acclaimed vegetarian Thai.

Nasser Elmassry (Map pp74–5; ☎ 0 2253 5582; 4/6 Soi 3/1, Th Sukhumvit; dishes 80–350B; ☺ 8am-5am; Skytrain Nana) One of several similar Middle Eastern restaurants on Soi 3/1, Nasser Elmassry is easily recognisable by its genuinely impressive floor-to-ceiling stainless-steel 'theme'.

Bed Supperclub (Map pp74–5; ☎ 0 2651 3537; www.bedsupperclub.com; 26 Soi 11, Th Sukhumvit; 3-course à la carte dinner Sun-Thu 1450B, 4-course set dinner Fri & Sat 1850B; ☺ 7.30-10.30pm Sun-Thu, dinner 9pm Fri & Sat; Skytrain Nana) Kiwi chef Paul Hutt and his army of talented Thai chefs are creating the most cutting-edge cuisine in town. Dinner is à la carte except on Friday and Saturday when Hutt does a four-course surprise menu at 9pm sharp.

LUMPHINI PARK & TH PHRA RAM IV

ourpick **Cy'an** (Map pp80–1; ☎ 0 2625 3333; Metropolitan Hotel, 27 Th Sathon Tai; 9-course set dinner 3100B; ☺ lunch & dinner; Metro Lumphini) Combining vibrant Mediterranean and Moroccan flavours, a healthy obsession with the finest seafood, and a stylish and intimate atmosphere, this is one of the best destinations for a splurge.

FOOD COURT FRENZY

Every Bangkok mall worth its escalators has some sort of food court. The following are some of the better choices.

- **Food Loft** (Map p68; 6th floor, Central Chit Lom, 1027 Th Ploenchit; ☺ 10am-10pm; Skytrain Chitlom) Central Chit Lom pioneered the concept of the upmarket food court, and mock-ups of the various Indian, Italian, Singaporean and other international dishes aid in the decision-making process.

- **MBK Food Court** (Map p68; 6th floor, MBK Center, cnr Th Phra Ram I & Th Phayathai; ☺ 10am-9pm; Skytrain National Stadium) The granddaddy of the genre offers dozens of vendors selling food from virtually every corner of Thailand and beyond.

BANGKOK

DRINKING

DRINKING
KO RATANAKOSIN & BANGLAMPHU

At night the natives deem it safe to join the crowds, giving the area an entirely different atmosphere. Bars tend to segregate into foreigner and Thai factions, but you can always reverse that trend. Here are a few popular options:

Buddy Bar (Map p66; Th Khao San; river ferry Tha Phra Athit) A spotless colonial-themed bar for when only air-conditioning will do.

Center Khao San (Map p66; Th Khao San; river ferry Tha Phra Athit) One of many front-row views of the human parade on Th Khao San; the upstairs bar hosts late-night bands.

Molly Bar (Map p66; Th Rambutri; river ferry Tha Phra Athit) Packed on weekends for Thai local bands; more mellow on weekdays with outdoor seating.

SILOM, SATHON & RIVERSIDE

Sirocco Sky Bar (Map pp80-1; ☎ 0 2624 9555; The Dome, 1055 Th Silom; Skytrain Saphan Taksin) Bangkok seems to be one of the only places in the world where nobody minds if you slap a bar right on top of a skyscraper. But be sure to dress the part; shorts and sandal wearers have to stay at ground level.

Moon Bar at Vertigo (Map pp80-1; ☎ 0 2679 1200; Banyan Tree Hotel, 21/100 Th Sathon Tai; Metro Lumphini) Also precariously perched on top of a skyscraper, Moon Bar at Vertigo offers a slightly different bird's-eye view of Bangkok. Things can get a bit crowded here come sunset, so be sure to show up a bit early to get the best seats.

Vino di Zanotti (Map pp80-1; ☎ 0 2636 3366; 41 Soi Yommarat; Skytrain Sala Daeng, Metro Silom) A branch of the nearby Italian restaurant of the same name, Vino keeps it casual with live music, a huge wine list and lots of delicious nibbles.

SIAM SQUARE & PRATUNAM

Diplomat Bar (Map pp80-1; ☎ 0 2690 9999; Conrad Hotel, 87 Th Withayu/Wireless Rd; Skytrain Ploenchit) This is one of the few hotel

Vino di Zanotti

AUSTIN BUSH

lounges that the locals make a point of visiting. Choose from an expansive list of innovative martinis and sip to live jazz, played gracefully at conversation level.

To-Sit (Map p66; ☎ 0 2658 4001; Soi 3, Siam Sq, Th Phra Ram 1; Skytrain Siam) To-Sit epitomises everything a Thai university student could wish for on a night out: sappy Thai music and cheap, spicy eats.

Café Trio (Map p68; ☎ 0 2252 6572; 36/11-12 Soi Lang Suan; Skytrain Chitlom) Spend an evening at this cosy jazz bar and you'll go home feeling like a local.

SUKHUMVIT

Tuba (Map pp52-3; ☎ 0 2622 0708; 30 Ekamai Soi 21, Soi Ekamai/63, Th Sukhumvit; Skytrain Ekamai) Part storage room for over-the-top vintage furniture, part friendly local boozer, this bizarre bar certainly doesn't lack in character.

Spring (Map pp74-5; ☎ 0 2392 2747; 199 Soi Promsri 2, Soi Phrompong/39, Th Sukhumvit; Skytrain Phrom Phong) Although not technically a bar, the expansive lawn of this smartly reconverted 1970s-era house is probably the only chance you'll ever have to witness Bangkok's fair and beautiful willingly exposing themselves to the elements.

Cheap Charlie's (Map pp74-5; Soi 11, Th Sukhumvit; ☿ Mon-Sat; Skytrain Nana) There's never enough seating, and the design concept is best classified as 'junkyard', but on most nights this chummy open-air beer corner is a great place to meet everybody, from package tourists to resident English teachers.

ENTERTAINMENT
LIVE MUSIC

Saxophone Pub & Restaurant (Map pp52-3; ☎ 0 2246 5472; 3/8 Th Phayathai; Skytrain Victory Monument) This nightlife staple is the big stage of Bangkok's live music scene. It's a

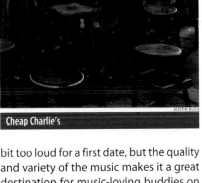
AUSTIN BUSH
Cheap Charlie's

bit too loud for a first date, but the quality and variety of the music makes it a great destination for music-loving buddies on a night out.

Tawan Daeng German Brewhouse (Map pp52-3; ☎ 0 2678 1114; cnr Th Phra Ram III & Th Narathiwat Ratchanakharin; taxi) It's Oktoberfest all year round at this hangar-sized music hall. The Thai-German food is tasty, the house-made brews are entirely potable, and the nightly stage shows make singing along an absolute necessity.

Brown Sugar (Map pp80-1; ☎ 0 2250 1825; 231/20 Th Sarasin; Skytrain Ratchadamri) Plant yourself in a corner of this cosy, mazelike pub, and bump to Zao-za-dung, the nine-piece house band.

DANCE CLUBS

Cover charges for clubs and discos range from 250B to 600B and usually include a drink. Don't even think about showing up before 11pm, and always bring ID. Most clubs close at 2am.

Club Culture (Map pp52-3; ☎ 0 89497 8422; Th Sri Ayuthaya; ☺ 7pm-late Wed, Fri & Sat; Skytrain Phayathai) Housed in a unique 40-year-old Thai-style building, Club Culture is the biggest and quirkiest recent arrival on Bangkok's club scene.

Nung-Len (Map pp52-3; ☎ 0 2711 6564; 217 Soi Ekamai/63; Skytrain Ekamai) Young, loud and Thai, Nung-Len (literally 'sit and chill') is a ridiculously popular sardine tin of live music and uni students on popular Th Ekamai. Make sure you get in before 10pm or you won't get in at all.

Bed Supperclub (Map pp74-5; ☎ 0 2651 3537; www.bedsupperclub.com; 26 Soi 11, Th Sukhumvit; Skytrain Nana) This illuminated tube has been a literal highlight of the Bangkok club scene for a good while now. Arrive early to squeeze in dinner, or if you've only got dancing on your mind, come on Tuesday for the hip-hop nights.

Royal City Avenue (RCA; Map pp52-3; off Th Phra Ram IX) Well and truly Club Alley.

CINEMAS

Escape the smog and heat at one of the city's high-tech cinemas. All movies screened in Thai cinemas are preceded by the Thai royal anthem and everyone is expected to stand respectfully for its duration.

EGV Grand (Map p68; ☎ 0 2515 5555; Siam Discovery Center, Th Phra Ram I; Skytrain Siam)

House (Map pp52-3; ☎ 0 2641 5177; www.houserama.com; UMG Bldg, Royal City Ave, near Th Petchaburi; Metro Phetburi)

Lido Cinema (Map p68; ☎ 0 2252 6498; Siam Sq, Th Phra Ram I; Skytrain Siam)

Paragon Cineplex (Map p68; ☎ 0 2515 5555; Siam Paragon, Th Phra Ram I; Skytrain Siam)

Scala Cinema (Map p68; ☎ 0 2251 2861; Siam Sq, Soi 1, Th Phra Ram I; Skytrain Siam)

GAY & LESBIAN BANGKOK

With out-and-open nightspots and annual pride events, the city's homosexual community enjoys an unprecedented amount of tolerance considering attitudes in the rest of the region.

Traipse on over to Soi 4 to find the old-timer conversation bars, such as **Balcony** (Map pp80-1; ☎ 0 2235 5891; 86-88 Soi 4, Th Silom; Skytrain Sala Daeng, Metro Silom) and **Telephone** (Map pp80-1; ☎ 0 2234 3279; 114/11-13 Soi 4, Th Silom; Skytrain Sala Daeng, Metro Silom).

Th Sarasin, behind Lumphini Park, is lined with more loungey options, such as **70s Bar** (Map pp80-1; ☎ 0 2253 4433; 231/16 Th Sarasin; no cover; ☺ 6pm-1am; Skytrain Ratchadamri), a small dance club that resuscitates the era of disco, and **Kluen Saek** (Map pp80-1; ☎ 0 2254 2962; 297 Th Sarasin; Skytrain Ratchadamri), both part of a strip of formerly 'hetero' bars that are becoming gayer by the day.

After all these years, Bangkok finally has something of a lesbian scene. **E Fun** (Map pp52-3; Royal City Ave/RCA, off Phra Ram IX; no cover; ☺ 10pm-2am; Metro Ram IX) and **Zeta** (Map pp52-3; ☎ 0 2203 0994; 29 Royal City Ave/RCA, off Phra Ram IX; no cover; ☺ 10pm-2am; Metro Ram IX) are both easy-going clubs for the girls with a nightly band doing Thai and Western covers.

Thai boxing

MICK ELMORE

SF Cinema City (Map p68; ☎ 0 2268 8888; 7th fl, MBK Center, cnr Th Phra Ram I & Th Phayathai; Skytrain National Stadium)

TRADITIONAL ARTS PERFORMANCES

Chalermkrung Royal Theatre (Sala Chaloem Krung; Map p66; ☎ 0 2222 0434; www.salachalermkrung.com; cnr Th Charoen Krung & Th Triphet; tickets 1000-2000B; river ferry Tha Saphan Phut) In a Thai art-deco building at the edge of the Chinatown-Phahurat district, this theatre provides a striking venue for *köhn* (masked dance-drama based on stories from the *Ramakian,* the Thai version of the *Ramayana). Köhn* performances last about two hours plus intermission; call for the schedule. The theatre requests that patrons dress respectfully, which means no shorts, tank tops or sandals.

Aksra Theatre (Map pp52-3; ☎ 0 2677 8888, ext 5604; www.aksratheatre.com; King Power Complex, 8/1 Th Rang Nam; tickets 800B; ☺ shows 7pm Tue-Fri, 1pm & 7pm Sat & Sun; Skytrain Victory Monument) The former Joe Louis Puppet Theatre has moved house and is starting a new life here as the Aksra Hoon Lakorn Lek. A variety of performances are now held at this modern theatre, but the highlight are performances of the Ramakian by using knee-high puppets requiring three puppeteers to strike humanlike poses.

Patravadi Theatre (Map p66; ☎ 0 2412 7287; www.patravaditheatre.com; 69/1 Soi Tambon Wanglang 1; tickets 500B; cross-river ferry from Tha Maharat) This open-air theatre is Bangkok's leading promoter of avant-garde dance and drama. The new Studio 9 annexe offers dinner theatre on Friday and Saturday nights.

THAI BOXING

Thai boxing's best of the best fight it out at Bangkok's two boxing stadiums: **Lumphini Stadium** (Sanam Muay Lumphini; Map pp80-1; ☎ 0 2251 4303; Th Phra Ram IV; tickets 3rd/2nd class/ringside 1000/1500/2000B; Metro Lumphini) and **Ratchadamnoen Stadium** (Sanam Muay Ratchadamnoen; Map p66; ☎ 0 2281 4205; Th Ratchadamnoen Nok; tickets 3rd/2nd class/ringside 1000/1500/2000B; bus 70, 503, 509).

LOCAL BUYS

- **D&O Shop** This open-air gallery is the first retail venture of an organisation created to encourage awareness of Thai design abroad. The items are modern and funky, and give a new breath of life to the concept of Thai design. Available at Gaysorn Plaza (right).
- **Harnn & Thann** Smell good enough to eat with botanical-based spa products: lavender massage lotion, rice bran soap and jasmine compresses. Available at Gaysorn Plaza (right).
- **Propaganda** Thai designer Chaiyut Plypetch dreamed up this brand's signature character, the devilish Mr P who appears in anatomically correct cartoon lamps and other products. Available at Siam Discovery Center (right) and Emporium (p91).

Ratchadamnoen hosts the matches on Monday, Wednesday and Thursday at 6pm and on Sunday at 5pm. Lumphini hosts matches on Tuesday, Friday and Saturday at 6pm. Aficionados say the best-matched bouts are reserved for Tuesday night at Lumphini and Thursday night at Ratchadamnoen.

SHOPPING

Despite the apparent scope and variety, Bangkok really only excels in one area when it comes to shopping: lots of cheap stuff.

ANTIQUES

River City Complex (Map pp80-1; Th Yotha, off Th Charoen Krung; river ferry Tha Si Phraya)

Near the Royal Orchid Sheraton Hotel, this multistorey shopping centre is an all-in-one stop for old-world Asiana. Many stores here close on Sunday.

House of Chao (Map pp80-1; ☎ 0 2635 7188; 9/1 Th Decho; ⏰ 9am-7pm; Skytrain Chong Nonsi) This three-storey antique shop, housed, appropriately, in an antique house, has everything necessary to deck out your fantasy colonial-era mansion.

DEPARTMENT STORES & SHOPPING CENTRES

Most shopping centres are open from 10am or 11am to 9pm or 10pm.

MBK Center (Mahboonkhrong; Map p68; ☎ 0 2217 9111; cnr Th Phra Ram I & Th Phayathai; Skytrain National Stadium) This colossal mall has become a tourist destination in its own right. This is the cheapest place to buy contact lenses, mobile phones and accessories, and name-brand knock-offs.

Siam Center & Siam Discovery Center (Map p68; cnr Th Phra Ram I & Th Phayathai; Skytrain National Stadium) These linked sister centres feel almost monastic in their hushed hallways compared to frenetic MBK, just across the street. Siam Discovery Center excels in home decor, with the whole 3rd floor devoted to Asian-minimalist styles and jewel-toned fabrics.

Siam Paragon (Map p68; ☎ 0 2610 8000; Th Phra Ram I; Skytrain Siam) The biggest, newest and glitziest of Bangkok's shopping malls, Siam Paragon is more of an urban park than shopping centre.

Gaysorn Plaza (Map p68; cnr Th Ploenchit & Th Ratchadamri; Skytrain Chitlom) A haute couture catwalk, Gaysorn Plaza's spiralling staircases and all-white halls preserve all of fashion's beloved designers in museum-curatorship style. Local fashion leaders occupy the 2nd floor, while the top floor is a stroll through chic home decor.

Emporium Shopping Centre (Map pp74-5; 622 Th Sukhumvit, cnr Soi 24; Skytrain Phrom Phong) Robust expat salaries and trust funds dwindle amid Prada, Miu Miu, Chanel and Thai brands such as Greyhound and Propaganda.

Pantip Plaza (Map p68; 604 Th Petchaburi; Skytrain Ratchathewi) North of Siam Square, this is five storeys of computer and software stores ranging from legit to flea market. Many locals come here to buy pirated software and computer peripherals, but the crowds and touts ('DVD sex?') make it among the more tiring shopping experiences in town.

FASHION & TEXTILES

Siam Square (Map p68; btwn Th Phra Ram I & Th Phayathai, Skytrain Siam) This low-slung commercial universe is a network of some 12 soi lined with trendy, fly-by-night boutiques, many of which are the first ventures of young local designers. It's a great place to find designs you won't find elsewhere.

Jim Thompson (Map pp80-1; ☎ 0 2632 8100; 9 Th Surawong; ☺ 9am-6pm; Skytrain Sala Daeng, Metro Silom) The surviving business of the international promoter of Thai silk, this, the largest Jim Thompson shop, sells colourful silk handkerchiefs, placemats, wraps and pillow cushions.

MARKETS

Th Khao San Market (Map p66; Th Khao San; ☺ 11am-11pm; river ferry Tha Phra Athit) The main guesthouse strip in Banglamphu is a day-and-night shopping bazaar for serious baht pinchers, with cheap T-shirts, bootleg CDs, wooden elephants, hemp clothing, fisherman pants and other goods that make backpackers go ga-ga.

Patpong Night Market (Map pp80-1; Patpong Soi 1 & 2, Th Silom; ☺ 7pm-1am; Skytrain Sala Daeng, Metro Silom) Drawing more crowds than the ping-pong shows, this market continues the street's illicit leanings with a deluge of pirated goods, particularly watches and clothing

Markets abound in Bangkok

RAY LASKOWITZ

GREG ELMS

Art stall, Chatuchak Weekend Market

↘ CHATUCHAK WEEKEND MARKET

Among the largest markets in the world, **Chatuchak Weekend Market** seems to unite everything buyable, from used vintage sneakers to baby squirrels. JJ, as it's also known, is the ideal place to finally pick up those gifts for people back home, not to mention a pretty item or two for your own home. The market is roughly divided into thematic sections, the best guide to these being *Nancy Chandler's Map of Bangkok*. Plan to spend a full day, as there's plenty to see, do and buy. But come early, ideally around 9am to 10am, to beat the crowds and the heat.

Things you need to know: Talat Nat Jatujak; Map pp52-3; ⏰ 9am-6pm Sat & Sun; Skytrain Mo Chit, Metro Chatuchak Park

GETTING THERE & AWAY
AIR
Bangkok has two airports. **Suvarnabhumi International Airport** (Map p94; ☎ 0 2723 0000; www.airportthai.com), 30km east of Bangkok, began commercial international and domestic service in September 2006 after several years of delay.

Bangkok's former international and domestic **Don Muang Airport** (Map p94; ☎ 0 2535 1111; www.airportthai.co.th), 25km north of central Bangkok, was retired from commercial service in September 2006, only to be partially reopened five months later to handle overflow from Suvarnabhumi. At the time of writing rumours of the airport's imminent closure had been circulating, but for now it's still serving some domestic flights.

AIRLINES
The following carriers service domestic destinations; a few also fly routes to international destinations.

Air Asia (☎ 0 2515 9999; www.airasia .com; Suvarnabhumi International Airport) Suvarnabhumi to Chiang Mai, Chiang Rai, Hat Yai, Krabi, Nakhon Si Thammarat, Narathiwat, Phuket, Ranong, Surat Thani, Ubon Ratchathani and Udon Thani.

Bangkok Airways (Map pp52-3; ☎ 0 2265 5555, call centre 1771; www.bangkokair.com; 99 Moo 14, Th Viphawadee) Suvarnabhumi to Chiang Mai, Phuket, Ko Samui, Sukhothai and Trat.

Nok Air (Map pp80-1; ☎ 1318; www.nokair .co.th; 17th fl, Rajanakarn Bldg, Th Sathon) This subsidiary of Thai flies from Don Muang to Chiang Mai, Hat Yai, Nakhon Si Thammarat, Phuket, Trang and Udon Thani. Nok Air also operates code-share flights with PB Air from Suvarnabhumi to Buriram, Lampang, Nakhon Phanom, Nan, Roi Et and Sakon Nakhon.

One-Two-Go (Map pp74-5; ☎ 0 2229 4260, call centre 1126; www.fly12go.com; 18 Th Ratchadaphisek) Domestic arm of Orient Thai; flies from Don Muang to Chiang Mai, Chiang Rai, Hat Yai, Nakhon Si Thammarat and Phuket.

PB Air (Map pp74-5; ☎ 0 2261 0222; www .pbair.com; UBC II Bldg, 591 Soi Daeng Udom/33, Th Sukhumvit) Suvarnabhumi to Buriram,

Chumphon, Lampang, Mae Hong Son, Nan, Nakhon Phanom, Roi Et and Sakon Nakhon.

SGA Airlines (Map pp52-3; ☎ 0 2664 6099; www.sga.co.th; 19/18-19 Royal City Ave/RCA, off Th Phra Ram IX) A subsidiary of Nok Air, SGA flies tiny prop planes from Suvarnabhumi to Hua Hin, and from Chiang Mai to Chiang Rai, Mae Hong Son and Pai.

Thai Airways International (THAI; ☎ 0 2356 1111; www.thaiairways.co.th) Silom (Map pp80-1; ☎ 0 2232 8000; temp address ground fl, BUI Building, 175-77 Soi Anuman Rachathon, permanent address 485 Th Silom); Banglamphu (Map pp80-1; ☎ 0 280 0110; 6 Th Lan Luang) Operates domestic air services to many provincial capitals.

BUS
BUS STATIONS
Allow one hour to reach all terminals from most parts of Bangkok.

Eastern bus terminal (Ekamai; Map pp52-3; ☎ 0 2391 6846; Soi Ekamai/40, Th Sukhumvit; Skytrain Ekamai) is the departure point for buses to Pattaya, Rayong, Chanthaburi and other points east.

Northern & Northeastern bus terminal (Mo Chit; Map pp52-3; ☎ for northern routes 0 2936 2852, ext 311/442, for northeastern routes 0 2936 2852, ext 611/448; Th Kamphaeng Phet) is just north of Chatuchak Park. Buses depart from here for all northern and northeastern destinations.

The city's new **Southern bus terminal** (Sai Tai Mai; Map pp52-3; ☎ 0 2435 1200; cnr Th Bromaratchachonanee & Th Phuttamonthon 1, Thonburi) lies quite far from the centre of Bangkok. Besides serving as the departure point for all buses south of Bangkok, transport to Kanchanaburi and western Thailand also departs from this new terminal.

TRAIN
Bangkok's **Hualamphong station** (Map pp80-1; ☎ 0 2220 4334, general information & advance booking 1690; www.railway.co.th; Th Phra Ram IV; Metro Hualamphong) is the terminus for

CHRISTOPHER GROENHOUT

Get around town in a túk-túk

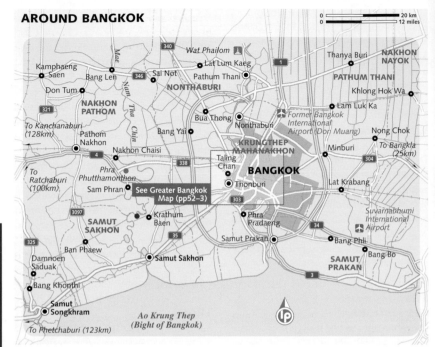

AROUND BANGKOK

the main rail services to the south, north, northeast and east.

GETTING AROUND
TO/FROM THE AIRPORT
SUVARNABHUMI INTERNATIONAL AIRPORT
AIRPORT BUS

Airport Express runs four useful routes between Suvarnabhumi and Bangkok. They operate from 5am to midnight and cost 150B, meaning a taxi will be a comparable price if there are two of you heading to central Bangkok, but slightly more expensive if you're going to Banglamphu.

SKYTRAIN

From late 2009 a new Skytrain line will run from downstairs at the airport to a huge new City Air Terminal in central

Bangkok, near Soi Asoke/21 and Th Petchaburi. There will be a new express service (pink line) that will take 15 minutes, and a local service (red line) taking 27 minutes.

TAXI

As you exit the terminal, ignore the touts and all the yellow signs pointing you to 'official airport taxis' (which cost 700B flat). Instead, walk outside on the arrivals level and join the fast-moving queue for a public taxi. Cabs booked through this desk should always use their meter, but they often try their luck so insist by saying, 'Meter, please'. You must also pay a 50B official airport surcharge and reimburse drivers for any toll charges (usually about 60B); drivers will always ask your permission to use the tollway. Depending on traffic, a taxi to Asoke should cost 200B to 250B, to Silom 300B to 350B and to Banglamphu 350B to 425B.

DON MUANG AIRPORT
There are no longer any express airport buses to/from Don Muang.

TAXI
As at Suvarnabhumi, public taxis leave from outside the arrivals hall and there is a 50B airport charge added to the meter fare. A trip to Banglamphu, including airport change and tollway fees, will set you back about 400B. The fare will be slightly less for a trip to Sukhumvit or Silom.

BOAT
Chao Phraya Express (Map pp80-1; ☎ 0 2623 6001; www.chaophrayaboat.co.th) provides one of the city's most scenic (and efficient) transport options, running passenger boats along Mae Nam Chao Phraya to destinations both south and north of Bangkok.

Tickets range from 13B to 34B and are generally purchased on board the boat, although some larger stations have ticket booths.

BUS
The city's public bus system is operated by **Bangkok Mass Transit Authority** (☎ 0 2246 4262; www.bmta.co.th); the website is a great source of information on all bus routes.

METRO (MRT)
Bangkok's first subway line opened in 2004 and is operated by the **Metropolitan Rapid Transit Authority** (MRTA; ☎ 0 2624 5200; www.mrta.co.th). Thais call the metro *rót fai fáh đâi din*.

Fares cost 15B to 39B; child and concession fares can be bought at ticket windows.

SKYTRAIN (BTS)
The most comfortable option for travelling in 'new' Bangkok (Silom, Sukhumvit and

Churning of the Sea of Milk sculpture, Suvarnabhumi International Airport

JOHN BORTHWICK

Siam Square) is the *rót fai fáh* (Skytrain), an elevated rail network that sails over the city's notorious traffic jams.

Fares vary from 10B to 40B, depending on your destination.

TAXI

Táak·see mee·đêu (metered taxis) were introduced in Bangkok in 1993 and the current flag fare of 35B is only a slight increase from that time, making us won- der how these guys (and there are a lot of them) earn any money. Fares to most places within central Bangkok cost 60B to 80B, and freeway tolls – 20B to 45B depending where you start – must be paid by the passenger.

TÚK-TÚK

A short trip on a túk-túk will cost at least 40B.

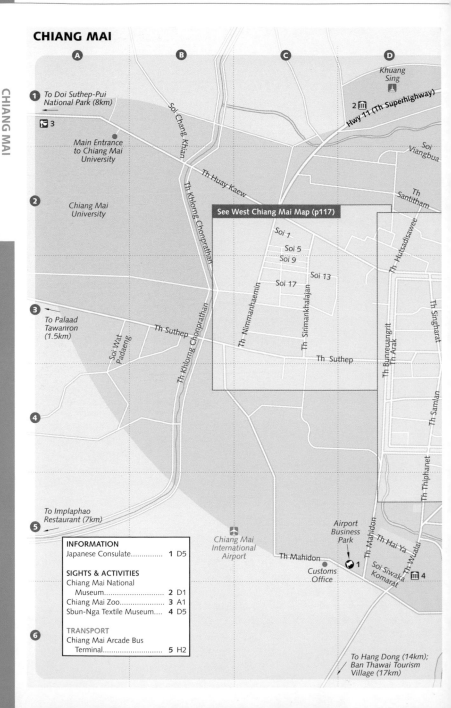

CHIANG MAI

CHIANG MAI

- **A** — To Doi Suthep-Pui National Park (8km)
- Main Entrance to Chiang Mai University
- Chiang Mai University
- Soi Chang Khian
- Th Khlong Chonprathan
- Th Huay Kaew
- Th Khlong Chonprathan
- To Palaad Tawanron (1.5km)
- Th Suthep
- Soi Wat Padaeng
- To Implaphao Restaurant (7km)
- Khuang Sing
- Hwy 11 (Th Superhighway)
- Soi Viangbua
- Th Santitham
- Th Hutsadisawee
- **See West Chiang Mai Map (p117)**
- Soi 1
- Soi 5
- Soi 9
- Soi 13
- Soi 17
- Th Nimmanhaemin
- Th Sirimankhalajan
- Th Suthep
- Th Bunreuangrit
- Th Arak
- Th Singharat
- Th Samlan
- Th Thiphanet
- Chiang Mai International Airport
- Airport Business Park
- Th Mahidon
- Customs Office
- Th Hai Ya
- Th Wualai
- Soi Siwaka Komarat
- Th Mahidon
- To Hang Dong (14km); Ban Thawai Tourism Village (17km)

INFORMATION
Japanese Consulate................ **1** D5

SIGHTS & ACTIVITIES
Chiang Mai National
  Museum........................... **2** D1
Chiang Mai Zoo..................... **3** A1
Sbun-Nga Textile Museum.... **4** D5

TRANSPORT
Chiang Mai Arcade Bus
  Terminal........................... **5** H2

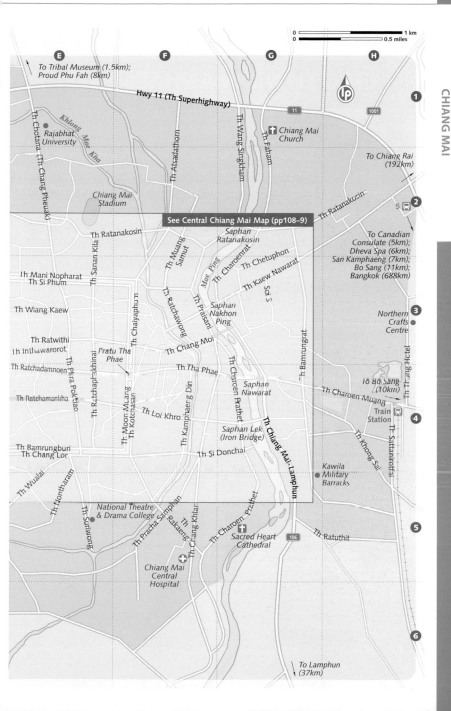

CHIANG MAI

0 — 1 km
0 — 0.5 miles

E F G H

To Tribal Museum (1.5km);
Proud Phu Fah (8km)

Hwy 11 (Th Superhighway)

11

1001

1

Chiang Mai
Church

To Chiang Rai
(192km)

Th Chotana (Th Chang Pheuak)

Khlong Mae Kha

Rajabhat
University

Th Atsadathorn

Th Wang Singkham

Th Faham

Th Ratanakacin

Chiang Mai
Stadium

5

2

See Central Chiang Mai Map (pp108–9)

Th Ratanakosin

Saphan
Ratanakosin

Th Muang Samut

Mae Ping

Th Charoenrat

Th Chetuphon

Th Sanan Kila

To Canadian
Consulate (5km);
Dheva Spa (6km);
San Kamphaeng (7km);
Bo Sang (11km);
Bangkok (688km)

Th Mani Nopharat
Th Si Phum

Th Kaew Nawarat

Soi 3

Th Wiang Kaew

Th Chaiyaphum

Th Ratchawong

Th Praisani

Saphan
Nakhon
Ping

Northern
Crafts
Centre

3

Th Ratwithi
Th Inthawarorot

Pratu Tha
Phae

Th Chang Moi

Th Bamrungrat

Th Ting Hotel

Th Ratchadamnoen

Th Phra Pok Klao

Th Ratchaphakhinai

Th Tha Phae

Th Charoen Prathet

To Bo Sang
(10km)

Th Charoen Muang

Th Ratchamankha

Th Moon Muang
Th Kotchasan

Th Loi Khro

Th Kamphaeng Din

Saphan
Nawarat

Train
Station

Th Sattanirotti

4

Th Bamrungburi
Th Chang Lor

Saphan Lek
(Iron Bridge)

Th Si Donchai

Th Chiang Mai–Lamphun

Kawila
Military
Barracks

Th Khlong Sai

Th Wualai

Th Hontharam

Th Sunwong

National Theatre
& Drama College

Th Pracha Samphan

Th Rakaeng

Th Chiang Khlan

Th Charoen Prathet

Sacred Heart
Cathedral

106

Th Ratuthit

5

Chiang Mai
Central
Hospital

6

To Lamphun
(37km)

CHIANG MAI HIGHLIGHTS

1 CHIC TH NIMMANHAEMIN

BY PIM KEMASINGKI, MANAGING EDITOR, *CITYLIFE CHIANG MAI*

The city has grown up right along with me: an innocent, backwater childhood; rebellious teenage years; and mature adulthood in a new millennium. Chiang Mai has cultural and historical significance but it is also vibrant and dynamic. It attracts artists, thinkers, activists, expats and Bangkok Thais for its creative, unpretentious lifestyle.

➤ PIM'S DON'T MISS LIST

❶ SHOPPING ON NIMMAN

My favourite place to shop is down Th Nimmanhaemin and its many soi. Soi 1, Th Nimmanhaemin is where you'll find exquisite textiles, ceramics, pewter, fashion and accessories. If I die, I want heaven to be decorated like Ginger (p120) – girlie accessories, pink tassels and all things feminine.

❷ NIMMANHAEMIN ART & DESIGN PROMENADE

This four-day event is held around the weekend of 5 December (HM the King's birthday). Soi 1 is closed to traffic so that designers, artists and businesses can show off their new products. Apart from shopping, there are dining and drinking zones, live music, fashion shows, games and gimmicks galore.

❸ NOSHING ON NIMMAN

Variety is the essence of Chiang Mai's dining scene. Café de Nimman (☎ 0 5321 8405; Rooms Boutique Mall, 61 Th Nimmanhaemin) has delicious Thai dishes at great prices. Su Casa Tapas Corner (Map p117; ☎ 0 5381 0088; 28 Soi

Clockwise from top: Fairy lights, Chiang Mai Night Bazaar (p120); Detail of terracotta ceramic; Streetside stall, Chiang Mai Night Bazaar (p120); Umbrella Factory, Bo Sang (p107)

11, Th Nimmanhaemin) is a charming little restaurant serving tapas, sangria and delightful champagne cocktails. **Khun Churn** (p117) is hands down the best vegetarian restaurant in town; the lunch buffets are hugely popular.

❹ NIGHTLIFE ON NIMMAN

Th Nimmanhaemin starts rocking at night when it's bursting with students. **Warm-Up** (p119) makes me feel ancient but is popular with the young and annoyingly beautiful crowd. **Glass Onion** (p119) is chic and slightly kitsch with fabulous martinis and wines.

❺ NIMMAN'S GALLERIES & SIGHTS

I am a city girl and I live on Th Nimmanhaemin. My advice? Simply

walk up and down the small soi and you will find charming and adorable little businesses. And don't miss **Look at This** (Map p117; ☎ 0 5340 0921; 6/6 Th Nimmanhaemin), a bold and active art gallery making waves for its monthly exhibitions.

➘ THINGS YOU NEED TO KNOW

Best Time to Visit Stores open around 11am and nightlife picks up around 10pm or 11pm **Top Tip** Pick up *Citylife Chiang Mai* for trends and happenings

CHIANG MAI HIGHLIGHTS

↘ TOUR THE OLD CITY

Chiang Mai's old city is packed with sacred spaces built during the heyday of the teak trade and reflect a sylvan aesthetic more akin to the temple architecture of Myanmar (Burma) and southern China. For a full dose, wander around Wat Phra Singh (p106), Wat Chedi Luang (p106) and Wat Chiang Man (p106).

↘ MAKE THE PILGRIMAGE TO DOI SUTHEP

Chiang Mai's guardian mountain ascends from the humid plains into a cool cloud belt where moss and ferns flourish. There are hiking and mountain biking trails to explore in this national park. But most Thais make the pilgrimage to Wat Phra That Doi Suthep (p112), built upon a site of mythical importance chosen by an auspicious relic mounted on a white elephant.

4

⬆ HUNT FOR CRAFTS

Chiang Mai is Thailand's handicraft centre. The Saturday Walking Street (p107) transforms the streets into an eating and shopping bazaar. Every evening the Chiang Mai Night Bazaar (p120) can be mined for souvenirs. Handicraft stores (p103) on Th Tha Phae, Th Charoenrat and Th Nimmanhaemin are good for daytime browsing.

5

⬆ MASTER THE MORTAR & PESTLE

You can study Thai cooking in every tourist town, but Chiang Mai has a little more spice for the aspiring chef: a laid-back approach, regional culinary twists and atmospheric old houses hosting cooking demos. Cooking classes (p113) introduce Thai culinary herbs and spices, tour a local market and prepare a menu of classic Thai dishes.

6

⬆ TREK THE NORTHERN MOUNTAINS

Chiang Mai is Thailand's base for outdoor activities (p112). There are the traditional treks to minority tribal villages, visits to elephant sanctuaries, zipline courses through the forest and rock climbing. Or you can rent your own wheels and head to Chiang Dao (p114) or the Mae Sa Valley (p114).

2 & 3 FELIX HUG; 4 JERRY ALEXANDER; 5 JERRY ALEXANDER; 6 FELIX HUG

2 Wat Phra Singh (p106); 3 Buddha statues, Wat Phra That Doi Suthep (p112); 4 Handicrafts at a night market; 5 Thai curry; 6 Chiang Mai Province countryside

CHIANG MAI'S BEST...

⬃ PLACES FOR ENLIGHTENMENT

- **Chiang Mai City Arts & Cultural Centre** (p107) Get educated on city history.
- **Chiang Mai National Museum** (p111) Sort out the characteristics of Lanna (northern Thai) art and architecture.
- **Wat Suan Dok** (p110) Do a two-day meditation retreat or chat with a monk about Buddhism.

⬃ PLACES TO GET A MASSAGE

- **Chiang Mai Women's Prison Massage Centre** (p111) Professional pummelling by ladies in the clink.
- **Dheva Spa** (p111) Luxurious treatment in a fairytale setting.
- **Ban Hom Samunphrai** (p111) Old-fashioned sauna and massage in a country setting.

⬃ PLACES TO SURROUND YOURSELF WITH SILK

- **Sbun-Nga Textile Museum** (p107) Textile museum for loom lovers.
- **Srisanpanmai** (p120) Stacks of antique-style silk sarongs.
- **Adorn with Studio Naenna** (p120) Shop for a cause at this village weaving cooperative.

⬃ PLACES TO HANG OUT

- **Riverside Bar & Restaurant** (p119) Everyone's favourite good-times spot.
- **Drunken Flower** (p118) Cosy bar for arty university students and beer-fuelled conversations.
- **Libernard Cafe** (p116) An eclectic cafe where breakfast turns into lunch.

Dining beside the river, Chiang Mai

ALAIN EVRARD

THINGS YOU NEED TO KNOW

⬆ VITAL STATISTICS

- **Population** 174,000
- **Best time to visit** November to February

⬆ NEIGHBOURHOODS IN A NUTSHELL

- **Old City** Historic quarter.
- **East of the Old City & Riverside** Craft shopping galore.
- **South of the Old City** Silversmiths on Th Wualai.
- **West of the Old City** New Chiang Mai and student hang out.
- **North of the Old City** Far-flung attractions.
- **Doi Suthep-Pui National Park** Forested playground and a holy temple.

⬆ ADVANCE PLANNING

- **One month before** Book accommodation and overnight train tickets from Bangkok.
- **One week before** Book meditation course and air tickets from Bangkok.
- **One day before** Book cooking course and outdoor activity tour.

⬆ RESOURCES

- **Citylife** (www.chiangmainews.com) Lifestyle magazine.
- **Golden Triangle Rider** (www.gt -rider.com) Maps of the countryside.
- **Nancy Chandler's Map of Chiang Mai** (www.nancychandler.net) Schematic city map.

- **Tourism Authority of Thailand** (TAT; ☎ 0 5324 8604; tatchmai@tat.or.th; Th Chiang Mai-Lamphun; ⏱ 8.30am-4.30pm) General tourist information and guide recommendations.
- **Tourist police** (☎ 0 5324 7318, 24hr emergency 1155; Th Faham; ⏱ 6am-midnight) Foreign-language liaisons for the police.

⬆ EMERGENCY NUMBERS

- **Fire** (☎ 199)
- **Police/Emergency** (☎ 191)
- **Tourist police** (☎ 1155; ⏱ 24hr)

⬆ GETTING AROUND

- **Bicycle** Easy and 'green' get-abouts for central Chiang Mai.
- **Motorcycle** Good self-touring option for outside central Chiang Mai.
- **Sörng·tăa·ou** Shared taxis go just about everywhere (20B to 40B).
- **Túk-túk** Chartered vehicles (60B to 80B); remember to bargain.

⬆ BE FOREWARNED

- **In temples** Dress and act respectfullys. Sit in the 'mermaid' position in front of Buddha figures.
- **Women travellers** Should not touch monks and should step off the footpath if passing by one.
- **Guides** Hire a guide through TAT to learn more about northern Thai temples.

CHIANG MAI

THINGS YOU NEED TO KNOW

DISCOVER CHIANG MAI

Snuggled into the foothills of northern Thailand, Chiang Mai is a sanctuary of sorts with a refreshing combination of city accoutrements and country sensibilities. It is a city of artisans and craftspeople, of university professors and students, of idealists and culture hounds – creating a disposition that is laid-back, creative and reverential.

The city is often lauded for its enduring Lanna characteristics; for the quaint, walled quarter filled with temples; and for the surrounding mountains with their legendary, mystical attributes.

But Chiang Mai isn't a pickled city, preserved to the point of inauthenticity. In reality, it is dynamic and modern without having lost its down-to-earth charm.

So enough praises. What can you do in Chiang Mai? First, be glad you aren't suffocating in Bangkok and then be a culture geek for a few days: do a cooking course, go temple spotting, shop for local handicrafts or explore some of the nearby natural attractions.

SIGHTS
OLD CITY

Chiang Mai's historic quarter is tightly bound by old ways with a semi-gloss of modernity.

WAT CHEDI LUANG

วัดเจดีย์หลวง

Another venerable stop on the temple trail, Wat Chedi Luang (Map pp108-9; ☎ 0 5327 8595; Th Phra Pokklao; donations appreciated) is built around a partially ruined Lanna-style *chedi* dating from 1441 that was believed to be one of the tallest structures in ancient Chiang Mai. The famed Phra Kaew (Emerald Buddha), now held in Bangkok's Wat Phra Kaew (p65), sat in the eastern niche here in 1475.

WAT PHAN TAO

วัดพันเตา

Near Wat Chedi Luang, Wat Phan Tao (Map pp108-9; ☎ 0 5381 4689; Th Phra Pokklao; donations appreciated) contains a beautiful old teak *wí·hǎhn* that was once a royal residence and is today one of the unsung treasures of Chiang Mai.

WAT PHRA SINGH

วัดพระสิงห์

Chiang Mai's most visited temple, Wat Phra Singh (Map pp108-9; ☎ 0 5381 4164; Th Singharat; donations appreciated) owes its fame to the fact that it houses the city's most revered Buddha image, Phra Singh (Lion Buddha), and it has a fine collection of classic Lanna art and architecture.

Phra Singh is housed in Wihan Lai Kham, a small chapel to the rear of the temple grounds next to the *chedi*.

WAT CHIANG MAN

วัดเชียงมั่น

Considered to be the oldest wat in the city, Wat Chiang Man (Map pp108-9; ☎ 0 5337 5368; Th Ratchaphakhinai; donations appreciated), is believed to have been established by the city's founder, Phaya Mengrai. The wát features typical northern Thai temple architecture.

CHIANG MAI CITY ARTS & CULTURAL CENTRE

หอศิลปวัฒนธรรมเชียงใหม่

The **Chiang Mai City Arts & Cultural Centre** (Map pp108-9; ☎ 053217793; www.chiang maicitymuseum.org; Th Ratwithi; adult/child 90/40B; ☺ 8.30am-5.30pm Tue-Sun) offers a fine primer on Chiang Mai history.

SUNDAY WALKING STREET

ถนนเดินวันอาทิตย์

A unique shopping experience, the **Sunday Walking Street** (pp108-9; Th Ratchadamnoen; ☺ 4pm-midnight Sun) offers better-than-average products and a good dose of provincial culture.

EAST OF THE OLD CITY & RIVERSIDE

Th Tha Phae is the main tourist drag filled with interesting craft shops and a few heritage-style buildings once belonging to British and Burmese teak merchants. The meandering Mae Ping is another historical attraction and the eastern riverside neighbourhood makes an interesting cycling tour.

SOUTH OF THE OLD CITY

Th Wualai is renowned for its silver shops and is often filled with the tapping sound of a decorative pattern being imprinted on to a plate of silver (or, more often, aluminium).

SATURDAY WALKING STREET

ถนนเดินวันเสาร์

The **Saturday Walking Street** (Map pp108-9; Th Wualai; ☺ 4pm-midnight Sat) is developing a reputation of having more authentic handicrafts and being less commercial than the Sunday Walking Street. This might be a bit of an exaggeration as most vendors work both markets without exclusion.

JERRY ALEXANDER

Chiang Mai Night Bazaar (p120)

⬊ IF YOU LIKE...

If you like the **weekend walking streets** (left), check out these handicraft villages:

- **Bo Sang** (off Map pp98-9) The 'umbrella village' is filled with craft shops selling tourist-grade painted umbrellas, fans, silverware, statuary, celadon pottery and lacquerware.
- **San Kamphaeng** (off Map pp98-9) Another craft village nearby, known for its cotton and silk weaving shops and textile show rooms.
- **Hang Dong** (off Map pp98-9) Rte 108 is a 'furniture highway' specialising in decorative arts, woodcarving, antiques and contemporary furniture.
- **Ban Thawai Tourism Village** (off Map pp98-9) A pedestrian-friendly tourist market with 3km of home decor shops.

SBUN-NGA TEXTILE MUSEUM

พิพิธภัณฑ์ผ้าโบราณสะบันงา

A surprisingly wonderful museum, **Sbun-Nga Textile Museum** (Map pp98-9; ☎ 0 5320 0655; www.sbun-nga.com; Chiang Mai Cultural Centre, 185/20 Th Wualai; admission 100B; ☺ 10.30am-6.30pm Thu-Tue) displays northern Thai textiles along with ethnocultural information about the different

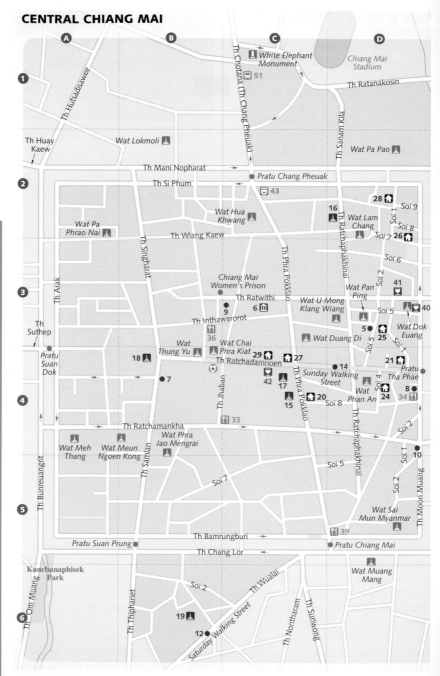

CENTRAL CHIANG MAI

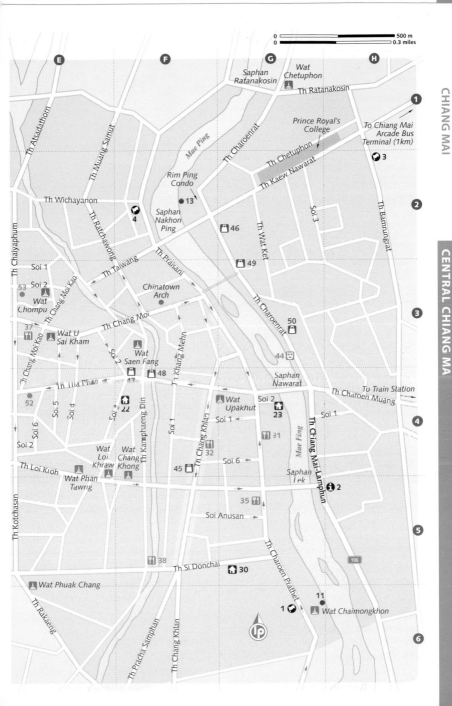

CHIANG MAI

CENTRAL CHIANG MA

500 m
0.3 miles

E F G H

Saphan
Ratanakosin

Wat
Chetuphon

Th Ratanakosin

1

Prince Royal's
College

To Chiang Mai
Arcade Bus
Terminal (1km)

3

Mae Ping

Th Charoenrat

Th Chetuphon

Th Kaew Nawarat

Rim Ping
Condo

Th Atsadathorn

Th Muang Samut

Th Wichayanon

Th Ratchawong

4

Saphan
Nakhon
Ping

13

46

Soi 3

Th Bamrungrat

2

Th Chaiyaphum

Soi 1

Th Taiwang

Th Praisani

Th Chiang Moi Kao

Chinatown
Arch

Th Wat Ket

49

Th Charoenrat

53 Soi 2
Wat
Chompu

Th Chang Moi

50

3

37 Wat U
Sai Kham

Th Chang Moi Kao

Soi 2

Wat
Saen Fang

Th Khang Mehn

44

47 48

Th Tha Phae

Saphan
Nawarat

To Train Station

Th Charoen Muang

52

So. 5

Soi 4

Soi 3

22

Th Kamphaeng Din

Soi 1

Th Chang Khlan

Wat
Upakhut

Soi 2

23

Soi 1

Mae Ping

Th Chiang Mai-Lamphun

Soi 1

4

Soi 6

Soi 2

Wat
Loi
Khraw

Wat
Chang
Khong

31

32

45

Soi 6

Th Loi Kroh

Wat Phan
Tawng

Saphan
Lek

2

Th Kotchasan

35

Soi Anusan

5

38

Th Si Donchai

30

106

Wat Phuak Chang

Th Charoen Prathet

11

Th Rakaeng

1

Wat Chaimongkhon

Th Pracha Samphan

Th Chang Khlan

6

INFORMATION
French Consulate 1 G6
Tourism Authority of Thailand (TAT) 2 H5
UK Consulate 3 H2
US Consulate 4 F2

SIGHTS & ACTIVITIES
Baan Thai 5 D3
Chiang Mai City Arts & Cultural Centre 6 C3
Chiang Mai Mountain Biking 7 B4
Chiang Mai Thai Cookery School 8 D4
Chiang Mai Women's Prison Massage Centre 9 C3
Elephant Nature Park Booking Office 10 D4
Gap's Thai Culinary Art School (see 24)
Mae Ping River Cruises 11 G6
Saturday Walking Street 12 B6
Scorpion Tailed River Cruise 13 F2
Sunday Walking Street 14 D4
Wat Chedi Luang 15 C4
Wat Chiang Man 16 D2
Wat Phan Tao 17 C4
Wat Phra Singh 18 B4
Wat Sisuphan 19 B6

SLEEPING
3 Sis 20 C4
Awanahouse 21 D4
Banthai Village 22 F4
Galare Guest House 23 G4
Gap's House 24 D4
Mini Cost 25 D3
Sri Pat Guest House 26 D2
Tamarind Village 27 C4
Tri Gong Residence 28 D2
U Chiang Mai 29 C4
Yaang Come Village 30 G5

EATING
Antique House 31 G4
Galare Food Centre 32 F4
Heuan Phen 33 C4
Jerusalem Falafel 34 D4
Just Khao Soy 35 G5
Kow Soy Siri Soy 36 B3
Libernard Cafe 37 E3
Tianzi Tea House 38 F5
Tien Sieng Vegetarian Restaurant 39 D5

DRINKING
Kafe 40 D3
UN Irish Pub 41 D3
Writer's Club & Wine Bar 42 C4

ENTERTAINMENT
North Gate Jazz Co-Op 43 C2
Riverside Bar & Restaurant 44 G3

SHOPPING
Chiang Mai Night Bazaar 45 F4
La Luna Gallery 46 G2
Lost Heavens 47 F4
Siam Celadon 48 F4
Sop Moei Arts 49 G3
Vila Cini 50 G3

TRANSPORT
Chang Pheuak Bus Terminal 51 C1
Journey 52 E4
North Wheels 53 E3

tribes that are categorised as Lanna: Tai Lue, Tai Kaun, Tai Yai and Tai Yuan.

WEST OF THE OLD CITY

Th Huay Kaew is the main thoroughfare to the western reaches of the city and it becomes more interesting as it enters the gravitational pull of Chiang Mai University (referred to in Thai by its initials *'Mor Chor'*). Th Nimmanhaemin is the city's most stylish avenue, a cross between Bangkok's Siam Square and Banglamphu.

RIVER CRUISES

The Mae Ping is rural and rustic in most parts with grassy banks and small stilted houses crouching alongside.

Scorpion Tailed River Cruise (**Map pp108-9; ☎ 08 1960 9308, 0 5324 5888; www.scorpiontailed.com; Th Charoenrat; fare 500B**) focuses on the history of the river using traditional-style craft, known as scorpion-tailed boats.

Mae Ping River Cruises (**Map pp108-9; ☎ 0 5327 4822; www.maepingriver cruise.com; Wat Chaimongkhon, Th Charoen Prathet**) offers daytime cruises (450B, two hours) in roofed long-tail boats.

WAT SUAN DOK

วัดสวนดอก

Built on a former flower garden in 1373, this **temple** (**Map p117; ☎ 0 5327 8967; Th Suthep; donations appreciated**) is not as architecturally interesting as the temples in the old city but it does have a very powerful photographic attribute: the temple's collection of whitewashed *chedi* sit in the foreground while the blue peaks of Doi Suthep and Doi Pui loom in the background.

Foreigners often come to Wat Suan Dok for the popular monk chat (see p115) and the English-language meditation retreats.

CHIANG MAI ZOO

สวนสัตว์เชียงใหม่

At the foot of Doi Suthep, the **Chiang Mai Zoo** (**Map pp98-9; ☎ 0 5335 8116;

www.chiangmaizoo.com; Th Huay Kaew; adult/child 100/50B, ⏰ 8am-6pm, ticket booth closes at 5pm) occupies a lush park setting that is often crowded with Thai families and school groups. The zoo boasts a fairly comprehensive assortment of animals plus two special attractions (pandas and an aquarium) that require separate admission fees.

NORTH OF THE OLD CITY

CHIANG MAI NATIONAL MUSEUM
พิพิธภัณฑสถานแห่งชาติเชียงใหม่

Operated by the Fine Arts Department and established in 1973, the Chiang Mai National Museum (Map pp98-9; ☎ 0 5322 1308; www.thailandmuseum.com; off Th Superhighway; admission 100B; ⏰ 9am-4pm Wed-Sun) functions as the primary caretaker of Lanna artefacts and as the curator of northern Thailand's history.

TRIBAL MUSEUM
พิพิธภัณฑ์ชาวเขา

Overlooking a lake in Suan Ratchamangkhala on the northern outskirts of the city, this octagonal museum (off Map pp98-9; ☎ 0 5321 0872; off Th Chang Pheauk; admission free; ⏰ 9am-4pm Mon-Fri) houses a collection of handicrafts, costumes, jewellery, ornaments, household utensils, agricultural tools, musical instruments and ceremonial paraphernalia. There are also informative displays showing the cultural features and background of each of the major hill tribes in Thailand; an exhibition on activities carried out by the Thai royal family on behalf of the hill tribes; and various bits of research and development sponsored by governmental and non-governmental agencies.

DOI SUTHEP-PUI NATIONAL PARK
อุทยานแห่งชาติดอยสุเทพ–ปุย

Chiang Mai's sacred peaks, Doi Suthep (1676m) and Doi Pui (1685m) loom over the city like guardian spirits and were used by the city's founders as a divine compass in locating an auspicious position.

Portions of the mountains form a 265 sq km national park (Map p117; ☎ 0 5321 0244; adult/child under 14 yr 200/100B; ⏰ 8am-sunset) that contains a mix of wilderness,

---

PAMPERING & PUMMELLING

Chiang Mai Women's Prison Massage Centre (Map pp108-9; ☎ 08 1706 1041; 100 Th Ratwithi; ⏰ 8.30am-4.30pm; 150-200B) offers fantastic full body and foot massages performed by inmates at the women's prison as a part of their rehabilitation training program.

Ban Hom Samunphrai (☎ 0 5381 7362; www.homprang.com; 93/2 Moo 12; treatments 500-800B) is a time capsule of old folk ways, 9km from Chiang Mai near the McKean Institute. Maw Hom ('Herbal Doctor') is a licensed herb practitioner and massage therapist, but learned most of her craft from her grandmother, a midwife and herbalist living near the Myanmar (Burmese) border. She runs a traditional herbal steam bath re-creating what was once a common feature of rural villages.

Dheva Spa (off Map pp98-9; ☎ 0 5388 8888; www.mandarinoriental.com/hotel; Mandarin Oriental Dhara Dhevi, 51/4 Th Chiang Mai-San Kamphaeng; treatments from 3400B) The grandest spa in all of Chiang Mai is an architectural treasure, built to look like the ancient Burmese palace located at Mandalay.

hill-tribe villages and tourist attractions, including Wat Phra That Doi Suthep.

One of the north's most sacred temples, **Wat Phra That Doi Suthep** (Map p117; admission 30B) sits majestically atop Doi Suthep's summit. Thai pilgrims flock here to make merit to the Buddhist relic enshrined in the picturesque golden *chedi*.

WALKING TOUR
OLD CITY TEMPLE TOUR

Starting with the best, **Wat Phra Singh** (**1**; p106) is home to the city's most revered Buddha image (Phra Singh) and is an excellent example of Lanna architecture. Trot down Th Ratchadamnoen and turn right on Th Phra Pokklao to **Wat Chedi Luang** (**2**; p106), another venerable temple. **Wat Phan Tao** (**3**; p106) is a teak temple that's more photo-

genic than venerated. If it isn't too hot, squeeze in one more temple by turning right on Th Ratchadamnoen and left on Th Ratchaphakhinai to **Wat Chiang Man** (**4**; p106), the oldest wat in the city.

You can use this opportunity to indulge your wheat tooth by turning right on Th Wiang Kaew and taking another right on Th Phra Pokklao to reach **Amazing Sandwich** (**5**), a popular expat antidote to rice. Head south on Th Phra Pokklao and turn right at Th Ratwithi where you can nod to the **Anusawari Sam Kasat** (**6**), the Three Kings Monument, on your way to the informative and air-conditioned **Chiang Mai City Arts & Cultural Centre** (**7**; p107).

If your feet are aching, carry on along Th Ratwithi until you reach Chiang Mai Women's Prison, where you'll find the **Chiang Mai Women's Prison Massage Centre** (**8**; p111).

ACTIVITIES

Most companies operating out of Chiang Mai offer the same type of tour: a one-hour mini-bus ride to Mae Taeng or Mae Wang (depending on the duration of the trip), a brief **hike** to an elephant camp, an hour **elephant ride** to a waterfall, another hour **rafting** down a river and an overnight in or near a hill-tribe village.

Chiang Mai is not the only base for **hill-tribe treks** but it is the most accessible. One-day treks usually cost around 1500B, while multi-day treks (three days and two nights) cost 2500B.

Flight of the Gibbon (☎ **08 9970 5511; www.treetopasia.com; Mae Kampong; tours from 2000B**) is a new adventure outfit in Chiang Mai operating a zipline through the forest canopy some 1300m above sea level.

Chiang Mai Mountain Biking (**Map pp108-9**; ☎ **08 1024 7046; www.mountainbiking**

OLD CITY TEMPLE TOUR

0 —— 200 m
0 —— 0.1 miles

Th Wiang Kaew

Chiang Mai Women's Prison

Th Singharat

Th Phra Pokklao

Th Ratchaphakhinai

Th Ratwithi

Th Inthawarorot

Th Ratchadamnoen

Th Phra Pokklao

END • 8 7 6

1 START

5 4

3

2

WALK FACTS

Start Wat Phra Singh
Finish Chiang Mai Women's Prison
Distance 2.5km
Duration Two to three hours

FELIX HUG
Elephant trekking

chiangmai.com; 1 Th Samlan; tours from 1450-1550B) offers a variety of guided mountain biking (as well as hike-and-bike) tours through Doi Suthep for all levels.

Click & Travel (☎ 0 5328 1553; www.clickandtravelonline.com; tours 950 1300B) specialises in half-day and full-day bicycle tours of Chiang Mai.

Elephant Nature Park (Map pp108-9; booking office: ☎ 0 5320 8246; www.elephantnaturepark.org; 1 Soi 1, Th Ratchamankha; full-day tour 2500B) Khun Lek (Sangduen Chailert) has won numerous awards for her elephant sanctuary in the Mae Taeng valley, 60km (1½-hour drive) from Chiang Mai.

Peak (☎ 0 5380 0567; www.thepeakadventure.com; climbing course 1500-2500B) teaches introductory and advanced rock-climbing courses at Crazy Horse Buttress. The Peak also leads a variety of soft adventure trips, including abseiling down Nam Tok Wachiratan at Doi Inthanon, as well as trekking, white-water rafting and a jungle survival cooking course.

COURSES
BUDDHIST MEDITATION
The following temples offer *vipassana* meditation courses and retreats to English-language speakers.

International Buddhism Center (IBC; ☎ 0 5329 5012; www.fivethousandyears.org; Wat Phra That Doi Suthep) is headquartered within the temple grounds on Doi Suthep. It offers beginner to advanced meditation retreats, lasting from three to 21 days.

Wat Suan Dok (Map p118; ☎ 0 5380 8411 ext 114; www.monkchat.net; Th Suthep) offers a two-day meditation retreat every Tuesday to Wednesday.

COOKING
Baan Thai (Map pp108-9; ☎ 0 5335 7339; www.baanthaicookery.com; 11 Soi 5, Th Ratchadamnoen) has an in-town location where you can select which dishes to prepare; its intensive courses include a menu of northern Thai specialities.

Chiang Mai Thai Cookery School (Map pp108 9; ☎ 0 5320 6388; www.thaicookeryschool

CHIANG MAI

SLEEPING

.com; booking office, 47/2 Th Moon Muang) is one of Chiang Mai's first cooking schools and holds classes at the Wok restaurant and in a rural setting outside of Chiang Mai.

Gap's Thai Culinary Art School (Map pp108-9; ☎ 0 5327 8140; www.gaps-house.com; 3 Soi 4, Th Ratchadamnoen) is affiliated with the guesthouse Gap's House (where you can make your booking) and holds its classes out of town at the owner's house.

SLEEPING
OLD CITY
BUDGET

Awanahouse (Map pp108-9; ☎ 053419005; www.awanahouse.com; 7 Soi 1, Th Ratchadamnoen; r 300-900B; 🍴 💻 🛋) Awana has large and bright rooms, some with balconies, TV and fridge. The top floor has been converted into a chill-out space with city views and a pool table.

Hill-tribe women, Chiang Dao

JERRY ALEXANDER

➘ IF YOU LIKE...

If you like the mountain landscape of Doi Suthep (p111), take a day trip to these outdoor escapes.

- **Doi Inthanon National Park** (Map p118; ☎ 0 5328 6730; adult/child 200/100B, car/motorbike 30/20B; 🕗 8am-sunset) contains Thailand's highest peak and gives locals a chance to shiver in the cool temps and spot the rare phenomenon of frost.
- **Chiang Dao** (Map p118) Plant yourself at the base of Doi Chiang Dao, which boasts hiking trails, birdwatching spots and a cave temple. Overnight at Chiang Dao Nest (☎ 08 6017 1985; www.chiangdao.com; r 700-1000B; 💻 🛋).
- **Mae Sa Valley** One of the easiest mountain escapes Rt 1096 travels 100km from the lowland's concrete expanse into the highlands' forested frontier. Stop at the Maesa Elephant Camp (☎ 0 5320 6247; www.maesaelephantcamp.com; Rte 1096; admission adult/child 120/80B) and eat lunch at Proud Phu Fah (off Map pp98-9; ☎ 0 5387 9389; www.proudphufah.com; Km17, Rte 1096; r 4500-7000B; 🍴 💻 🛋), boasting a panoramic view of the valley.

Gap's House (Map pp108-9; ☎ 0 5327 8140; www.gaps-house.com; 3 Soi 4, Th Ratchadamnoen; r 350-800B; 🔀 🖵) A quirky little gem, Gap's House has Thai-style wooden rooms planted in a thick jungle garden cluttered with statuary, cabinets of trinkets and a *săh·lah* (open-air pavilion, often spelt as *sala*). Bring your mozzie spray.

Tri Gong Residence (Map pp108-9; ☎ 0 5321 4754; www.trigong.com; 8 Soi 1, Th Si Phum; r 700-1000B; 🔀 🖵) Built around a courtyard, the large rooms have better-than-average furniture, cable TV and fridge.

Mini Cost (Map pp108-9; ☎ 0 5341 8787; www.minicostcm.com; 19-19/4 Soi 1, Th Ratchadamnoen; s 550B, d 750-1050B; 🔀 🖵) This apartment-style spot has modern rooms with easy chairs, calming colours and a few touches of Thai-style decor.

MIDRANGE

ourpick **Sri Pat Guest House** (Map pp108-9; ☎ 0 5321 8716; www.sri-patguesthouse.com; 16 Soi 7, Th Moon Muang; r 1000B; 🔀) Sri Pat has just the right dose of personality. Rooms have sunny outlooks, celadon-coloured tiles, folksy cotton drapes and balconies.

3 Sis (Map pp108-9; ☎ 0 5327 3243; www.3sisbedandbreakfast.com; 1 Soi 8, Th Phra Pokklao; r 1350-1650B; 🔀 🖵) Get all the comfort of a hotel without all the fuss at this new flashpacker place.

TOP END

U Chiang Mai (Map pp108-9; ☎ 0 5332 7000; www.uchiangmai.com; 70 Th Ratchadamnoen; r from 4500B; 🔀 🖵 🏊) Golf clubs and briefcases are shuttled in and out of this corporate-friendly hotel, a rare find in the heart of the old city.

Tamarind Village (Map pp108-9; ☎ 0 5341 8896-9; www.tamarindvillage.com; 50/1 Th Ratchadamnoen; r 6000-18,000B; 🔀 🖵 🏊) Considered to be one of the first of the 'Lanna revival' hotels, Tamarind Village has

---

MONK CHAT

Wat Suan Dok (Map p118; ☎ 0 5380 8411-3; Th Suthep; ⏱ 5-7pm Mon, Wed & Fri) has a dedicated room where foreigners can interact with the monastic students.

Wat Chedi Luang (Map pp108-9; ☎ 0 5327 8595; Th Phra Pokklao; ⏱ 1-6pm Mon-Fri) and **Wat Sisuphan** (Map pp108-9; ☎ 0 5320 0332; 100 Th Wualai; ⏱ 5.30-7pm Tue, Thu & Sat) have monk chat tables on certain days.

---

re-created the quiet spaces of a temple with galleried buildings and garden courtyards on the grounds of an old tamarind orchard.

EAST OF THE OLD CITY
MIDRANGE & TOP END

ourpick **Banthai Village** (Map pp108-9; ☎ 0 5325 2789; www.banthaivillage.com; 19 Soi 3, Th Tha Phae; r from 4500B; 🔀 🖵 🏊) With only 33 rooms, it also strikes the right balance between intimacy and privacy. Rooms occupy several Lanna-style terraced rowhouses with generously sized beds and glass-fronted bathrooms with mini soak-tubs.

Yaang Come Village (Map pp108-9; ☎ 0 5323 7222; www.yaangcome.com; 90/3 Th Si Donchai; r 6000-9000B; 🔀 🖵 🏊) A clever twist on the Lanna reproduction hotel is this homage to a Tai Lue village, based on the owner's travels to the Yunnan region of China. Rooms are large and tastefully decorated with murals, textiles and teak furniture.

RIVERSIDE

ourpick **Galare Guest House** (Map pp108-9; ☎ 0 5381 8887; www.galare.com; 7/1 Soi 2, Th Charoen Prathet; r 1100B; 🔀) With an affordable riverside setting, Galare is a repeat

Market food, Chiang Mai

FELIX HUG

visitor's favourite. Although the rooms don't have river views, they are spacious, if a tad dated, and open on to a wide shared veranda.

EATING
OLD CITY

ourpick **Tien Sieng Vegetarian Restaurant** (Map pp108-9; ☎ 0 5320 6056; Th Phra Pokklao; dishes 20B; ✆ 6.30am-5pm) This Buddhist society–affiliated restaurant serves a variety of pre-made vegetarian dishes over rice.

Kow Soy Siri Soy (Map pp108-9; ☎ 0 5321 0944; Th Inthawarorot; dishes 30-35B; ✆ 7am-3pm Mon-Fri) This simple shop prepares a rich and hearty broth for its *kôw soy*, served with or without chicken.

Heuan Phen (Map pp108-9; ☎ 0 5327 7103; 112 Th Ratchamankha; dishes 60-150B; ✆ 8am-3pm & 5-10pm) At this well-known restaurant everything is on display, from the northern Thai food to the groups of culinary visitors and the antique-cluttered dining room.

ourpick **Jerusalem Falafel** (Map pp108-9; ☎ 0 5327 0208; 35/3 Th Moon Muang; dishes 100-280B) A lively place to assemble with friends and nosh on a meze platter of falafel, shashlik, hummus and tabouli.

EAST OF THE OLD CITY

Galare Food Centre (Map pp108-9; Galare Night Bazaar, Th Chang Khlan; dishes 50-80B; ✆ 6pm-midnight) A classic food court, the Galare Food Centre offers a stress-free version of a night market. There's also nightly entertainment, including Thai classical dancing.

Just Khao Soy (Map pp108-9; ☎ 0 5381 8641; 108/2 Th Charoen Prathet; dishes 100B) This is the gourmet version of *kôw soy*.

Antique House (Map pp108-9; ☎ 0 5327 6810; 71 Th Charoen Prathet; dishes 130-260B; ✆ 11am-midnight) The menu is mainly northern Thai with all the central Thai classics, but the dishes are just window dressing for the Thai-style ambience.

Libernard Cafe (Map pp108-9; ☎ 0 5323 4877; 36 Th Chaiyaphum; dishes 50-110B; ✆ 8am-5pm Tue-Sun) A low-key cafe, Libernard serves fresh Arabica coffee grown in Thailand. Try the *gaang mát·sà·màn* (Muslim-style curry).

Tianzi Tea House (Map pp108-9; ☎ 0 5344 9539; Th Kamphaeng Din; dishes 60-120B; ⏱ 10am-10pm) Such hard-core health food is usually found in dirt-floor hippy shacks, but Tianzi has adopted the ascetic's meal to an aesthetic surrounding.

WEST OF THE OLD CITY

Khun Churn (Map p118; ☎ 0 5322 4124; Soi 17, Th Nimmanhaemin; dishes 50-70B) You might think that vegetarian means rustic, but Khun Churn has kept up with the times with its 21st-century minimalist dining space.

Implaphao Restaurant (off Map pp98-9; ☎ 0 5380 6603; Rte 121; dishes 80-160B) Dining by the water is an appetising feature for Thais and this barn-like restaurant lures in the supping parties for *blah pŏw* (broiled fish stuffed with aromatic herbs) and *ɖôm yam gûng* (spicy prawn soup). It isn't the easiest restaurant to reach since it is 10km southwest of Chiang Mai, across from Talat Mae Huay, but it is an undiluted Thai experience.

Palaad Tawanron (off Map pp98-9; ☎ 0 5321 6039; Th Suthep; dishes 90-350B; ⏱ 11.30am-midnight) Set in the woods near Doi Suthep,

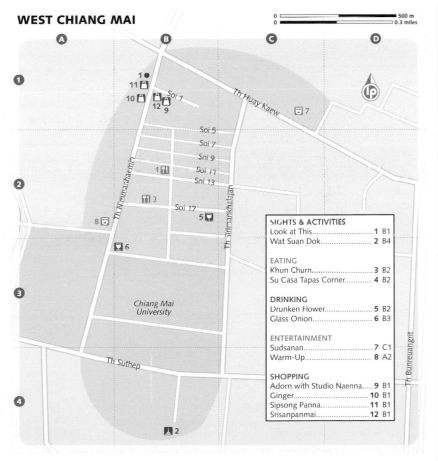

WEST CHIANG MAI

0 — 500 m
0 — 0.3 miles

CHIANG MAI

EATING

this restaurant draws in Thais and foreigners alike for the Thai food and the spectacular views over twinkly Chiang Mai.

DRINKING

Writer's Club & Wine Bar (Map pp108-9; ☎ 08 1928 2066; 141/3 Th Ratchadamnoen) Run by an ex-foreign correspondent, this unassuming traveller hang-out hosts an informal Friday night gathering of Chiang Mai's reporters and writers.

UN Irish Pub (Map pp108-9; ☎ 0 5321 4554; 24/1 Th Ratwithi) A standard-issue backpacker joint, this two-storey bar and restaurant is an old favourite for its Thursday quiz night and match nights.

Kafe (Map pp108-9; Th Moon Muang) A cosy bar snuggled in beside Soi 5, Kafe is often crowded with Thais and backpackers when every other place is empty. It offers a simple formula: cheap cold beer and efficient service.

Drunken Flower (Map p117; ☎ 0 5389 4210; 28/3 Soi 17, Th Nimmanhaemin) The closet-sized bar invokes an antique mood where the shaggy-headed students might have drunk and noshed away their haircut money.

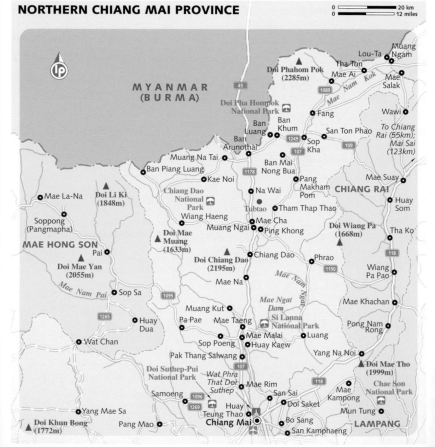

NORTHERN CHIANG MAI PROVINCE

Glass Onion (Map p117; ☎ 0 5321 8479; Rooms Boutique Mall, Th Nimmanhaemin) While the barely legals try to blow their eardrums out at Nimmanhaemin's dance clubs, this is the domain of grown-ups desiring cocktails and conversation.

ENTERTAINMENT

Riverside Bar & Restaurant (Map pp108-9; ☎ 0 5324 3239; 9-11 Th Charoenrat) In a twinkly setting on Mae Ping, Riverside is a one of the longest-running live-music venues in Chiang Mai. The cover bands made up of ageing Thai hippies stake out centre stage and fill the room with all the singalong tunes from the classic-rock vault.

North Gate Jazz Co-Op (Map pp108-9; Th Si Phum) This tight little jazz club packs in more musicians than patrons, especially for its Tuesday open-mic night.

Sudsanan (Map p117; ☎ 08 5038 0764; Th Huay Kaew) Long-haired Thais and expats (who know how to use a squat toilet) come here to applaud the adept acoustic performances that jog from samba to *pleng pêu·a chee·wít* (songs for life).

Warm-Up (Map p117; ☎ 0 5340 0676; 40 Th Nimmanhaemin) The perennial favourite of the dance-floor divas, Warm-Up aims to please with a little bit for everybody, including an interior courtyard filled with seating for dancers who need a breather.

SHOPPING

Lost Heavens (Map pp108-9; ☎ 0 5325 1557; 228-234 Th Tha Phae; ⏰ 10am-6pm) This store specialises in museum-quality tribal arts, including textiles, carpets and antiques, as well as ritual artefacts from the Yao (also known as Mien) tribe.

Siam Celadon (Map pp108-9; 0 5324 3518; 158 Th Tha Pae) This established company sells pieces from its fine collection of cracked-glazed celadon ceramics in a lovely teak building.

La Luna Gallery (Map pp108-9; ☎ 0 5330 6678; www.lalunagallery.com; 190 Th Charoenrat) In the old shophouse row on the east bank of the river, this professional gallery picks a fine bouquet of emerging Southeast Asian artists.

CHRIS MELLOR

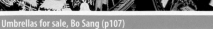
Umbrellas for sale, Bo Sang (p107)

CHIANG MAI

> ## COMMERCE AFTER DARK
>
> **Chiang Mai Night Bazaar** (Map pp108-9; Th Chang Khlan; ⏰7pm-midnight) is one of the city's main night-time attractions, especially for families, and is the modern legacy of the original Yunnanese trading caravans that stopped here along the ancient trade route between Simao (in China) and Mawlamyaing (on Myanmar's Gulf of Martaban coast). Today the night bazaar sells the usual tourist souvenirs, like what you'll find at Bangkok's street markets. The quality and bargains aren't especially impressive, but the allure is the variety and concentration of stuff and the dexterity and patience it takes to trawl through it all.

GETTING THERE & AWAY

Vila Cini (Map pp108-9; ☎ 0 5324 6246; www.vilacini.com; 30-34 Th Charoenrat) Villa Cini sells high-end, handmade silks and cotton textiles that are reminiscent of the Jim Thompson brand.

Sop Moei Arts (Map pp108-9; ☎ 0 5332 8143; www.sopmoeiarts.com; 150/10 Th Charoenrat) Lots of shops sell hill-tribe crafts, but this one has put a modern makeover on the traditional crafts of the Pwo Karen, a tribal group living in Mae Hong Son Province.

Sipsong Panna (Map p117; ☎ 0 5321 6096; Nantawan Arcade, 6/19 Th Nimmanhaemin) Opposite the Amari Rincome Hotel, this upmarket shop is the place for jewellery collected in Thailand, Laos, Myanmar and southwestern China.

Srisanpanmai (Map p117; ☎ 0 5389 4717; 6 Soi 1, Th Nimmanhaemin) From the technicolour rainbow patterns of Burma to the wide-hem panel style of Chiang Mai, Srisanpanmai specialises in silks made in the old tradition.

Adorn with Studio Naenna (Map p117; ☎ 0 5389 5136; 22 Soi 1, Th Nimmanhaemin) The pensive colours of the mountains have been woven into these naturally dyed silks and cottons, part of a village weaving project pioneered by Patricia Cheeseman, an expert and author on Thai-Lao textiles.

Ginger (Map p117; ☎ 0 5321 5635; 6/21 Th Nimmanhaemin) For something more night-on-the-townish, check out the shimmery dresses, sparkly mules, fabulous jewellery and colourful accessories.

GETTING THERE & AWAY
AIR

Regularly scheduled flights arrive at and depart from **Chiang Mai International Airport** (Map pp98-9; ☎ 0 5327 0222), which is 3km south of the centre of the old city. Unless otherwise noted the following airlines use the Suvarnabhumi Airport for travel from and to Bangkok.

Air Asia (☎ 0 2515 9999; www.airasia.com) Flies to Bangkok (1660B, six daily) and Kuala Lumpur (from 4000B, one daily).

Bangkok Airways (☎ 0 2265 5556; www.bangkokair.com) Flies to Bangkok (3400B; two daily) and continues to Samui (7300B).

China Airlines (☎ 0 5320 1268; www.china-airlines.com) Flies to Taipei (12,000B, two per week).

Lao Airlines (☎ 0 5322 3401; www.laoairlines.com) Flies to Vientiane (8400B, two daily) and Luang Prabang (5600B, one daily).

Nok Air (☎ 1318; www.nokair.com) Flies to Bangkok's Don Muang (2440B, four to five daily); note that Nok Air is a subsidiary of THAI. It also operates a code-share flight from Chiang Mai to Pai (660B, one daily) and Mae Hong Son (1090B, one daily) with SGA.

One-Two-Go (☎ 1141, ext 1126; www.fly 12go.com) Flies to Bangkok's Don Muang (1950B, three daily).

Siam GA (SGA; ☎ 0 5328 0444; www.sga.co .th) Flies to Pai (660B, one daily) and Mae Hong Son (1090B, one daily); these are code-share flights with Nok Air.

Silk Air (☎ 0 5390 4985; www.silkair.com) Flies to Singapore (16,000B, one daily).

Thai Airways International (THAI; ☎ 0 5321 1044/7; www.thaiair.com) Flies to Bang-

kok (1700B); there are eight daily flights to Suvarnabhumi Airport. Also flies to Mae Hong Son (1300B, three daily).

BUS

Chiang Mai's long-distance terminal is known as **Arcade Bus Terminal** (Map pp98-9; ☎ 0 5324 2664; Th Kaew Nawarat) and is about 3km from the old city.

For buses to destinations within Chiang Mai Province, use the **Chang Pheuak Bus Terminal** (Map pp108-9; ☎ 0 5321 1586; Th Chang Pheuak), which is north of the old city.

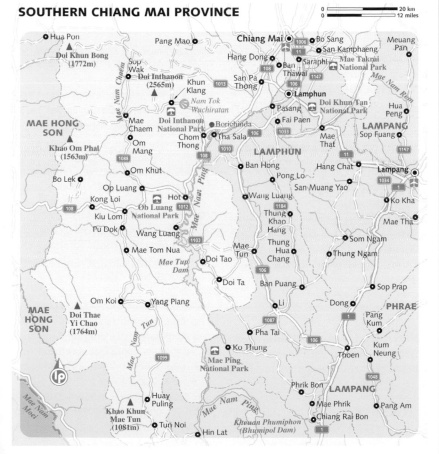

SOUTHERN CHIANG MAI PROVINCE

Săhm-lór driver (p389)

FELIX HUG

TRAIN

Chiang Mai's **train station** (Map pp98-9; ☎ 0 5324 5364, 0 5324 7462; Th Charoen Muang) is about 2.5km east of the old city. For information on schedules and fares contact the station or the **State Railway of Thailand** (☎ free hotline 1690; www.railway .co.th; ☽ 24 hr).

GETTING AROUND

TO/FROM AIRPORT

There is only one licensed airport taxi service charging a flat 150B fare. Many guesthouses and hotels also provide airport transfers.

From any point within the city, you can charter a túk-túk or red *sŏrng·tăa·ou* to the airport for 60B or 70B.

BICYCLE

Rickety cruiser bikes with a fixed gear can be rented for around 50B a day from some guesthouses or from various places along the east moat.

CAR & TRUCK

Two of the most well-regarded agencies are **North Wheels** (Map pp108-9; ☎ 0 5387 4478;

www.northwheels.com; 70/4-8 Th Chaiyaphum) and **Journey** (Map pp108-9; ☎ 0 5320 8787; www .journeycnx.com; 283 Th Tha Phae).

The highly recommended **Alternative Travel** (☎ 08 1784 4856, 08 9632 6556; noree9000@hotmail.com) offers customised tours with English-speaking drivers in Toyota sedans, 4WD trucks or vans (1500B to 2000B a day, plus petrol). Contact Winai to discuss car or itinerary options.

MOTORCYCLE

Agencies along Th Moon Muang and some guesthouses rent Honda Dream 100cc step-through manual/automatic bikes for about 150/200B a day.

SŎRNG·TĂA·OU & TÚK-TÚK

The *sŏrng·tăa·ou* are shared taxis: you can flag them down, tell them your destination and if they are going that way they'll nod.

Túk-túks work only on a charter basis and are about 20B per trip more expensive than *sŏrng·tăa·ou*. In entertainment areas at night most túk-túk drivers will ask for an optimistic 100B.

CENTRAL THAILAND

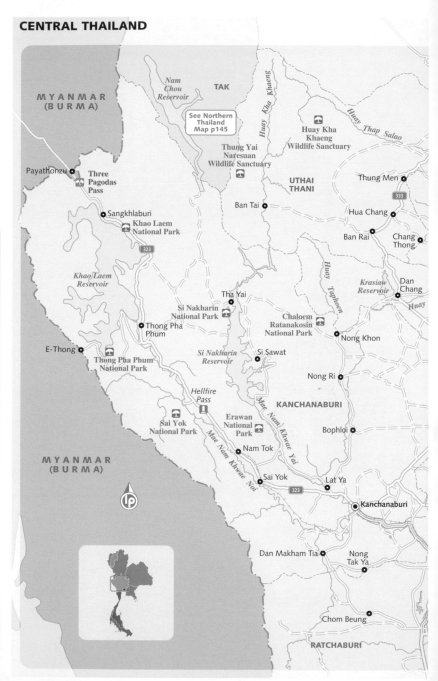

MYANMAR
(BURMA)

Nam Chou Reservoir

TAK

Huay Kha Khaeng

See Northern Thailand Map p145

Huay Thap Salao

Huay Kha Khaeng Wildlife Sanctuary

Thung Yai Naresuan Wildlife Sanctuary

Thung Men

333

Payathonzu

Three Pagodas Pass

Ban Tai

UTHAI THANI

Hua Chang

Sangkhlaburi

Khao Laem National Park

Ban Rai

Chang Thong

323

Huay Tapihoen

Krasiaw Reservoir

Dan Chang

Khao Laem Reservoir

Tha Yai

Huay

Si Nakharin National Park

Chaloem Ratanakosin National Park

Nong Khon

Thong Pha Phum

Si Sawat

E-Thong

Si Nakharin Reservoir

Nong Ri

Thong Pha Phum National Park

Hellfire Pass

KANCHANABURI

Sai Yok National Park

Erawan National Park

Bophloi

Nam Tok

Mae Nam Khwae Yai

MYANMAR
(BURMA)

Sai Yok

Lat Ya

323

Mae Nam Khwae Noi

Kanchanaburi

Dan Makham Tia

Nong Tak Ya

Chom Beung

RATCHABURI

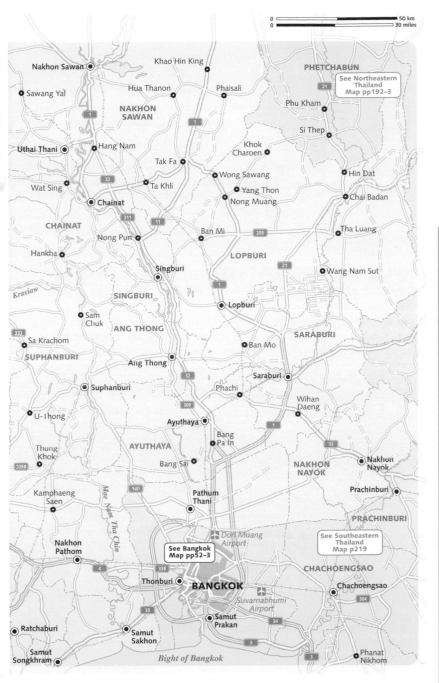

CENTRAL THAILAND

CENTRAL THAILAND HIGHLIGHTS

1 | AYUTHAYA

BY LAITHONGRIEN (OM) MEEPAN, FOUNDER/ DIRECTOR OF AYUTHAYA ELEPHANT PALACE AND ROYAL ELEPHANT KRAAL VILLAGE

Ayuthaya was the capital of Siam for over 400 years and elephants helped build the city and the country into what it is today. I became aware of the problems elephants faced after buying an elephant for my daughter's 7th birthday. Now I work on elephant conservation in the former royal city.

⬂ PI OM'S DON'T MISS LIST

❶ ROYAL ELEPHANT KRAAL

The Royal Elephant Kraal (p135) is the only one left in Thailand. It was here that elephants were rounded up and trained for war. We initially bought seven elephants. Now there are over 180. We provide a safe haven for them and support the mahout culture. That is where the knowledge is.

❷ ELEPHANT TAXI THROUGH THE HISTORIC CITY

We set up this program to get a few elephants off the streets as beggars and give them safe, legal, easy work. The elephants carry tourists through the historic park and its World Heritage–listed ruins. It is a very beautiful city and in the past elephants were a common mode of transport.

Clockwise from top: Elephants out for a stroll; Up close and personal; Elephant ride at Ayuthaya (p134); Mahouts and their elephants

CLOCKWISE FROM TOP: ANDERS BLOMQVIST; FRANK CARTER; OLIVER STREWE; FELIX HUG

❸ ELEPHANTSTAY PROGRAM

Creating a sustainable future for elephants is not easy and requires many solutions. Our non-profit Elephantstay program (p135), started and operated by Michelle Reedy and Ewa Narkiewicz, supports retired elephants through tourism. Visitors stay in the elephant village and learn about mahout life and get to bond with elephants. We love to see young children in the program because elephants need their help in the future. The elephants get a very high standard of care.

❹ ELEPHANT CONSERVATION

The history of elephants and people living and working together spans 5000 years. We work to preserve this history by training the elephants in the old tradition (as military machines) and the mahouts as proud elite warriors. Elephants need to work and be productive to keep them stimulated in captivity. Many of our elephants went to work in the tsunami-devastated area of Khao Lak in 2004. If it was not for the tourists supporting elephants, there would not be any left in Thailand.

↘ THINGS YOU NEED TO KNOW

Getting Started Check out the Elephantstay website (www.elephantstay .com) for program details **Top Tip** Hire an elephant taxi to take you to the famous Ayuthaya ruins **Top Souvenir** Elephant art created by artistic elephants putting trunk and brush to paper

CENTRAL THAILAND HIGHLIGHTS

⬎ 'RUIN' YOUR VACATION IN AYUTHAYA

An easy day trip north of Bangkok, the former Siamese capital of Ayuthaya (p134) is now an Unesco-designated World Heritage Site with hundreds of temple ruins in and around the modern provincial town. Visit the most famous sites aboard an elephant, once a common site in old Siam, and then board a long-tail boat for a river tour of further-flung attractions.

⬎ FIND WWII HISTORY IN KANCHANABURI

The foothills northwest of Bangkok hosted a dramatic WWII sub-plot that was made famous by the book *The Bridge Over the River Kwai,* and the similarly named movie. The town of Kanchanaburi (p138) hosts two maintained war cemeteries, several interesting museums and the bridge itself over the Mae Nam Khwae Yai ('Khwae' is pronounced more like 'quack' minus the final consonant sound).

4

↘ LOOP AROUND LOPBURI

Lopburi (p137) is a charming, walkable town where gravity-worn ruins, some dating back to the Khmer empire, sit comfortably beside daily Thai life. The best-looking ruin is the unofficial residence of a troop of mischief-making monkeys, who get an undeserved feast in November during their very own festival.

5

↘ ADVENTURE SOFTLY IN KANCHANABURI

If you like to dabble but not dawdle in the great outdoors, then Kanchanaburi is a good fit. Tour providers pack in a full day of elephant rides, bamboo river-rafting and a visit to the waterfall at Erawan National Park (p142). Adventure that doesn't require too much exertion.

6

↘ HEAD FOR THE HILLS

Western Thailand is a stunning landscape of dragon-scaled mountains – remote and jungle clad with small ethnic villages reflecting the area's proximity to Myanmar (Burma). But few foreign tourists follow the road to the final outpost at Sangkhlaburi (p141), a lakeside town sitting on the edge of a national park system.

2 OLIVER STREWE; 3 DENNIS JOHNSON; 4 ERIC WHEATER; 5 IMAGEBROKER / ALAMY; 6 AUSTIN BUSH

2 Wat Chai Wattanaram, Ayuthaya (p134); 3 Death Railway Bridge, Kanchanaburi (p139); 4 Woman in temple, Lopburi (p137); 5 Waterfall, Erawan National Park (p142); 6 Vachiralongkorn Dam, Sangkhlaburi (p142)

CENTRAL THAILAND'S BEST...

⤵ PLACES TO WANDER

- **Ayuthaya** (p134) Rent a squeaky bike and tackle the ruins in your own time.
- **Lopburi** (p137) Watch out for the roof-jumping monkeys as you poke around town.
- **Thong Pha Phum** (p140) Climb up to the hilltop temple for bucolic views.

⤵ PLACES FOR HISTORY BUFFS

- **Thailand-Burma Railway Centre** (p138) Get the facts on Kanchanaburi's small but interesting role in WWII.
- **Ayuthaya Historical Study Centre** (p137) Imagine the city when foreign ships came to call and the temples were topped with gold.
- **Hellfire Pass Memorial** (p140) Walk the rugged terrain that Allied POWs laboured through to build the Death Railway.

⤵ PLACES TO BE PROVINCIAL

- **Hua Raw Night Market** (p135) Eat with the people at Ayuthaya's night market.
- **Saisowo** (p140) Master the ubiquitous noodle soup at this Kanchanaburi restaurant.

⤵ PLACES TO RIDE ELEPHANTS

- **Ayuthaya** (p134) Tour the sites like royalty.
- **Kanchanaburi** (p138) Hitch a ride through the jungle.
- **Sangkhlaburi** (p141) Dive into the forest on a four-legged tour.

LEFT: STAEVEN VALLAK; RIGHT: ANDREW BAIN

Left: A row of buddhas, Ayuthaya (p134); Right: Hellfire Pass walking trail, Kanchanaburi (p141)

THINGS YOU NEED TO KNOW

⩗ VITAL STATISTICS

- Population 2.3 million
- Best time to visit October to December

⩗ TOWNS IN A NUTSHELL

- Ayuthaya A required stop on the culture trail.
- Lopburi Monkey around the temple ruins.
- Kanchanaburi Easy jungle tours and WWII history.
- Thong Tha Phum Tiny town cradled by the mountains.
- Sangkhlaburi Remote border town for end-of-the-road sojourns.

⩗ ADVANCE PLANNING

- One month before Watch the movie *Bridge On the River Kwai* or read the book *Bridge Over the River Kwai*.
- One week before Book your accommodation if you're going midrange or top end.
- One day before Buy train tickets.

⩗ RESOURCES

- Tourism Authority of Thailand (TAT; ☎ 0 3532 2730, 0 3524 6076; 108/22 Th Si Sanphet, ◷ 8.30am-4.30pm) In central Ayuthaya.
- TAT (☎ 0 3642 2768-9; Th Phraya Kamjat; ◷ 8.30am-4.30pm) In central Lopburi.
- TAT (☎ 0 3451 1200; Th Saengchuto; ◷ 8.30am-4.30pm) In Kanchanaburi.

⩗ EMERGENCY NUMBERS

- Fire (☎ 199)
- Police/Emergency (☎ 191)
- Tourist police (☎ 1155; ◷ 24hr)

⩗ GETTING AROUND

- Bus Best way to get from Bangkok to Kanchanaburi and beyond.
- Bicycle & Motorcycle Good self-touring option in the cities.
- Sŏrng·tăa·ou Small pick-up trucks that act as shared taxis and public buses.
- Train Slow but scenic way to Ayuthaya and Lopburi.
- Sǎhm·lór & Túk·túk Chartered vehicles for trips from the bus/train stations to hotels (around 40B to 50B) for sightseeing tours. Negotiate the price beforehand.

⩗ BE FOREWARNED

- Dress modestly Cover to the elbows and the ankles when visiting temples in Ayuthaya and don't pose for pictures in front of Buddha images.
- Waterfalls Kanchanaburi's waterfalls are at their peak during and just after the rainy season (June to December).
- Monkeys Keep your distance from Lopburi's monkeys as they might snatch your belongings or cause bodily harm; refrain from feeding them.

CENTRAL THAILAND ITINERARIES

ANCIENT MONUMENTS Three days

The fertile central plains have long nurtured monument builders, from the local Mon Dvaravati to the far-reaching Khmer empire. And at an auspicious island-like confluence of rivers, the emerging Thai nation established Ayuthaya, which ruled the plains and beyond for 400 years.

(1) Ayuthaya (p134) is the first stop on the culture trail that traces the origins of the modern Thai state. Though many of the great monuments have been destroyed or stolen, Ayuthaya remains historically important and some of its glory is still evident at Wat Phra Si Sanphet, displaying three elongated *chedi* (stupa) that epitomize Ayuthaya architecture.

A short train trip north leads to **(2) Lopburi** (p137), one of Thailand's oldest cities. Crumbling brick ruins built by the Khmers dot the city, which can be visited in a day en route to points north, if you time the train right. Alternatively you can overnight in one of the old town's modest hotels for a taste of provincial life.

RIVERS, FORESTS & HISTORY Five Days

Just a half-day journey from Bangkok, Kanchanaburi offers a quick jungle escape and attractions for WWII history buffs.

(1) Kanchanaburi (p138) was a base for a WWII Japanese-run POW camp. The town today provides a respectful commemoration to fallen Allied soldiers through several cemeteries and museums.

(2) Erawan National Park (p142) is best known for its seven-tiered waterfall said to resemble Erawan, the three-headed elephant of Hindu mythology. Walking to the first three tiers is simple, but you'll be huffing and puffing to complete the entire 1.5km hike. Most tourist tours stop here in the morning but you can make a day of it with your own transport.

During WWII, the Japanese military forced their POW captives to build a rail line to Burma, a task that resulted in thousands of deaths. Today trains travel over surviving portions of the **(3) Death Railway Line** (p140) from Kanchanaburi across Mae Nam Khwae Noi (River Kwai) to Nam Tok station.

The **(4) Hellfire Pass Memorial** (p140) has transformed one of the Death Railway's most difficult cuttings into a walking trail. The forbidding name refers to glow from the crews burning torches that cast eerie shadows on the inhumane labour, reminiscent of medieval underworld scenes.

CENTRAL THAILAND

CENTRAL THAILAND ITINERARIES

BORDER BOUND One Week

Beyond Kanchanaburi, Thailand's western frontier reflects neighbouring Myanmar (Burma) and its porous border. Mon, Karen and Burmese ethnic groups have long sought refuge in Thailand from their troubled homeland.

Explore the scenic and historic riverside town of (1) Kanchanaburi (p138), a gateway to the western frontier.

A sleepy mountain hamlet, (2) Thong Pha Phum (p140) is where Thais go to get 'back to nature'. The nearby Kheuan Khao Laem supplies plenty of Thai-style entertainment: karaoke and whisky drinking by the water. It's worth an overnight for deep-immersion types, who can wander to the hilltop temple or sample ethnic Mon and Burmese-style curries.

An ethnically diverse border town, (3) Sangkhlaburi (p141) is perched beside a scenic lake where morning boats swim through the mist to look at half-submerged temples.

If the border is open, peep into Myanmar (Burma) through the crossing at (4) Three Pagodas Pass (p142). Foreigners can pay US$10 (500B) for a day-pass permit allowing them access to a small Burmese market town and a bit of Burma bragging rights.

DISCOVER CENTRAL THAILAND

Both the geographic and cultural heart of the kingdom, the central region is the birthplace of modern-day Thailand.

Just north of Bangkok is the former Siam royal capital of Ayuthaya, home to fabled palace and temple ruins. Slightly further north is the small town of Lopburi, where monkeys play and scavenge among the Khmer-style ruins.

Northwest from Bangkok is Kanchanaburi, the country's third-largest province. Its natural beauty makes it a popular destination for Thais and tourists, who come to bathe in waterfalls, trek through jungles and kayak along rivers. War veterans make pilgrimages here to remember those who died in WWII when Japanese forces used prisoners of war to build the 'Death Railway'.

In the mountains of northwest Kanchanaburi are sleepy Thong Pha Phum and Sangkhlaburi. Few travellers make it this far, but those that do are richly rewarded with a fascinating blend of cultures and beliefs.

AYUTHAYA PROVINCE

AYUTHAYA
พระนครศรีอยุธยา
pop 137,600

Ayuthaya was the capital of Siam for 417 years, between 1350 and 1767, and had strong links to several European nations. Its glorious reign ended in 1767 when the invading Burmese army sacked the city, looting most of its treasures.

SIGHTS

A one-day pass for most sites on the island is available for 220B and can be bought at the museums or ruins.

WAT PHRA SI SANPHET
วัดพระศรีสรรเพชญ์

The three dominant *chedi* (stupas) at **Wat Phra Si Sanphet** (admission 50B) make it a must-see location on any temple tour. Built in the late 14th century, this was the largest temple in Ayuthaya and was used by several kings.

WAT PHRA MAHATHAT
วัดพระมหาธาตุ

Built in 1374 during the reign of King Borom Rachathirat I, the most famous part of **Wat Phra Mahathat** (admission 50B) is a Buddha head embedded among a tree's maze of roots.

WAT RATBURANA
วัดราชบูรณะ

Immediately north of Wat Phra Mahathat, this **temple** (Ratcha-burana; admission 50B) has one of the best preserved *prang* in the city. It was built in the 15th century by King Borom Rachathirat II on the cremation site for his two brothers who both died while fighting each other for the throne.

WAT CHAI WATTANARAM
วัดไชยวัฒนาราม

Just 40 years ago this **temple** (admission 50B) was immersed in thick jungle. Today it's one of Ayuthaya's most-photographed sites, thanks to its impressive Khmer-style central *prang*, which stands 35m high.

ROYAL ELEPHANT KRAAL
เพนียดคล้องช้าง

Wild elephants were once rounded up and kept in this stockade. Each year the king would look on here as the finest beasts were chosen and either put to work or used as war machines.

TOURS

Several guesthouses offer night tours of the ruins (200B per person).

A variety of cycling tours are available on and off the island through **Ayutthaya Boat & Travel** (☎ 02 2746 1414; www.ayutthaya-boat.com), off Th Rotchana.

SLEEPING

Wieng Fa Hotel (☎ 0 3524 3252; 1/8 Th Rotchana; r 400-500B; ☒) Retro furniture and an outdoor patio add character to this professionally run hotel.

our pick **Baan Lotus Guest House** (☎ 0 3525 1988; 20 Th Pamaphrao; r 400-600B; ☒) This charming family-run guesthouse is the pick of the crop.

DENNIS JOHNSON

Floating restaurant, Kanchanaburi (p138)

River View Place Hotel (☎ 0 3524 1444; 35/5 Th U Thong; r from 2000B; ☒ 🖳 ☒) The best of the on-island hotels, the River View Place Hotel has large, comfortable rooms and a raft of amenities.

HELPING AN OLD FRIEND

The **Ayuthaya Elephant Palace** (☎ 08 0668 7727; www.elephantstay.com) does its part to raise the profile of the animal, and the mahout. It provides rides for tourists around the city ruins, runs a successful breeding program and holds several innovative promotional activities.

The centre aims to protect Thailand's remaining elephants by buying sick or abused animals.

Laithongrien Meepan opened the centre in 1996 after buying his daughter an elephant as a present. Australians Michelle Reedy, a former zoo keeper, and Ewa Narkiewicz run an **Elephantstay program** (www.elephantstay.com; 4000B per day) at the site, where visitors learn how to ride, bathe and earn the trust of the animals over several days or weeks.

AYUTHAYA

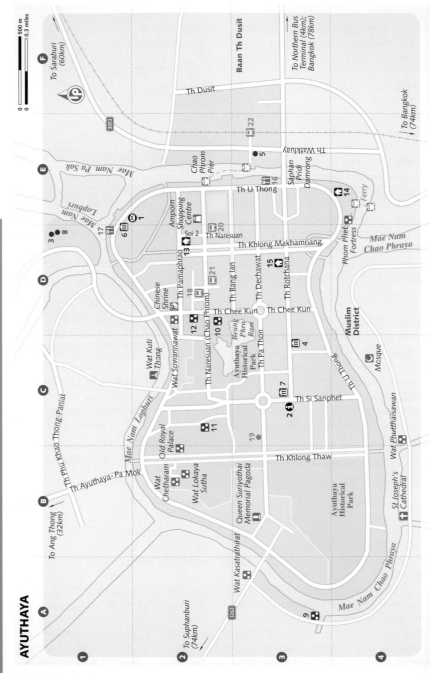

EATING

ourpick **Hua Raw Night Market** (Th U Thong) A great evening option, with simple riverfront seating.

Baan Khun Phra (☎ 0 3524 1978; dishes 80-140B; 48/2 Th U Thong) Behind the guesthouse of the same name, this restaurant has a pleasant riverside atmosphere and good Thai, Western and vegetarian choices.

GETTING THERE & AWAY

BOAT

Boat Step Travel (☎ 08 9744 2672, 1500B) runs daily trips, leaving Ayuthaya at 11.30am and arriving in Bangkok at 4.30pm.

BUS

The provincial bus stop is on Th Naresuan, a short walk from the guesthouse area. Buses from Bangkok arrive two blocks away from the main bus terminal.

Buses to Lopburi (40B, two hours, every 45 minutes) also depart from the terminal on Th Naresuan.

TRAIN

The train station is east of central Ayuthaya and is accessible by a quick cross-river ferry (4B).

GETTING AROUND

The main ruins are close together, so the most environmentally friendly way to see them is by bicycle or elephant. The elephants stay at a kraal on Th Pa Thon.

LOPBURI PROVINCE
LOPBURI

ลพบุรี

Laid-back Lopburi is a small, charming town where temple ruins sit alongside noodle stalls and street markets.

Chao Sam Phraya National Museum

OLIVER STREWE

➘ IF YOU LIKE...

If you would like to know more about Ayuthaya's past, hire a guide through TAT (☎ 0 3524 6076; 108/22 Th Si Sanphet; ⏰ 8.30am-4.30pm) and check out these museums:

- **Ayuthaya Historical Study Centre** (☎ 0 3524 5124; Th Rotchana; adult/student 100/50B; ⏰ 9am-4.30pm Mon-Fri, to 5pm Sat & Sun)
- **Chao Sam Phraya National Museum** (admission 150B; ⏰ 9am-4pm Wed-Sun)
- **Chantharakasem National Museum** (Th U Thong; admission 100B; ⏰ 9am-4pm Wed-Sun)

CENTRAL THAILAND

LOPBURI PROVINCE

Buddha statue, Prang Sam Yot

The easygoing pace only shifts a gear when locals chase away Lopburi's most notorious residents – a troop of monkeys.

SIGHTS

PHRA NARAI RATCHANIWET
พระนารายณ์ราชนิเวศน์

This **former royal palace** (entrance Th Sorasak; admission 150B; ☉ gallery 8.30am-4pm Wed-Sun, palace grounds 7am-5.30pm) is the best place to begin your walking tour of Lopburi's ruins.

The palace grounds house the **Lopburi Museum** (officially called the Somdet Phra Narai National Museum), which has interesting displays explaining the history of the province.

PRANG SAM YOT
ปรางค์สามยอด

This **shrine** (Th Wichayen; admission 50B; ☉ 8am-6pm) is the old town's best-known and most-photographed feature. The three linked towers originally symbolised the Hindu Trimurti of Shiva, Vishnu and Brahma.

GETTING THERE & AWAY

Lopburi's **bus station** (Th Naresuan) is nearly 2km away from the old town.

The **train station** (Th Na Phra Kan) is within walking distance of the old town and its guesthouses.

KANCHANABURI PROVINCE
KANCHANABURI
กาญจนบุรี

pop 63,100

The natural beauty of Kanchanaburi attracts tourists looking for an alternative to the bustle of Bangkok, 130km away.

During WWII the town experienced darker times. Japanese forces used Allied prisoners of war and conscripted Southeast Asian labourers to build a rail route to Myanmar.

SIGHTS

THAILAND-BURMA RAILWAY CENTRE
ศูนย์รถไฟไทย–พม่า

This informative **museum** (☎ 0 3451 0067; www.tbrconline.com; 73 Th Chaokunen; adult/child 100/50B; ☉ 9am-5pm) is the ideal place to begin your look at Kanchanaburi's role in WWII.

ALLIED WAR CEMETERY
สุสานทหารสัมพันธมิตรดอนรัก

Across the street from the museum is the **Allied War Cemetery** (Th Saengchuto; ☉ 8am-6pm), which is immaculately maintained by the War Graves Commission. Of the 6982 prisoners of war buried here, nearly half were British.

DEATH RAILWAY BRIDGE (BRIDGE OVER THE RIVER KWAI)

สะพานข้ามแม่น้ำแคว

This 300m **railway bridge** (Th Mae Nam Khwae) is one huge tourist trap. The centre of the bridge was destroyed by Allied bombs in 1945 so today only the outer curved spans are original.

ACTIVITIES

For those with more time and stamina, cycling tours, canoeing and jungle trekking can all be booked from Kanchanaburi.

SLEEPING

Blue Star Guest House (☎ 0 3451 2161; 241 Th Mae Nam Khwae; r 150-650B; 🖳) Accommodation here ranges from backpacker simplicity to comfy rooms with air-con and TV.

Ploy Guesthouse (☎ 0 3451 5804; www .ploygh.com; 79/2 Th Mae Nam Kwai; r 600-950B; 🖳) Stylish and chic, this guesthouse stands head and shoulders above its budget style neighbours.

Royal River Kwai Resort & Spa (☎ 0 3465 3297; 88 Kanchanaburi-Saiyok Rd; r from 2450B; 🖳 🖳) Beautiful grounds and chic rooms make this a splendid resort.

EATING

The **market** (Th Saengchuto) near the bus station is well known for its excellent *hŏy tôrt* (fried mussels in an egg batter).

Saisowo (no roman-script sign; Th Chaokunen; dishes 20-30B; 🕙 8am-4pm) A long-running noodle emporium with some of the finest *gŏo·ay ĕe·o mŏo* for miles around.

Jukkru (no roman-script sign; Th Song Khwae; dishes 50-120B) It lacks the glamour of the floating restaurants opposite, but Jukkru compensates with superb Thai cuisine.

GETTING THERE & AWAY

Kanchanaburi's **bus station** (☎ 0 3451 5907; Th Saengchuto) is to the south of the town.

AROUND KANCHANABURI

TIGER TEMPLE (WAT LUANG TA BUA YANNA SAMPANNO)

วัดหลวงตาบัวญาณสัมปันโน

Kanchanaburi's most expensive tourist attraction is also its most controversial. This

DENNIS JOHNSON

Jeath War Museum

🢂 IF YOU LIKE...

If you like Kanchanaburi's WWII history, there are more sites to explore:

- **Jeath War Museum** (Th Wisuttharangsi; admission 30B; 🕙 8.30am-6pm) Resembles the bamboo huts in which POWs were kept.
- **Chung Kai Allied War Cemetery** Across the river and a scenic resting place for Allied soldiers.
- **Death Railway Line** Portions of this historic train line are still functioning and depart from Kanchanaburi to Nam Tok, 2km from Sai Yok Waterfall. The trip takes two hours and costs 100B.

KANCHANABURI

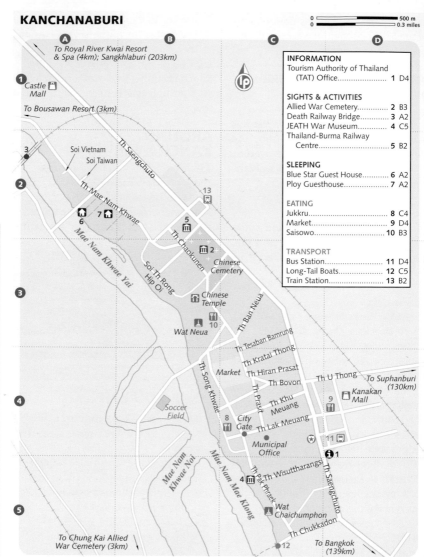

INFORMATION		
Tourism Authority of Thailand (TAT) Office.....................	**1**	D4
SIGHTS & ACTIVITIES		
Allied War Cemetery.............	**2**	B3
Death Railway Bridge.............	**3**	A2
JEATH War Museum.............	**4**	C5
Thailand-Burma Railway Centre................................	**5**	B2
SLEEPING		
Blue Star Guest House............	**6**	A2
Ploy Guesthouse....................	**7**	A2
EATING		
Jukkru....................................	**8**	C4
Market....................................	**9**	D4
Saisowo.................................	**10**	B3
TRANSPORT		
Bus Station............................	**11**	D4
Long-Tail Boats.....................	**12**	C5
Train Station.........................	**13**	B2

monastery (☎ 0 3453 1557; admission 500B; ☽ noon-3.30pm) affords incredible photo opportunities for visitors to get up close and personal with the big cats. Some of the temple's 30 tigers pose for pictures in a canyon while visitors are shepherded in and out in quick succession.

The temple is 38km from Kanchanaburi on Hwy 323. Most travellers book an afternoon tour with a travel company.

Hellfire Pass walking trail, Kanchanaburi

ANDREW BAIN

HELLFIRE PASS MEMORIAL

ช่องเขาขาด

This museum (www.dva.gov.au/commem /oawg/thailand.htm; admission by donation; 9am-4pm) is a joint Thai-Australian project that remembers the tragedy of the 'Death Railway' in a simple and dignified manner. A 4km-long walking trail (which takes three hours round-trip) runs along the original railbed.

The museum is 80km northwest of Kanchanaburi on Hwy 323 and can be reached by Sangkhlaburi-Kanchanaburi bus (50B, 1½ hours, frequent departures). The last bus back to Kanchanaburi passes here at 4.30pm.

THONG PHA PHUM

ทองผาภูมิ

Surrounded by cloud-capped mountains and dense forests, this tiny town is a great place to sample a quieter way of life. Thong Pha Phum acts as a stop-off point for those heading north to Sangkhlaburi,

and also as an access point for nearby natural attractions.

SLEEPING & EATING

Ban Suan (☎ 0 3459 9841?; off Hwy 3272; r 650-1200B; ⊠) Outside of town, Ban Suan has great views of the dam, good facilities and an English-speaking manager, something of a rarity in these parts.

Restaurants around town reflect the large Burmese and ethnic communities who live here: the large metal pots full of tempting curries are typically Mon.

SANGKHLABURI

สังขละบุรี

pop 47,200

Few places in Thailand have such a blend of ethnic identities, with Burmese, Karen, Mon, Thai and some Lao each calling this home. Many cross the Myanmar (Burmese) border, driven by economic need or through fear of oppression.

ANTONY GIBLIN

Waterfall, Erawan National Park

ERAWAN NATIONAL PARK

อุทยานแห่งชาติเอราวัณ

The seven-tiered waterfall at the 550-sq-km Erawan National Park is the best-known attraction, but there are several other natural features worth seeking out.

Tham Phra That boasts a large variety of limestone formations. Guides with paraffin lamps lead visitors through the unlit cave, pointing out the translucent rocks, glittering crystals and bat-covered caverns.

Things you need to know: ☎ 0 3457 4222; admission 200B; ☺ 8am-4pm, levels 1 & 2 to 5pm

SIGHTS

KHAO LAEM RESERVOIR

เขื่อนเขาแหลม

This enormous lake was formed when the Vachiralongkorn Dam (known locally as Khao Laem Dam) was constructed across Mae Nam Khwae Noi in 1983. In the dry season it's still possible to see the spires of the village's Wat Sam Prasop protruding from the lake.

Canoes, long-tail boats and jet-skies can be found on the lake.

SLEEPING & EATING

P Guest House (☎ 0 3459 5061; www .pguesthouse.com; 8/1 Mu 1; r 252-909; ⊠) With English-speaking staff and rooms with fabulous lake views, P Guest House is a safe choice. Trips can be arranged from here, along with motorbike, bicycle and canoe hire.

Baan Unrak Bakery (snacks 25-90B) Vegetarians will love this meatless cafe, which has excellent pastries and Thai dishes.

GETTING THERE & AWAY

Right across from the market is a bare patch of land that serves as Sangkhlaburi's bus station.

The distance between Kanchanaburi and Sangkhlaburi is about 230km.

AROUND SANGKHLABURI

THREE PAGODAS PASS

ด่านเจดีย์สามองค์

The pagodas (Phrá Jedii Săam Ong) after which the town is named are unremarkable, and the main reason many come here is to gain a day pass into secretive Myanmar (Burma).

It's important to check with locals before coming, as the Myanmar (Burmese) government habitually shuts its side of the border due to fighting between Burmese military and ethnic armies.

Sŏrng·tăa·ou leave from Sangkhlaburi's bus station (40B) every 45 minutes between 6.40am and 5.20pm.

NORTHERN THAILAND

Wat Mahathat (p172), Sukhothai Historical Park

NORTHERN THAILAND

0 — 100 km
0 — 60 miles

MYANMAR
(BURMA)

LAOS

Tachileik
Mae Sai
Chiang Saen
Mae Salong
Mae Chan
Chiang Khong
Huay Xai

See Golden Triangle & Around Map (p168)

Doi Ang Khang (1300m)
Tha Ton
Fang
Wawi
Chiang Rai
1020

Mekong River

Ban Huay Kon

Huay Nam Dang National Park
CHIANG MAI
CHIANG RAI
Phan

Soppong (Pangmapha)
Doi Chiang Dao (2195m)
Pai
Chiang Dao
Mae Hong Son

Doi Luang National Park
Mae Chai
PHAYAO
Thung Chang

MAE HONG SON
Wang Neua
1021
Chiang Klang
Pua

Mae Rim
Mae Taeng
Phayao
Pong
Ban Bo Luang

Khun Yuam
Chae Son National Park
LAMPANG
Mae Yom National Park
NAN

Doi Inthanon (2595m)
See Chiang Mai Map pp98-9
Doi Saket
Jae Hom
Ngao
Nan

Chiang Mai
Kheuan Mae Chang
Tham Pha Thai
Wiang Sa
1125

Doi Inthanon National Park
Lamphun
Pasang
Doi Khun Tan National Park
Song
103
101

Salawin National Park
Chom Thong
PHRAE

Mae Sariang
Hot
Ban Hong
Lampang
1023
Phrae
1022

Mae Ngao National Park
Ob Luang National Park
Thai Elephant Conservation Center
Mae Wang
Den Chai
Fak Tha

CHIANG MAI
106
Kheuan Sirikit
UTARADIT
1268
LAOS

LAMPHUN
Thoen
Utaradit
Mae Nam Yom
Wang Pa Chun

Ban Tha Song Yang
Mae Ping National Park
LAMPANG
Si Satchanalai
Dan Sai

Mae Sarit
Sawankhalok
PHITSANULOK

Tha Song Yang
Si Samrong
Nakhon Thai
Lom Sak

TAK
SUKHOTHAI
2013

MYANMAR
(BURMA)
Mae Ramat
Sukhothai
Phitsanulok
Lam Nam Khek
Khao Kho
203

Tak
Mae Nam Ping
Krabeu
12

Myawadi
Mae Sot
101
Mae Nam Yom

Phop Phra
1090
Kamphaeng Phet
115
Phichit
Phetchabun

Khlong Lan National Park
Khlong Khlung
PHICHIT
PHETCHABUN

Um Phang
KAMPHAENG PHET
Khanu Woralaksaburi
117
See Northeastern Thailand Map pp192-3

Palatha
Mae Wong National Park
Chumsaeng
Nong Phai
Nong Bua
225

TAK
Letongkhu
See Central Thailand Map pp124-5
Nakhon Sawan
11

Huay Thap Salao
NAKHON SAWAN
Tak Fa

Payathonzu
Three Pagodas Pass
Sangkhlaburi
Uthai Thani
Ta Khli
LOPBURI

Kheuan Khao Kaem
323
UTHAI THANI
Chainat
11
Ban Mi
205

Huay Kha Khaeng
CHAINAT
333
Hankha
SINGBURI
21

KANCHANABURI

NORTHERN THAILAND HIGHLIGHTS

1   CHIANG RAI PROVINCE

BY URUPHONG (TOI) RAKSASAD, INDEPENDENT FILMMAKER

Chiang Rai is connected to Laos and Myanmar (Burma) and has beautiful scenery that makes it special in Thailand. It is quieter than Chiang Mai and will allow you to live in peace. I grew up in Theong district, a lowland rice-growing area outside of Chiang Rai town, and this is where I film my movies, including *Agrarian Utopia* (2009).

↘ TOI'S DON'T MISS LIST

❶ COUNTRY SCENERY

Chiang Rai Province is filled with beautiful mountains and rice paddies. There is a triangle-shaped mountain near my home that points to the sky. I like to climb to the top to look out towards Laos and see the Mekong River below. But there are many other mountains in the province, like **Doi Tung** (p166), which is outside of Mae Sai.

❷ NORTHERN THAI FOOD

In Chiang Rai town, I would advise trying Lanna-style food, like *nám prík nùm* (grilled green-chilli paste), *nám prík ong* (pork and tomato chilli dip) eaten with sticky rice and *sâi òo·a* (northern-style sausages).

Clockwise from top: Hill-tribe woman and child, Mae Hong Son (p180); Hill-tribe village; Dicing chillies; Mountains, Chiang Rai Province (p157)

❸ WAT PHRA KAEW

Whenever you visit a Thai town, you must visit the most famous temple. In Chiang Rai town, this is **Wat Phra Kaew** (p155), the oldest one in town. Spend some time talking with the abbot or other monks. This temple used to be the home of a very famous Buddha figure in Thailand.

❹ WAT RONG KHUN

Chiang Rai province has many temples but the one I would suggest you see is **Wat Rong Khun** (p162). This white temple is still being built by Thai artist Chalermchai Kositpipat but you can visit some part of it to see the relationship between religion and art.

❺ HILL-TRIBE VILLAGES

Many tourists come to Chiang Rai Province to visit minority hill-tribe villages; there are many **trekking companies** (p159), but I'm a lowland person and I still don't understand the mountain people. You will enjoy the beautiful landscape of mountains and rice paddies too.

↘ THINGS YOU NEED TO KNOW

Best Time to Visit November to February (winter season) when the weather is cool and the forest is green **Best Photo Op** Farmers working in the fields

NORTHERN THAILAND HIGHLIGHTS

2

⬎ FIND PEACE AMONG THE RUINS

You may have gotten your fill of tumbled down bricks in Ayuthaya but the ancient capital of **Sukhothai** (p171) is worth the extra effort. The old city is sheltered in a quiet park-like setting that creates a meditative calm. The surviving Buddha figures are elegant and fluid despite their stationary position – a hallmark of Sukhothai's artistic tradition. And rarely are the ruins crowded.

3

⬎ CLIMB THROUGH MAE HONG SON PROVINCE

The winding roads are gruelling and time-consuming but this remote province is a stunning landscape of mountains, lush forests and villages that hardly seem Thai. Start off in **Pai** (p184); continue to **Mae Hong Son** (p180) for Burmese-style markets and treks into true wilderness; detour to **Soppong** (p188) and its curious cave; and squeeze in one more forest foray in **Mae Sariang** (p180).

4

↘ MAKE A RUN FOR CHIANG RAI PROVINCE

Looking for border adventures but short on time? Look no further than easy-to-reach **Chiang Rai** (p157), a convenient base for eco-tours to hill-tribe villages. Nearby are the towns and farming villages that once comprised the infamous **Golden Triangle** (p166).

5

↘ UNCOVER NORTHERN THAI HISTORY

Sukhothai might have been the first 'Thai' kingdom but the valleys through which the Thai people migrated from southern China cultivated many minor regional kingdoms. There are monuments to powers now past in **Lamphun** (p154), **Kamphaeng Phet** (p178) and **Chiang Saen** (p165).

6

↘ LUMBER THROUGH LAMPANG

Lampang (p154) is an easy detour for Bangkok–Chiang Mai bound travellers, and has a bit of everything for which northern Thailand is famous. Horse-drawn carts can deliver you to Lanna-style temples built during the teak trade. Or venture outside of town to the elephant conservation centre, where you can train to be a mahout.

2 PATRICK HORTON; 3 AUSTIN BUSH; 4 MICK ELMORE; 5 AUSTIN BUSH; 6 AUSTIN BUSH

2 Detail of buddha statue, Sukhothai (p171); 3 Hillside Buddhist temple, Mae Hong Son Province (p180); 4 Rafting, Chiang Rai Province (p157); 5 Temple ruins, Kamphaeng Phet Historical Park (p179); 6 Temple, Lampang (p154)

NORTHERN THAILAND'S BEST...

⬎ SCENIC JOURNEYS

- **Mae Salong–Chiang Mai** (p162) Slide down the ridge road from this ethnic Chinese village.
- **Mae Hong Son Loop** (p180) A famous motorcycle ride along mountain switchbacks and vistas.
- **Doi Tung-Mae Sai** (p166) Tiptoe past Myanmar (Burma) en route to this former opium-growing area.

⬎ PLACES TO SLEEP

- **Ruean Thai Hotel** (p175) Pretend you're Thai aristocracy at this restored teak house.
- **Pai Treehouse** (p186) Sleep in the trees at this riverside hotel.
- **Red Rose Hotel** (p160) Kooky theme rooms sprinkle a little Thai *sà·nùk* (fun) into slumberland.

⬎ PLACES FOR TREKKING

- **Chiang Rai** (p157) An easy departure point for treks that have a philanthropic hook.
- **Mae Sariang** (p188) Remote trekking with eco- and culturally sensitive guides.
- **Mae Hong Son** (p180) Nature hikes without the crowds.

⬎ PLACES TO TAKE THE CURE

- **Phra Ruang Hot Springs** (p179) Boil on purpose in the thermal pools.
- **Tha Pai Hot Springs** (p185) Soak to point of pruning at this Pai highlight.
- **Pooklon Country Club** (p182) Plaster yourself with home-grown, mineral-rich mud.

LEFT: JOHN ELK III; RIGHT: AUSTIN BUSH

Left: Buddha statues, Wat Phra Si Ratana Mahathat (p167), Phitsanulok; Right: Winding roads, Mae Salong (p162)

THINGS YOU NEED TO KNOW

⤷ VITAL STATISTICS

- **Population** 7.8 million
- **Best time to visit** November to March

⤷ PROVINCES IN A NUTSHELL

- **Chiang Rai** Border province known for coffee and the Golden Triangle.
- **Kamphaeng Phet** Detour for temple buffs.
- **Lampang** A mini-version of Chiang Mai.
- **Lamphun** Temple-spotting day trip.
- **Mae Hong Son** Rugged landscape, Burmese influences and bohemian Pai.
- **Phitsanulok** Famous Buddhist temple and rail access to Sukhothai.
- **Sukhothai** Ancient Thai capital; a must-see on the culture trail.

⤷ ADVANCE PLANNING

- **One month before** Book accommodation.
- **One week before** Plan your itinerary.
- **One day before** Buy bus and/or train tickets.

⤷ RESOURCES

- **Golden Triangle Rider** (www.gt -rider.com) Motorcycle touring maps.
- **Tourism Authority of Thailand** (TAT; ☎ 0 5374 4674, 0 5371 1433; Th Singkhlai, Chiang Rai; ◷ 8.30am-4.30pm)
- **TAT offices** Phitsanulok (☎ 0 5525 2742/2743; 209/7-8 Th Borom Trailokanat;

◷ 8.30am-4.30pm); Mae Hong Son (☎ 0 5361 2982; Th Khumlum Praphat; ◷ 8.30am-4.30pm Mon-Fri)

⤷ EMERGENCY NUMBERS

- **Fire** (☎ 199)
- **Police/Emergency** (☎ 191)
- **Tourist police** (☎ 1155; ◷ 24hr)

⤷ GETTING AROUND

- **Air** Fly to Chiang Rai or Mae Hong Son.
- **Bicycle** A great way to see the towns.
- **Bus** Best option for Chiang Rai and Mae Hong Son provinces.
- **Motorcycle/car** Good self-touring option.
- **Sŏrng·tăa·ou** Small pick-up trucks that shuttle to small border towns.
- **Train** Bangkok–Chiang Mai with detours at Phitsanulok, Lampang or Lamphun.
- **Túk-túk** Chartered vehicles for in-town trips; remember to bargain.

⤷ BE FOREWARNED

- **Rainy season** Remote parts of Mae Hong Son are inaccessible from June to October.
- **Hot season** Between April and June the valleys can be smoky from agriculture-related fires.
- **Checkpoints** Bring an ID to show at military checkpoints near the border.
- **Guides** Use a TAT-licensed guide for treks and tours.

NORTHERN THAILAND ITINERARIES

CONNECT TO THE CULTURE TRAIL Three Days

As you travel north from Bangkok, you pass through the cradle of the Thai nation. The ancient capital of Sukhothai is the most important stop, but there are other former satellite cities and independent kingdoms that had a hand in shaping the country's identity.

If you're travelling by train, disembark at **(1) Phitsanulok** (p167), an average provincial town with bus access to Sukhothai. Thai tourists stop in Phitsanulok to make merit at Wat Phra Si Ratana Mahathat and eat *gŏoay·đĕe·o hôy kăh* (literally, 'legs-hanging' noodles).

Continue on to **(2) Sukhothai** (p171) for two day's of ruin reconnaissance. Sukhothai's dynasty lasted 200 years and included the reign of King Ramkhamhaeng (1275–1317), credited with developing the first Thai script. Deeper into the countryside is **(3) Si Satchanalai-Chaliang Historical Park** (p177), a Sukhothai satellite. The rural setting offers glimpses into the country's agricultural rice basket.

If you've got a day to spare, detour to **(4) Kamphaeng Phet** (p178), a pleasant provincial town with a handful of Sukhothai-era ruins.

STOMP AROUND CHIANG RAI Five Days

Thailand's northernmost province, Chiang Rai has always been a conduit – for the ancestral migration of the Thai people, the pony caravans during the Silk Rd-era and the pack mules carrying opium from the Golden Triangle. Today goods and people continue to migrate through this culturally diverse province.

Start off in **(1) Chiang Rai** (p157) for a multi-day trek led by NGOs that have *real* connections to hill-tribe villages.

Do a day trip to **(2) Mae Salong** (p162), an ethnic Chinese village that teeters on the mountain ridge.

Bus to the scruffy border town of **(3) Mae Sai** (p164), a gateway to the Golden Triangle and entry point into Myanmar (Burma). Day trip to **(4) Doi Tung** (p166), where coffee now grows instead of opium poppies.

Move on to the Mekong border town of **(5) Chiang Saen** (p165), the first Lanna capital. Day trip to **(6) Sop Ruak** (p166), the Golden Triangle's official 'centre'.

ZIGZAG THROUGH MAE HONG SON One Week

Bordering the Myanmar (Burmese) frontier, Mae Hong Son Province has alluring mountain scenery and seemingly unchartered wilderness. The modest villages are a mix of cross-border ethnicities, further adding to the sense of remoteness and adventure.

ROUTES
— Connect to the Culture Trail
— Stomp Around Chiang Rai
— Zigzag Through Mae Hong Son

From Chiang Mai it is a stomach-wrenching ride to (1) Pai (p184), set in a pretty mountain valley. Most folk just take it easy in Pai – a little yoga, a trip to the hot springs, some nibbling and imbibing, maybe a trek or an elephant ride.

Do an overnight in (2) Soppong (p188) to explore its famous cave. You can also arrange hill-tribe treks and rafting trips in Soppong if the tourist crowds in Pai seem like a distraction.

Continue on to (3) Mae Hong Son (p180), the provincial capital with picturesque lakeside temples, markets selling Burmese specialties and less-trodden trekking tours.

Or swing down to (4) Mae Sariang (p188), which has a well-respected sustainable trekking industry: fees are paid directly to the host villages, or knowledgeable guides provide minority culture immersions. The road winds out of the mountains and swings back to Chiang Mai.

DISCOVER NORTHERN THAILAND

Despite the centuries that have passed since early Tai tribes from southern China are thought to have settled here, northern Thailand continues to cling to its roots, and for many Thais the area still maintains an aura of the 'real' Thailand.

In addition to the Thai majority, the north is the most ethnically diverse part of the country, with well-known hill tribes such as Hmong and Akha, to lesser known groups such as the unique Chinese community of Mae Salong and Mae Hong Son's small Muslim communities.

Put all this together and it's clear that these old hills are the perfect destination for seeking out a special cultural experience. And for those seeking something more vigorous, the region's geography and climate ensure that there is also ample opportunity for more active pursuits.

LAMPHUN PROVINCE
LAMPHUN
ลำพูน

pop 56,800

The old fortress wall and ancient temples are surviving examples of Lamphun's former life as the northernmost outpost of the ancient Mon Dvaravati kingdom then known as Hariphunchai (AD 750–1281).

SIGHTS
WAT PHRA THAT HARIPHUNCHAI
วัดพระธาตุหริภุญชัย

This **temple** (Th Inthayongyot; admission 20B) enjoys an exalted status because it dates back to the Mon period, having been built on the site of Queen Chama Thewi's palace in 1044 (or 1108 or 1157 according to some datings).

HARIPHUNCHAI NATIONAL MUSEUM
พิพิธภัณฑสถานแห่งชาติลำพูน

Just across the street from Wat Phra That Hariphunchai is the informative

Hariphunchai National Museum (☎ 0 5351 1186; Th Inthayongyot; admission 100B; ☺ 9am-4pm Wed-Sun). Run by the national Fine Arts Department, this museum has a collection of Mon and Lanna artefacts and Buddhas from the Dvaravati kingdom, as well as a stone inscription gallery with Mon and Thai Lanna scripts.

GETTING THERE & AWAY
Blue *sŏrng·tăa·ou* and white buses to Lamphun (20B, every 30 minutes) leave Chiang Mai from a stop on Th Praisani in front of Talat Warorot and from another stop on the east side of the river on Th Chiang Mai-Lamphun, just south of the Tourist Authority of Thailand (TAT).

LAMPANG PROVINCE
LAMPANG
ลำปาง

pop 148,200

Boasting lumbering elephants, elegant mansions of former lumber barons and impressive (and in many cases, lumber-based) Lanna-era temples, Lampang seems to unite every northern Thai cliché – but in a good way.

SIGHTS
WAT PHRA KAEW DON TAO
วัดพระแก้วดอนเต้า

From 1436 to 1468, this **wat** (admission 20B; ⏱ 7am-6pm) was among four in northern Thailand to previously house the Emerald Buddha (now in Bangkok's Wat Phra Kaew, see p65).

OTHER TEMPLES
Wat Si Rong Meuang and **Wat Si Chum** are two wats built in the late 19th century by Burmese artisans. Both have temple buildings constructed in the Burmese 'layered' style, with tin roofs gabled by intricate woodcarvings.

BAAN SAO NAK
บ้านเสานัก

In the old Wiang Neua (North City) section of town, **Baan Sao Nak** (☎ 0 5422 7653; 85 Th Ratwathana; admission 50B; ⏱ 10am-5pm)

was built in 1895 in the traditional Lanna style. The entire house is furnished with Burmese and Thai antiques, but the real treasure is the structure itself and its manicured garden.

WALKING STREET
Perhaps wanting to emulate the success of Chiang Mai's street markets, Lampang now has its own along the charming **Th Talat Kao** (also known as Kat Korng Ta). Dotted with old shophouses showcasing English, Chinese and Burmese architectural styles, the street is closed to traffic on Saturday and Sunday from 4pm to 10pm and fills up with souvenir, handicraft and food stalls.

ACTIVITIES
HORSE CARTS
Lampang is known throughout Thailand as Meuang Rot Mah (Horse Cart City) because it's the only town in Thailand where horse carts are still found, although nowadays they are exclusively used for tourists. A 15-minute horse cart tour around

AUSTIN BUSH

Horse cart, Lampang

town costs 150B; for 200B you can get a half-hour tour that goes along the Mae Wang.

TRADITIONAL MASSAGE

The **Samakhom Samunphrai Phak Neua** (☎ 08 9758 2396; 149 Th Pratuma; massage per hr 200B, sauna 100B; ☼ 8am-7.30pm), next to Wat Hua Khuang in the Wiang Neua area, offers traditional northern-Thai massage and herbal saunas.

SLEEPING

Tip Inn Guest House (☎ 0 5422 1821; 143 Th Talat Kao; r 150-350B; ⌘) Although the cheapies are little more than a bed in a box, Tip Inn is a homey alternative to the city's overwhelmingly characterless budget hotels.

AUSTIN BUSH

Traditional Thai massage

ourpick Riverside Guest House (☎ 0 5422 7005; www.theriversidelampang.com; 286 Th Talat Kao; r 300-800B; ⌘) Although still within budget range, this leafy compound of refurbished wooden houses is by far the most pleasant place to stay in Lampang.

EATING

Lampang is known for its addictive *kôw đaan,* deep-fried rice cakes drizzled with palm sugar, the making of which can be observed at **Khun Manee** (☎ 0 5431 2272; 35 Th Ratsada).

ourpick Aroy One Baht (☎ 08 970 0944; cnr Th Suan Dok & Th Talat Kao; dishes 20-90B; ☼ 4pm-midnight) Some nights it can seem like just about everybody in Lampang has gathered at this rambling wooden house, and understandably so; the food is delicious and embarrassingly cheap, the service lightning fast and the setting in a wooden house-cum-balcony-cum-garden heaps of fun.

Grandma's Café (☎ 0 5432 2792; 361 Th Thip Chang; dishes 30-40B; ☼ 10am-9pm) Well-worn teak chairs and doily window shades suggest grandma's influence, but we doubt she had any role in the slate greys and minimalist feel of this trendy coffee shop.

Khawng Kin Ban Haw (72 Th Jama Thewi; dishes 50-110B; ☼ lunch & dinner) This is a good place to try northern Thai staples such as *gaang kaa gòp* (a herb-laden soup with frog) or *lâhp kôo·a* (*lâhp* that has been stir-fried with local spices).

GETTING THERE & AWAY

AIR

Nok Air (☎ nationwide call centre 1318; www .nokair.co.th; Lampang airport) and **PB Air** (☎ 0 5422 6238, Bangkok ☎ 0 2261 0220; www.pbair.com; Lampang airport) conduct code-share daily flights between Lampang and Bangkok (3025B, one hour, three times daily).

BUS

The bus terminal in Lampang is some way out of town, at the corner of Asia 1 Hwy and Th Chantarasurin – 15B by shared *sŏrng·tăa·ou*.

TRAIN

Lampang's historic **train station** (☎ 0 5421 7024; **Th Phahonyothin**) dates back to 1916 and is located a fair hike from most accommodation.

CHIANG RAI PROVINCE

Chiang Rai, Thailand's northernmost province, has a bit of everything: the mountains in the far east of the province are among the most dramatic in the country, the lowland Mekong River floodplains to the northeast are not unlike those one would find much further south in Isan, and the province shares borders with Myanmar (Burma) and Laos, allowing relatively easy access to China.

CHIANG RAI

เชียงราย

pop 61,200

If you take the time to know it, Chiang Rai is a small but delightful city with a relaxed atmosphere, good value accommodation and some tasty eats.

SIGHTS
WAT PHRA KAEW

วัดพระแก้ว

Originally called Wat Pa Yia (Bamboo Forest Monastery) in local dialect, this is the city's most revered Buddhist temple. Legend has it that in 1434 lightning struck the temple's octagonal *chedi*, which fell apart to reveal the Phra Kaew Morakot, or Emerald Buddha (actually

ANDREW BAIN

Elephants and their mahouts

➘ THAI ELEPHANT CONSERVATION CENTER

ศูนย์อนุรักษ์ช้างไทย

Located in Amphoe Hang Chat, 33km from Lampang, this facility promotes the role of the Asian elephant in ecotourism, and provides medical treatment and care for sick elephants from all over Thailand.

For those keen on delving deeper into pachyderm culture, the TECC's Mahout Training School offers an array of scholarships ranging in duration from one day to one month, all with the aim of making you a bona-fide mahout.

Accommodation at the centre is available in the form of activity-packed homestays with mahouts in basic huts, or in bungalows at the Chang Thai Resort.

Things You Need to Know: Thai Elephant Conservation Center (**Map p145**; ☎ 0 5424 7875; www.changthai.com; child/adult incl shuttle bus 30/70B; ☺ elephant bathing 9.45am & 1.15pm, public shows 10am, 11am & 1.30pm) Mahout Training School (☎ 0 5424 7875; 1/2/3/6/10 days 3500/8000/12,000/20,000/35,000B) Chang Thai Resort (☎ 08 618 1545; bungalows 1/2 bedroom 1000/1500B)

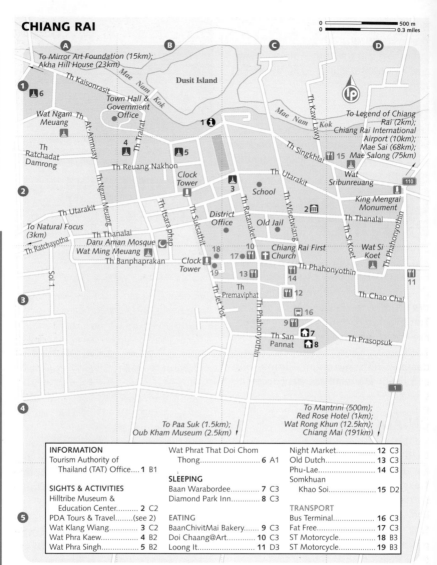

CHIANG RAI

0   500 m
0   0.3 miles

made of jade). After a long journey that included a long stopover in Vientiane, Laos, this national talisman is now ensconced in the temple of the same name in Bangkok.

WAT PHRA SINGH
วัดพระสิงห์

A sister temple to Chiang Mai's Wat Phra Singh, its original buildings are typical northern Thai-style wood structures with low, sweeping roofs.

Wat Phra Singh

AUSTIN BUSH

WAT PHRA THAT DOI CHOM THONG

This hilltop wat has partial views of the river and gets an occasional river breeze. The Lanna-style *chedi* here most likely dates from the 14th to 16th centuries, and may cover an earlier Mon *chedi* inside. King Mengrai, Chiang Rai's founder, first surveyed the site for the city from this peak.

OUB KHAM MUSEUM

พิพิธภัณฑ์อูบคำ

This privately owned **museum** (☎ 0 5371 3349; www.oubkhammuseum.com; 81/1 Military Front Rd; admission adult/child 300/100B; ☽ 8am-5pm) houses an impressive collection of paraphernalia from virtually every corner of the former Lanna kingdom.

HILLTRIBE MUSEUM & EDUCATION CENTER

พิพิธภัณฑ์และศูนย์การศึกษาชาวเขา

This **museum and handicrafts centre** (☎ 0 5374 0088; www.pda.or.th/chiangrai; 3rd fl, 620/1 Th Thanalai; admission 50B; ☽ 8.30am-6pm Mon-Fri, 10am-6pm Sat & Sun) is a good place

to visit before undertaking any hill-tribe trek. The centre, run by the nonprofit Population & Community Development Association (PDA), is underwhelming in its visual presentation, but contains a wealth of information on Thailand's various tribes and the issues that surround them.

ACTIVITIES
TREKKING

The following agencies have a reputation for operating responsible treks and cultural tours, and in some cases profits from the treks go directly to community-development projects.

Akha Hill House (☎ 08 9997 5505; www.akhahill.com) Wholly owned and managed by Akha tribespeople, this outfit offers one- to seven-day treks.

Mirror Art Foundation (☎ 0 5373 7412-3; www.mirrorartgroup.org; 106 Moo 1, Ban Huay Khom, Tambon Mae Yao) Trekking with this group encourages real interaction with the villagers.

Natural Focus (☎ 08 5888 6869; www.naturalfocus-cbt.com; 129/1 Mu 4, Th Pa-Ngiw,

Soi 4, Rop Wiang) Formerly a project of the Hill Area and Community Development Foundation (www.hadf.org), this now-private company offers tours ranging from one to 15 days that concentrate on nature and hill-tribe living.

PDA Tours & Travel (☎ 0 5374 0088; crpda tour@hotmail.com; 620/1 Th Thanalai, Hilltribe Museum & Education Center; 620/1 Th Thanalai) Culturally sensitive treks are led by Population & Community Development Association–trained hill-tribe members.

SLEEPING

our pick **Baan Warabordee** (☎ 0 5375 4488; 59/1 Th San Pannat; r 500-700B; ✄ ☐) A delightful small hotel has been made from this modern three-storey Thai villa. The owners are friendly and can help with local advice.

Lanna-style chedi, Wat Phra Kaew (p157)

Diamond Park Inn (☎ 0 5375 4960; www .diamondparkinn.com; 74/6 Moo 18, Th San Pannat; r incl breakfast 900-1050B; ste incl breakfast 1500B; ✄ ☐) Rooms are large and attractive, with modern furniture and beds on an elevated platform.

our pick **Red Rose Hotel** (☎ 0 5375 6888; www.redrosehotel.com; 14 Th Prachasanti; r incl breakfast 900-1050B; ste incl breakfast from 1600B; ✄ ☐) Think Disneyland on acid; the Red Rose is by far northern Thailand's wackiest place to stay. The owner was inspired by US-style amusement parks, and rooms here feature themes such as UFO, Jungle House and Love Boat (we suggest the Thai Boxing room, complete with ringside bed and punching bags).

Mantrini (☎ 0 5360 1555-9; www.mantrini .com; 292 Moo 13, Robwiang on the Superhighway; r 2880-3290B; ste 9700B; ✄ ☐ ☎) Rooms are delightfully chic, some boasting bathrooms with super-inviting recessed tubs. The hotel is located about 2km outside the city centre but operates a shuttle downtown.

our pick **Legend of Chiang Rai** (☎ 0 5391 0400; www.thelegend-chiangrai.com; 124/15 Moo 21, Th Kohloy; r 3900-5900B, villa 8100B; ✄ ☐ ☎) One of the few hotels in town to take advantage of a river location, this upmarket resort feels like a traditional Lanna village. The riverside infinity pool and spa are the icing on the comfort-filled cake.

EATING

The night market has a decent collection of food stalls offering snacks and meals, from deep-fried won tons to fresh fish.

Paa Suk (no roman-script sign; ☎ 0 5375 2471; Th Sankhongnoi; dishes 10-25B; ⏲ 8am-3pm Mon-Sat) This popular third-generation restaurant specialises in the local dish *kà·nŏm jeen nám ngée·o,* a thin broth of pork or beef and tomatoes served over fresh rice noodles.

Somkhuan Khao Soi (no roman-script sign; Th Singkhlai; dishes 25B; 8am-3pm Mon-Fri) Friendly Mr Somkhuan sells Chiang Rai's tastiest *kôw soy*, a curry noodle dish, from a basic street stall under two giant trees.

our pick **Loong It** (Local Food; Th Wat Phranorn; dishes 30-60B; 8am-3pm) To eat like a local, look no further than this rustic but delicious northern-style food shack.

Old Dutch (541 Th Phahonyothin; dishes 50-1000B; 8am-midnight) This cosy, foreigner-friendly restaurant is a good choice for those not quite ready for the city's more authentic Thai offerings.

Phu-Lae (0 5360 0500; 612/6 Th Phahonyothin; dishes 60-150B; lunch & dinner) This air-conditioned restaurant is exceedingly popular among Thai tourists for its yummy northern Thai dishes.

GETTING THERE & AWAY
AIR
Chiang Rai Airport (0 5379 8000) is 8km north of the city. Taxis run into town from the airport for 200B. To the airport you can get a túk-túk for approximately 250B.

Air Asia (0 5379 3545/8275; www.airasia.com; Chiang Rai Airport) Flies between Bangkok and Chiang Rai (from 1800B, 1¼ hours, three times daily).

Nok Air (nationwide call centre 1318; www.nokair.co.th; Chiang Rai Airport) With its subsidiary **SGA Airlines** (0 5379 8244; www.sga.co.th), operates flights between Chiang Rai and Chiang Mai (from 1690B, 40 minutes, twice daily).

One-Two-Go (nationwide call centre 1126; www.fly12go.com; Chiang Rai Airport) Flies between Bangkok's Don Muang airport and Chiang Rai (from 2100B, 1¼ hours, once daily).

THAI City Centre (0 5371 1179; www.thaiair.com; 870 Th Phahonyothin; 8am-5pm

CAFE CULTURE, CHIANG RAI STYLE

For such a relatively small town, Chiang Rai has an abundance of high-quality, Western-style cafes. This is largely due to the fact that many of Thailand's best coffee beans are grown in the more remote corners of the province.

- **BaanChivitMai Bakery** (08 1764 7020; www.baanchivitmai.com; Th Prasopsuk; 7am-9pm Mon-Sat, 2-9pm Sun) Profits go to BaanChivitMai, an organisation that runs homes and education projects for vulnerable, orphaned and AIDS-affected children.
- **Doi Chaang@Art** (0 5375 2918; 542/2 Th Rattanakhet; 7am-10pm) Doi Chaang is the leading brand among Chiang Rai coffees, and its beans are now sold as far abroad as Canada and Europe.

Mon-Fri); airport office (0 5379 8202/3; 8am-8pm) Flights to/from Bangkok (3745B, 1¼ hours, three times daily).

BUS
Chiang Rai's bus terminal is in the centre of town.

GETTING AROUND
Bicycles rental can be arranged at **Fat Free** (0 5375 2532; 542/2 Th Banphaprakan; per day city/mountain bike 80/250B; 9am-8pm). Motorcycles can be hired at **ST Motorcycle** (0 5371 3652; Th Banphaprakan; per day Yamaha TTR motorcycles less than 115cc 150-300B, less than 250cc 700-1000B; 8am-6pm), which has another outlet on Th Wat Jet Yot – it takes good care of its bikes.

AROUND CHIANG RAI

WAT RONG KHUN
วัดร่องขุ่น

Thirteen kilometres south of Chiang Rai is the unusual and popular **Wat Rong Khun** (☎ 0 5367 3579), aka the 'White Wat'. Whereas most temples have centuries of history, this one's construction began in 1997 by noted Thai painter-turned-architect Chalermchai Kositpipat.

Seen from a distance, the temple appears to be made of glittering porcelain; a closer look reveals that the look is due to a combination of whitewash and clear-mirrored chips. To get to the temple, hop on one of the regular buses that run from Chiang Rai to Chiang Mai and ask to get off at Wat Rong Khun (15B).

HOME AWAY FROM HOME

Mae Salong was originally settled by the 93rd Regiment of the Kuomintang (KMT), who'd fled to Myanmar (Burma) from China after the 1949 Chinese revolution. Crossing into northern Thailand with their pony caravans, the ex-soldiers and their families settled into mountain villages and recreated a society like the one they'd left behind in Yunnan.

Infamous Khun Sa made his home in nearby Ban Hin Taek (now Ban Thoet Thai) until the early 1980s when he was finally routed by the Thai military.

In an attempt to quash opium activity, and the more recent threat of *yah bâh* (methamphetamine) trafficking, the Thai government has created crop-substitution programs to encourage hill tribes to cultivate tea, coffee, corn and fruit trees.

MAE SALONG (SANTIKHIRI)
แม่สลอง (สันติคีรี)

pop 25,400

For a taste of China without crossing any international borders, head to this atmospheric village perched on the back hills of Chiang Rai.

SIGHTS

A tiny but interesting **morning market** convenes from 6am until 8am at the T-intersection near Shin Sane Guest House. An **all-day market** forms at the southern end of town, and unites vendors selling hill-tribe handicrafts, shops selling tea and a few basic restaurants.

To soak up the great views from **Wat Santakhiri** go past the market and ascend 718 steps (or drive if you have a car). The wat is of the Mahayana tradition and Chinese in style.

Past the Khumnaiphol Resort and further up the hill is a **viewpoint** with some teashops, and a famous Kuomintang (KMT) general's **tomb**. In the same vein and south of the turn-off to the tomb is the **Chinese Martyr's Memorial Museum**, an elaborate Chinese-style building that is more memorial than museum.

ACTIVITIES
TREKKING

Shin Sane Guest House has a free map showing approximate routes to Akha, Lisu, Mien, Lahu and Shan villages in the area. It also arranges four-hour horseback treks to four nearby villages for 500B per day.

SLEEPING

Shin Sane Guest House (☎ 0 5376 5026; 32/3 Th Mae Salong; s/d from 50/100B, bungalows 300B; ▢) Although Mae Salong's first hotel is starting to show its 40 years, it still remains an atmospheric place to stay.

Wat Rong Khun

JOHN BORTHWICK

our pick Little Home Guesthouse (☎ 0 5376 5389; www.maesalonglittlehome.com; 31 Moo 1, Th Mae Salong; s/d from 50/100B, bungalows 600B; 💻) Located next door to Shin Sane, this delightful wooden house holds a few basic but cosy rooms and a handful of sparkling new bungalows out back. The owner is extremely friendly and has put together one of the more accurate maps of the area.

Maesalong Mountain Home (☎ 08 4611 9508; www.maesalongmountainhome.com; bungalows 800-1500B) Located down a dirt road 1km east of the town centre (signs say 'Maesalong Farmstay'), this is a great choice if you've got your own wheels. The nine new bungalows here are located in the middle of a working farm and are bright and airy, with huge bathrooms.

EATING

The very Chinese breakfast of *ƀah·tôrng·gŏh* (deep-fried fingers of dough) and hot soybean milk at the morning market is an inspiring way to start the day.

In fact, many Thai tourists come to Mae Salong simply to eat Yunnanese dishes such as *màn·tŏh* (steamed Chinese buns) served with braised pork leg and pickled vegetables, or black chicken braised with Chinese-style herbs. All of these and more are available at **Sue Hai** (no roman-script sign; ☎ 08 9429 4212; 288 Moo 1, Th Mae Salong; dishes 60-150B; 🕙 7am-9pm), located in a light blue building 100m west of Sweet Maesalong. **Nong Im Phochana** (☎ 0 5376 5309; Th Mae Salong; dishes 60-150B; 🕙 lunch & dinner), directly across from Khumnaiphol Resort, has a similar menu with an emphasis on local veggies, and the restaurant at **Mae Salong Villa** (☎ 0 5376 5114; Th Mae Salong; dishes 60-150) is said to do the most authentic Yunnanese food in town, including a delicious duck smoked over tea leaves.

Countless teahouses sell locally grown teas (mostly oolong and jasmine) and offer complimentary tastings.

GETTING THERE & AWAY

Mae Salong is accessible via two routes. The original road, Rte 1130, winds west from Ban Basang. Newer Rte 1234 approaches from the south, allowing easier access from Chiang Mai. The older route is more spectacular.

To get to Mae Salong by bus, take a Mae Sai bus from Chiang Rai to Ban Basang (20B, 30 minutes, every 15 minutes from 6am to 4pm). From Ban Basang, *sŏrng·tăa·ou* head up the mountain to Mae Salong (60B, one hour).

MAE SAI

แม่สาย

pop 21,800

At first glance, Thailand's northernmost town, Mae Sai, appears to be little more than a large open-air market. But the city can be used as a starting point for exploring the Golden Triangle, Doi Tung and Mae Salong, and its position across from Myanmar (Burma) also makes it a stepping-off point for those wishing to explore some of the more remote parts of Shan State.

SLEEPING

our pick **Khanthongkham Hotel** (☎ 0 5373 4222; 7 Th Phahonyothin; r 950B, ste 1190-1390B; ✴) This brand new hotel features huge rooms that have been tastefully decorated in light woods and brown textiles. A downside is that many rooms don't have windows.

Piyaporn Place Hotel (☎ 0 5373 4511-3; www.piyaporn-place.com; 77/1 Th Phahonyothin; r 1000B; ✴ ⚙ ⌨) On the main road by Soi 7, this seven-storey hotel is good value. The large, contemporary-styled rooms have wooden floors, a small sofa and the usual four/five-star amenities like bath, cable TV and minibar.

EATING

A decent night market unfolds every evening along Th Phahonyothin.

Khrua Bismillah (no roman-script sign; ☎ 08 1530 8198; Soi 4, Th Phahonyothin; dishes 25-40B; ☯ 6am-6pm) Run by Burmese Muslims, this tiny restaurant does an excellent biryani, not to mention virtually everything else Muslim, from roti to samosa. There's no English sign, simply look for the green halal sign.

Kik Kok Restaurant (Th Phahonyothin; dishes 30-120B; ☯ 6am-8pm) This restaurant prepares a huge selection of Thai dishes and has an English menu.

Mae Sai Riverside Resort (☎ 0 5373 2630; Th Wiengpangkam; dishes 40-139B) Recommended for its Thai dishes, like the tasty lemongrass fried fish, this restaurant has a great location looking out over the river to Myanmar.

GETTING THERE & AWAY

On the main Th Phahonyothin road, by Soi 8, is a sign saying 'bus stop'. From here *sŏrng·tăa·ou* run to Sop Ruak (45B, every 40 minutes from 9am to 2pm), terminating in Chiang Saen (50B).

For Doi Tung take one of the *sŏrng·tăa·ou* that park by Soi 10 to Ban Huay Khrai (25B), then another *sŏrng·tăa·ou* to Doi Tung (60B, one hour).

Mae Sai's government **bus station** (☎ 0 5364 437) is 4km south of the frontier immigration office, a 15B shared *sŏrng·tăa·ou* ride from the corner of Th Phahonyothin and Soi 2.

For the same prices as at the bus station you can buy tickets in advance at **Chok Roong Tawee Tour** (no roman-script sign; ☎ 0 5364 0123) . There is no sign in English so look for the large red 'International Telephone' sign.

GETTING AROUND

Sŏrng·tăa·ou around town are 15B shared. Motorcycle taxis cost 20B to 30B.

Myanmar (Burma)–Thailand border, Mae Sai

AUSTIN BUSH

Honda Dreams can be rented at **Pornchai** (☎ 0 5373 1136; 4/7 Th Phahonyothin) for 150B a day.

AROUND MAE SAI
CROSS-BORDER TRIPS TO TACHILEIK

Foreigners are ordinarily permitted to cross the bridge over the Nam Sai into Tachileik. On occasion the border may close temporarily for security reasons, so be prepared for possible disappointment if the political situation between Thailand and Myanmar (Burma) deteriorates again.

The Thai immigration office is officially open from 6.30am to 6.30pm. After taking care of the usual formalities, cross the bridge and head to the Myanmar (Burma) immigration office. Here you pay US$10 or 500B and your picture is taken for a temporary ID card that allows you to stay in town for 14 days; your passport will be kept at the office. On your return to Thailand, the Thai immigration office at the bridge will give you a new 15-day tourist visa.

There is little to do in Tachileik apart from sample Burmese food and shop – the prices are about the same as on the Thai side and everyone accepts baht.

CHIANG SAEN

เชียงแสน

pop 10,800

The dictionary definition of a sleepy river town, Chiang Saen was the site of a Thai kingdom thought to date back to as early as the 7th century. Scattered throughout the modern town are the ruins of the former empire – surviving architecture includes several *chedi*, Buddha images, *wí·hǎhn* pillars and earthen city ramparts.

SIGHTS & ACTIVITIES

Near the town entrance, the **Chiang Saen National Museum** (☎ 0 5377 7102; 702 Th Phahonyothin; admission 100B; ☀ 8.30am-4.30pm Wed-Sun) is a great source of local information considering its relatively small size.

About 200m from the Pratu Chiang Saen (the historic main gateway to the town's western flank) are the remains of **Wat Pa Sak**, where the ruins of seven monuments are visible in a **historical park** (admission 50B). The main mid-14th-century *chedi* combines elements of the Hariphunchai and Sukhothai styles with a possible Bagan influence, and still holds a great deal of attractive stucco relief work.

SLEEPING

Gin's Guest House (☎ 0 5365 0847; 71 Mu 8; r 300-700B, bungalows 200B) Located 1km north of the centre of town, this place has a variety of rooms (all with attached bathroom) and a variety of prices. Mountain bike and motorcycle rentals are available, as are a variety of tours.

Mekong River at the convergance of Thailand, Laos and Myanmar (Burma) borders
AUSTIN BUSH

⭲ IF YOU LIKE…

If you like **Chiang Saen** (p165), then delve deeper into the infamous Golden Triangle:

- **Doi Tung** Atop 'Flag Mountain' is a **royal summer palace** (☎ 0 5376 7011; www.doitung.org; admission 70B; ⏲ 6.30am-5pm) and agricultural initiative that helped transition local farmers from opium production to legal cash crops. The 24km road between Doi Tung and Mae Sai's Soi 7 hugs the rugged border between Thailand and Myanmar (Burma). Overnight at **Ban Ton Nam 31** (☎ 0 5376 7003; www.doitung.org; Doi Tung Development Project, Mae Fah Luang District; r incl breakfast 2500-3000B; ⛌ 🖳) that once housed the royal staff.

- **Sop Ruak** The borders of Myanmar (Burma), Thailand and Laos meet at this official 'centre' of the Golden Triangle. To commemorate those lawless days there's both a **House of Opium** (Baan Phin; ☎ 0 5378 4060; www.houseofopium.com; admission 50B; ⏲ 7am-8pm) and a **Hall of Opium** (☎ 0 5378 4444; www.golden trianglepark.com; Mu 1 Baan Sobruak; admission 300B; ⏲ 10am-3.30pm) plus **Mekong River Cruises** (1hr cruise max 5 people per boat 400B). Overnight at **Anantara Golden Triangle Resort & Spa** (☎ 0 5378 4084; www.anantara.com; Sop Ruak; r/ste from 10,900/15,200B; ⛌ 🖳 ⛌), an award-winning resort.

Sunshine Kitchen (Khrua Ban Rot Fai; ☎ 0 5365 0605; Rte 1129; bungalows 600-800B, caboose 1200B; ❄) Named after the riverfront restaurant that also shares this compound, lodging here takes the form of three bamboo bungalows and, of all things, an authentic train caboose.

Chiang Saen River Hill Hotel (☎ 0 5365 0826; www.chiangsaenriverhill.net; 714 Th Sukapibansai 2; r incl breakfast 1200B; ❄) Although the pink exterior and floor tiles don't exactly compliment the northern Thai furnishing touches, this is still probably the best place in town. Rooms are large, and equipped with TV, fridge and a small area for relaxing.

EATING & DRINKING

our pick **Jinda's Kitchen** (no roman-script sign; ☎ 08 6654 3116; Rte 1290; dishes 20-50B; ❄ 7am-8pm) Try the famous northern noodle dishes *kôw soy* or *kà·nŏm jeen nám ngée·o*, or choose a curry or homemade sausage from the English-language menu. Jinda's Kitchen is located roughly halfway between Chiang Saen and Sop Ruak, near Km31; look for the Pepsi sign.

Ah Ying (no roman-script sign; ☎ 08 9655 3468; 778/1 Th Rimkhong; dishes 25-60B; ❄ 7am-10pm) This tiny family-run restaurant specialises in delicious hand-pulled noodles. There's no English sign; simply look for the Chinese cooks busy stretching and flinging lengths of dough.

Kiaw Siang Hai (no roman-script sign; 44 Th Rimkhong; dishes 60-120B; ❄ 6.30am-8.30pm) Serving the workers of Chinese boats that dock at Chiang Saen, this authentic Chinese restaurant prepares a huge menu of dishes in addition to the namesake noodle and wonton dishes.

GETTING THERE & AWAY

Blue *sŏrng·tăa·ou* that travel to Sop Ruak (20B) and Mae Sai (50B) wait at the eastern end of Th Phahonyothin during daylight hours. The green *sŏrng·tăa·ou* bound for Chiang Khong (100B) park on Th Rimkhong, south of the riverside immigration office.

Chiang Saen has no proper bus terminal, rather there is a covered bus shelter at the eastern end of Th Phahonyothin where buses pick up and drop off passengers. From this stop there are frequent buses between Chiang Rai and Chiang Saen (35B, 1½ hours, 5.30am to 5.30pm).

GETTING AROUND

Motorbike taxis and *săhm·lór* will do short trips around town for 20B.

Mountain bikes (per day 50B) and motorcycles (per day 200B) can be rented at Gin's Guest House and **Angpao Chiangsean Tour** (☎ 0 5365 0143; www .angpao-r3a.com; Th Phahonyothin; ❄ 9am-8pm). The latter can also provide a vehicle with driver, and conducts a variety of local tours.

PHITSANULOK PROVINCE
PHITSANULOK
พิษณุโลก

pop 80,300

Phitsanulok sees relatively few independent travellers, but a fair amount of package tourists, perhaps because the city is a convenient base from which to explore the attractions of historical Sukhothai, Si Satchanalai and Kamphaeng Phet.

SIGHTS
WAT PHRA SI RATANA MAHATHAT
วัดพระศรีรัตนมหาธาตุ
The full name of this temple is Wat Phra Si Ratana Mahathat, but the locals call it Wat Phra Si or Wat Yai. The main

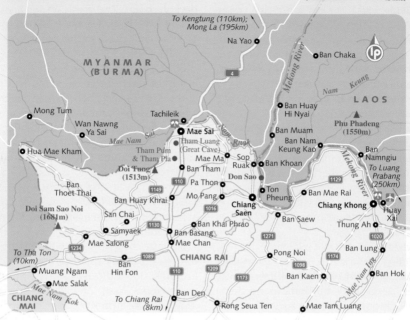

wí·hǎhn appears small from the outside, but houses the Phra Phuttha Chinnarat, one of Thailand's most revered and copied Buddha images. This famous bronze statue is probably second in importance only to the Emerald Buddha in Bangkok's Wat Phra Kaew.

OTHER SIGHTS

A nationally acclaimed expert on Thai folkways, a former military cartographer and Buddha statue caster, and apparent bird aficionado, Sergeant Major Thawee Buranakhet has taken from his diverse experiences and interests to create three very worthwhile attractions in Phitsanulok.

The **Sergeant Major Thawee Folk Museum** (26/43 Th Wisut Kasat; child/adult 20/50B; ☼ 8.30am-4.30pm Tue-Sun) displays a remarkable collection of tools, textiles and photographs from Phitsanulok Province. To get here take bus 8.

Across the street and also belonging to Dr Thawee is a small **Buddha Casting Foundry** (☼ 8am-5pm) where bronze Buddha images of all sizes are cast.

Attached to the foundry is Dr Thawee's latest project, **Garden Birds of Thailand** (☎ 0 5521 2540; child/adult 20/50B; ☼ 8.30am-5pm). This collection of aviaries contains indigenous Thai birds including some endangered species, like the very pretty pink-chested jamu fruit-dove, and the prehistoric-looking helmeted hornbill.

ACTIVITIES
MASSAGE

Relaxation takes an entirely new form at **Phae Hatha Thai Massage** (☎ 0 5524 3389; Th Wangchan; massage per hr with fan/air con 120/150B; ☼ 9am-10pm), a Thai massage centre housed on a floating raft.

SLEEPING

Phitsanulok Youth Hostel (☎ 0 5524 2060; www.tyha.org; 38 Th Sanam Bin; d 120, r 200-400B; ❄) There's no clear sign to identify this place; simply look for the large '38' out front. At the rear of the leafy compound you'll find several rooms decked out in aged teak. The rooms have their own rustic charm, but the entire compound could use a bit of TLC.

ourpick Casa Holiday (☎ 0 5530 4340; www .mycasaholiday.com; 305/2 Th Phichaisongkhram; r 380-650B; ❄ 🖳) Located 2km outside the centre of town, if you've got your own wheels this character-laden place is a no-brainer. Several of the 42 bright and airy rooms in the ranch-style complex feature fun design extras such as outdoor showers or 'Japanese beds' (futons).

Golden Grand Hotel (☎ 0 5521 0234; www.goldengrandhotel.com; 66 Th Thammabucha, r 790-950B; ❄ 🖳) The rooms are so tidy we're wondering if they've ever even been slept in, and friendly staff and great views of the city from the upper floors are even more incentive to stay here.

Pailyn Hotel (☎ 0 5525 2411; 38 Th Borom Trailokanat; s/d/ste incl breakfast 900/1000/3500B; ❄) The rooms are spacious, have cable TV and minibar, and are well decorated apart from very loud batik panels above the beds. Some have great river views.

Yodia Heritage Hotel (☎ 08 1613 8496; www.yodiaheritage.com; Th Phuttha Bucha; r 3750-6000B; ste 15,000B; ❄ 🖳 🕾) Located near a quiet stretch of the Mae Nam Nan, but still conveniently close to the centre, the 21 rooms here will follow several different design themes, all luxurious.

EATING

The city is particularly obsessive about night markets, and there are no fewer than three dotted in various locations around town. The most well known, Phitsanulok's **Night Bazaar** (dishes 40-80B; ☼ 5pm-3am), focuses mainly on clothing,

Offerings of incense, Wat Phra Si Ratana Mahathat (p167), Phitsanulok

GLENN BEANLAND

but a few riverfront restaurants specialise in *pàk bûng loy fáh* (literally 'floating-in-the-sky morning glory vine'), where the cook fires up a batch of *pàk bûng* in the wok and then flings it through the air to a waiting server who catches it on a plate.

Another dish that is associated with Phitsanulok is *gŏoay·đĕe·o hôy kǎh* (literally, 'legs-hanging' noodles). The name comes from the way customers sit on the floor facing the river, with their legs dangling below. **Rim Nan** (☎ 08 1379 3172; 5/4 Th Phaya Sua; dishes 20-35B; ☻ 9am-4pm), north of Wat Phra Si Ratana Mahathat, is one of a few similar restaurants along Th Phutta Bucha that offer noodles and 'alternative' seating.

Fah-Kerah (786 Th Phra Ong Dam; dishes 5-20B; ☻ 6am-2pm) There are several Thai-Muslim cafes near the mosque on Th Phra Ong Dam, and this is a popular one.

Rin Coffee (☎ 0 5525 2848; 20 Th Salreuthai; dishes 20-85B; ☻ 7.30am-9pm Mon-Fri, 9.30am-9pm Sat & Sun) This light-filled, glass-fronted cafe is popular with young Thais.

Karaket (☎ 0 5525 8193; Th Phayalithai; dishes 25-40B; ☻ 1-8pm) Opposite Lithai Guest House, this simple restaurant has a variety of Thai curries, soups and stir-fries on display. Simply point to whatever looks good.

our pick **Ban Mai** (☎ 08 6925 5018; 93/30 Th U Thong; dishes 70-140B; ☻ 11am-2pm & 5-10pm) Don't expect home cooking though; Ban Mai specialises in unusual, but perfectly executed dishes that aren't easily found elsewhere, like the *gaang pèt ʉ̀bèt yâhng*, a curry of smoked duck, or *yam đà·krái*, lemongrass 'salad'.

DRINKING & ENTERTAINMENT

A few floating pubs can be found along the strip of Th Wangchan directly in front of the Grand Riverside Hotel including **Sabai Boat** (Th Wangchan; dishes 40-140B; ☻ 11am-11pm) and **Wow!** (Th Wangchan; dishes 50-150B; ☻ 5pm-midnight), both proffering food as well as drink.

Wood Stock (☎ 08 1785 1958; 148/22-23 Th Wisut Kasat; dishes 35-70B; ☻ 5pm-midnight) combines funky '60s and '70s-era furni-

AUSTIN BUSH

Wat Phra Si Ratana Mahathat (p167), Phitsanulok

ture, live music, and a brief and cheap menu of *gàp glâam* (Thai-style nibbles).

GETTING THERE & AWAY
AIR
Phitsanulok's **airport** (☎ 0 5530 1002) is 5km south of town.

THAI (☎ 0 5524 2971-2; 209/26-28 Th Borom Trailokanat) operates flights between Phitsanulok and Bangkok (3185B, 55 minutes, twice daily).

BUS
Transport options out of Phitsanulok are good, as it's a junction for bus routes both north and northeast. Phitsanulok's bus station is 2km east of town on Hwy 12.

TRAIN
Phitsanulok's train station is within walking distance of ample accommodation and offers a left-luggage service.

GETTING AROUND
Ordinary city buses cost 8B to 11B and there are several routes, making it easy to get just about anywhere by bus. The main bus stop for city buses is next to the Asia Hotel on Th Ekathotsarot, and there is a chart with the various bus routes in English.

Run by the TAT, the Phitsanulok Tour Tramway (PTT) is a quick way to see many sights. The **tram** (child/adult 20/30B) leaves from Wat Yai and stops at 15 sights before returning to the same temple.

SUKHOTHAI PROVINCE
SUKHOTHAI
สุโขทัย

pop 17,500

The Sukhothai (Rising of Happiness) Kingdom flourished from the mid-13th century to the late-14th century. This period is often viewed as the 'golden age' of Thai civilisation – the religious art and architecture of the era are considered to be the most classic of Thai styles. The remains of the kingdom, today known as the *meuang gòw* (old city), feature around 45 sq km of partially rebuilt ruins, which are one of the most visited ancient sites in Thailand.

Located 12km east of the historical park on the Mae Nam Yom, the market town of New Sukhothai is not particularly interesting. Yet its friendly and relaxed atmosphere, good transport links and attractive accommodation make it a good base from which to explore the old city ruins.

SIGHTS
SUKHOTHAI HISTORICAL PARK
อุทยานประวัติศาสตร์สุโขทัย

The **Sukhothai ruins** (Map p172; admission 100-350B, plus per bicycle/motorcycle/car 10/20/50B; ☼ 6am-6pm) are one of Thailand's most impressive World Heritage sites. The park includes remains of 21 historical sites and four large ponds within the old walls, with an additional 70 sites within a 5km radius.

The ruins are divided into five zones – central, north, south, east and west – each of which has a 100B admission fee. For 350B you can buy a single ticket that allows entry to all the Sukhothai sites, plus Sawanworanayok Museum (p177), Ramkhamhaeng National Museum (below) and the Si Satchanalai and Chaliang (p177).

RAMKHAMHAENG NATIONAL MUSEUM
พิพิธภัณฑสถานแห่งชาติรามคำแหง

A good starting point for exploring the historical park ruins is **Ramkhamhaeng National Museum** (Map p172; ☎ 0 5561

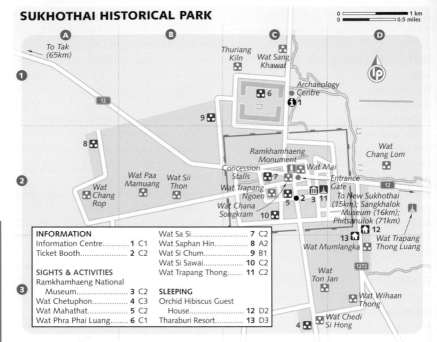

SUKHOTHAI HISTORICAL PARK

INFORMATION			Wat Sa Si...................... **7** C2
Information Centre...........**1** C1			Wat Saphan Hin............. **8** A2
Ticket Booth....................**2** C2			Wat Si Chum...................**9** B1
			Wat Si Sawai................. **10** C2
SIGHTS & ACTIVITIES			Wat Trapang Thong....... **11** C2
Ramkhamhaeng National			
Museum......................**3** C2			SLEEPING
Wat Chetuphon...............**4** C3			Orchid Hibiscus Guest
Wat Mahathat.................**5** C2			House........................ **12** D2
Wat Phra Phai Luang........**6** C1			Tharaburi Resort............. **13** D3

2167; admission 150B; ☺ 9am-4pm). A replica
of the famous Ramkhamhaeng inscription, said to be the earliest example
of Thai writing, is kept here among an
impressive collection of the Sukhothai
artefacts.

WAT MAHATHAT
วัดมหาธาตุ
Completed in the 13th century, Wat
Mahathat (Map p172), the largest wat
in Sukhothai, is surrounded by brick
walls (206m long and 200m wide) and
a moat that is believed to represent the
outer wall of the universe and the cosmic ocean. The *chedi* spires feature the
famous lotus-bud motif, and some of
the original stately Buddha figures still
sit among the ruined columns of the old
wí·hǎhn.

WAT SI CHUM
วัดศรีชุม
This wat (Map p172) is northwest of
the old city and contains an impressive
mon·dòp with a 15m, brick-and-stucco
seated Buddha. This Buddha's elegant, ta-
pered fingers are much photographed.

WAT SAPHAN HIN
วัดสะพานหิน
Four kilometres to the west of the old city
walls in the west zone, Wat Saphan Hin
(Map p172) is on the crest of a hill that rises
about 200m above the plain. The site gives
a good view of the Sukhothai ruins and the
mountains to the north and south.

All that remains of the original temple
are a few *chedi* and the ruined *wí·hǎhn*,
consisting of two rows of laterite columns
flanking a 12.5m-high standing Buddha
image on a brick terrace.

WAT SI SAWAI

วัดศรีสวาย

Just south of Wat Mahathat, this shrine (Map p172), dating from the 12th and 13th centuries, features three Khmer-style towers and a picturesque moat. It was originally built by the Khmers as a Hindu temple.

WAT SA SI

วัดสระศรี

Also known as 'Sacred Pond Monastery', Wat Sa Si (Map p172) sits on an island west of the bronze monument of King Ramkhamhaeng (the third Sukhothai king). It's a simple, classic Sukhothai-style wat containing a large Buddha, one *chedi* and the columns of the ruined *wí·hăhn*.

WAT TRAPANG THONG

วัดตระพังทอง

Next to the museum, this small, still-inhabited wat (Map p172) with its fine stucco reliefs is reached by a footbridge across the large lotus-filled pond that surrounds it. This reservoir, the original site of Thailand's **Loi Krathong** festival, supplies the Sukhothai community with most of its water.

WAT PHRA PHAI LUANG

วัดพระพายหลวง

Outside the city walls in the northern zone, this somewhat isolated wat (Map p172) features three 12th-century Khmer-style towers, bigger than those at Wat Si Sawai.

WAT CHETUPON

วัดเชตุพน

Located 2km south of the city walls, this temple (Map p172) once held a four-sided *mon·dòp* featuring the four classic poses of the Buddha (sitting, reclining, standing and walking). The graceful lines of the walking Buddha can still be made out today.

SANGKHALOK MUSEUM

พิพิธภัณฑ์สังคโลก

This small but comprehensive **museum** (off Map p172; ☎ 0 5561 4333; 203/2 Mu 3 Th

Wat Sa Si

NOBORU KOMINE

Muangkao; child/adult 50/100B; 🕙 8am-5pm) is an excellent introduction to ancient Sukhothai's most famous product and export, its ceramics.

ACTIVITIES

Belgian cycling enthusiast Ronny offers a variety of fun and educational **bicycle tours** (Map p174; ☎ 0 5561 2519; half/full day 550/650B, sunset tour 250B) of the area. Ronny is based near Sabaidee Guest House, and he also offers free transport for customers.

SLEEPING

Sukhothai Guest House (Map p174; ☎ 0 5561 0453; www.sukhothaiguesthouse.net; 68 Th Vichien Chamnong; r 350-750B; 🔀 🖵) This long-running guesthouse has 12 bungalows with terraces packed into a shaded garden. The communal area is filled with an eclectic mix of bric-a-brac and the owners are friendly and very helpful.

ourpick At Home Sukhothai (Map p174; ☎ 0 5561 0172; www.athomesukhothai.com; 184/1 Th Vichien Chamnong; r 500-750B; 🔀 🖵) Located in the 50-year-old childhood home of the

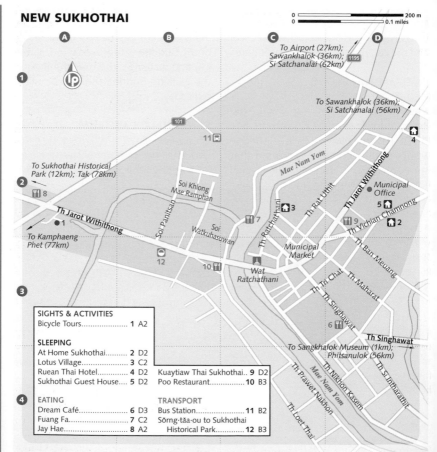

NEW SUKHOTHAI

0 ————— 200 m
0 ————— 0.1 miles

To Airport (27km);
Sawankhalok (36km);
Si Satchanalai (62km)

To Sawankhalok (36km);
Si Satchanalai (56km)

To Sukhothai Historical
Park (12km); Tak (78km)

Mae Nam Yom

Soi Khlong
Mae Ramphan

Th Jarot Withithong

Soi Panitsan

Soi
Watkuhasuwan

To Kamphaeng
Phet (77km)

Municipal
Office

Th Rat Uthit

Th Jarot Withithong

Th Vichian Chamnong

Th Ratchathani

Municipal
Market

Th Ban Meuang

Wat
Ratchathani

Th Tri Chat
Th Maharat

Th Singhawat

Th Singhawat

To Sangkhalok Museum (1km);
Phitsanulok (56km)

Mae Nam Yom

Th Nikhon Kasem

Th Prawet Nakhon

Th Loet Thai

Th Si Intharathit

SIGHTS & ACTIVITIES		
Bicycle Tours	**1**	A2
SLEEPING		
At Home Sukhothai	**2**	D2
Lotus Village	**3**	C2
Ruean Thai Hotel	**4**	D2
Sukhothai Guest House	**5**	D2
EATING		
Dream Café	**6**	D3
Fuang Fa	**7**	C2
Jay Hae	**8**	A2
Kuaytiaw Thai Sukhothai	**9**	D2
Poo Restaurant	**10**	B3
TRANSPORT		
Bus Station	**11**	B2
Sŏrng·tăa·ou to Sukhothai		
Historical Park	**12**	B3

proprietor, the attractive structure could easily pass as a newborn after recent renovations.

our pick **Ruean Thai Hotel** (Map p174; ☎ 0 5561 2444; www.rueanthaihotel.com; 181/20 Soi Pracha Ruammit, Th Jarot Withithong; rooms 1350-3200B; ❄ ▯ ☎) At first glance, you may mistake this eye-catching complex for a temple or museum. The rooms on the upper level are very Thai, and feature worn teak furnishings and heaps of character. Poolside rooms are slightly more modern, and there's a concrete building with simple air-con rooms out the back.

Lotus Village (Map p174; ☎ 0 5562 1484; www.lotus-village.com; 170 Th Ratchathani; r 790-1540B; ❄ ▯) Village is an apt label for this peaceful compound of elevated wooden bungalows.

Orchid Hibiscus Guest House (Map p172; ☎ 0 5563 3284; orchid _hibiscus_guest house@hotmail.com; 407/2 Rte 1272; r 800B, bungalows 1200B; ❄ ☎) This collection of rooms and bungalows is set in relaxing manicured grounds with a swimming pool as a centrepiece. Rooms are spotless and fun, featuring various design details and accents. The guesthouse is on Rte 1272 about 600m off Hwy 12 – the turn-off is between Km48 and Km49 markers.

our pick **Tharaburi Resort** (Map p172; ☎ 0 5569 7132; www.tharaburiresort.com; 321/3 Moo 3, Rte 1272; r 1200-4200B, ste 5000-6500B; ❄ ▯ ☎) Near the historical park, this boutique hotel features three main structures divided up into 20 individually and beautifully styled rooms and suites. The cheaper rooms are simpler, the suites feel like a small home, and there are also two-floor family rooms. Definitely the most stylish hotel in Sukhothai.

EATING

Sukhothai's signature dish is *gŏo·ay dĕe·o sù·kŏh·tai*, 'Sukhothai-style noodles',

AUSTIN BUSH

Celebrations for Loi Krathong festival (p49)

featuring a slightly sweet broth with different types of pork, ground peanuts and thinly sliced green beans. There are several places in town to try the dish, including **Kuaytiaw Thai Sukhothai** (Map p174; Th Jarot Withithong; dishes 20-30B; ❤ 9am-8pm), about 200m south of the turn-off for Ruean Thai Hotel. For many visiting Thais, you haven't been to Sukhothai if you haven't tried the noodles at **Jay Hae** (Map p174; ☎ 0 5561 1901; Th Jarot Withithong; dishes 25-40B; ❤ 7am-4pm), an extremely popular restaurant that also serves *pàt tai* and tasty coffee drinks.

Poo Restaurant (Map p174; ☎ 0 5561 1735; 24/3 Th Jarot Withithong; dishes 25-80B; ❤ breakfast, lunch & dinner) Deceptively simple, this restaurant offers a diverse menu of breakfasts, hearty sandwiches and even a few

Thai women at a festival, Sukhothai

CLAVER CARROLL

Thai dishes. A good source of information, this is also the place to rent motorbikes in town.

Fuang Fa (Map p174; ☎ 08 1284 8262; 107/2 Th Khuhasuwan; dishes 60-120B; ☺ lunch & dinner) Pretend you're a local in the know and stop by this riverside restaurant specialising in Sukhothai's abundant and delicious freshwater fish. The English-language menu is limited, so be sure to ask about recommended dishes.

our pick Dream Café (Map p174; ☎ 0 5561 2081; 86/1 Th Singhawat; dishes 80-150B; ☺ lunch & dinner) A meal at Dream Café is like dining in a museum or an antique shop. Eclectic but tasteful furnishings and knick-knackery abound, staff are equal parts competent and friendly, and most importantly of all, the food is good.

GETTING THERE & AWAY
AIR
Sukhothai's airport is 27km from town off Rte 1195, about 11km from Sawankhalok. **Bangkok Airways** (☎ 0 5564 7224; www .bangkokair.com) operates a daily flight from Bangkok (2870B, 70 minutes, once daily). There is a minivan service (120B) between the airport and Sukhothai.

BUS
Sukhothai's bus station is located almost 1km northwest of the centre of town on Rte 101.

GETTING AROUND
A ride by *sāhm·lór* around New Sukhothai should cost no more than 40B. *Sŏrng·tăa·ou* run frequently from 6.30am to 6pm between New Sukhothai and Sukhothai Historical Park (20B, 30 minutes), leaving from Th Jarot Withithong near Poo Restaurant (p175).

The best way to get around the historical park is by bicycle, which can be rented at shops outside the park entrance for 30B per day.

Motorbikes can be rented at Poo Restaurant (p175) and many guesthouses in New Sukhothai.

AROUND SUKHOTHAI

SI SATCHANALAI-CHALIANG HISTORICAL PARK

อุทยานประวัติศาสตร์ศรีสัชนาลัย/ชะเลียง

If you have the time, don't skip this portion of the Sukhothai World Heritage site. Bring your imagination and sense of adventure and you're sure to love this more rustic collection of impressive ruins.

The **park (admission 220B or free with 350B inclusive ticket from Sukhothai, usable for 30 days, plus per bike/motorbike/car 10/30/50B;** ⏰ **8.30am-5pm)** covers roughly 720 hectares and is surrounded by a 12m-wide moat. Chaliang, 1km southeast, is an older city site (dating to the 11th century), though its two temples date to the 14th century.

An **information centre** (⏰ **8.30am-5pm)** at the park distributes free park maps and has a small exhibit outlining the history and major attractions.

WAT CHANG LOM

วัดช้างล้อม

This fine temple, marking the centre of the old city of Si Satchanalai, has elephants surrounding a bell-shaped *chedi* that is somewhat better preserved than its counterpart in Sukhothai.

WAT KHAO PHANOM PHLOENG

วัดเขาพนมเพลิง

On the hill overlooking Wat Chang Lom to the right are the remains of Wat Khao Phanom Phloeng, including a *chedi*, a large seated Buddha and stone columns that once supported the roof of the *wí·hǎhn*. From this hill you can make out the general design of the once-great city.

WAT PHRA SI RATANA MAHATHAT

วัดพระศรีรัตนมหาธาตุ

These ruins at Chaliang consist of a large laterite *chedi* (dating back to 1448–88) between two *wí·hǎhn*. One of the *wí·hǎhn*

holds a large seated Sukhothai Buddha image, a smaller standing image and a bas-relief of the famous walking Buddha, exemplary of the flowing, boneless Sukhothai style. The other *wí·hǎhn* contains some less distinguished images.

There's a separate 10B admission for Wat Phra Si Ratana Mahathat.

WAT CHAO CHAN

วัดเจ้าจันทร์

These wat ruins are about 500m west of Wat Phra Si Ratana Mahathat in Chaliang. The central attraction is a large Khmer-style tower similar to later towers built in Lopburi and probably constructed during the reign of Khmer King Jayavarman VII (1181–1217).

SAWANKHALOK KILNS

เตาเผาสังคโลก

The Sukhothai-Si Satchanalai area was once famous for its beautiful pottery, much of which was exported to countries throughout Asia.

At one time, more than 200 pottery kilns lined the banks of Mae Nam Yom in the area around Si Satchanalai. Several have been carefully excavated and can be viewed at the **Si Satchanalai Centre for Study & Preservation of Sangkalok Kilns (admission 100B)**. Admission is included in the 220B all-inclusive ticket.

Ceramics are still made in the area, and several open-air shops can be found around the kiln centre in Chaliang. One local ceramic artist continues to fire his pieces in an underground wood-burning oven.

SAWANWORANAYOK NATIONAL MUSEUM

พิพิธภัณฑสถานแห่งชาติสวรรควรนายก

In Sawankhalok town, near Wat Sawankhalam on the western riverbank,

NORTHERN THAILAND

KAMPHAENG PHET PROVINCE

Kamphaeng Phet Historical Park

JOHN ELK III

this state-sponsored **museum** (☎ 0 5564 1571; 69 Th Phracharat; admission 50B; ⏰ 9am-4pm) houses an impressive collection of 12th- to 15th-century artefacts. The ground floor focuses on the area's ceramic legacy, while the 2nd floor features several beautiful bronze and stone Sukhothai-era Buddha statues.

GETTING THERE & AWAY

Si Satchanalai-Chaliang Historical Park is off Rte 101 between Sawankhalok and new Si Satchanalai. From New Sukhothai, take a Si Satchanalai bus (38B, two hours) and ask to get off at 'meuang gòw' (old city). Alternatively, you could catch the 9am bus to Chiang Rai, which costs the same but makes fewer stops. The last bus back to New Sukhothai leaves at 4.30pm.

There are two places along the left side of the highway where you can get off the bus and reach the ruins in the park; both involve crossing Mae Nam Yom. The first, mentioned above, leads to a footbridge over Mae Nam Yom to Wat Phra Si Ratana

Mahathat at Chaliang; the second crossing is about 2km further northwest just past two hills and leads directly into the Si Satchanalai ruins.

GETTING AROUND

You can rent bicycles (per day 20B) from a shop at the gateway to Wat Phra Si Ratana Mahathat as well as near the food stalls at the entrance to the historical park.

KAMPHAENG PHET PROVINCE
KAMPHAENG PHET

กำแพงเพชร

pop 30,100

Located halfway between Bangkok and Chiang Mai, Kamphaeng Phet literally means 'Diamond Wall', a reference to the apparent strength of this formerly walled city's protective barrier. The modern city stretches along a shallow section of the Mae Nam Ping and is one of Thailand's pleasanter provincial capitals.

SIGHTS

KAMPHAENG PHET HISTORICAL PARK

อุทยานประวัติศาสตร์กำแพงเพชร

A Unesco World Heritage site, this **park** (☎ 0 5571 1921; inclusive admission 100-150B, bicycle/motorbike/sǎhm·lór/car 10/20/30/50B; ⏰ 8am-5pm) features the ruins of structures dating back to the 14th century, roughly the same time as the better-known kingdom of Sukhothai. The park is divided into two parts; an inclusive ticket allows entry to both areas. The **old city** (admission 100B) is surrounded by a wall (the 'Diamond Gate' of the city's name) and was formerly inhabited by monks of the *gamavasi* ('living in the community') sect.

The majority of Kamphaeng Phet's ruins are found a few hundred metres north of the city walls in an area previously home to monks of the *aranya* ('living in forests') sect. An inclusive ticket purchased at the old city also allows entrance here, and there is an excellent **visitor centre** (admission 100B; ⏰ 8.30am-4.30pm) at the entrance. There are more than 40 temple compounds in this area, including **Wat Phra Si Iriyabot**, which has the shattered remains of standing, sitting, walking and reclining Buddha images all sculpted in the classic Sukhothai style.

KAMPHAENG PHET NATIONAL MUSEUM

พิพิธภัณฑสถานแห่งชาติกำแพงเพชร

The **national museum** (☎ 0 5571 1570; Th Pindramri; admission 100B; ⏰ 9am-noon & 1-4pm Wed-Sun) has the usual survey of Thai art periods downstairs.

KAMPHAENG PHET REGIONAL MUSEUM

พิพิธภัณฑ์เฉลิมพระเกียรติกำแพงเพชร

The **regional museum** (☎ 0 5572 2341; Th Pindramri; admission 10B; ⏰ 9am-4pm) is a series of Thai-style wooden structures on stilts set among nicely landscaped grounds. There are three main buildings in the museum featuring displays ranging from history and prehistory to the various ethnic groups that inhabit the province.

PHRA RUANG HOT SPRINGS

บ่อน้ำร้อนพระร่วง

Located 20km outside Kamphaeng Phet along the road to Sukhothai, this complex of natural **hot springs** (⏰ 8.30am-4pm) is the Thai version of a rural health retreat. There is no public transport to the hot springs, but transport can be arranged at Three J Guest House.

SLEEPING

Three J Guest House (☎ 0 5571 3129; threejguest@hotmail.com; 79 Th Rachavitee; r 300-600B; ⏰ 🖥) This pleasant collection of bungalows in a pretty garden has a very hospitable and friendly host. There's heaps of local information, bicycles and motorcycles are available for rent, and the owner can also arrange visits to his country resort near Klong Wang Chao National Park.

Phet Hotel (☎ 0 5571 2810-5; www.phethotel.com; 189 Soi Pracha Hansa; r 500-650B; ⏰ 🖥 ⚡) Near the morning market, this comfortable hotel features spacious, well-maintained, modern rooms with views over Kamphaeng Phet. Look for the sign on the top of the building. The street-side sign is only in Thai script.

Chakungrao Riverview (☎ 0 5571 4900-8; www.chankungraoriverview.com; 149 Th Thesa; r 1000-1200B, ste 5000B; ⏰ 🖥 ⚡) Kamphaeng Phet's poshest digs has some nice rooms despite its unremarkable facade. Rooms are tastefully decked out in dark woods and forest green and feature balconies with river or city views.

EATING

Bamee Chakangrao (no roman-script sign; ☎ 0 5571 2446; Th Ratchadamnoen; dishes 25-30B ☻ 8.30am-3pm) Thin wheat and egg noodles *(bà·mèe)* are a speciality of Kamphaeng Phet, and this famous restaurant is one of the best places to try them.

Phayao Bakery (Th Thesa 1; dishes 45-120B; ☻ breakfast, lunch & dinner) This air-conditioned place is a great place to escape from the heat.

A busy night market sets up every evening near the river just north of the Navarat Hotel. There are also some cheap restaurants near the roundabout near the main bridge over the Mae Nam Ping, Including the exceedingly popular **Kamphaeng Phet Phochana** (no roman-script sign; ☎ 0 5571 3035; dishes 25-50B; ☻ 6am-1am), which puts out just about every Thai fave from *pàt tai* to *kôw man gài*. There's no English-language sign, so look for the rainbow-coloured facade.

GETTING THERE & AWAY

The bus terminal is about 1km west of town. If coming from Sukhothai or Phitsanulok get off in the old city or at the roundabout on Th Tesa to save getting a *sŏrng·tăa·ou* back into town.

GETTING AROUND

The least expensive way to get from the bus station into town is to hop on a shared *sŏrng·tăa·ou* (15B per person) to the roundabout across the river.

It is worth renting a bicycle or motorbike to explore areas outside of the old city – Three J Guest House (p179) has both for rent (per day bicycle/motorcycle 50/200B).

MAE HONG SON PROVINCE

Accessible only by incredibly windy mountain roads or a dodgy flight to the provincial capital, this is Thailand's most remote province.

MAE HONG SON

แม่ฮ่องสอน

pop 6000

Mae Hong Son, with its remote setting and surrounding mountains, fits many travellers' preconceived notion of how a

---

DETOUR: THE MAE HONG SON LOOP

One of the most popular motorcycle tours in northern Thailand is the circuitous route that begins in Chiang Mai and passes through the length of Mae Hong Son province before looping back to the city – a round trip of nearly 1000km.

The Mae Hong Son loop really begins 34km north of Chiang Mai when you turn onto Rte 1095 and lean into the first of its 1864 bends. Convenient overnight stops include Pai, 130km from Chiang Mai, Soppong, another 40km up the road, and Mae Hong Son, 65km from Soppong.

Upon reaching Khun Yuam, 70km south of Mae Hong Son, you can opt to take Rte 1263 to Mae Chaem, before continuing back to Chiang Mai via Doi Inthanon, the country's highest peak, or you can continue south to Mae Sariang and follow Rte 108 all the way back to Chiang Mai via Hot, although the distances between towns here are greater and best done on a more powerful and more comfortable motorcycle.

Wat Jong Kham and Wat Jong Klang
AUSTIN BUSH

northern Thai city should be. A palpable Burmese influence and an edgy border town feel don't dispel this image, and best of all, there's hardly a túk-túk or tout to be seen.

SIGHTS
WAT PHRA THAT DOI KONG MU
วัดพระธาตุดอยกองมู

Climb the hill west of town, Doi Kong Mu (1500m), to visit this Shan-built wat, also known as Wat Plai Doi. The view of the sea of fog that collects in the valley each morning is impressive; at other times of the day you get a view of the town.

WAT JONG KHAM & WAT JONG KLANG
วัดจองคำ/วัดจองกลาง

Wat Jong Kham was built nearly 200 years ago by Thai Yai (Shan) people, who make up about half of the population of Mae Hong Son Province. Wat Jong Klang houses 100-year-old glass *jataka* paintings and a **museum** (admission by donation; ☉ 8am-6pm) with 150-year-old wooden dolls from

Mandalay that depict some of the more gruesome aspects of the wheel of life. Wat Jong Klang has several areas that women are forbidden to enter – not unusual for Burmese-Shan Buddhist temples.

ACTIVITIES
TREKKING & RAFTING

Mae Hong Son's location at the edge of mountainous jungle makes it an excellent base for treks into the countryside. Trekking trips can be arranged at several guesthouses and travel agencies.

Long tail boat trips on the nearby Mae Pai are gaining popularity, and the same guesthouses and trekking agencies that organise treks from Mae Hong Son can arrange river excursions.

Friend Tour (☎ 0 5361 1647; 21 Th Pradit Jong Kham; trek per person per day 700-900B) With nearly 20 years' experience, this recommended outfit offers trekking, elephant riding and rafting, as well as day tours.

Nature Walks (☎ 0 5361 1040, 08 9552 6899; www.trekkingthailand.com; natural_walks @yahoo.com) Treks here range from day

'Coffin cave' (p189), Soppong

AUSTIN BUSH

long nature walks (1000B) to multi-day journeys across the province (per person per day 2500B).

MUD SPA

Pooklon Country Club (☎ 0 5328 2579; www.pooklon.com; Ban Mae Sanga; ⏰ 8am-6.30pm) is touted as Thailand's only mud treatment spa.

Pooklon is 16km north of Mae Hong Son in Mok Champae district.

SLEEPING

Romtai (☎ 0 5361 2437; Th Chumnanatit; r 500-900B, bungalows 1200B; ⚡) Behind the lakeside temples, this place has a huge variety of accommodation, ranging from spacious, clean rooms to bungalows looking over a lush garden with fishponds.

ourpick Sang Tong Huts (☎ 0 5362 0680; www.sangtonghuts.com; Th Makhasanti; r 700B, bungalows 800-3000B; ⚡) This popular set of bungalows in a wooded area outside of town is one of the more character-filled places to stay. It's popular among repeat

visitors to Mae Hong Son, so it pays to book ahead.

Jongkham Place (☎ 0 5361 4294; 4/2 Th Udom Chao Nites; bungalows 800B, ste 2000B; ⚡) This new family-run place by the lake has four attractive wooden bungalows and one penthouse-like suite. All accommodation includes TV, fridge and air-con.

ourpick Residence@MaeHongSon (☎ 0 5361 4100; www.theresidence-mhs.com; 41/4 Th Nives Pisarn; r 900-1400B; ⚡ 💻) One of the more recent places to go up, this cheery yellow building houses eight stylish and inviting rooms. There's also a sunny communal rooftop area, a friendly English-speaking owner and bicycles provided free of charge.

ourpick Fern Resort (☎ 0 5368 6110; www .fernresort.info; 64 Moo 10 Tambon Pha Bong; bungalows 2500-3500B; ⚡ 💻 🏊) The 40 Shan-style wooden bungalows are set among tiered rice paddies and streams and feature stylishly decorated interiors. Nearby nature trails lead to the adjacent Mae Surin National Park, and to encourage community-based tourism, most of the employees come from local villages.

EATING

Mae Hong Son's morning market is a fascinating place to have breakfast. Several vendors at the north end of the market sell unusual dishes such as *tòo·a òon*, a Burmese noodle dish supplemented with thick gram porridge and deep-fried bits of vegetables, gram flour cakes and tofu. Other vendors along the same strip sell a local version of *kà·nŏm jeen nám ngée·o*, often topped with *kahng pòrng*, a Shan snack of battered and deep-fried vegetables.

Mae Si Bua (☎ 0 5361 2471; 51 Th Singhanat Bamrung; dishes 20-30B 8.30am-6.30pm) Like the Shan grandma you never had, Auntie Bua prepares more than a dozen different Shan curries, soups and dips on a daily basis.

Pa Tim (Th Khunlum Praphat; dishes 25-80B; 9am-10pm) Everyone loves this place for its extensive variety of well-priced Thai and Chinese options.

Salween River Restaurant (☎ 0 5361 2050; Th Singhanat Bamrung; dishes 50-160B; 7am-midnight) The menu here spans just about everything, ranging from excellent organic hill-tribe coffee to baked goods, local-style Shan specialities and imaginative Western dishes. The owners are very friendly and a good source of information.

Fern Restaurant (Th Khunlum Praphat; dishes 60-120B; 10.30am-midnight) The Fern is probably Mae Hong Son's most upmarket restaurant, but remember, this is Mae Hong Son.

DRINKING

Sunflower Café (☎ 0 5362 0549; Th Pradit Jong Kham; 7am-midnight) This open-air place

NORTHERN NOSH

- *Gaang hang·lair* – Burmese in origin (*hang* is a corruption of the Burmese *hin*, meaning curry), this rich pork curry is often seen at festivals and ceremonies.
- *Kâap möo* – deep-fried pork crackling is a common – and delicious – side dish in northern Thailand.
- *Kôw soy* – this popular curry-based noodle dish is most likely Burmese in origin, and was probably introduced to northern Thailand by travelling Chinese merchants.
- *Kà·nŏm jeen nám ngée·o* – fresh rice noodles served with a spaghetti-like pork- and tomato-based broth.
- *Lâhp kôo·a* – literally 'fried *lâhp*', this dish takes the famous Thai minced-meat 'salad' and fries it with a mixture of local bitter/hot dried spices and herbs.
- *Nám prík nùm* – green chillies, shallots and garlic that are grilled then mashed into a paste served with sticky rice, parboiled veggies and deep-fried pork crackling.
- *Sâi òo·a* – a grilled pork sausage supplemented with copious fresh herbs.
- *đam sôm oh* – the northern Thai version of *sôm·đam* substitutes pomelo for green papaya.

combines draught beer, live lounge music and views of the lake.

GETTING THERE & AWAY

AIR

For many people the time saved flying from Chiang Mai to Mae Hong Son versus bus travel is worth the extra baht.

Nok Air (☎ nationwide call centre 1318; www .nokair.co.th; Mae Hong Son airport) and its subsidiary, **SGA Airlines** (☎ 0 5379 8244; www.sga.co.th; Mae Hong Son airport), conduct a code-share flight to/from Chiang Mai (1800B, 35 minutes, once daily).

THAI (☎ 0 5361 2220; www.thaiair.com; 71 Th Singhanat Bamrung; ⏰ 8.30am-5.30pm Mon-Fri) also fly to/from Chiang Mai (1365B, 35 minutes, twice daily), from where they have connections to Bangkok (3600B).

BUS

Mae Hong Son's bus station has been moved 1km outside the city and **Prempracha Tour** (☎ 0 5368 4100) conducts bus services within the province, including south to Khun Yuam (ordinary/air-con 70/110B, two hours, 6am, 8am, 10.30am, 8pm and 9pm) with a stop in Mae Sariang (ordinary/air-con 100/180B, four hours) before culminating in Chiang Mai (ordinary/air-con 190/340B, eight hours).

GETTING AROUND

The centre of Mae Hong Son can easily be covered on foot, and it is one of the few towns in Thailand that doesn't seem to have a motorcycle taxi at every corner.

Because most of Mae Hong Son's attractions are outside of town, renting a vehicle is a good option here.

PA Motorbike (☎ 0 5361 1647; 21 Th Pradit Jong Kham), opposite Friend House, rents motorbikes (150B to 200B per day), cars and jeeps (1000B to 2500B per day).

PAI

ปาย

pop 2300

Spend enough time in northern Thailand and eventually you'll hear rumours that Pai is the Khao San Rd of northern Thailand. Although this is definitely a stretch, in re-

Rice fields, Pai

AUSTIN BUSH

cent years the small town has started to resemble a Thai island getaway – without the beaches.

Despite all this, the town's popularity has yet to impact its setting in a nearly picture-perfect mountain valley. There's heaps of quiet accommodation outside the main drag, a host of natural, lazy activities to keep visitors entertained, a vibrant art and music scene, and the town's Shan roots can still be seen in its temples, quiet back streets and fun afternoon market.

SIGHTS & ACTIVITIES
WAT PHRA THAT MAE YEN
วัดพระธาตุแม่เย็น

This temple sits atop a hill and has good views overlooking the valley. Walk 1km east from the main intersection in town, across a stream and through a village, to get to the stairs (353 steps) that lead to the top.

THA PAI HOT SPRINGS
Across Mae Nam Pai and 7km southeast of town via a paved road is **Tha Pai Hot Springs** (admission 200B; ☽ 7am-6pm), a well-kept local park 1km from the road. A scenic stream flows through the park; the stream mixes with the hot springs in places to make pleasant bathing areas. There are also small public bathing houses into which hot spring water is piped.

TREKKING & RAFTING
Most guesthouses in Pai can provide information on local trekking and a few offer guided treks for as little as 700B per day if there are no rafts or elephants involved. Among the more established local agencies are **Back-Trax** (☎ 0 5369 9739; backtraxinpai@yahoo.com; Th Chaisongkhram) and **Duang Trekking** (Duang Guest House; ☎ 0 5369 9101; 8 Th Rangsiyanon).

Rafting along the Mae Nam Pai during the wet season is also a popular activity. Back-Trax offers rafting options, but **Thai Adventure Rafting** (☎ 0 5369 9111; www .thairafting.com; Th Rangsiyanon) is generally considered the most professional outfit. The main rafting season typically runs from mid-June to mid-February.

ELEPHANT RIDING
The most established of these, and with an office in town, is **Thom's Pai Elephant Camp** (☎ 0 5369 9286; www.thomelephant.com; Th Rangsiyanon; elephant rides per person 500-1200B). Thom's can also arrange a variety of trips, including bamboo or rubber rafting, hill-tribe village stays or any combination of the aforementioned for about 1000B per person per day.

MASSAGE & SPA TREATMENTS
Pai Traditional Thai Massage (PTTM; ☎ 0 5369 9121; 68/3 Soi 1, Th Wiang Tai; massage per 1/1½/2hr 180/270/350B, sauna per visit 80B, 3-day massage course 2500B; ☽ 9am-9pm) This established and locally owned outfit offers very good northern-Thai massage, as well as a sauna where you can steam yourself in *sà·mŭn·prai* (medicinal herbs).

Mr Jan's Massage (Mr Jan's Bungalows; Soi Wanchaloem 18; per hr 150B) For those into the rougher stuff, this place employs a harder Shan-Burmese massage technique.

COURSES
Mam Yoga House (☎ 08 9954 4981; Th Rangsiyanon; 1-day course 200-550B) Just north of the police station, Mam offers Hatha Yoga classes and courses in small groups.

SLEEPING
Keep in mind that prices fluctuate immensely in Pai, and nearly all the midrange and top-end accommodation cut

their prices, sometimes by as much as 60%, during the off season.

During the height of the Thai tourist season (December to January), tents are available in abundance for about 100B.

IN TOWN

Baan Tawan Guest House (☎ 0 5369 8116/7; www.baantawan-pai.com; 117 Mu 4, Th Wiang Tai; r 500-1500B; ✗ 🖵) The older, more charming, more expensive, riverside two-storey bungalows made with salvaged teak are the reason to stay here, but there are also spacious rooms in a large two-storey building. Motorcycles and inner tubes (for floating down the river) are available for rent.

Pai Pura (☎ 08 1891 1771; Th Ratchadamnoen; r 600-1200B; ✗) Although the rooms don't follow the rather decadent external design theme of stones, fountains and bricks, they're still a good value. A highlight is the herbal sauna and adjacent dipping pool.

ourpick Baan Pai Village (☎ 0 5369 8152; www.baanpaivillage.com; Th Wiang Tai; bungalows 1000-1600B; ✗ 🖵) This well-maintained place has a collection of wooden bungalows set among winding pathways. There are also several cheaper, but simpler, riverside bungalows under the name Baan Pai Riverside.

ourpick Rim Pai Cottage (☎ 0 5369 9133; www.rimpaicottage.com; Th Chaisongkhram; bungalows incl breakfast 1500-5000B; ✗ 🖵) The homelike bungalows here are spread out along a secluded and beautifully wooded section of the Nam Pai. There are countless cosy riverside corners to relax at, and a palpable village-like feel about the whole place.

OUT OF TOWN

Southeast of town are a number of places to stay along the road that leads to the hot springs, not very far from Wat Phra That Mae Yen.

Sun Hut (☎ 0 5369 9730; www.thesunhut .com; 28/1 Ban Mae Yen; r 350-1350B) Located in a jungle-like setting with a stream running through it, this is one of the more unique places in the area. Bungalows are nicely spaced apart and more expensive ones have porches and lots of charm.

Pairadise (☎ 0 5369 8065; www.pairadise .com; 98 Mu 1, Ban Mae Hi; bungalows 850-1350B) Popular with the Western yoga-and-meditation set, this resort looks over the Pai Valley from atop a ridge just outside town. Bungalows surround a waterfall-fed pond that is suitable for swimming.

ourpick Pai Treehouse (☎ 08 1911 3640; www.paitreehouse.com; 90 Moo 2 Mae Hi; bungalows 1000-5500B; 🖵) It's every child's fantasy hotel: wooden bungalows suspended from a giant old tree. Even if you can't score one of the three elusive treehouse rooms (they're popular), there are several other attractive bungalows, many near the river. On the vast grounds you'll also find elephants and floating decks on the Mae Nam Pai, all culminating in a family-friendly atmosphere.

EATING

Je-In Pai (Pure Vegetarian Food; Th Ratchadamnoen; dishes 25-80B; ⏰ 10am-8pm) Opposite the District Office, this simple open-air place serves tasty and cheap vegan and vegetarian Thai food.

Nong Beer (☎ 0 5369 9103; cnr Th Khetkalang & Th Chaisongkhram; dishes 30-60B; ⏰ 10am-10pm) The atmosphere at this extremely popular place is akin to a food court (you have to exchange cash for tickets, and everything is self-serve), but it's a good place for cheap and authentic Thai eats ranging from *kôw soy* to curries ladled over rice.

ourpick Baan Phleng (Local Northern Thai food; cnr Th Khetkalang & Th Chaisongkhram; dishes

30-60B; ◷ 10am-10pm) A branch of the excellent Mae Hong Son restaurant of the same name, this popular place does a mix of northern Thai and Mae Hong Son–specific dishes.

our pick **Laap Khom Huay Pu** (no roman-script sign; ☎ 0 5369 9126; Ban Huay Pu; dishes 35-60B; ◷ 9am-10pm) Escape the dreadlocks and tofu crowd and get your meat at this unabashedly carnivorous local eatery. The restaurant is about 1km north of town, on the first street just past the turn-off to Belle Villa and Baan Krating.

Mama Falafel (Soi Wanchaloem; dishes 60-90B; ◷ 11am-8pm) Since 2002 this friendly native of Pai has been cooking up tasty felafel, hummus, schnitzel and other Jewish/Israeli faves.

The Sanctuary (☎ 0 5369 8150; 115/1 Moo 4 Th Wiang Tai; dishes 80-290B) The local/organic dishes at this new-agey quasi-veggie restaurant are rather expensive by local standards, but the cakes and coffee are tasty, and the free wi-fi and, yes, free yoga lessons (10.30am Tuesday, Thursday and Saturday) are a good deal.

DRINKING & ENTERTAINMENT

Pai boasts a small but happening live-music scene.

Bebop (Th Rangsiyanon; ◷ 6pm-1am) This legendary box is popular with travellers and has live music nightly (from about 9.30pm), playing blues, R&B and rock.

Phu Pai Art Café (Th Rangsiyanon; ◷ 5pm-midnight) This attractive wooden house is another highlight of Pai's live-music scene.

GETTING THERE & AWAY

AIR

Pai's airport is around 2km north of town along Rte 1095.

SGA Airlines (☎ nationwide call centre 0 2264 6099, 0 5369 8207; www.sga.co.th; Pai airport), a subsidiary of Nok Air, operates propeller-powered flights between Pai and Chiang Mai (from 1930B, 30 minutes, twice daily).

BUS

From Pai it's easy to get to Soppong (ordinary/air-con/minivan 40/80/100B,

Night market, Pai

AUSTIN BUSH

1½ hours, 8.30am to 2pm) and Mae Hong Son (ordinary/air-con/minivan 80/100/150B).

A couple of ordinary buses depart from Pai's bus station for Chiang Mai (112B, four hours, 8.30am and 10.30am).

Book your ticket in advance at **aYa Service** (☎ 0 5369 9940; 22/1 Moo 3 Th Chaisongkhram); it runs hourly air-con minivan buses to Chiang Mai (150B, three hours, from 7.30am to 4.30pm), as well as less frequent departures to Chiang Rai (550B, five hours), Mae Sai (700B, six hours) and Chiang Khong (750B, 10 hours).

SOPPONG & AROUND

สบปอง

There's not much to see in town, but the surrounding area is defined by dense forests, rushing rivers and dramatic limestone outcrops and is *the* place in northern Thailand for **caving**.

THAM LOT

ถ้ำลอด

About 9km north of Soppong is Tham Lot (pronounced *tâm lôrt* and also known as *tâm nám lôrt*), a large limestone cave with impressive stalagmites and 'coffin caves' (see boxed text, p189), and a wide stream running through it.

Tham Lot is a good example of community-based tourism as all of the guides at the cave are from local Shan villages.

SLEEPING

our pick **Cave Lodge** (☎ 0 5361 7203; www.cavelodge.com; dm 90-120B, r 250B, bungalows 300-2000B) Open since 1986, this is one of the more legendary places to stay in northern Thailand (and was probably the first guesthouse in Mae Hong Son). Run by the unofficial expert on the area, John Spies, the 11 bungalows here are basic but unique and varied. Choose from caving and kayaking trips, guided or unguided treks (good maps are available) or just hang out in the beautiful communal area.

MAE SARIANG

แม่สะเรียง

pop 10,000

Little-visited Mae Sariang is gaining a low-key buzz for its attractive riverside

Cultivating rice fields, Soppong

AUSTIN BUSH

setting and potential as a launching pad for sustainable tourism and trekking opportunities.

SIGHTS & ACTIVITIES

Mae Sariang Man, as the owner of **Mae Sariang Tours** (☎ 08 2032 4790; www.maesariangtravel.multiply.com; Th Laeng Phanit; 1-day trek 1200B plus expenses) prefers to be known, is an experienced trekker who leads environmentally conscious and community-based treks and rafting trips in the jungles and national parks surrounding his native city.

The ex-teacher running **Kanchana Tour** (☎ 08 1952 2167; www.orchidhomestay.com; half-day cycling tour 600B, 1-day tour 1000B) offers half- and full-day cycling tours around Mae Sariang, as well as other tours ranging from boat trips along the Mae Nam Salawin, to visits to local hill tribes.

Mr Salawin and his brothers have been leading tours in the area for 16 years. Their trips at **Salawin Tour & Trekking** (☎ 08 2181 2303; Th Laeng Phanit; 1-/3-day trek 1300/2500B) typically involve activities such as elephant riding, rafting and hiking.

SLEEPING

Road Side Guest House (☎ 0 5368 2713; road-sidegh@hotmail.com; 44 Th Mae Sariang; r 200B) The owner, an experienced trekking guide, leads various tours of the area.

Riverside Guest House (☎ 0 5368 1188; 85 Th Laeng Phanit; r 250-550B; 🖳) This friendly, ramshackle guesthouse keeps growing and improving. Some rooms feel cramped but most share large terraces with great views of a turn in the river and the valley beyond.

our pick Riverhouse Hotel (☎ 0 5362 1201; www.riverhousehotels.com; 77 Th Laeng Phanit; r incl breakfast 1000-1300B; 🖳 🖳) The combination of nostalgia-inducing teak and stylish decor makes this riverside hotel the best spot in town. Air-conditioned 2nd-floor rooms have huge verandas overlooking the river, as well as floor-to-ceiling windows.

THE CAVES OF PANGMAPHA

The 900-sq-km area of Pangmapha district is famous for its high concentration of cave systems, where over 200 have been found.

Many of the caves are essentially underground river systems, some of which boast waterfalls, lakes and 'beaches'.

More than 85 of the district's 200 limestone caverns are known to contain ancient teak coffins carved from solid teak logs. Up to 9m long, the coffins are typically suspended on wooden scaffolds inside the caves. The coffins have been carbon-dated and shown to be between 1200 and 2200 years old.

It is not known who made them or why they were placed in caves, but as most caves have fewer than 10 coffins it indicates that not everyone was accorded such an elaborate burial.

EATING & DRINKING

Inthira Restaurant (☎ 0 5368 1529; Th Wiang Mai; dishes 30-150B; 🕑 8am-10pm) Probably the town's best restaurant, this place features a strong menu of dishes using unique ingredients such as locally grown shiitake mushrooms and fish from the Mae Nam Moei.

Sawadee Restaurant & Bar (Th Laeng Phanit; dishes 40-150B; 🕑 8am-midnight) Like a beachside bar, this is a great place to recline with a beer and watch the water (in this case the Mae Nam Yuam). There's a lengthy menu with lots of options for vegetarians.

GETTING THERE & AROUND

Located at the bus station, **Prempracha Tour** (☎ 0 5368 1347) conducts buses between Mae Sariang and Mae Hong Son (ordinary/air-con 100/180B, four hours, five departures from 7am to 5.30pm), with a stop midway in Khun Yuam (ordinary/air-con 70/110B, two hours). There are also buses to Chiang Mai (ordinary/air-con 100/180B, four hours, five departures from 7am to 3pm).

Destinations anywhere in town are 20B by motorcycle taxi.

NORTHEASTERN THAILAND

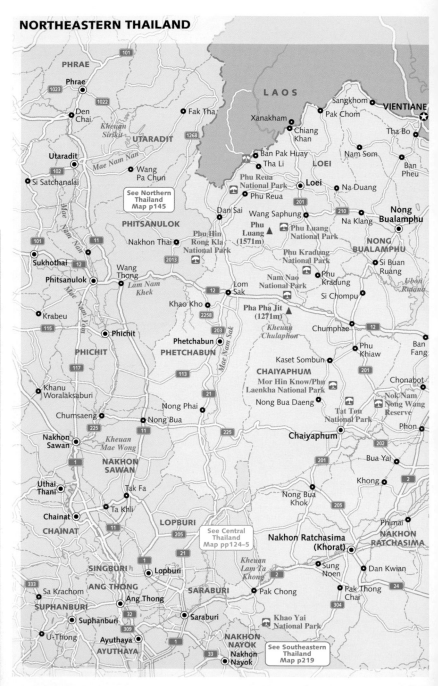

See Northern Thailand Map p145

See Central Thailand Map pp124–5

See Southeastern Thailand Map p219

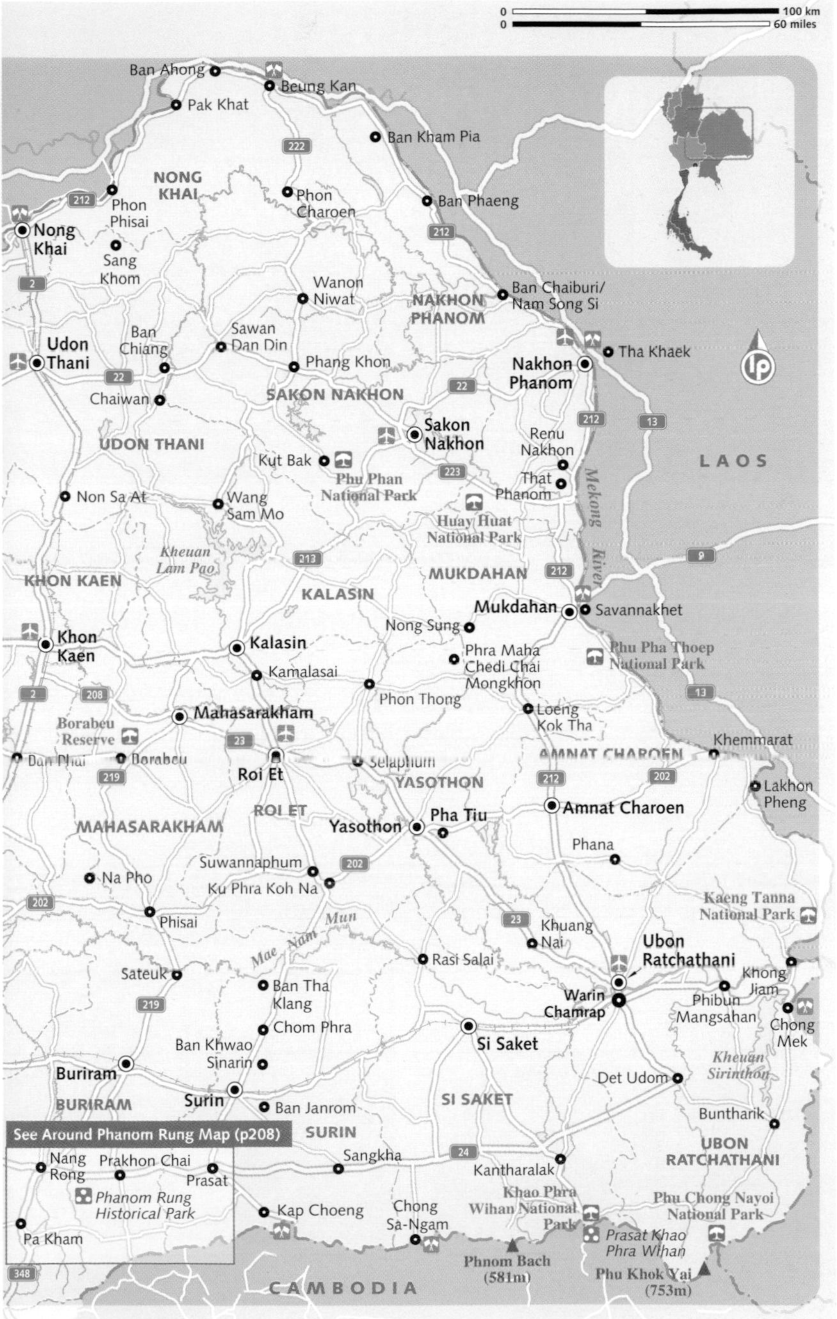

0 _____ 100 km
0 _____ 60 miles

Ban Ahong
Beung Kan
Pak Khat
Ban Kham Pia
222
NONG KHAI
Phon Charoen
Ban Phaeng
212
Phon Phisai
212
Nong Khai
2
Sang Khom
Wanon Niwat
NAKHON PHANOM
Ban Chaiburi/ Nam Song Si
Udon Thani
Ban Chiang
Sawan Dan Din
Phang Khon
Nakhon Phanom
Tha Khaek
22
Chaiwan
SAKON NAKHON
22
Sakon Nakhon
Renu Nakhon
212
13
LAOS
Non Sa At
Kut Bak
Phu Phan National Park
223
That Phanom
Mekong River
Wang Sam Mo
Huay Huat National Park
KHON KAEN
Kheuan Lam Pao
213
MUKDAHAN
212
9
KALASIN
Nong Sung
Mukdahan
Savannakhet
Khon Kaen
Kalasin
Phra Maha Chedi Chai Mongkhon
Phu Pha Thoep National Park
2
208
Kamalasai
Phon Thong
Loeng Kok Tha
13
Borabeu Reserve
23
Mahasarakham
AMNAT CHAROEN
Khemmarat
Dan Phai
Borabeu
219
Roi Et
Selaphum
YASOTHON
212
202
Amnat Charoen
Lakhon Pheng
MAHASARAKHAM
ROI ET
Yasothon
Pha Tiu
Phana
Na Pho
Suwannaphum
202
Ku Phra Koh Na
Kaeng Tanna National Park
202
Phisai
Mae Nam Mun
23
Khuang Nai
Ubon Ratchathani
Khong Jiam
Sateuk
Ban Tha Klang
Rasi Salai
Warin Chamrap
Phibun Mangsahan
Chong Mek
219
Chom Phra
Ban Khwao Sinarin
Si Saket
Kheuan Sirinthon
Buriram
Surin
Det Udom
Buntharik
BURIRAM
Ban Janrom
SI SAKET
UBON RATCHATHANI
SURIN
Sangkha
24
See Around Phanom Rung Map (p208)
Kantharalak
Nang Rong
Prakhon Chai
Prasat
Khao Phra Wihan National Park
Phu Chong Nayoi National Park
Phanom Rung Historical Park
Kap Cheong
Chong Sa-Ngam
Prasat Khao Phra Wihan
Pa Kham
348
CAMBODIA
Phnom Bach (581m)
Phu Khok Yai (753m)

NE THAILAND HIGHLIGHTS

1 SURIN PROVINCE

BY DUANGDAO (JUNE) NIAMPAN, FOUNDER LEMONGRASS VOLUNTEERING

The people in the northeast are very friendly and kind-hearted. There aren't a lot of tourists here but there are many cultural attractions. In fact Surin is composed of three cultures – Thai, Khmer and Suay – living together peacefully. I grew up in a Thai-Khmer village and now run a volunteering agency in Surin.

JUNE'S DON'T MISS LIST

❶ KHMER RUINS

Because the region is very rural it doesn't seem like there is a lot of architecture here but there are many Khmer ruins, including **Phanom Rung** (p209) and **Prasat Meuang Tam** (p210) that are only an hour's drive from Surin town.

❷ SURIN ELEPHANT ROUND-UP

Surin is famous across Thailand for its annual **Elephant Round-Up festival** (p208). There are over 250 elephants that come for activities and it is very

spectacular to see so many in one place. Also during the festival you get to see the local culture, like traditional Thai dancing.

❸ ELEPHANT VILLAGE

Ban Tha Klang (p211) is a traditional village where elephants live together with their mahouts. But my favourite elephant village is nearby Ban Taa Tid where I'm friends with the village chief, Khun Lee. I often take my volunteers to Khun Lee's house where we feed the animals and ride them through the vil-

Clockwise from top: Elephant Round-Up festival, Surin (p208); Silk-weaver at work; Silk cocoons; Phanom Rung Historical Park (p209)

lage past the local primary school to the jungle. Once the students see so many foreigners passing through town they become curious, so we usually stop by the school and play games.

❹ CRAFT VILLAGES

Surin is famous for silk-weaving and silver-jewellery making and craft villages (p211) show how the intricate designs are made and how much hard work is put into just one piece of silk. Now you'll see why silk is expensive; it takes time and technique to make something so beautiful.

❺ VOLUNTEERING

Local schools are eager to have native English speakers visit so that the schoolchildren have someone

to practice their English skills with. There are also day-care centres where visitors with only a few hours to spare can play with pre-school aged kids. It is great fun and helps the community. Plus volunteering provides memorable experiences.

↘ THINGS YOU NEED TO KNOW

Getting Started Check out LemonGrass Volunteering (www.lemongrass -volunteering.com) for volunteering options **Top Survival Tip** Foreigners are an oddity here and children (and some adults too) might stare at you; just wave and smile and their surprise will change to friendliness

NE THAILAND HIGHLIGHTS

↘ TRACK DOWN ANGKOR RUINS

Smaller versions of Angkor Wat dot the countryside of the northeast. Temples, including **Phimai** (p203) and **Phanom Rung** (p209) linked the distant empire's capital to trading posts that today seem like the middle of nowhere. In addition to great architecture, the scenery is a fascinating look at rural Thailand: rice paddies, ladies in sarongs and water buffaloes submerged in muddy ponds.

↘ DO A NATURE ESCAPE TO KHAO YAI

Close to Bangkok but devoid of concrete, **Khao Yai National Park** (p205) is a delightful retreat into the Thai wilderness. There are the usual outdoor pursuits of hiking and waterfall-spotting but the park is also a beloved picnic outing for Thais: you might find that for all your plans to get back to nature, you've actually spent more time eating *sôm·đam* (green papaya salad) with strangers.

4

⬃ RELAX BY THE RIVER

Nong Khai (p214) is a lovely little town beside the Mekong River with flower-festooned gardens, a busy riverside market, and plenty of wandering and cycling opportunities. The main event is the Sala Kaew Ku Sculpture Park (p214), filled with surreal statuary that would look more at home in an avant-garde gallery in Bangkok.

5

⬃ CELEBRATE ISAN FESTIVALS

The northeast is lean on tourist-worthy attractions but it abounds with cultural festivals (p198). The beginning and end of Buddhist Lent are recognised with much fanfare in this region. Ubon Ratchathani, Nong Khai and Nakhon Phanom all have citywide parades and events that showcase traditional dance and music.

6

⬃ SURVEY SURIN PROVINCE

The countryside of Surin (p208) is peppered with Angkor ruins and villages that have survived into the modern era with ancient professions – like elephant herding and silk weaving – intact. The provincial capital is an ordinary Thai town that assembles around the night market as if it were a communal dinner table.

2 BILL WASSMAN; 3 & 4 JOHN ELK III; 5 ANDREW WATSON; 6 ALAIN EVRARD

2 Detail of temple relief, Phimai (p203); 3 Giant ficus, Khao Yai National Park (p205); 4 Sala Kaew Ku Sculpture Park (p214); 5 Dancers celebrate òrk pan-säh (the end of Buddhist lent; p48); 6 Local transport, Surin (p208)

NORTHEASTERN THAILAND

NORTHEASTERN THAILAND'S BEST...

⬆ FESTIVALS

- **Candle Parade** (p213) Ubon Rat-chathani marks the start of Buddhist Lent (July) with elaborate candle sculptures.
- **Elephant Round-Up** (p213) Surin's traditional elephant herders show off their pachyderms.
- **Naga Fireballs** (p216) The Mekong's gaseous burps attracts thousands to Nong Khai.

⬆ LOCAL DISHES

- **Pàt mèe koh·râht** Khorat's local version of *pàt tai*.
- **Sôm·đam & gài yâhng** Cornerstones of Isan cuisine.
- **Năam neu·ang** A culinary import from Vietnam.

⬆ MEKONG TOWNS

- **Nong Khai** (p214) A riverside darling.
- **Chiang Khan** (p213) Small and sleepy.
- **Nakhon Phanom** (p213) Picturesque town with a Vietnamese influence.

⬆ CRAFT VILLAGES & SHOPS

- **Dan Kwian** (p203) Distinctive pottery village outside Khorat.
- **Ban Khwao Sinarin** (p211) Silk-weaving village using ancient Khmer techniques; outside of Surin.
- **Camp Fai Ubon** (p213) Ubon-style loomed cotton.

LEFT: RICHARD I'ANSON; RIGHT: JOHN ELK III

Left: Monk studying; Right: Sunset over the Mekong River, Chiang Khan (p213)

THINGS YOU NEED TO KNOW

⬎ VITAL STATISTICS

- **Population** 22 million
- **Best time to visit** November to February

⬎ TOWNS IN A NUTSHELL

- **Nakhon Ratchasima** Region's biggest and most urban centre.
- **Surin** A good base for visiting Angkor temple ruins.
- **Ubon Ratchathani** Friendly and pleasant Isan city.
- **Nong Khai** Adorable riverside town.

⬎ ADVANCE PLANNING

- **One day before** Buy bus tickets directly from Bangkok's Northern & Northeastern (Mo Chit) bus station (p93). Buy train tickets from Bangkok's Hualamphong station (p93).

⬎ RESOURCES

- **Tourism Authority of Thailand** (TAT; ☎ 0 4421 3666; 2102-2104 Th Mittaphap; Nakhon Ratchasima; ⏱ 8.30am-4.30pm)
- **TAT Offices** (⏱ 8.30am-4.30pm) Surin (☎ 0 4451 4447; tatsurin@tat.or.th; 355/3-6 Th Thesaban 1); Nong Khai (☎ 0 4242 1326; Hwy 2); Ubon Ratchathani (☎ 0 4524 3770; www.tatubon.org; 264/1 Th Kheuan Thani)

⬎ EMERGENCY NUMBERS

- **Fire** (☎ 199)
- **Police/Emergency** (☎ 191)
- **Tourist police** (☎ 1155; ⏱ 24hr)

⬎ GETTING AROUND

- **Bus** Best way to get from town to town and to link with northern Thailand through Phitsanulok.
- **Motorcycle** Good self-touring option for visiting Khmer temples.
- **Sŏrng·tăa·ou** Small pick-up trucks that act as public buses.
- **Train** Two lines connect to Bangkok.
- **Túk-túk** Chartered vehicles for trips within towns; remember to bargain.

⬎ BE FOREWARNED

- **Amenities** Spoken English is very limited and tourist amenities are lean.
- **Hot season** From March to May temperatures climb to over 40°C.
- **Accommodation** Can be limited during local festivals.
- **Dress modestly** Cover shoulders and knees.

NORTHEASTERN THAILAND

THINGS YOU NEED TO KNOW

NORTHEASTERN THAILAND ITINERARIES

MONKEY AROUND IN KHAO YAI Three Days

Thailand's first national park shelters an impressive slice of wilderness within striking distance to urban Bangkok. **(1) Khao Yai National Park** (p205) includes a 1351m summit, five vegetative zones, herds of elephants, troops of monkeys and waterfalls. The best time to visit is just after the rainy season in October or November when the waterfalls are still thundering and the landscape is still lush. Beware of leeches though.

With your own transport you can also visit Thailand's very own wine country (p207), where small wineries are tending to tropical grapes.

If you need a civilisation after the park, stop in at **(2) Nakhon Ratchasima** (Khorat; p202). Like all Thai cities, the best place to absorb its character is at the various night markets. Just outside of town is Dan Kwian (p203), a famous pottery village.

FOLLOW THE ANGKOR TEMPLE TRAIL Five days

Starting in the 11th century, the great Khmer kingdom extended deep into modern-day Thailand, building a temple-studded highway that linked to the Angkor capital.

One of the northeast's biggest towns, **(1) Nakhon Ratchasima** (p202) is a convenient base for exploring Phimai and connecting to other Isan towns.

Of all the Khmer ruins in northeast Thailand, **(2) Phimai** (p203) is one of the easiest to reach and has the best tourist infrastructure. Delving deeper into ethnic Khmer territory, **(3) Surin** (p208) is a handy base for arranging tours to more far-flung ruins.

Widely considered the apex of Khmer architecture, **(4) Phanom Rung** (p209) is the most elaborate and elegant structure this dusty corner of the country has seen in centuries. Nearby, **(5) Prasat Meuang Tam** (p210) provides a counterpoint to renovated Phanom Rung. It is a time-worn complex, sitting among the rice fields that tickle villagers' imaginations with mystical tales.

Built upon a sacred summit, **(6) Prasat Khao Phra Wihan** (p210) is technically in Cambodia, though the border has long been contested. Its no-man's-land status and views into former Khmer Rouge territory are reason enough to visit.

MEET THE MEKONG IN NONG KHAI One Week

The mighty Mekong River swells and contracts with the seasonal rains as it defines an ever-changing border between Thailand and Laos. But

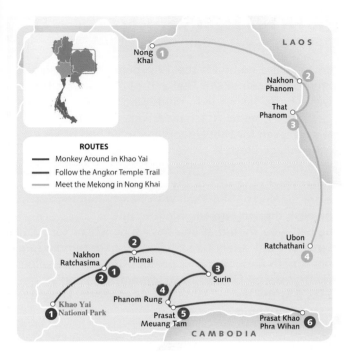

the muddy conduit continues to bind the people on either side of the international border.

An overnight train ride from Bangkok, (1) Nong Khai (p214) is the only northeast town that has a traveller's 'scene' thanks to the border crossing into Laos, making it a little less lonely than the rest of the region. After you've cycled every nook in Nong Khai, hop on a bus to (2) Nakhon Phanom (p213), a handsome provincial capital with Indochinese architecture and a Vietnamese community displaced from their homeland during the 20th-century conflicts.

Bus over to (3) That Phanom (p213), a speck of a place where the river is as prominent as the people, and the tallest building in town is the Lao-style stupa.

Start the slow trip home through (4) Ubon Ratchathani (p211), a surprisingly large town with heaps of Lao character. Ubon is on the rail so book a berth for the overnight ride to Bangkok.

DISCOVER NORTHEASTERN THAILAND

Isan (*ee·săhn*), the collective name for the 19 provinces that make up the northeast, offers a glimpse of the Thailand of old: rice fields run to the horizon, water buffaloes wade in muddy ponds, silk weaving remains a cottage industry, pedal-rickshaw drivers pull passengers down city streets, and, even for those people who've had to seek work in the city, the village lifestyle prevails.

If you spend even just a little time here you'll start to find as many differences as similarities to the rest of the country. The language, food and culture are more Lao than Thai, with hearty helpings of Khmer and Vietnamese thrown into the melting pot.

And spend time here you should. If you have a penchant for authentic experiences, it will surely be satisfied: Angkor temple ruins pepper the region, superb national parks protect some of the wildest corners of the country, sleepy villages host some of Thailand's wildest celebrations and the scenery along parts of the Mekong is often nothing short of stunning.

NAKHON RATCHASIMA PROVINCE

NAKHON RATCHASIMA (KHORAT)

นครราชสีมา(โคราช)

pop 215,000

A bumper dose of urban hubbub reflects the city's growing affluence, and Khorat's one-time historic charm has been largely smothered under a duvet of homogenous development.

SLEEPING

ourpick Sansabai House (Map pp204-5; ☎ 0 4425 5144; 335 Th Suranari; r 270-500B; ☒) Walk into the welcoming lobby at Sansabai House and you half expect the posted prices to be a bait-and-switch ploy. But no, all rooms are bright and spotless and come with good mattresses, mini-fridges and little balconies.

Chaophaya Inn (Map pp204-5; ☎ 0 4426 0555; www.chaophayainn.com; 62/1 Th Jomsurangyat; r 500-1000B; ☒ ▣) Rising beyond the jailhouse vibes endemic in most of Khorat's midrange options, the Chaophaya offers cleanliness, comfort, free in-room wi-fi and a little atmosphere for a very reasonable price.

EATING

One speciality not to miss during your stay is *pàt mèe koh·râht*. It's similar to *pàt tai*, but boasts more flavour and is made with a local style of rice noodle (*mèe koh·râht*). It's available at most restaurants. You can also sample it, along with deep-fried crickets, pork sausages and other Isan specialities, at the **Wat Boon Night Bazaar** (Map pp204-5; Th Chomphon).

ourpick Rabieng-Pa (Map pp204-5; ☎ 0 4424 3137; 284 Th Yommarat; dishes 45-220B; ☾ dinner) The leafiest and loveliest restaurant on this stretch of Th Yommarat (and arguably all of Khorat) is also one of the most low key.

GETTING THERE & AWAY
BUS
Khorat has two bus terminals. **Terminal 1** (Map pp204-5; ☎ 0 4424 2899; Th Burin) in the city centre serves Bangkok and towns within the province. Buses to other destinations, plus more for Bangkok, use **Terminal 2** (Map pp204-5; ☎ 0 4425 6006) off Hwy 2.

TRAIN
Eleven trains leave Khorat **train station** (Map pp204-5; ☎ 0 4424 2044) daily for Bangkok (3rd/2nd/1st class 50/115/230B) taking four to six hours – in other words, much longer than the bus. There are also seven trains (3rd/2nd class air-con 60/425B, four to six hours) to/from Ubon Ratchathani.

AROUND NAKHON RATCHASIMA
DAN KWIAN
ด่านเกวียน
Just a quick trip out of Khorat, this village has been producing pottery for hundreds of years and its creations are famous for their rough texture and rust-like hue. Only kaolin sourced from this district produces such results. Myriad shops line the highway and some are as much art gallery as shop.

To get here from Khorat, hop on a bus (14B, 30 minutes) from near the south city gate, the east gate or Terminal 2.

PHIMAI
พิมาย
Reminiscent of Cambodia's Angkor Wat, Prasat Phimai once stood on an important trade route linking the Khmer capital of Angkor with the northern reaches of the realm.

NICHOLAS REUSS

Prasat Phimai

SIGHTS
PHIMAI HISTORICAL PARK
อุทยานประวัติศาสตร์พิมาย
Started by Khmer King Jayavarman V (AD 968–1001) during the late 10th century and finished by King Suriyavarman I (AD 1002–49) in the early 11th century, this Hindu-Mahayana Buddhist temple projects a majesty that transcends its size. Although pre-dating Angkor Wat by a century or so, **Prasat Phimai** (Map p206; ☎ 0 4447 1568; Th Anantajinda; admission 100B; ⏲ 7.30am-6pm) shares a number of design features with its more famous cousin, not least the roof of its 28m-tall main shrine.

SLEEPING & EATING
Old Phimai Guesthouse (Map p206; ☎ 0 4447 1918; www.phimaigh.com; 214/14 Th

NAKHON RATCHASIMA (KHORAT)

Ⓐ   Ⓑ   Ⓒ   Ⓓ

❶

Mae Nam Mun

Th Mittaphap

❷   Soi Sawai Riang   Trok Samorai   Trok Sao Thanonong   Th Kingran

Th Suranari

Soi Lampru   Th Mukkhamontri   Th Jomsurangyat

Th Mukkhamontri

❸   Th Seup Siri   Soi 4

Soi 3

Wat Pa Salawan

Th Mittaphap

❹

To Bangkok
(250km)

INFORMATION		Wat Boon Night	
Tourism Authority of Thailand		Bazaar................................ **5** H2	
(TAT)................................ **1** A3			
		TRANSPORT	
SLEEPING		Bus Terminal 1.................... **6** E2	
Chaophaya Inn.................... **2** F3		Bus Terminal 2.................... **7** E1	
Sansabai House.................... **3** E2		Bus to Dan Kwian................ **8** H3	
		Bus to Dan Kwian................ **9** H3	
EATING		Nakhon Ratchasima (Khorat)	
Rabieng Pa.......................... **4** H2		Train Station.................... **10** C3	

Chomsudasadet; dm 90B, s 150-350B, d 180-450B;
❄ 🖥) The backpacker vibe prevails in
this historic wooden house tucked away
down a quiet soi. The friendly hosts are a
great source of information about Phimai
and also run reasonably priced day trips
to Phanom Rung.

   Baiteiy Restaurant (Map p206; ☎ 0 4428
7103; Th Phimai-Chumpuang; dishes 45-200B;
🕑 breakfast, lunch & dinner) Appropriately
decorated with some pseudo-Khmer
carvings, this pleasant outdoor eatery,
located about 500m south of Pratu Chai
(Victory Gate), does a decent spread of

Thai-Isan-Chinese fare, as well as a few
international staples.

   Phimai also has a small **night bazaar**
(Map p206; Th Anantajinda; 🕑 4-10pm).

GETTING THERE & AWAY
Phimai has a bus station, but there's no
need to use it as all buses pass near Pratu
Chai, the clock tower and the museum on
their way in and out of town.

   Buses for Phimai leave from Khorat's
Bus Terminal 2 (ordinary/2nd class 45/50B,
1¼ hours), off Hwy 2, every half-hour until
7pm.

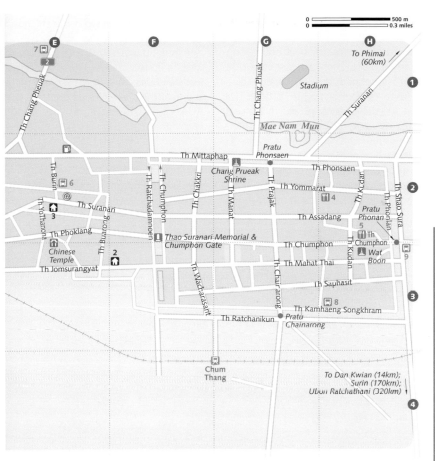

KHAO YAI NATIONAL PARK

อุทยานแห่งชาติเขาใหญ่

Up there on the podium with some of the world's greatest parks, **Khao Yai** (☎ 08 1877 3127; admission 400B) is Thailand's oldest and most visited reserve. Covering 2168 sq km, Khao Yai incorporates one of the largest intact monsoon forests remaining in mainland Asia, which is why it was named a Unesco World Heritage site (as part of the Dong Phayayen-Khao Yai Forest Complex).

There are two primary entrances to the park. One is the northern entrance through Nakhon Ratchasima Province, with most travellers passing through the town of Pak Chong (see 207 for transport information).

SIGHTS & ACTIVITIES

Many of the hotels and resorts around Khao Yai offer **park tours** and this is really the ideal way to visit.

SLEEPING & EATING

ourpick **Greenleaf Guesthouse** (☎ 0 4436 5024; www.greenleaftour.com; Th Thanarat, Km7.5; r 200-300B) Step past the slightly chaotic

NORTHEASTERN THAILAND

common areas and you'll be surprised by the great-value rooms (all with private bathrooms) at the back of this long-running place. These are just about the only budget beds outside Pak Chong.

Khao Yai Garden Lodge (☎ 0 4436 5178; www.khaoyai-gardenlodge.com; Th Thanarat, Km7; r 350-2600B, f 3800-6800B; 🞕 💻 🖵) This friendly and funky place offers a very different experience from the big, fancy resorts up the road. Rooms have individual character (except the 350B shared bathroom ones) and are spread out around a

lush garden. It's a bit worn, but still good value by area standards.

Juldis (☎ 0 4429 7297; www.juldiskhaoyai .com; Th Thanarat, Km17; r 1760-4800B, bungalows 4800-7200B; 🞕 💻 🖵) This plush place is one of the Khao Yai area originals, but it's kept up with the times with a 2008 renovation.

Kirimaya (☎ 0 4442 6000; www.kirimaya .com; Rte 3052; r 7600-14,300B, pool villas 15,400B, tented villas 22,200B; 🞕 💻 🖵) Step 'through' the wooden front doors and you're greeted by a towering stilted restaurant

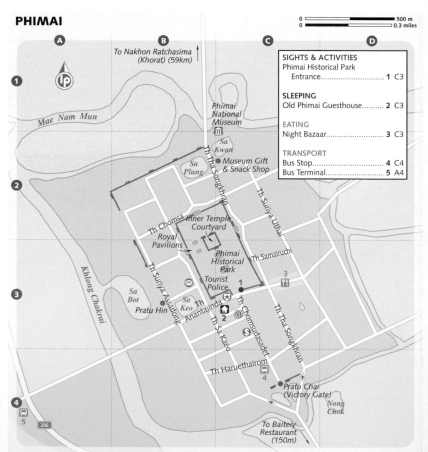

PHIMAI

0   500 m
0   0.3 miles

SIGHTS & ACTIVITIES		
Phimai Historical Park		
Entrance	1	C3
SLEEPING		
Old Phimai Guesthouse	2	C3
EATING		
Night Bazaar	3	C3
TRANSPORT		
Bus Stop	4	C4
Bus Terminal	5	A4

To Nakhon Ratchasima (Khorat) (59km)

Mae Nam Mun

Phimai National Museum

Sa Kwan

Museum Gift & Snack Shop

Sa Plung

Th Tha Songkhran

Th Suriya Uthai

Th Chomsuda   Inner Temple Courtyard

Royal Pavilions

Phimai Historical Park

Th Samairuchi

Th Suriya Atsadong

Tourist Police

Khlong Chakrai

Sa Bot

Pratu Hin

Sa Keo

Th Anantajinda

Th Sa Keo

Th Chomsudasadet

Th Tha Songkhran

Th Haruethairom

To Baiteiy Restaurant (150m)

Pratu Chai (Victory Gate)

Nong Chok

NAKHON RATCHASIMA PROVINCE

BEYOND THE FOREST

Thailand is the pioneer of 'New Latitude Wines'. Two of the leaders, **Khao Yai Winery** (☎ 0 3622 6416; www.khaoyaiwinery.com; ⏰ 9am-8pm Sun-Thu, to 10pm Fri & Sat), which corked its first bottle in 1998, and **GranMonte** (☎ 0 3622 7334; www.granmonte.com; ⏰ 11am-8pm), which got in the game three years later, lie along Pansuk-Kudkla Rd, the direct route from Bangkok to Khao Yai (exit Km144).

and other Thai-Bali fusion buildings, all rising from a lotus- and reed-filled pond and backed by the mountains.

The best setting for sleeping is, of course, in the park itself. There are two **campsites** (per person with own tent 30B, 2-4 person tent 150-250B) and a variety of **rooms and bungalows** (☎ 0 2562 0760; www.dnp .go.th/parkreserve; 2-8 people 800-3500B).

GETTING THERE & AWAY

Just about all buses between Bangkok (2nd/1st class 100/140B, two hours) and Khorat (2nd/1st class 60/75B, one hour) stop in Pak Chong. Ayuthaya, on the other hand, has no direct bus service, so the train (3rd class 175B, 2nd class 200-330B; two hours), of which there are 11 daily, is the best option.

BURIRAM PROVINCE
NANG RONG

นางรอง
pop 20,300

This workaday city is even more forgettable than Buriram, 45km to the north, but it's the most convenient base for visiting Phanom Rung.

SLEEPING & EATING

`our pick` **Honey Inn** (☎ 0 4462 2825; www.honey inn.com; 8/1 Soi Si Kun; r 200-400B; ❄ 💻) This welcoming guesthouse, 1km from the bus station, is run by a knowledgeable retired English teacher. The rooms are simple but bright and travel tips get shared around the dinner table. Motorcycle hire, guided tours and food (with advance notice) are all available at good prices.

`our pick` P **California Inter Hostel** (☎ 0 4462 2214; www.nangronghomestay.com; 59/9 Th Sangkakrit; r 250-700B; ❄ 💻) The California is somewhat shinier than the Honey Inn, although some of the rooms are a little more cramped. Khun Wicha, who is a wealth of knowledge about the area, also hires bikes and motorcycles and leads tours.

ANDERS BLOMQVIST

Phanom Rung Historical Park (p209)

GETTING THERE & AWAY

Nang Rong's **bus terminal** (☎ 0 4463 1517) is on the west side of town.

SURIN & SI SAKET PROVINCES
SURIN

สุรินทร์

pop 41,200

Surin doesn't have much to say for itself until November, when the provincial capital explodes into life for the **Surin Elephant Round-up**. Arguably the festival's best event is the elephant buffet on the Friday before the big show.

TOURS

Pirom, at Pirom-Aree's House (right), offers a wide range of tours, from a half-day in Ban Tha Klang and the craft villages (per person 1400B with four people) to a three-day Isan immersion experience (per person per day 2400B with four people). Tours to all the well-known Khmer temples (and many others) are also available.

Saren Travel (☎ 0 4452 0174; 202/1-4 Th Thesaban 2; ⏱ 8.30am-6pm Mon-Sat) offers customised day tours in and around Surin Province from 1600B.

SLEEPING

Hotels fill up fast during the Elephant Round-Up and prices skyrocket, so book as far in advance as you can.

our pick **Pirom-Aree's House** (☎ 0 4451 5140; Soi Arunee, Th Thungpo; s/d 120/200B) The location for this long-time budget favourite, 1km west of the city, is inconvenient but very peaceful. Aree cooks some pretty good food and Pirom is one of the best sources of information on the region you'll meet.

Kritsada Grand Palace (☎ 0 4471 3997; Th Suriyarat; r 400-450B; 🅿 💻) Sitting on a quiet side street behind city hall, this newly opened property is a bit hard to find, but that makes for a very quiet downtown location. Rooms are rather plain, but good value.

Treehouse Resort (☎ 08 9948 4181; sboonyoi@gmail.com; Hwy 226; r 350-1000B; 🅿) This peculiar place, under slow-mo construction since 1998, is a combination of

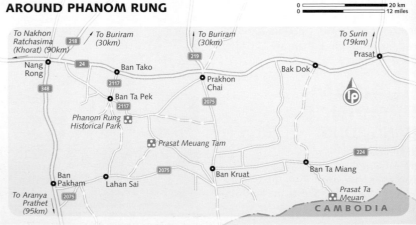

AROUND PHANOM RUNG

0 — 20 km
0 — 12 miles

To Nakhon Ratchasima (Khorat) (90km)
218
To Buriram (30km)
To Buriram (30km)
219
To Surin (19km)
Prasat

Nang Rong
24
Ban Tako
Prakhon Chai
Bak Dok

348
2117

Ban Ta Pek
2117
2075

Phanom Rung Historical Park

Prasat Meuang Tam

224

Ban Pakham
Lahan Sai
2075
Ban Kruat
Ban Ta Miang

To Aranya Prathet (95km)
2075
Prasat Ta Meuan

CAMBODIA

JOHN ELK III

Phanom Rung Historical Park

PHANOM RUNG HISTORICAL PARK

อุทยานประวัติศาสตร์เขาพนมรุ้ง

Phanom Rung has a knock-me-dead location. Crowning the summit of a spent volcano, this sanctuary sits a good 70 storeys above the paddy fields below. The Phanom Rung temple complex is the largest and best restored Khmer monument in Thailand.

The Phanom Rung temple was erected between the 10th and 13th centuries, the bulk of it during the reign of King Suriyavarman II (r AD 1113–50), which by all accounts was the apex of Angkor architecture. The complex faces east, towards the original Angkor capital.

Below the main sanctuary, after the long row of gift shops, an **information centre** houses artefacts found at the site and displays about both the construction and restoration. You can pick up a free informative brochure or arrange a guide (fees are negotiable) here.

The easiest way to the ruins from Nang Rong is to arrange a ride from your hotel (expect to pay about 800B).

Things You Need to Know: Phanom Rung (Big Mountain; ☎ 0 4478 2715; admission 100B; ⏰ 6am-6pm); information centre (admission free; ⏰ 9am-4.30pm)

Gilligan's Island and your grandparents' dishevelled basement. Khun Boonyai, the cheerful owner and creator, prefers that you book a day in advance; in return, he'll pick you up in town for free when you arrive.

EATING

Petmanee 2 (no roman-script sign; ☎ 08 4451 6024; Th Murasart; dishes 20-60B; ⏰ lunch) This simple spot south of Ruampaet Hospital and next to Wat Salaloi (look for the chicken grill in front) is Surin's most famous purveyor of *sôm·đam* and *gài yâhng*.

Guardian-figure relief, Prasat Meuang Tam

JOE CUMMINGS

⬦ IF YOU LIKE...

If you like the **Phanom Rung** (p209), then you'll like these ancient Khmer temples that formed a temple trail from Phimai to Cambodia's Angkor Wat.

- **Prasat Meuang Tam** (Map 208; Lower City; admission 100B; ☻ 7am-6pm) was once a shrine to Shiva and dates back to the late 10th or early 11th century under King Jayavarman V. Accessible from Phanom Rung.
- **Prasat Ta Meuan** (Map 208; admission free; ☻ daylight hr), in Tambon Ta Miang, is a secluded complex on the Thai–Cambodian border built in the Jayavarman VII period (AD 1181–1210) as a rest stop for pilgrims. It's 55km from Phanom Rung; arrange a tour from Surin (p208).
- **Prasat Khao Phra Wihan** (Preah Vihear in Khmer; Map pp192-3) is one of the region's great Angkor-period monuments. It straddles a 600m-high cliff on the Thai–Cambodian border in disputed territory. It is accessible from Thailand's adjacent **national park** (☎ 0 4581 8021; admission 200B, car fee 30B). To get here take a bus from Surin to Kantharalak (45B, 1½ hours) and then catch a *sŏrng·tǎa·ou* to Phum Saron (35B, 40 minutes); both depart about every half-hour until 3pm. From Phum Saron you'll have to hire a motorcycle taxi to the park.

Larn Chang (☎ 0 4451 2869; 199 Th Siphathai Saman; dishes 35-200B; ☻ dinner) Tasty and low-priced Thai and Isan dishes are served in and around an old wooden house overlooking a surviving stretch of the city moat.

Surin's principal **night market** (Th Krung Si Nai; ☻ 5-10pm) is a block south of the fountain.

GETTING THERE & AWAY
BUS

From Surin's **bus terminal** (☎ 0 4451 1756; Th Jit Bamrung) buses head to/from Si Saket (ordinary 60B, 1½ hours, hourly), Ubon Ratchathani (2nd/1st class 145/215B, three hours, hourly), Roi Et (2nd class 100B, three hours, hourly), Khorat (2nd/ 1st class 120/180B, four hours, every half-hour), Chiang Mai (2nd class/32-seat VIP 700/900B, 14 hours, six daily) and Pattaya (2nd class/32-seat VIP 415/585B, eight hours, hourly).

TRAIN

Surin is on the Bangkok–Ubon line. There are 10 daily services to both places.

GETTING AROUND

Surin is a very convenient city for travellers; virtually everything you'll want or need is within a few blocks of the bus and train stations.

AROUND SURIN

BAN THA KLANG

บ้านตากลาง

To see Surin's elephants during the low season, visit the **Elephant Study Centre** (☎ 0 4414 5050; admission free; ⏰ 9.30am-4.30pm) in Ban Tha Klang, about 50km north of Surin.

There are daily one-hour **talent shows** (donations expected; ⏰ 10am & 2pm, not during the festival) with painting and basketball among the many tusker tricks.

Sŏrng·tăa·ou run from Surin's bus terminal (45B, two hours, hourly) with the last one returning at 4pm. If you're driving, take Rte 214 north for 40km and follow the 'Elephant Village' signs down Rte 3027.

CRAFT VILLAGES

There are many silk-weaving villages in easy striking distance of Surin town. The province's distinct fabrics – principally *pâh hoh,* a tightly woven *mát·mèe* – have a Khmer influence. They use only natural dyes and the most delicate silk fibres from the insides of the cocoons.

Ban Khwao Sinarin and **Ban Chok**, next-door neighbours 18km north of Surin via Rtes 214 and 3036, are known for silk and silver respectively. The silver stand-

out is *ʾbrà keuam,* a Cambodian style of bead brought to Thailand by Ban Chok's ancestors many centuries ago.

UBON RATCHATHANI PROVINCE

UBON RATCHATHANI

อุบลราชธานี

pop 115,000

Located against Mae Nam Mun, Thailand's second-longest river, the southern portions of the city have a sluggish character rarely found in the region's big conurbations. Few cities in Thailand reward aimless wandering as richly as Ubon.

AUSTIN BUSH

Local fisherman

SIGHTS
UBON NATIONAL MUSEUM
พิพิธภัณฑสถานแห่งชาติอุบลราชธานี

Don't miss the informative **Ubon National Museum** (☎ 0 4525 5071; Th Kheuan Thani; admission 100B; ⏰ 9am-4pm Wed-Sun). This is the place to swot up on background information before venturing out int othe wider province.

The museum is on the edge of Thung Si Meuang Park, the centrepiece of which is a huge concrete replica of an elaborate

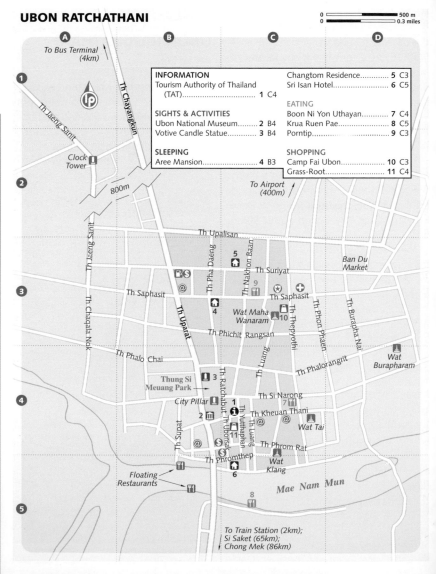

UBON RATCHATHANI

```
0            500 m
0          0.3 miles
```

INFORMATION
Tourism Authority of Thailand
(TAT)................................. 1 C4

SIGHTS & ACTIVITIES
Ubon National Museum......... 2 B4
Votive Candle Statue............. 3 B4

SLEEPING
Aree Mansion....................... 4 B3

Changtom Residence............ 5 C3
Sri Isan Hotel....................... 6 C5

EATING
Boon Ni Yon Uthayan............ 7 C4
Krua Ruen Pae...................... 8 C5
Porntip................................ 9 C3

SHOPPING
Camp Fai Ubon.................... 10 C3
Grass-Root.......................... 11 C4

To Bus Terminal (4km)

Th Jaeng Sanit
Th Chayangkun

Clock Tower

800m

To Airport (400m)

Th Upalisan

Th Pha Daeng
Th Nakhon Baan
Th Suriyat

Ban Du Market

Th Saphasit   Th Saphasit
Th Chagala Nok
Th Uparat

Wat Maha Wanaram
Th Thepyothi
Th Phom Phaen
Th Burapha Nai

Th Phichit Rangsan

Th Phalo Chai
Th Luang
Th Phalorangrit

Wat Burapharam

Thung Si Meuang Park
City Pillar
Th Ratchabut
Th Ubonsak
Th Vutthaphan

Th Si Narong
Th Kheuan Thani

Th Supat
Th Luang
Wat Tai

Th Phromthep
Th Phrom Rat

Wat Klang

Floating Restaurants

Mae Nam Mun

To Train Station (2km);
Si Saket (65km);
Chong Mek (86km)

votive candle representing Ubon's annual Candle Parade.

FESTIVALS
Ubon's famous Candle Parade (Hae Tian) began during the reign of King Rama V when the governor decided the city's rocket festival was too dangerous. The festival is very popular with Thai tourists and the city's hotels are booked out long in advance.

SLEEPING
Aree Mansion (☎ 0 4526 5518; 208-212 Th Pha Daeng; r 250-350B; 🅿 🖳) The clear pick of the pack for shoestring travellers can't hide its age, but it deserves credit for trying.

Changtom Residence (☎ 0 4526 5525; 216 Th Suriyat; r 400B; 🅿 🖳) Not only does this mid-sized place have clean, comfortable rooms, but the friendly English-speaking owner will pick you up for free when you arrive in town.

ourpick **Sri Isan Hotel** (☎ 0 4526 1011; www.sriisanhotel.com; 62 Th Ratchabut; r 650-1400B; 🅿 🖳) The rooms are small and the decor is a little twee (a knitted toilet-roll cover wouldn't be out of place) but standards are high and an orchid comes gratis on every pillow.

EATING
Boon Ni Yon Uthayan (☎ 0 4524 0950; Th Si Narong; per plate 10-15B; 🕑 breakfast & lunch Tue-Sun) Run by the ascetic Sisa Asoka group, this restaurant has an impressive vegetarian buffet under a giant roof.

Porntip (☎ 08 9720 8101; Th Saphasit; dishes 20-100B, ½ chickens 60-80B; 🕑 9am-6pm) This relocated restaurant, formerly Gai Yang Wat Jaeng, is considered by many to be Ubon's premier purveyor of *gài yâhng*, *sôm·đam*, sausages and other Isan food.

ourpick **Krua Ruen Pae** (no roman-script sign; ☎ 0 4532 4342; dishes 40-300B; 🕑 lunch &

Chiang Khan
TOM COCKREM

🔌 IF YOU LIKE...
If you like the Mekong setting of Nong Khai (p214), follow the river road to these towns.

- **Chiang Khan** Traditional timber houses line the streets, with old ladies sitting nattering in their shadows, and the Mekong drifts slowly by. Stop in at Chiang Khan Guesthouse (☎ 0 4282 1691; www.thailandunplugged.com; 282 Th Chai Khong; r 300-400B; 🖳). West of Nong Khai, transfer through Loei.

- **Nakhon Phanom** Once a refuge for Ho Chi Minh, this city has a photogenic view of the Laos mountains across the river. Overnight at iHotel (☎ 0 4254 3355; Th Chayanghoon; r 450-800B; 🅿 🖳). East of Nong Khai, accessible via direct bus.

- **That Phanom** A small speck of place known for its Lao-style stupa. Overnight at Kritsada Rimkhong Resort (☎ 0 4254 0088; 90-93 Th Rimkhong; r 400-600B; 🅿 🖳). East of Nong Khai, accessible via Nakhon Phanom.

dinner) One of several floating restaurants on the Mun River, Krua Ruen Pae serves up tasty Thai and Isan food and a relaxed atmosphere.

SHOPPING

The speciality of Ubon Province is natural-dyed, hand-woven cotton, and you'll find a fantastic assortment of clothing, bags and fabric here. First stop should be **Camp Fai Ubon** (☎ 0 4524 1821; 189 Th Thepyothi; ☺ 8am-5pm), which is signed as Peaceland. Smaller, but also good is **Grass-Root** (☎ 0 4524 1272; 87 Th Yutthaphan; ☺ 9am-5pm).

GETTING THERE & AWAY

THAI (www.thaiairways.com) has two daily flights to/from Bangkok (one way 2020B); **Air Asia** (www.airasia.com) has one (1400B).

Ubon's **bus terminal** (☎ 0 4531 6085) is north of the town; take *sŏrng·tǎa·ou* 2, 3 or 10 to the centre. The **train station** (☎ 0 4532 1588) is in Warin Chamrap; take *sŏrng·tǎa·ou* 2 from Ubon.

NONG KHAI PROVINCE
NONG KHAI

หนองคาย

pop 61,500

Lady Luck certainly smiles on the location, spread out along the edge of the Mekong River. Seduced by its dreamy pink sunsets, sluggish pace of life and surrounding attractions, many who mean to stay a day end up bedding down for many more.

SIGHTS

SALA KAEW KU SCULPTURE PARK

ศาลาแก้วกู่

One of Thailand's most enigmatic attractions, **Sala Kaew Ku Sculpture Park** (admission 20B; ☺ 8am-6pm) is a surreal, sculptural journey into the mind of a mystic shaman. Built over a period of 20 years by Luang Pu Boun Leua Sourirat, who died in 1996, the park features a weird and wonderful array of gigantic sculptures ablaze with Hindu-Buddhist imagery.

The park is a smorgasbord of bizarre cement statues of Shiva, Vishnu, Buddha and every other Hindu and Buddhist deity imaginable (as well as numerous secular figures), all supposedly cast by unskilled artists under Luang Pu's direction.

SLEEPING

ourpick Mut Mee Garden Guesthouse (☎ 0 4246 0717; www.mutmee.com; off Th Kaew

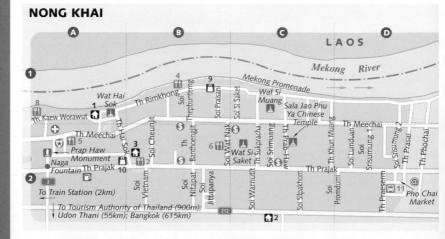

NONG KHAI

Worawut; dm 100B, r 140-750B; 🗷) Occupying a sleepy stretch of the Mekong, Nong Khai's budget old-timer has a garden so relaxing it's intoxicating, and most nights it's packed with travellers. A huge variety of rooms are clustered around a thatched-roof restaurant where the owner, Julian, holds court with his grip of local legend and his passion for all things Isan.

Pantawee Hotel (☎ 0 4241 1568; www .pantawee.com; 1049 Th Hai Sok; s 600-900B, d 700-1000B, q 1400-2200B; 🗷 💻 🗷) The efficiently run Pantawee is almost a village unto itself, with various lodging blocks plus a spa, travel agency and 24-hour restaurant.

Nong Khai Grand (☎ 0 4242 0033; www .nongkhaigrand.com; Hwy 212; r 1290-1700B, ste 2700-3700B; 🗷 💻 🗷) A big hit with passing suits, 'executive' standards are maintained throughout.

EATING

For quick, colourful eats swing by the **Hospital Food Court** (no roman-script sign; Th Meechai; 🗷 breakfast, lunch & dinner) where about a dozen cooks whip up the stand-

EATING ISAN

Isan's culinary creations are a blend of Lao and Thai cooking styles that make use of local ingredients. The holy trinity of northeastern cuisine – *gài yâhng* (grilled chicken), *sôm·đam* (papaya salad) and *kôw něe·o* (sticky rice) – is integral to the culture.

ards, or visit the **night market** (Th Prajak; 🗷 4-11pm) between Soi Cheunjit and Th Hai Sok. During the day, grilled fish reigns supreme at the lunch-only **riverside restaurants** (Th Rimkhong) tucked behind Tha Sadet Market.

Khrua Sukapap Kwan Im (☎ 0 4246 0184; Soi Wat Nak; dishes 30B; 🗷 breakfast & lunch) The food is Thai and Chinese standards (from a buffet counter and an English-language menu) plus some excellent juices.

Nung-Len Coffee Bar (☎ 08 3662 7686; 1801/2 Th Kaew Worawut; dishes 35-180B; 🗷 breakfast, lunch & dinner) One of the friendliest places in Nong Khai, this petite place has good java and juices plus an eclectic

Th Kawnkan Uhit

Th Prajak

To Sala Kaew Ku Sculpture Park (2km);
Phon Phisai (45km);
Nakhon Phanom (315km)

0   500 m
0   0.3 miles

GREAT BALLS OF FIRE

Since 1983 (or for ages, depending on who you ask), the sighting of the *bâng fai pá·yah·nâhk* (loosely translated, 'naga fireballs') has been an annual event. Sometime in the early evening, at the end of the Buddhist Rains Retreat (October), which coincides with the 15th waxing moon of the 11th lunar month, small reddish balls of fire shoot from the Mekong River just after dusk and float a hundred or so metres into the air before vanishing without a trace.

Every year some 40,000 people invade little Phon Phisai, the locus of fireball watching, and thousands more converge on dozens of other riverside spots between Sangkhom and Khong Jiam in hopes of sightings. Several hotels run their own buses where you'll get a guaranteed seat, plus Mut Mee Garden Guesthouse sails its boat there and back (2500B, including lunch and dinner).

The fireball experience is much more than just watching a few small lights rise from the river; it's mostly about watching Thais watching a few small lights rise from the river.

menu of Thai and *fa·ràng* food, and even a few fusions of the two, like spaghetti fried chilli with chicken.

Daeng Namnuang (☎ 0 4241 1961; 526 Th Rimkhong; dishes 35-180B; ☻ breakfast, lunch & dinner) This Vietnamese place has grown into an Isan institution and hordes of out-of-towners head home with car boots and carry-on bags (there's an outlet at Udon Thani's airport) stuffed with Vietnamese *năam neu·ang* (pork spring rolls).

SHOPPING

Tha Sadet Market (Th Rimkhong) This huge market runs for most of the day and offers the usual mix of dried food, electronic items, souvenirs and assorted bric-a-brac, most of it imported from Laos and China.

Village Weaver Handicrafts (☎ 0 4242 2652; 1020 Th Prajak; ☻ 8am-6pm) This place sells high-quality, hand-woven fabrics and clothing (ready-made or made-to-order) to fund development projects around Nong Khai. The *mát·mèe* cotton is particularly good here.

GETTING THERE & AWAY
BUS
Nong Khai's bus terminal (☎ 0 4241 1612) is located just off Th Prajak, about 1.5km from the main pack of riverside guesthouses.

TRAIN
Express trains leave Bangkok daily at 6.30pm and 8pm, arriving in Nong Khai at 5.05am and 8.25am respectively. Going the other way, the express train services depart from Nong Khai at 6am (arriving at 5.10pm) and 6.20pm (arriving at 6.25am). The fares range from 1320B for a 1st-class sleeper cabin to 255/390B for a 3rd-/2nd-class seat. There's also one rapid train (215/350B 3rd/2nd class) leaving Bangkok at 6.40pm (arriving at 7.35am) and leaving for Bangkok at 7.15pm (arriving at 8am).

KIMBERLEY COOLE

Fire show on the beach, Ko Samet (p229)

SOUTHEASTERN THAILAND

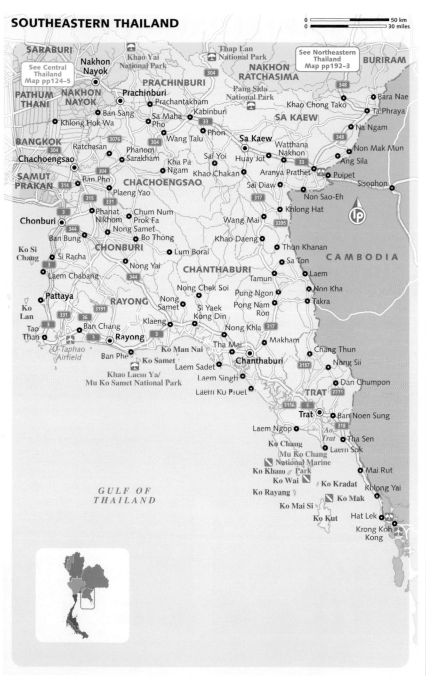

0 ━━━━━ 50 km
0 ━━━━━ 30 miles

SARABURI

Khao Yai National Park

Thap Lan National Park

See Central Thailand Map pp124–5

See Northeastern Thailand Map pp192–3

BURIRAM

Nakhon Nayok

304

NAKHON RATCHASIMA

PRACHINBURI

348

PATHUM THANI

NAKHON NAYOK

Prachinburi

Prachantakham

Pang Sida National Park

Bara Nae

Khao Chong Tako

Ta Phraya

Ban Sang

Kabinburi

SA KAEW

Sa Maha Pho

33

Na Ngam

Khlong Hok Wa

348

BANGKOK

3076

304

Wang Talu

Phon

Sa Kaew

Watthana Nakhon

Non Mak Mun

Ratchasan

Phanom Sarakham

Sai Yoi

Huay Jot

33

Ang Sila

Chachoengsao

304

Kha Pa Ngam

Khao Chakan

Aranya Prathet

Poipet

Sisophon

SAMUT PRAKAN

314

Ban Pho

CHACHOENGSAO

Sai Diaw

Non Sao-Eh

315

Plaeng Yao

317

Khlong Hat

331

Phanat Nikhom

Chum Num Prok Fa

Wang Mai

3395

Chonburi

3

344

Nong Samet

Khao Daeng

Thun Khanan

Ban Bung

Bo Thong

CAMBODIA

CHONBURI

Lum Borai

Khao Daeng

Sa Ton

Ko Si Chang

Si Racha

Nong Yai

CHANTHABURI

Laem

3

344

Tamun

Laem Chabang

Nong Chek Soi

Non Kha

RAYONG

Nong Samet

Pung Ngon

Takra

Pattaya

3191

Si Yaek Kong Din

Pong Nam Ron

Ko Lan

331

36

Ban Chang

Klaeng

Nong Khla

317

Tao Than

3

Rayong

3

Makham

Chang Thun

U-Taphao Airfield

Ban Phe

Ko Man Nai

Tha Mai

Nong Sii

3157

Ko Samet

Chanthaburi

Laem Sadet

Dan Chumpon

Khao Laem Ya/ Mu Ko Samet National Park

Laem Singh

TRAT

2371

Laem Ko Proet

3156

3

Trat

Ban Noen Sung

Laem Ngop

Ao Trat

318

Tha Sen

GULF OF THAILAND

Ko Chang

Laem Sok

Mu Ko Chang National Marine Park

Ko Kham

Mai Rut

Ko Wai

Ko Kradat

Khlong Yai

Ko Rayang

Ko Mak

Ko Mai Si

Ko Kut

Hat Lek

Krong Koh Kong

SOUTHEASTERN THAILAND

SE THAILAND HIGHLIGHTS

SE THAILAND HIGHLIGHTS

1 KO CHANG

BY LEK MEELAP, CO-OWNER OF JUNGLE WAY

Ko Chang has a thick jungle right next to the beach – that's why people come. It is easy to get to and is still undeveloped in places. I grew up here and remember the days before electricity and paved roads. Those were carefree days when we knew about real life.

⬎ LEK'S DON'T MISS LIST

❶ JUNGLE TREKKING

My company leads treks into the jungle around my home village, Ban Khlong Son. It's filled with pristine rainforest, orchids, lizards, some monkeys, snakes and a lot of birds. Ban Kwan Chang Elephant Camp (p234) is next door to my house, if trekkers want to try elephant riding too.

❷ VILLAGE LIFE

In Ban Khlong Son and in Salak Phet you can see local Ko Chang life. In a few shops they still sell local *nám prík gà·bì* (a thick shrimp paste) and the dessert *lôrt chông gà·tí* (green rice noodles in coconut milk). Both are delicious on Ko Chang. Also nearby is Koh Chang Animal Project (www.kohchang animalfoundation.org), a veterinary clinic that helps the island's pets

Clockwise from top: Snorkelling, Ko Wai (p234); Hat Sai Khao, Ko Chang (p233); Cycling, Ko Chang (p233); Ban Kwan Chang Elephant Camp (p234), Ko Chang

CLOCKWISE FROM TOP: JOHN BORTHWICK; CRAIG PERSHOUSE; JOHN BORTHWICK; DAVID GREEDY

❸ SNORKELLING

I also work for a company doing snorkelling tours to **Ko Wai** (p234), which is my favourite place. The coral is in pretty good shape and there are a lot of fish. Ko Wai is also very quiet and isn't too busy.

❹ BEACHES

Hat Yao (Long Beach; p236) on the east coast is a chill place to go when you want to feel private. It is far away from everything and isn't like Hat Sai Khao (White Sands Beach), which is like a city with all the people and the noise.

⬇ **THINGS YOU NEED TO KNOW**

Top Tip Stop into Jungle Way Restaurant, where Lek's mum is the cook **Avoid** Long weekends and public holidays: they're popular for Thai beach tourists who like to relax with late-night karaoke parties

SE THAILAND HIGHLIGHTS

⤜ WEEKEND ON KO SAMET

Just a few hours west of Bangkok, **Ko Samet** (p229) is a blissful break from the urban tangle, with nary a túk-túk or skyscraper in sight. Float in the warm amniotic water or follow the footpaths over rocky headlands to the next picturesque cove. Dine under the stars at one of the numerous beachside barbecues and tap into the old backpacker tradition of watching movies in an open-air restaurant.

⤜ TACKLE THE JUNGLE ON KO CHANG

The mountainous interior of **Ko Chang** (p233) is an undisturbed landscape of thick vegetation, silvery waterfalls and challenging terrain. Get a better view of the forest canopy aboard an elephant, Thailand's original 4x4 machines. Or hire a guide to lead you along the forest floor to spectacular coastal viewpoints. Afterwards, cool off in one of the waterfalls' refreshing plunge pools.

4

↘ KICK BACK ON KO MAK

Do a whole lot of nothing on unassuming Ko Mak (p237). Soak up the sun on the low-key beaches, wander around the fishing villages, become a sunset connoisseur and enjoy the nightly insect serenade. Sup and sip at modest thatched-roof huts as everyone around seems to be seconds away from a nap.

5

↘ DETOUR ON THE MAINLAND

En route to your island idyll, make a detour to one of Southeastern Thailand's mainland towns for a glimpse into a workaday region. Schedule a visit to Chanthaburi (p232) and its weekend gem market; Si Racha (p228), famous for seafood and its namesake spicy sauce; and Trat (p233), filled with bustling provincial markets.

6

↘ MEDITATE ON KO SI CHANG

Hardly a blip on the tourist radar, Ko Si Chang (p228) has a little of everything. There are temples, a meditation retreat, cave shrines, a Thai-Chinese fishing village, small sandy beaches, kayak tours of mangrove forests and bike routes around the island. There's also a local restaurant that helps tourists get turned on to Si Chang.

2 RICHARD NEBESKY; 3 SARA-JANE CLELAND; 4 WOODS WHEATCROFT; 5 & 6 RICHARD NEBESKY

2 Hat Sai Kaew (p229), Ko Samet; 3 Hiking (p234), Ko Chang; 4 Swinging around, Ko Mak (p237); 5 Sunset over Trat (p233); 6 Fishing boats, Ko Si Chang (p228)

SOUTHEASTERN THAILAND'S BEST...

⬐ PLACES FOR R&R

- **Hat Sai Khao** (p234) Ko Chang's widest beach is perfect for bar-hopping and sunbathing.
- **Ao Phutsa** (p230) This Ko Samet bay offers a break from sunbathers and hawkers.
- **Bailan Herbal Sauna** (p234) Sweat without lifting a muscle on Ko Chang.

⬐ PLACES TO SPOT WILDLIFE

- **Rayong Turtle Conservation Centre** (p230) Learn about Thailand's marine turtles at this protected breeding site.
- **Salak Kok Kayak Station** (p234) Paddle through Ko Chang's critter-filled mangrove bay.
- **Ban Kwan Chang Elephant Camp** (p234) Feed, bathe and ride aboard elephants on Ko Chang.

⬐ PLACES TO DIVE & SNORKEL

- **Ko Chang** (p233) Dive shops and coral aplenty.
- **Ko Kut** (p237) Gin-clear waters and quiet coves for snorkelling.
- **Ko Mak** (p237) Laid-back diving and living.

⬐ PLACES TO SUP ON SEAFOOD

- **Si Racha** (p228) Bangkok Thais often pit-stop here for a seafood feast.
- **Ban Bang Bao** (p236) Dine in Ko Chang's former fishing village.

LEFT: DAVID GREEDY; RIGHT: JOHN HAY

Left: Mahout and elephant, Ban Kwan Chang Elephant Camp (p234), Ko Chang; Right: Tempt your tastebuds

THINGS YOU NEED TO KNOW

◥ VITAL STATISTICS

- **Population** 3.6 million
- **Best time to visit** November to May

◥ TOWNS IN A NUTSHELL

- **Si Racha** Seaside town known for seafood and spicy sauce.
- **Ko Si Chang** Fishing-village island filled with temples.
- **Ko Samet** Bangkok's quick and easy beach playground.
- **Chanthaburi** Small town, big gem market.
- **Trat** Transit town to Ko Chang.
- **Ko Chang** Beach retreat for mod-cons and outdoor sports.

◥ ADVANCE PLANNING

- **One month before** Book your accommodation.
- **One week before** Book your dive trip.
- **One day before** Buy bus tickets directly from Bangkok's Eastern bus station (p93).

◥ RESOURCES

- **Tourism Authority of Thailand** (TAT; ☎ 0 3959 7259; tattrat@tat.or.th; 100 Mu 1, Th Trat-Laem Ngop; ⊙ 8.30am-4.30pm) Near the pier in Laem Ngop.
- **Koh Si Chang** (www.koh-sichang .com) An excellent source of local information.

◥ EMERGENCY NUMBERS

- **Fire** (☎ 199)
- **Police/Emergency** (☎ 191)
- **Tourist police** (☎ 1155; ⊙ 24hr)

◥ GETTING AROUND

- **Boat** Frequent ferries from Ban Phe to Ko Samet and Trat-Laem Ngop to Ko Chang; less frequent in wet season (June to October).
- **Bus** Best way to get from Bangkok to mainland towns.
- **Motorcycle** Good self-touring option on Ko Samet but not on hilly Ko Chang.
- **Sörng·tǎa·ou** Small pick-up trucks that act as shared taxis on the islands and public buses on the mainland.
- **Túk-túk** Chartered vehicles for trips within towns; remember to bargain.

◥ BE FOREWARNED

- **Boat tickets** Buy tickets directly from ticket offices, not from touts.
- **National Parks** Keep your national park admission receipt.
- **Wet season** Some parts of Ko Chang and nearby islands close down in the wet season.
- **Topless sunbathing & nudity** Are illegal in Thailand's national marine parks.

SOUTHEASTERN THAILAND ITINERARIES

QUICK BEACH BREAK Three Days

Southeastern Thailand doesn't have the beaches that rank Thailand as a global vacation spot but it is an excellent area if you need a quick shot of coastal R&R.

Take a slight detour to **(1) Ko Si Chang** (p228), off the coast of Si Racha, for a day's sightseeing tour. It's a favourite weekend spot for locals, and part of the charm is seeing Thais at leisure: picnicking in the shade, swimming fully clothed, and climbing the steep temple steps. Talk to the owners of Pan & David Restaurant if you want to overnight.

Bangkok's backyard swimming hole, **(2) Ko Samet** (p229), is part of a national marine park and is relatively rustic and undeveloped compared to the famous Thai beach resorts. There are no high-rises or busy roads to detract from two days' worth of watching the waves roll in.

A SPORTY BEACH Five Days

If you get bored lazing in a beach chair, then the Ko Chang archipelago is calling. Thailand's most 'sporty' beach is a national marine park that has 'lollipop' dives (easy and colourful underwater spectacles), jungle treks and kayaking.

From Bangkok, catch a bus to **(1) Trat** (p233), a typical provincial town with bustling markets and buzzing motorcycles. Without much effort, you'll be herded on to the *sŏrng·tăa·ou* heading to the piers with a ferry service to Ko Chang. Resist the escape route and hunt down the town's famous herbal cure-all (known as *nám·man lĕu·ang*), an indispensable Trat souvenir.

(2) Ko Chang (p233) has a full menu of marine and jungle activities. Spend a day or two exploring the island's rainforest-covered interior and then strap on a tank and trace the underwater contours. Or hang out in Hat Sai Khao at the convivial beachfront pubs.

If you need more resting than recreation, hop across to **(3) Ko Kut** (p237), to enjoy quiet star-gazing nights.

SURF & TURF One Week

Past the industrial suburbs of Bangkok, the southeast becomes a pleasant patchwork of fruit orchards, coastal fishing villages and laid-back provincial towns. Without much delay, you can hop off the beach-bound trail to experience ordinary Thai life and still have enough time to frolic in the ocean.

(1) Chanthaburi (p232) is a pretty piece of old Siam with old teak shophouses and Indochinese architecture, a legacy of a brief French

rule in the 19th century and successive waves of Vietnamese refugees in the 20th century. The town's best spectacle is the gem market that unfolds on Th Si Chan on Friday and Saturday. You can stroll along the river, eat at simple restaurants and shop at the markets for locally grown rambutans and mangosteens.

Trot through (2) Trat (p233), the transfer point to the piers serving Ko Chang ferries. Once on (3) Ko Chang (p233), escape to the remote east coast for a bit of solitude.

Arrange an overnight trip to the nearby and less-developed island of (4) Ko Mak (p237), where you can cycle around a buffet of beaches and listen to the wind passing through the coconut palms.

DISCOVER SOUTHEASTERN THAILAND

The razzle-dazzle of jewels lures dealers to Chanthaburi's gem markets. Equally alluring are Ko Samet's aquamarine waters and white beaches, which once earned it a name that translates to 'Vast Jewel Isle', and on weekends you can watch – or join – Bangkok locals as they make a different kind of trade: weekday anxieties for weekend amusements.

More subdued but no less attractive are the region's subtle hints of old Siam: teak houses and pier buildings scattered along the coast. Si Racha's pier-front looks across the cargo ship–studded water to Ko Si Chang, a quiet island with hillside temples often overlooked by weekend Bangkok escapees. Trat Province, with its riverside ambience and excellent budget lodgings, invites backpackers en route to Mu Ko Chang and Cambodia to ease off the travellers' accelerator.

CHONBURI PROVINCE

SI RACHA

ศรีราชา

pop 141,400

Si Racha is famous for seafood, and a sprawling night market kicks off around 5pm on Th Si Racha Nakorn 3.

Moom Aroy (dishes 100-350B; ☽ lunch & dinner), across from Samitivej Hospital, means 'delicious corner', and we have to agree. Turn left at the hospital and look for the tank with the 2m fish out front.

Perched on the Ko Loi jetty, the humble **seafood stalls** (dishes 40-160B; ☽ lunch & dinner) specialise in fresh seafood. There is no English menu but the food is all good.

GETTING THERE & AROUND

Frequent buses travelling to Si Racha depart from both Bangkok's Eastern (Ekamai) and Northern (Mo Chit) Stations from 5am to 9pm (ordinary/air-con 73/94B, 1¾ hours).

KO SI CHANG

เกาะสีชัง

pop 4500

With its fishing-village atmosphere, gentle hills studded with Chinese and Thai temples, and beachfront reminders of a stately royal palace, Ko Si Chang is practically the anti-Thai island. No sweeping sandy beaches, no coconut groves – and no hoards of tourists.

SIGHTS & ACTIVITIES

The Buddhist **Tham Yai Phrik Vipassana Monastery** (☎ 0 3821 6104; ☽ dawn to dusk) is built around several meditation caves running into the island's central limestone ridge, and offers fine views from its hilltop *chedi* (stupa).

Sea kayaks are available for rent (150B per hour) on Hat Tham Phang. Recharge at the **Si Chang Healing House** (☎ 0 3821 6467; 167 Mu 3 Th Makham Thaew; ☽ 8am-6pm Thu-Tue), which offers massage and beauty treatments (400B to 800B) in a garden labyrinth opposite Pan & David Restaurant.

EATING

our pick Pan & David Restaurant (☎ 0 3821 6629; 167 Mu 3 Th Makham Thaew; dishes 40-260B; breakfast, lunch & dinner Wed-Mon) With free-range chicken, homemade ice cream (we thoroughly enjoyed the maple-pecan), French-pressed coffee, a wine list and excellent Thai dishes, the menu can't go wrong. Phoning ahead for a booking is recommended.

GETTING THERE & AROUND

Boats to Ko Si Chang leave hourly from 7am to 8pm from the Ko Loi jetty in Si Racha (60B).

Ko Si Chang's túk-túks are big and bad and they'll take you anywhere for 40B to 60B. Island tours are available for around 300B: you might need to haggle.

BAN PHE

บ้านเพ

The little port of Ban Phe is only on the map thanks to its role as a launch pad for nearby Ko Samet.

There are two air-conditioned bus stations in Ban Phe that have buses to Bangkok's Eastern (Ekamai) bus terminal. Fifty metres west of Ban Phe pier, buses depart four times a day starting in the afternoon at 12.30pm; they leave Bangkok as many times in the mornings beginning at 7am (138B, 2½ hours).

For information about boats to and from Ko Samet see p232.

RAYONG PROVINCE

KO SAMET

เกาะเสม็ด

What happens when an island blessed with 14 white-sand beaches is just half a day's travel from a Southeast Asian super city?

If it's pretty Ko Samet it becomes a weekend and holiday getaway for the good people of Bangkok – locals and ex-pats alike.

SLEEPING

EAST COAST

Known as 'Diamond Sand', Hat Sai Kaew is the island's biggest and busiest beach.

FRANK CARTER

Ko Samet

It's a favourite for Thais from Bangkok, and at the weekends expect a cacophony of jet skis and karaoke.

Saikaew Villa (☎ 0 3864 4144; r 500-1550B; 🏊) Big rooms or small rooms, fan or air-conditioning, Saikaew Villa conjures up a wide range of accommodation options amid a manicured space that (almost) goes too far with the holiday-camp atmosphere.

RICHARD NEBESKY

Hat Sai Kaew (p229), Ko Samet

↘ IF YOU LIKE...

If you like **Ko Samet's beaches** and want to learn more about the marine environment, check out these activities:

- **Rayong Turtle Conservation Centre** (☎ 0 3861 6096; Ko Man Nai; ☾ 9am-4pm) Visit this sea turtle breeding site on a daytrip from Ko Samet with **Jimmy's Tours** (☎ 08 9832 1627). You can also volunteer at the centre through **Starfish Ventures** (www.starfish ventures.co.uk).
- **Diving & Snorkelling** Ko Chang's surrounding marine park shelters several protected and easy dives. Contact **Scuba Evolution** (☎ 08 7926 4973; www .scuba-evolution.com) on Ko Chang or **Kok Mak Divers** (☎ 08 3297 7724) on Ko Mak for more information.

AO HIN KHOK

This is the island's traditional backpacker hub, and while the ambience is slowly moving towards the upmarket, there's still loads of energy from independent travellers to make it a fun spot – especially after dark.

Jep's Bungalows (☎ 0 3864 4112; www.jepbungalow.com; r 600-2600B; 🏊 🖥) Spearheading the evolution of Ao Hin Khok, the long-established Jep's offers rooms ranging from dingy fan bungalows to air-con rooms with satellite TV.

AO PHAI

Around the next headland Ao Phai is another shallow bay with a wide beach, but it can get crowded during the day.

Samed Villa (☎ 0 3864 4094; www.samed villa.com; r 1800-4000B; 🏊) A Swiss-run place, and it shows. Everything is spick and span, and the architects allocated a substantial budget to make the inside of some of the rooms as flash as the outside.

AO PHUTSA

Also known as Ao Tub Tim, this small and secluded beach is popular with return travellers and Bangkok weekenders.

Tubtim Resort (☎ 0 3864 4025; www .tubtimresort.com; r 600-1500B; 🏊) A range of bungalows, from fan-cooled to fab, fill a garden that's edging slowly towards jungle status.

AO WONG DEUAN

This crescent-shaped bay has good night-life and a chilled after-dark vibe, but your daytime soundtrack may be jet skis and speedboats.

Blue Sky (☎ 08 1509 0547; r 600-800B; 🏊) One of the last budget spots on Ao Wong Deuan, Blue Sky has simple bungalows set on a rocky headland. The restaurant does tasty things with seafood.

Dining on Ko Samet

FRANK CARTER

Vongduern Villa (☎ 0 3864 4260; www
.vongduernvilla.com; r 1200-3000B; ❄)
Sprawling along the bay's southern edge,
Vongduern's bungalows are either near
the beach or higher on the clifftop for
better views.

AO THIAN
Better known by its English name,
Candlelight Beach, Ao Thian has stretches
of sand with rocky outcrops.

Tonhard Bungalow (☎ 08 1435 8900;
r 700-1500B; ❄) On a wooded and sandy
part of the beach, this place is quiet,
friendly and somewhat private. Most
bungalows differ from each other.

Viking Holiday Resort (☎ 0 3864 4353; r
from 2000B; ❄) Rooms are large and luxurious, and there's only nine of them so book
ahead.

AO WAI
Lovely Ao Wai is about 1km from Ao
Thian, but can be reached from Ban Phe
by chartered speedboat (1500B for two
people).

Samet Ville Resort (☎ 0 3865 1682; www
.sametvilleresort.com; r incl breakfast 2000-5300B;
❄) Under a forest canopy, it's a case of
'spot the sky' at the very secluded Samet
Ville.

EATING & DRINKING
Look for nightly beach barbecues, particularly along Ao Hin Khok and Ao Phai.

Silver Sand Bar (☎ 0 6530 2417; Ao Phai;
dishes 60-180B; ❄ breakfast, lunch & dinner) As
well as a regular menu, Silver Sand offers fresh crêpes, a juice bar and nightly
movies. Once the movies end, the action
progresses (regresses?) to cocktail buck-
ets and fire shows on the beach.

Baywatch Bar (☎ 08 1826 7834; Ao Wong
Deuan; kebabs 190-290B; ❄ breakfast, lunch & dinner) The cocktails are strong and it's a fun
evening crowd.

Tok's Little Bar (☎ 0 3864 4072; Ao Hin
Khok) With sticks-and-straw decor, a few
locals who fancy themselves as ladykillers,
and nightly drinking games, you won't
mistake this place for a sophisticated
cocktail bar.

FRANK CARTER

Beachside accommodation, Ko Chang

GETTING THERE & AWAY

Ferries (one way/return 50/100B, 40 minutes) depart hourly between 7am and 5pm from Ban Phe's Saphan Nuan Tip pier – opposite the 7-Eleven, where the buses and *sŏrng·tăa·ou* stop.

From Ban Phe, two scheduled ferries (9am and noon) also make the run to Ao Wong Deuan (one way/return 70/110B, one hour).

GETTING AROUND

A network of dirt roads connects the western beach and most of the southern bays, while walking trails snake over the boulders and headlands that separate beaches all the way to the southernmost tip.

CHANTHABURI PROVINCE
CHANTHABURI

จันทบุรี

pop 86,400

Buyers from across Southeast Asia come to Chanthaburi to deal in sapphires and rubies, and from Friday to Sunday the city is bustling and cosmopolitan.

Peering through magnifying glasses in **gem shops** along Th Si Chan and Th Thetsaban 4, the city's gem dealers are Chanthaburi's living, breathing highlight. This is strictly a spectator sport – great deals can be clinched by the savvy, but amateurs are likely to go home with a bagful of worthless rocks. You're better off filling up at the food stalls surrounding the commercial bustle; there'll be more guarantee of satisfaction.

EATING

To try the famous Chanthaburi *gŏo·ay dĕe·o sên jan* (noodles), head for the Chinese-Vietnamese part of town along Mae Nam Chanthaburi where you'll see variations on the basic rice-noodle theme, including delicious crab with fried noodles.

GETTING THERE & AWAY

Buses operate between Chanthaburi and Bangkok's Eastern (Ekamai) bus station

(200B, 4½ hours) every half hour from 4.30am to 11:30pm. If you're heading to Ko Chang, you can ride all the way to Laem Ngop.

Motorbike taxis around town cost 20B to 30B.

TRAT PROVINCE

TRAT

ตราด

pop 20,100

For too many travellers, all they see of Trat is the shiny new bus station before they are shunted onto a *sŏrng·tăa·ou* to the Ko Chang ferry.

Trat is overpopulated with markets. The **indoor market** beneath the municipal shopping centre off Th Sukhumvit, the old day market off Th Tat Mai, and another nearby day market are all worth a look. The latter becomes an excellent **night market** in the evening.

Though it's no longer on the corner since the original building burned down in 2008, the hip artist/owner of **Cool Corner** (☎ 08 4159 2030; 49-51 Th Thana Charoen; dishes 50-150B; ☙ breakfast, lunch & dinner) still serves

up great vibes, phat beats and darn good mango lassies.

GETTING THERE & AWAY

Bangkok Airways (☎ Trat Airport 0 3952 5767, in Bangkok 0 2265 5555; www.bangkokair .com) flies three times a day to and from Trat and Bangkok (one way/return 2575/5150B).

Note that most Mo Chit buses also stop at Bangkok's Suvarnabhumi Airport, so if you're leaving Thailand you don't need to double back to Bangkok.

Sŏrng·tăa·ou for Laem Ngop and Centrepoint Pier (40B to 60B) leave Trat from a stand on Th Sukhumvit, in front of the pharmacy (don't get confused with the ones a block north near the market – you'll end up chartering your own), and also from the bus station.

Laem Ngop is the jumping-off point for Ko Chang.

KO CHANG

อุทยานแห่งชาติเกาะช้าง

With steep, jungle covered peaks erupting from the sea and ringed with swirls of white-sand beaches, verdant Ko Chang

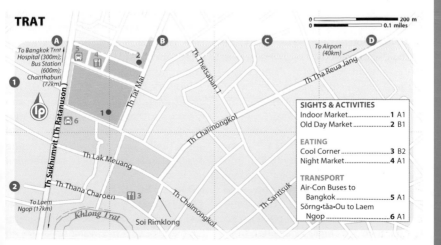

TRAT

To Bangkok Trat Hospital (300m); Bus Station (600m); Chanthaburi (72km)

To Airport (40km)

Th Tat Mai

Th Thetsaban 1

Th Tha Reua Jang

Th Chaimongkol

Th Sukhumvit (Th Ratanuson)

Th Lak Meuang

Th Thana Charoen

Th Chaimongkol

Th Santisuk

To Laem Ngop (17km)

Khlong Trat

Soi Rimklong

0 ——— 200 m
0 ——— 0.1 miles

SIGHTS & ACTIVITIES	
Indoor Market	1 A1
Old Day Market	2 B1

EATING	
Cool Corner	3 B2
Night Market	4 A1

TRANSPORT	
Air-Con Buses to Bangkok	5 A1
Sŏrng·tăa·Ou to Laem Ngop	6 A1

is in many ways the ideal tropical island. Thus, if your time on other Thai islands has included just a few too many days lying on the beach, on Ko Chang you can get nicely active and brush off any holiday cobwebs.

ACTIVITIES
DIVING & SNORKELLING
Southwest of Ao Salak Phet, reef-fringed **Ko Wai** features a good variety of colourful hard and soft corals at depths of 6m to 15m.

By far the best diving, however, is around **Ko Rang**. Protected from fishing by its marine-park status, this place has some of the most pristine coral in Thailand.

ELEPHANT TREKKING
There are several elephant camps on Ko Chang where you can get up close and personal with former working elephants. Of these, the award-winning (2007 TAT eco-awards for community involvement) **Ban Kwan Chang Elephant Camp** (☎ 08 1919 3995; changtone@yahoo.com; ⏰ 8.30am-5pm), near Ban Khlong Son, is the best option.

HIKING
A combination of steep terrain and year-round streams creates a wealth of scenic waterfalls on Ko Chang. The ranger stations around the island aren't very useful for solo trekkers, but you can arrange guides at **Evolution Tour** (☎ 0 3955 7078; www.evolutiontour.com; Khlong Prao). Lek from **Jungle Way** (☎ 08 9223 4795; www.jungleway.com) runs one-day (800B) and two-day (950B) treks into the island's interior. **Salak Phet Kayak Station** (☎ 08 7834 9489) guides overnight treks (one night 1500B) to the highest point on Ko Chang, the 744m Khao Salak Phet, from

where it's possible to view both sunrise and sunset.

KAYAKING
The **Salak Kok Kayak Station** (☎ 08 1919 3995; Ban Salak Kok), in a traditional stilt village in the island's southeast, hires kayaks for viewing the mangrove-forested bay.

OTHER ACTIVITIES
Bailan Herbal Sauna (☎ 08 6252 4744; Ban Bailan; ⏰ 4-8pm) has a round earthen sauna set amid lush greenery where you can get healthy with different herbal concoctions for 200B.

SLEEPING
HAT SAI KHAO
The long beach at Hat Sai Khao is not the island's best, but a wide range of eating and sleeping options, and a lively nightlife keep it popular.

Rock Sand Beach Resort (☎ 0 8712 0044; r 400-1500B; ❄) Rock Sand takes budget accommodation up a notch. Simple fan bungalows share bathrooms, while the highest-priced air-con rooms look out over the sea.

HAT KAI MOOK
Laid-back Hat Kai Mook (Pearl Beach) is a quieter alternative to Hat Sai Khao and features mostly midrange accommodation.

Remark Cottage (☎ 0 3955 1261; www.remarkcottage.com; r 2000-3500B; ❄) An overgrown garden conceals 15 Balinese-style bungalows that look simple at first, but are actually accented with interesting design details.

AO KHLONG PRAO
our pick **Blue Lagoon Resort** (☎ 08 1940 0649; r 600-1000B; ❄) Whitewashed bungalows with private decks and softly striped

curtains sit right above a calm lagoon, and further back two-story air-con bungalows stand in a shady grove. A wooden walkway leads to the beach and there's even a hand-pulled raft across the water.

HAT KAIBAE

South of the lagoon, Hat Kaibae is an expanding scene of midrange places and former backpacker spots moving upmarket.

Garden Resort (☎ 03955 7260; www.garden resortkohchang.com; r 2200B; 🖾 🖳 🖭) In a quiet location off the busy main road, Garden Resort has individually decorated bungalows, in-room internet access and arty touches such as bamboo piping in the sinks and showers.

HAT THA NAM (LONELY BEACH) & BAILAN BAY

South from Hat Kaibae is Hat Tha Nam – more commonly known as Lonely Beach. If you're looking for peace and quiet you're in the wrong place. Just south, Bailan Bay is still nicely low-key.

Magic Garden (☎ 08 3756 8827; www .magicgardenresort.com; Hat Tha Nam; r 500-750B; 🖳) The Magic Garden's not for everyone, but this place is perfect for sociable 21st-century neo-hippies. Two-story round bungalows resemble tree houses; the smaller huts are your basic backpacker model.

Mangrove (☎ 08 1949 7888; Bailan Bay; r 1000B) Cascading down a hill to a private beach and an architecturally designed restaurant, the bungalows are round and spacious, with skylights and accordion doors that open to the views.

Warapura Resort (☎ 08 9122 9888; Hat Tha Nam; r incl breakfast 1500-3500B; 🖾 🖭) Bringing Hat Tha Nam up a notch (but on a contained scale), these sculpted concrete bungalows are whitewashed and bright. All have open porches, and a few are seafront.

EAST COAST

This part of the island can feel isolated with most resorts catering to Thai customers. Transport is limited.

DAVID GREEDY

Snorkellers, Ko Chang

A road now runs from just south of Judo Resort to Hat Yao (Long Beach), a quiet, pristine slip of sand with minimal development.

Treehouse Lodge (☎ 08 1847 8215; www .tree-house.org; Hat Yao; r 300B) A true backpacker paradise, travellers often stay longer than they planned. Basic huts (which share super-basic bathrooms) sit along a hillside, looking down to a softly sanded slice of beach.

EATING & DRINKING
HAT SAI KHAO

Tonsai (☎ 08 9895 7229; dishes 40-150B; ☺ lunch & dinner) Settle down on the funky cushions in this tree house/restaurant built in a sturdy banyan tree (*đôn sai* in Thai). There's a good selection of Thai and Western eats amid a nicely relaxed ambience. Make an afternoon of it.

Oodie's Place (☎ 0 3955 1193; pizza 170-260B; ☺ lunch & dinner) Local musician Oodie runs a nicely diverse operation with excellent French food, tasty Thai specialities and live music from 10pm.

AO KHLONG PRAO

Blue Lagoon Resort (☎ 08 1940 0649; dishes 60-220B; ☺ breakfast, lunch & dinner) With a cooking school on the premises, you know the food has to be good. Even better are the private eating pavilions perched over the lagoon and joined by wooden walkways.

HAT KAIBAE

Kharma (☎ 08 1663 3286; ☺ breakfast, lunch & dinner) Eclectic music, a wide-ranging menu featuring Thai, Mexican and vegetarian food, and a few inflated blowfish are all good reasons to head to this gay-friendly spot.

BAN BANG BAO

Ruan Thai (☎ 08 7000 162; dishes 80-300B; ☺ lunch & dinner) The seafood is a little pricey, but it's about as fresh as it gets

RICHARD NEBESKYLOCATION

Children playing, Hat Sai Kaew (p229), Ko Samet

(note your future dinner swimming around as you walk in) and the portions are large. The doting service is beyond excellent – they'll even help you crack your crabs.

GETTING THERE & AWAY

During the high season, Tha Laem Ngop is the main pier to many of the Ko Chang National Marine Park islands.

From Tha Ko Chang Centrepoint, there are hourly ferries to and from Ko Chang's Tha Dan Kao from 6am until 7pm daily (one way/return 80/160B, 45 minutes). A *sŏrng·tăa·ou* from Trat to Tha Ko Chang Centrepoint costs around 60B per person, though be wary of drivers who don't want to take you straight to the pier.

Another way to get to Ko Chang is via the hourly vehicle ferry from Tha Thammachat. This ferry arrives at Ao Sapparot on Ko Chang (per person/car 60/120B, 30 minutes) and may be the only boat running during rough seas.

GETTING AROUND

The *sŏrng·tăa·ou* meeting the boats at Tha Dan Kao and Ao Sapparot charge 60B per person to Hat Sai Khao, 70B to Ban Khlong Prao, 80B to Hat Kaibae and 100B to Hat Tha Nam along the west coast. You may need to negotiate.

AROUND KO CHANG
KO KUT

The water is clear, the palms are shady, and the beaches are top-notch; there's nothing in the form of nightlife or even dining, really, but those are the reasons for visiting.

There are no banks or ATMs around, though major resorts can exchange money.

SLEEPING

Ko Kut lacks decent transport infrastructure, and most resorts cater to package tourists.

Koh Kood Ngamkho Resort (☎ 08 1825 7076; www.kohkood-ngamkho.com; Ao Ngam Kho; hut/bungalow 300/650B) 'Uncle Joe' runs a great setup that's the best budget option around – though the quarters are rustic, they're made fun with colourful tiles and mosaics. Super-simple huts hold only a mattress and mosquito net; they're snug and a step above camping.

Dusita (☎ 08 1523 7369; Ao Ngam Kho; r 700-1200B; 🗙) With a sandy beach, leafy surroundings, and pavilions and restaurants open to the sea breeze, the bungalows at Dusita are good value.

Shantaa (☎ 08 1817 9648; www.shantaa kohkood.com; Hat Khlong Yai Ki; r incl breakfast 5000B; 🗙) Stylish bungalows top a sunny cliff at what is probably the classiest spot on the island.

GETTING THERE & AROUND

During the low season, transport to the islands can be nonexistent.

From Ko Chang, **Bang Bao Boats** (☎ 08 7054 4300) runs a 'fast ferry' twice a day in the high season between Bang Bao and the other islands.

Speedboat Dan Kao departs Tha Dan Kao, 5km east of Trat (not to be confused with Ko Chang's Tha Dan Kao), at 9am daily during the high season (550B, 1¼ hours).

On-island transport is thin on the ground, and you're better off renting a motorbike or mountain bike.

KO MAK

Pretty little Ko Mak is only 16 sq km and doesn't have the jungled peaks and valleys of Ko Chang or Ko Kut, but its small size and lack of drama just means it's a lot more relaxed.

There are no banks or ATMs on Ko Mak, so stock up on cash before visiting.

SLEEPING & EATING

Monkey Island (☎ 08 9501 6030; www .monkeyislandkohmak.com; Ao Khao; r 600-3000B; 🗙 🖵 🗶) All budgets are catered for at what is probably the best backpacker accommodation on the island.

Baan Koh Maak (☎ 0 3952 4028; www .baan-koh-mak.com; Ao Khao; r 700-1400B; 🗙) Competing for most stylish flashpacker digs on the island, Baan Koh Maak's bungalows are bright and funky.

Ko Mak Coco-Cape (☎ 08 1937 9024; www.kohmakcococape.com; r 1000-4500B; 🗙 🗶) Owned by a couple of Bangkok architects (and it shows), this sprawling place is kind of Ko Med with its crisply whitewashed walls in the flashier bungalows and villas.

GETTING THERE & AROUND

All boats passing from the mainland and Ko Chang to Ko Kut will stop at Ko Mak. Expect to pay 200B to 400B for transport between Ko Kut and Ko Mak.

Motorbikes go for 60B to 80B per hour or 300B to 450B per day.

AUSTIN BUSH

Seafood market, Ko Samui (p254)

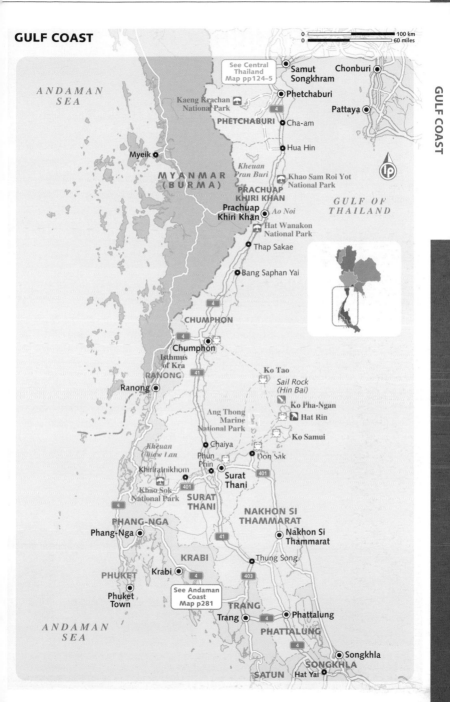

GULF COAST

GULF COAST HIGHLIGHTS

1 KO SAMUI

BY THITIMA (TI) FATHAVEEPORN, OWNER ZAZEN BOUTIQUE RESORT & SPA

Ko Samui is a tropical paradise that offers beautiful beaches, amazing inland jungle and authentic fishing villages. Most of the fishing families (like my own) built simple bungalow guesthouses for the first tourists. Today our boutique resort is where my parent's original guesthouse used to be, and I know all about Samui's hidden places.

↘ TI'S DON'T MISS LIST

❶ BO PHUT

I was born and live today in **Bo Phut** (p258). The village is composed of Thais with Chinese heritage and we were fisherfolk (that's why the village is called Fisherman's Village). It has changed a lot since then but the historic spirit is still alive in the international restaurants, bars and shops.

❷ OLD SAMUI

Visiting the village of **Mae Nam** is like going back in time. Many of the locals are coconut plantation farmers. There is always thick smoke from the coconut skins being burned in the garden and the children run around the yard without looking for traffic because there isn't any. It reminds me of my childhood.

Clockwise from top: Zazen restaurant (p259); Children playing on a pile of coconuts; Morning market; Boats, Bo Phut (p258)

CLOCKWISE FROM TOP: AUSTIN BUSH; JERRY ALEXANDER; AUSTIN BUSH; RICHARD NEBESKY

❸ WAT SAMRET

This scenic **temple** (p256) is in the middle of a coconut plantation and is very remote and quiet. If you can find a monk, ask him to open the secret room where antique Buddha statues are kept away. And take the time to explore nearby in the southern part of the island; it is much quieter than Chaweng.

❹ SAMUI MEALS

I will tell you about the local restaurants that tourists don't know about. Pa-Sri Restaurant (in Fisherman's Village close to the I-junction) sells local dishes like *gaang mát·sà·màn gài* (Muslim curry) and *gaang pá·naang* (Penang curry) in takeaway bags for the children's school lunches. Pa-Maitri Restaurant (in

Mae Nam en route to Phu Kao Thong temple) is known for Samui and southern Thailand specialties. Jee-Mui serves *kà·nŏm jeen* (rice noodles doused in a thin curry); it is on Mae Nam's main road next to the police station and Soi 1.

↘ THINGS YOU NEED TO KNOW

Getting Started Stay or sup at Zazen (p259), Ti's resort and restaurant smack dab on the beach **Top Tip** Rent a motorcycle to explore the roadside curry shops and untouristed corners of the island

GULF COAST HIGHLIGHTS

2

⬐ SWIM WITH THE FISH ON KO TAO

Get schooled in scuba on **Ko Tao** (p272). Dive shops compete with unrestrained capitalistic spirit for your business, meaning that prices are low, quality is high and accommodation at affiliated guesthouses is nearly free. Ko Tao's location make it ideal for beginners: waters are clear and relatively calm, the neon reefs are filled with marine life and the ocean temperatures are like bathwater.

3

⬐ HANG OUT IN A HAMMOCK ON KO PHA-NGAN

Ko Pha-Ngan (p264) has mythic status among generations of globetrotters. It is an easy-going island known for picturesque surroundings and amnesiac days of doing nothing. The north and the east coast are the sleepiest, while the west coast is more 'civilised'. The sandy peninsula of Hat Rin is party-central most days and a full-on rave during the monthly Full Moon parties.

4 ↘ PLEASE EVERYBODY ON KO SAMUI

Often competing with Phuket for package tourists and holiday-makers, **Ko Samui** (p254) aims to please everyone. There's the rowdy but spectacular beach of Chaweng; the mellow northern beaches of Mae Nam and Bo Phut that appeal to young families, yuppies and working-class Lamai; and a handful of resorts.

5 ↘ HEAD TO HUA HIN

A favourite weekend getaway for Bangkok's elite (and the royal family), **Hua Hin** (p250) is a friend indeed if beach time is short and the need for comfort is high. It is the closest resort town to the capital and is geared toward older families, retirees and golf addicts.

6 ↘ SLEEP UNDER THE STARS ON A SLOW BOAT

Sometimes the journey can leave as much of an impression as the destination. The **overnight ferry** (p254) from Chumphon to Ko Tao is slow and bare-bones, but you can sleep under the stars, swim past bright squid boats and watch the sun rise over the hulking island as you slip into the harbour.

2 RICHARD NEBESKY; 3 KRISTIN PILJAY; 4 AUSTIN BUSH; 5 NOBORU KOMINE; 6 AUSTIN BUSH

2 Sairee Beach (p273), Ko Tao; 3 Full Moon party (p270), Ko Pha-Ngan; 4 Library resort (p258), Ko Samui; 5 Buddha statue, Hua Hin (p250); 6 Travelling by ferry along the Gulf Coast

GULF COAST

GULF COAST'S BEST...

↘ PLACES TO DIVE & SNORKEL

- **Ko Tao** (p272) First stop for beginners to get dive certified; snorkel spots steps from shore.
- **Ko Pha-Ngan** (p264) Less crowded 'fun' dives.
- **Ang Thong Marine National Park** (p277) Snorkel and kayak tours are just an excuse for sightseeing in this surreal landscape.

↘ PLACES TO 'DETOXIFY'

- **Spa Resort** (p256) Ko Samui's first health retreat for fasting and health regimes.
- **Tamarind Retreat** (p256) Spa among the trees and the boulders at this Ko Samui resort.
- **Sanctuary** (p268) Ko Pha-Ngan's homage to all things healthy.

↘ PLACES TO SUP ON SEAFOOD

- **Hua Hin** (p251) Pick your supper from the iced trays at the Chatchai Market.
- **Prachuap Khiri Khan** (p253) An unassuming provincial town feeds local Thais with a feast from the sea.
- **Ko Samui** (p260) An island resort that doesn't dumb down the cuisine.

↘ PLACES TO PARTY

- **Ark Bar** (p262) Ko Samui's popular beachside bar brings all the party people together.
- **Full Moon Parties** (p270) Day-glo body paint, fire-twirlers, chest-thumping beats and drunken revelry abound at Ko Pha-Ngan's monthly raves.
- **Dining on the Rocks** (p260) A scenic and sophisticated spot for a sundowner on Ko Samui.

LEFT: AUSTIN BUSH; RIGHT: AUSTIN BUSH

Left: Sila Evason Hideaway (p256), Ko Samui; Right: Ark Bar (p262), Ko Samui

THINGS YOU NEED TO KNOW

⬑ VITAL STATISTICS

- **Population** 3.86 million
- **Best time to visit** December to June

⬑ TOWNS IN A NUTSHELL

- **Hua Hin** Seaside town for seafood and aristocrats.
- **Prachuap Khiri Khan** Seaside hamlet far from the tourist trail.
- **Chumphon** Mainland transfer to Samui islands.
- **Ko Tao** Dive-centric island.
- **Ko Pha-Ngan** Mellow hang-out island.
- **Ko Samui** Well-rounded resort island.
- **Surat Thani** Mainland transfer to Samui islands and Andaman coast.

⬑ ADVANCE PLANNING

- **One month before** Book accommodation and train/air tickets.
- **One week before** Book dive trip.
- **One day before** Buy bus tickets directly from Bangkok's Southern bus station (p93).

⬑ RESOURCES

- **Tourist Authority of Thailand** (TAT; ☎ 0 7728 8817-9; tatsurat@samart .co.th; 5 Th Talat Ma, Surat Thani)
- **TAT office** (☎ 0 7742 0504; Na Thon, Ko Samui)
- **Backpackers Information Centre** (☎ 0 7737 5535; www.backpackers thailand.com; Hat Rin, Ko Pha-Ngan)
- **Koh Tao Community** (www.kohtao -community.com)

⬑ EMERGENCY NUMBERS

- **Fire** (☎ 199)
- **Police/Emergency** (☎ 191)
- **Tourist police** (☎ 1155; ☽ 24hr)

⬑ GETTING AROUND

- **Boat** From the mainland (Chumphon and Surat Thani) to the Samui islands; inter-island too.
- **Bus** Mainland journeys.
- **Motorcycle** Self-touring on Ko Samui (150B to 250B).
- **Sŏrng·tăa·ou** Small pick-up trucks that act as shared taxis and public buses.
- **Train** Good for mainland overnight journeys.
- **Taxi** Convenient on Ko Samui but remember to bargain (200B to 400B).
- **Túk·túk** Chartered vehicles for trips within towns; remember to bargain (40B to 60B).

⬑ BE FOREWARNED

- **Motorcycle travel** Wear a helmet and protective clothing when riding a motorcycle.
- **Drugs** Don't buy drugs on Ko Pha-Ngan.
- **Women travellers** Should be cautious when returning home from Ko Samui's and Ko Pha-Ngan's bars.
- **Bus tickets** Buy Bangkok beach-bound bus tickets directly from government bus stations to avoid unscrupulous private operators.
- **Crowds** Expect large crowds between December and April.

GULF COAST

THINGS YOU NEED TO KNOW

GULF COAST ITINERARIES

QUICK BEACH BREAK Three Days

When Bangkok's hi-sos (high-society) head to the beach for a long weekend, they point their BMWs south towards Hua Hin, which has been hosting bluebloods since King Rama VII built a seaside palace here in 1922.

If you're short on time, **(1) Hua Hin** (p250) is ideal as it is a quick and easy drive from Bangkok and doesn't require a ferry transfer. The beachfront hotels boast international standards and the nightly food markets provide just enough Thai ambience to feel exotic.

Take a break from the beach with a day trip to **(2) Khao Sam Roi Yot National Park** (p252), a mountainous preserve with limestone caves, the country's largest freshwater marsh and ample opportunities for bird-watching.

SEASON YOURSELF IN SAMUI Five Days

Travellers shopping for a resort island often face a dilemma: to vacation in Phuket or in Ko Samui. When compared, Ko Samui might not have the dramatic scenery of the Andaman coast but it retains a pleasant rural personality, despite its rapid transformation from backwater coconut plantation to global destination.

The Gulf coast's premier island, **(1) Ko Samui** (p254) is well-rounded enough to appeal to every kind of traveller. Base yourself in Chaweng to be close to the action and an amazing half-moon beach. Or retreat to the northern beaches of Mae Nam and Bo Phut, which aren't as stunning but have more 'village' characteristics. Consider a dabble with the island's various health treatments, from beachside yoga to three-day fasts.

Swim among the craggy and curiously shaped limestone islands of the **(2) Ang Thong Marine National Park** (p277), a popular day trip from Samui.

If your timing is right, you can ferry over to **(3) Ko Pha-Ngan** (p264) for the monthly beachside rave party. Welcome the rising sun and hop on a ferry back to Samui for some well-earned sleep.

DO THE SAMUI SISTERS One Week

Most travellers bounce through the three islands of the Samui archipelago (Ko Tao, Ko Pha-Ngan and Ko Samui) like a bikini-clad Goldilocks. It is a prerequisite to sample all three and proclaim one the 'best'.

From Bangkok, **(1) Chumphon** (p253) is the closest jumping-off point to the islands. Transit packages (bus/boat or train/boat) will get you to Ko Tao – shop carefully as unscrupulous operators often overcharge and under-deliver.

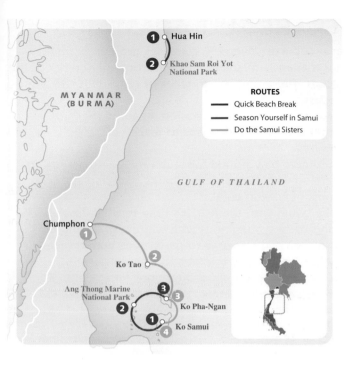

(2) Ko Tao (p272) is the smallest and most rustic of all the islands, but most visitors hardly notice since they're submerged with dive-certification programs. Escape to the rocky coves of the east coast for island solitude or strike out on a solo snorkelling trip.

Next stop is (3) Ko Pha-Ngan (p264), for those wanting to take it easy. Watch the waves, devour a book, sleep late. Then howl at the moon during the infamous Full Moon parties, based on the party beach of Hat Rin.

(4) Ko Samui (p254) is the final and most mature stop before returning to the mainland town of Surat Thani, which is well-equipped for transit to the Andaman coast.

DISCOVER THE GULF COAST

It really isn't fair – there are over 200 countries around the globe and Thailand has managed to snag a disproportionate number of the world's top beaches. These creamy stretches of sand undulate along the paper-thin coast.

It's simple. If you're plagued by indecision, head to Thailand's Gulf Coast and follow three simple steps to reach your ultimate beach-holiday nirvana.

Ko Tao is the ultimate playground for scuba neophytes, sporting shallow reefs teeming with slippery reef sharks, skulking stingrays and radiant blooms of waving coral.

Now that you've swum with the fish, it's time to drink like one. Ko Pha-Ngan has long been synonymous with white nights, and on the eve of every full moon, pilgrims pray to party gods with trance-like dancing, glittery body paint and bucket-sized beverages.

An intensive detox session is a must after your lunar romp. Ko Samui is the ultimate place to pamper yourself silly, and five-star luxury is the name of the game.

PRACHUAP KHIRI KHAN PROVINCE

HUA HIN

อำเภอหัวหิน

pop 42,000

Once a humble fishing village, Hua Hin owes its roots as Thailand's first glamorous getaway to King Rama VII.

Today all the big hotel chains have properties in Hua Hin, and in recent years a growing number of expats have chosen to live in the seaside town that's fast becoming one of Thailand's most cosmopolitan cities.

Compared to Pattaya, the other main beach destination near Bangkok, Hua Hin is (relatively) serene, and is a favourite with families and older travellers.

ACTIVITIES

A long-time favourite golf-holiday destination for Thais, Hua Hin has recently started receiving attention from international golfers.

The **Royal Hua Hin Golf Course** (☎ 0 3251 2475; green fee 2000B) is only one of several golf courses but it's definitely the best. Near the train station, it offers ocean and temple views on an elegant course.

SLEEPING

ourpick **Pattana Guest House** (☎ 0 3251 3393; 52 Th Naresdamri; r 350-550B) This restored fisherman's house has small rooms, but a lusciously verdant bar and courtyard area. Note the whimsically carved teak sinks in the bathroom. Book ahead as it's very popular.

ChaLeLarn (☎ 0 3253 1288; www.chalelarn.com; 11 Th Chomsin; r 1200-1300B; ❄ ▯) ChaLeLarn has a beautiful lobby with wooden floors, while big rooms are equipped with king-sized beds. Verandahs, breakfast and free wi-fi are all part of the perks.

City pillar, Prachuap Khiri Khan (p252)

NOBORU KOMINE

Jed Pee Nong (☎ 0 3251 2381; www.jed peenonghotel-huahin.com; 17 Th Damnoen Kasem; r 1500-1800B; ) Family-oriented, this place has a small kid-friendly pool (they'll love the water slides) and larger three-bed family rooms to squeeze the whole clan into. Cartoon-character shower curtains make bath-time fun. It's centrally located and within walking distance of the beach.

Baan Bayan (☎ 0 3253 3544; www.beach fronthotelhuahin.com; 119 Th Phetkasem; r 6000-11,000B;) A colonial beach house built in the early 20th century, Baan Bayan is perfect for travellers seeking a luxury experience without the overkill of a big, flashy resort. The airy, high-ceilinged rooms are painted a relaxing buttery yellow, the staff are super attentive and the location is absolute beachfront.

EATING

One of Hua Hin's major attractions is the inexpensive Chatchai Market in the centre of town, where vendors gather nightly to cook fresh seafood for hordes of hungry Thais.

Chalasai (7 Th Naletmanley; mains 50-120B; 9am-9pm) With a small patio and a seaside location, Chalasai (no roman-script sign – it's across from Monsoon) doesn't need to put any energy into ambience. Instead, it puts it all into the delicious, cheap Thai seafood.

Sidewalk Café (☎ 08438 5518-7; Soi Selakam; coffee 50B, breakfast 70-130B; 8.30am-1am) Welcoming owner Tim advertises 'probably the best coffee in town', and we have to concede that he's probably right.

Moon Smile (Th Phunsuk; dishes 80-200B; lunch & dinner) The best in an enclave of well-priced Thai restaurants on Th Phunsuk that will respect your request for 'Thai spicy, please'.

Monsoon (☎ 0 3253 1062; 62 Th Naresdamri; dishes 120-300B, afternoon tea 120B; 2pm-midnight) An excellent wine list and mood lighting make this Vietnamese restaurant, located in a lovingly restored two-storey teak house, Hua Hin's most romantic (and expensive) spot.

GETTING THERE & AWAY

Air-con buses to/from Bangkok's southern bus station (140B to 165B, three hours) leave 70m north of Rajana Garden House on Th Sasong (outside the Siripetchkasem Hotel), every hour from 4am to 10pm.

The new main bus station is south of town, on Th Phetkasem, and has air-con buses to many destinations throughout the country.

There are frequent trains running to/from Bangkok's Hualamphong train station (2nd class 292B to 382B, 3rd class 100B to 234B, four hours) and other stations on the southern railway line.

KHAO SAM ROI YOT NATIONAL PARK

อุทยานแห่งชาติเขาสามร้อยยอด

Towering limestone cliffs, caves and beaches produce a dramatic landscape at this 98-sq-km **park** (☎ 0 3282 1568; **adult/child 200/100B**), which means Three Hundred Mountain Peaks in English. The park's lagoons and coastal marshlands are excellent for birdwatching, and with a little exercise you'll be rewarded with magnificent views of the gulf coastline.

There are three park headquarter locations: Hat Laem Sala, Ban Rong Jai and Ban Khao Daeng. There are also visitor centres at Hat Laem Sala, Hat Sam Phraya and Ban Khao Daeng. A nature-studies centre lies at the end of a 1km road leading north from Ban Rong Jai. There are a couple of checkpoints – on the road south from Pranburi and on the road east of Hwy 4. You'll need to pay admission or show proof that you already have.

The park is about 40km south of Hua Hin, and best visited by car. Transport can also be arranged at travel agencies in Hua Hin, most of which also run tours. **Hua Hin Adventure Tour** (☎ 0 3253 0314; www.hua hinadventuretour.com) has the best selection of more intrepid activities.

PRACHUAP KHIRI KHAN

ประจวบคีรีขันธ์

pop 27,700

This sleepy seaside town is actually the provincial capital, but the ambience is

Khao Sam Roi Yot National Park

NOBORU KOMINE

nicely small-town relaxed. Attractions, with a small 'a', include climbing to a hilltop wat while being shadowed by a troop of curious monkeys, taking a leisurely motorbike ride to the excellent beaches north and south of town, or just enjoying some of Thailand's freshest (and cheapest) seafood.

SIGHTS & ACTIVITIES
Visible from almost anywhere in Prachuap Khiri Khan is **Khao Chong Krajok** (Mirror Tunnel Mountain – named after the hole in the mountain that appears to reflect the sky). At the top of a long flight of stairs up the small mountain is **Wat Thammikaram**, established by Rama VI. At the base of the mountain, the more fastidious monkeys bathe in a small pool.

Continue 4km north along the beach road and you'll come to the small village of **Ao Bang Nang Lom**, where wooden fishing vessels are still made using traditional Thai methods. A couple of kilometres north of Ao Bang Nang Lom is another bay, **Ao Noi**, with a small fishing village and the comfortable Aow Noi Sea View hotel (p253).

SLEEPING
AO NOI BEACH
Heading 5km north from town, you reach Ao Noi Beach, where there's a small market and blue fishing boats cluttered at the southern end.

Aow Noi Sea View (☎ 0 3260 4440; www .aownoiseaview.com; 202/3 Mu 2; r 800B; 🆒) A three-storey beachfront hotel that has sea breezes, large bathrooms and linen drying on the line outside.

AO KHLONG WAN
To the south of town is Ao Khlong Wan.
Baan Forty (☎ 0 3266 1437; www.baanforty resort.com; 555 Th Prachuap-Khlong Wan; bunga-

lows 800-1200B; 🆒) Spend your nights in concrete bungalows on a private beach, and spend your days relaxing on the sand or in the shady garden waiting for another huge meal. The friendly owner arranges tours and will hire you bicycles or motorbikes.

EATING
Because of its reputation for fine seafood, Prachuap Khiri Khan has many restaurants. A local specialty is *blah săm·lee dàat dee·o* whole cotton fish that's sliced lengthways and left to dry in the sun for half a day. It's then fried quickly and served with mango salad.

Ma Prow (☎ 08 5293 7278; 48 Th Chai Thaleh; dishes 80-160B; 🕑 lunch & dinner) An airy wooden pavilion across from the beach that cooks up excellent *blah săm·lee dàat dee·o*. The music is an intriguing mix of Western and Thai – kind of like the clientele you'll see here on a busy weekend.

GETTING THERE & AWAY
There are frequent air-con buses to/from Bangkok (190B to 256B, five hours), Hua Hin (80B, 1½ hours), Cha-am (90B, 2½ hours) and Phetchaburi (95B to 105B, three hours) leaving from Th Phitak Chat near the centre.

There are frequent train services to/ from Bangkok (2nd class 210B to 357B, 3rd class 168B, six hours).

CHUMPHON PROVINCE
CHUMPHON
ชุมพร
pop 48,600
Chumphon features as a blip on many travellers' itinerary as they flit in and out of the busy transport hub en route to Ko Tao, or head west for Ranong and Phuket.

GETTING THERE & AWAY
BOAT
You have many options for getting to the small island of Ko Tao (p272), as several piers service different types of boats. Most travel agencies provide free transfers for all but the slowest, cheapest ferries.

From Tha Yang a slow night boat (200B, six hours) departs at midnight.

A car ferry leaves Tha Yang at 11pm (with cabin 300B, six hours). It's possible to get a bunk or mattress on this boat, making it a more comfortable (and fun) option than the other night ferry.

From Talaysub, the Songsrem Express (450B, 2½ hours) departs at 7am.

The **Lomprayah express catamaran** (www.lomprayah.com) leaves Tummakam pier (25km from town) at 7am and 1pm (550B, 1½ hours). Seatran Discovery run a catamaran out of Pak Nam pier (or Seatran Jetty), 10km from Chumphon, at 7am (550B, two hours).

A shared taxi to Tha Yang pier costs 50B. *Sŏrng·tăa·ou* to Tha Yang and Pak Nam piers are 30B.

BUS
Most Bangkok buses stop in town so get off there and save yourself the *sŏrng·tăa·ou* fare from the bus station.

TRAIN
There are frequent services to/from Bangkok (2nd class 292B to 382B, 3rd class 235B, 7½ hours). Overnight sleepers range from 440B to 770B.

Southbound rapid and express trains – the only trains with 1st and 2nd class – are less frequent and can be difficult to book out of Chumphon from November to February.

SURAT THANI PROVINCE
KO SAMUI
เกาะสมุย

pop 45,800

Ko Samui is a choose-your-own-adventure kinda place that strives, like a genie, to grant every tourist their ultimate holiday wish. You want ocean views, daily mas-

Ko Samui

AUSTIN BUSH

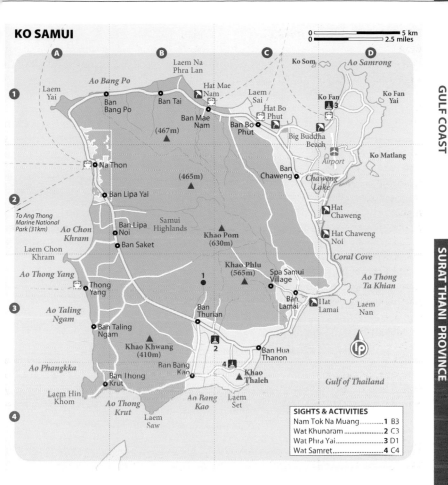

KO SAMUI

SIGHTS & ACTIVITIES

Nam Tok Na Muang	**1** B3
Wat Khunaram	**2** C3
Wat Phra Yai	**3** D1
Wat Samret	**4** C4

GULF COAST

SURAT THANI PROVINCE

sages and personal butlers? Poof – here are the keys to your private poolside villa. It's a holistic aura-cleansing vacation you're after? Shazam – take a seat on your yoga mat before your afternoon colonic. Wanna party like a rock star? Pow – trance your way down the beach with the throngs of whisky bucket–toting tourists.

SIGHTS

At the southern end of **Lamai**, the second-largest beach, you'll find the infamous **Hin Ta** and **Hin Yai** stone formations (also known as Grandfather and Grandmother Rocks). These genitalia-shaped rocks provide endless mirth to giggling Thai tourists.

At 30m, **Nam Tok Na Muang** is the tallest waterfall on Samui and lies in the centre of the island about 12km from Na Thon. The water cascades over ethereal purple rocks, and there's a great pool for swimming at the base. This is the most scenic, and somewhat less frequented, of Samui's falls.

At Samui's northern end, on a small rocky island linked by a causeway, is **Wat**

GULF COAST

SURAT THANI PROVINCE

AUSTIN BUSH

Tamarind Retreat, Ko Samui

⬊ IF YOU LIKE...

If you like all things New Age, then you'll love Samui and its full range of spas and health retreats.

- **Absolute Sanctuary** (☎ 0 7760 1190; www.absoluteyogasamui.com; Chaweng North) A wellness resort offering detox programs and every type of yoga.
- **Spa Resort** (☎ 0 7723 0855; www.spasamui.com; Lamai North) The island's original health resort for 'clean me out' fasting regime and a bevy of other thera-peutic programs.
- **Tamarind Retreat** (☎ 0 7723 0571; www.tamarindretreat.com; Lamai; ⊠ ⛶) Tucked into a coconut grove, Tamarind Retreat operates Tamarind Springs, an award-winning day spa with rock pools and massage pavilions set in the canopy.
- **Sila Evason Hideaway** (☎ 0 7724 5678; www.sixsenses.com) Defines the term 'barefoot elegance'. Its spa centre, nestled within a rocky promontory, overlooks ocean deep.
- **Health Oasis Resort** (☎ 0 7742 0124; www.healthoasisresort.com; ⊠) Will cleanse your aura or your colon. Guests can choose from a variety of healing pack-ages involving everything from meditation to fasting.

Phra Yai (Temple of the Big Buddha). Erected in 1972, the modern Buddha (sit-ting in the Mara posture) stands 15m high and makes an alluring silhouette against the tropical sky and sea.

Several temples have the mummified remains of pious monks including **Wat Khunaram**, which is south of Rte 4169 between Th Ban Thurian and Th Ban Hua.

The monk, Luang Phaw Daeng, has been dead for over two decades but his corpse is preserved sitting in a meditative pose and sporting a pair of sunglasses.

At **Wat Samret**, near Th Ban Hua, you can see a typical Mandalay sitting Buddha carved from solid marble – a common sight in India and northern Thailand, but not so common in the south.

ACTIVITIES

If you're serious about diving, head to Ko Tao and base yourself over there for the duration of your diving adventure.

For those interested in snorkelling and kayaking, book a day trip to the stunning Ang Thong Marine National Park (p255). Blue Stars Kayaking (☎ 077413231; www.blue stars.info), based in Chaweng on Ko Samui, offers guided sea-kayak trips (2000B) in the park.

SLEEPING

CHAWENG

Packed end-to-end with hotels and bungalows, this beach is the eye of the tourist storm. Despite the chaos, there's a striking stretch of beach, and most resorts are well protected from street noise. At the south end of the beach, a small headland separates a sliver of sand (called Chaweng Noi) from the rest of the hustle.

Queen Boutique Resort (☎ 0 7741 3148; queensamui@yahoo.com; Soi Colibri; s/d from 600/800B; ⌗ ▢) Yes, these rooms really are less than 1000B (although probably not for long)! Queen is a brand new place to hang your hat and is luring travellers by the boatload with boutique digs at backpacker prices.

Jungle Club (☎ 0 1894 2327; bungalows 600-2900B, villas 3500B; ⌗ ▢ ▣) The perilous drive up the slithering dirt road is totally worthwhile once you get a load of the awesome views from the top. Call ahead for a pick-up; you don't want to spend your precious jungle vacation in a body cast.

Chaweng Center Hotel (☎ 0 7741 3747; chawengcenter@hotmail.com; r 1200B; ⌗ ▣) Although the views of McDonald's across the street are far from charming, this central cheapie has freshly refurbished rooms that are well-priced and pull off 'minimal chic' instead of feeling spartan.

Akwa (☎ 08 4660 0551; www.akwaguest house.com; r 999-2599B; ⌗ ▢) A charming B&B-style sleeping spot, Akwa has a few funky rooms decorated with bright colours.

Chaweng Garden Beach (☎ 0 7796 0394; www.chawenggardnessamui.com; r from

Relaxing poolside, Ko Samui

AUSTIN BUSH

1600B; 🗙 💻 🏊) A popular 'flashpacker' choice, this campus of accommodation has a large variety of room types serviced by an extra-smiley staff.

Nora Chaweng (☎ 0 7791 3666; www.nora chawenghotel.com; r from 2500B; 🗙 💻 🏊) It's not on the beach, but this new addition to the Chaweng bustle has a great price-to-comfort ratio.

Baan Chaweng Beach Resort (☎ 0 7742 2403; www.baanchawengbeachresort.com; bungalows 4000-7000B; 🗙 💻 🏊) The immaculate rooms are painted in various shades of peach and pear, with teak furnishings that feel both modern and traditional.

our pick **Library** (☎ 0 7742 2407; www.the library.name; bungalows 9000-12,000B; 🗙 💻 🏊) The entire resort is a sparkling white mirage accented with black trimming and slatted curtains. The large rectangular pool is not to be missed – it's tiled in piercing shades of red, making the term 'bloodbath' suddenly seem appealing.

LAMAI

Ten years ago, people in the know used to say 'skip Chaweng and head to Lamai', but these days Lamai has become the island's has-been and the unofficial HQ of Samui's girly bar scene. South of Lamai, Hua Thanon is a small, quieter beach with a couple of standout resorts.

New Hut (☎ 0 7723 0437; newhut@hotmail .com; Lamai North; huts 200-500B) New Hut is a rare beachfront cheapie with tiny-but-charming A-frame huts.

Sunrise Bungalow (☎ 0 7742 4433; www .sunrisebungalow.com; Lamai South; bungalows 400-1300B; 🗙) Steps away from the awkward giggles at Hin Ta and Hin Yai (the island's infamous genital-shaped rocks), Sunrise offers budget travellers a relaxing place to hang their backpack.

Amity (☎ 0 7742 4084; bungalows 350-1500B; 🗙) Amity offers alluring modern bunga-

lows and a few ramshackle cheapies with shared bathroom – there's no theme, just a mishmash of accommodation that changes style depending on the price range (we liked the 700B huts). The aircon cottages are a welcome addition to the repertoire.

Lamai Wanta (☎ 0 7742 4550, 0 7742 4218; www.lamaiwanta.com; r & bungalows 1600-3400B; 🗙 💻 🏊) The pool area feels a bit retro, with its swatch book of beige- and blue-toned tiles, but in the back there are modern motel rooms and bungalows with fresh coats of white paint.

our pick **Rocky Resort** (☎ 0 7741 8367; www.rockyresort.com; Hua Thanon; r 4200-14000B; 🗙 🏊) Our favourite spot in Lamai (well, actually just south of Lamai), Rocky finds the right balance between an upmarket ambience and an unpretentious, sociable atmosphere.

NORTHERN BEACHES

The beach isn't breathtaking, but Bo Phut has the most dynamic lodging in all of Samui. A string of vibrant boutique cottages starts deep within the clutter of Fisherman's Village and radiates outward along the sand.

Khuntai (☎ 0 7724 5118, 08 6686 2960; r 600-850B; 🗙) A block away from the beach, on the outskirts of Fisherman's Village, Khuntai's 2nd-floor rooms are drenched in afternoon sunshine and feature outdoor lounging spots.

Cactus (☎ 0 7724 5565; cactusbung@hotmail .com; bungalows 700-1590B; 🗙) The palpable backpacker buzz means that rooms err on the basic side, but they're still clean, comfy and sport loads of charm (the fan bathrooms could benefit from an air freshener though).

Lodge (☎ 0 7742 5337; www.apartment samui.com; r 1350-1900B; 🗙 🏊) Another great choice in Bo Phut, the Lodge feels like a

AUSTIN BUSH

Library resort, Ko Samui

colonial hunting chalet with pale walls and dark wooden beams jutting across the ceiling. Reservations are a must – this place always seems to be full.

ourpick **L'Hacienda** (☎ 0 7721 5943; www .samui-hacienda.com; r 1400-3000B; 🞪 🞵) Polished terracotta and rounded archways give the entrance a Spanish-mission motif. Similar decor permeates the eight adorable rooms, which sport loads of personal touches like pebbled bathroom walls and translucent bamboo lamps.

Red House (☎ 0 7742 5686; www.design -visio.com; r 2000B; 🞪) To reach the small reception area at the back, guests must pass through a shoe shop that looks like a sleek Chinese bordello. The four rooms are decorated with a similar spiciness. A cache of reclining beach chairs and potted plants is the perfect rooftop escape.

ourpick **Zazen** (☎ 0 7742 5085; www.samui zazen.com; r 5300-12,800B; 🞪 🞏 🞵) Zazen is the boutique-iest boutique resort on Samui – every inch of this charming getaway has been thoughtfully and creatively designed.

MAE NAM

Shangrilah (☎ 0 7742 5189; bungalows 300-2000B; 🞪) A backpacker's Shangri-La indeed – these are some of the cheapest huts around and they're in decent condition!

Coco Palm Resort (☎ 0 7742 5095; bungalows 1200B; 🞪) The bungalows at Coco Palm have been crafted with tons of rattan. A rectangular pool is the centrepiece along the beach – and the price is right for a resort-like atmosphere.

Maenam Resort (☎ 0 7742 5116; www .maenamresort.com; bungalows 1200-2700B; 🞪 🞏) Palm-bark cottages are set in several rows amid a private, junglelike garden. Suites are a steal for families.

Harry's (☎ 0 7742 5447; www.harrys-samui .com; bungalows 1200-3000B; 🞪 🞵) Arriving here is like entering sacred temple grounds. Polished teak wood abounds in the lobby and the classic pitched roofing reaches skyward.

Sea Fan (☎ 0 7742 5204; www.seafanresort .com; r 2200-2700B; 🞪 🞵) Offering huge thatch and wood bungalows connected by wooden walkways, with colourful flora abounding, this is a fine place to stay. The beautiful beachside pool has a small kids' area.

EATING
CHAWENG
For the best ambience, get off the road and head to the beach, where many bungalow operators set up tables on the sand and have glittery fairy lights at night.

Laem Din Market & Night Market (dishes from 30B; ☻ 4am-6pm, night market 6pm-2am) A busy day market, Laem Din is packed with stalls selling fresh fruits, vegetables and meats that stock local Thai kitchens. For dinner, come to the adjacent night market and sample the tasty southern-style fried chicken and curries.

Wave Samui (☎ 0 7723 0803; dishes from 60B; ☻ breakfast, lunch & dinner) This jack-of-all trades (guesthouse-bar-restaurant) serves honest food at honest prices and fosters a travellers' ambience with an in-house library and a popular happy hour (3pm to 7pm).

Bellini (☎ 0 7741 3831; www.bellini-samui .com; dishes from 200B; ☻ dinner) A staple on Soi Colibri, Bellini sizzles under designer mood lighting. There's Italian on the menu, but not in a pizza-pasta kind of way – think veal, rock lobster and a dainty assortment of tapas.

ourpick Page (☎ 0 7742 2767; dishes 180-850B; ☻ breakfast, lunch & dinner) If you can't afford to stay at the ultra-swank Library (p258), have a meal at its beachside restaurant. Lunch is a bit more casual and affordable, but you'll miss the designer lighting effects in the evening.

Betelnut (☎ 0 7741 3370; mains 600-800B; ☻ dinner) The menu is a pan-Pacific mix of curries and chowder, papaya and pancetta.

LAMAI
Hua Thanon Market (☎ 0 7742 4630; dishes from 30B; ☻ 6am-6pm) Slip into the rhythm of this village market slightly south of Lamai; it's a window into the food ways of southern Thailand. Follow the market road to the row of food shops delivering edible southern culture: chicken biryani, fiery curries, or toasted rice with coconut, bean sprouts, lemongrass and dried shrimp.

Lamai Night Food Centre (☎ 0 7742 4630; dishes from 30B; ☻ dinner) The vendor stalls whip up all the Thai standards – a spectacle in itself. And then the hostesses at the nearby girly bars crank up the music for pole dancing or a few rounds of *muay thai* (Thai boxing).

NORTHERN BEACHES
Boho Bo Phut has several trendy eateries to match the string of yuppie boutique hotels.

CHOENG MON & BIG BUDDHA BEACH (BANG RAK)
ourpick Dining on the Rocks (☎ 0 7724 5678; reservations-samui@sixsenses.com; menus from 1500B; ☻ dinner) The Sila Evason's ultimate dining experience takes place on nine cantilevered verandahs of weathered teak and bamboo that yawn over the gulf. After sunset (and a glass of wine), guests feel like they're dining on a wooden barge set adrift on a starlit sea.

BO PHUT
Starfish & Coffee (☎ 0 7742 7201; dishes 130-180B; ☻ breakfast, lunch & dinner) Evenings feature standard Thai fare and sunset views of rugged Ko Pha-Ngan.

Karma Sutra (dishes 130-260B; ☻ breakfast, lunch & dinner) A haze of purples and pillows, this charming chow spot in the heart of Bo Phut's Fisherman's Village

Rocky Resort (p258), Ko Samui

AUSTIN BUSH

serves up international and Thai eats listed on colourful chalkboards. Karma Sutra doubles as a clothing boutique.

Villa Daudet (dishes from 130-380B; ☺ lunch & dinner Mon-Sat) Villa Daudet is French-owned (so you know the food's gonna be good) and sits in a quaint garden decorated with a flower trellis and elephant-themed paintings.

Zazen (☎ 0 7742 5085; dishes 550-850B, set menus from 1300B; ☺ lunch & dinner) The chef describes the food as 'organic and orgasmic'. This romantic dining experience comes complete with ocean views, dim candle lighting and soft music. Reservations recommended.

MAE NAM & BANG PO

Angela's Bakery (☎ 0 7742 7396; dishes 80-200B; ☺ breakfast & lunch) Duck through the screen of hanging plants into this beloved bakery, smelling of fresh bread and hospitality. Her sandwiches and cakes have kept many Western expats from wasting away in the land of rice.

ourpick Ko-Seng (☎ 0 7742 5365; dishes 100-300B; ☺ dinner) Hidden down a narrow side street near Mae Nam's Chinese temple, Ko Samui's best-kept secret is a welcome escape from the island's restaurants that fuss over the decor instead of their food.

Bang Po Seafood (☎ 0 7742 0010; dishes from 100B; ☺ dinner) It's one of the only restaurants that serves traditional Ko Samui fare (think of it as island road-kill, well, actually it's more like local sea-kill): recipes call for ingredients such as raw sea urchin roe, baby octopus, sea water, coconut and local turmeric.

WEST COAST

Na Thon has a giant day market on Th Thawi Ratchaphakdi – it's worth stopping by to grab some snacks before your ferry ride.

About Art & Craft Café (☎ 08 9724 9673; Na Thon; dishes 80-180B; ☺ breakfast & lunch) An artistic oasis in the midst of hurried Na Thon, this cafe serves an eclectic assortment of healthy and wholesome food, gourmet coffee and, as the name states, art and craft, made by the owner and her friends.

Wiesenthal (☎ 0 7723 5165; Taling Ngam; dishes 90-250B; ☺ breakfast, lunch & dinner) Wiesenthal is a casual open-air restaurant overlooking a quiet beach. Devour a scrumptious assortment of international cuisine in the shade of a bamboo umbrella.

Big John Seafood (☎ 0 7742 3025; www .bigjohnsamui.com; Thong Yang; dishes 60-300B; ☺ breakfast, lunch & dinner) The seafood is freshly caught everyday from various fishing hot spots off the coast of Samui. Dinnertime is particularly special – live entertainment kicks in at 6pm just as the sun plunges below the watery horizon.

DRINKING & ENTERTAINMENT
CHAWENG

Making merry in Chaweng is a piece of cake. Most places are open until 2am and there are a few places that go strong all night long. Soi Green Mango has loads of girly bars. Soi Colibri and Soi Reggae Pub are raucous as well.

Ark Bar (☎ 0 7742 2047; www.ark-bar.com) The 'it' destination for a Wednesday-night romp on Samui. Drinks are dispensed from the multicoloured bar draped in paper lanterns, and guests lounge on pyramidal pillows strewn down the beach. The party usually starts around 4pm.

Bar Solo (☎ 0 7741 4012) The evening drink specials lure in the front-loaders preparing for a late, late night at the dance clubs on Soi Solo and Soi Green Mango.

Tropical Murphy's (☎ 0 7741 3614; dishes 50-300B) Come night time, the live music kicks on and this place turns into the most popular Irish bar on Samui (yes, there are a few).

Green Mango (☎ 0 7742 2661) Green Mango has blazing lights, expensive drinks and masses of sweaty bodies swaying to dance music.

Q-Bar (☎ 08 1956 2742; www.qbarsamui .com) Overlooking Chaweng Lake, Q Bar is a little piece of Bangkok nightlife planted among the coconut trees. The upstairs lounge opens just before sunset treating cocktail connoisseurs to various highbrow

Q-Bar, Ko Samui

AUSTIN BUSH

tipples and a drinkable view of southern Chaweng – mountains, sea and sky. After 10pm, the night-crawlers descend upon the downstairs club where DJs spin the crowd into a techno amoeba.

NORTHERN BEACHES

Frog & Gecko Pub (☎ 0 7742 5248) This tropical British watering hole and food stop is famous for its noodle-bending 'Wednesday Night Pub Quiz' competitions and its wide selection of music.

Pier (☎ 0 7743 0681; dishes 200-390B; ☺ lunch & dinner) It's the hippest address in Fisherman's Village, sporting multi-level terraces, a lively bar and plenty of wide furniture to lounge around on and watch the rickety fishing vessels pull into the harbour.

GETTING THERE & AWAY
AIR
Samui's airport is located in the northeast of the island near Big Buddha Beach.

Bangkok Airways (www.bangkokair .com) operates flights roughly every 30 minutes between Samui and Bangkok (2000B to 4000B, one to 1½ hours). **Thai Airways** (in Bangkok ☎ 0 2134 5403; www .thaiair.com) operates between Samui and Bangkok (5600B, twice a day). Both airlines land at Bangkok's Suvarnabhumi Airport.

Bangkok Air also flies from Samui to Phuket (2000B to 3000B, one hour, three daily), Pattaya (3000B, one hour, three daily), Krabi (1600B, one hour, three times a week) and Chiang Mai (4500B to 6500B, 2½ hours, twice a week). International flights go directly from Samui to Singapore (4200B to 5400B, three hours, daily) and Hong Kong (12,000B to 6000B, four hours, five days a week).

During the high season, make your flight reservations far in advance as seats

BUFFALO TANGO
Thai bullfighting is known to take on circus proportions. Flowers are placed on the bulls' horns and sacred ropes are hung around their necks. Eventually the two contestants will lock horns and connect in a brief bout of head-wrestling – the first animal to turn and run is declared the loser. Fights are usually over in minutes and the animals are rarely injured.

Events are arranged on a rotating basis at several rustic fighting rings around the island. Tourists are usually charged from 200B to 500B.

do sell out. If Samui flights are full, try flying into Surat Thani from Bangkok and taking a short ferry ride to Samui.

BOAT
The ferry situation is rather convoluted: schedules and prices are always in flux, and there are tons of entry and exit points on Samui and the mainland. On Samui, the three oft-used ports are Na Thon, Mae Nam and Big Buddha.

There are frequent daily boat departures between Samui and Surat Thani. The hourly Seatran ferry is a common option. Ferries cost between 110B and 190B, and take one to three hours, depending on the boat. The slow night boat to Samui (150B) leaves from central Surat Thani each night at 11pm, reaching Na Thon around 5am.

There are almost a dozen daily departures between Samui and Ko Pha-Ngan.

BUS & TRAIN
The government bus fares from Bangkok's Southern bus terminal include the cost of the ferry. These are 500B for

2nd-class passengers. Most private buses from Bangkok charge around 450B for the same journey and include the ferry fare.

GETTING AROUND

You can rent motorcycles (and bicycles) from almost every resort on the island.

Sŏrng·tăa·ou drivers love to try to overcharge you, so it's always best to ask a third party for current rates, as they can change with the season. These vehicles run regularly during daylight hours only. It costs about 30B to travel along one coast, and no more than 75B to travel halfway across the island.

TO/FROM THE AIRPORT

Ask your resort about complimentary airport transfers or try the **Samui Shuttle** (www.samuishuttle.com). Taxis typically charge 300B to 500B for airport transfer. Some Chaweng travel agencies arrange minibus taxis for less.

KO PHA-NGAN

เกาะพะงัน

pop 12,100

In the family of southern Gulf islands, Ko Pha-Ngan sits in the crystal sea between Ko Samui, its business-savvy older brother, and little Ko Tao, the spunky younger brother full of dive-centric energy. Ko Pha-Ngan is the slacker middle child: a chilled out beach bum with tattered dreadlocks, a tattoo of a Chinese serenity symbol, and a penchant for white nights and bikini-clad pool parties.

SIGHTS & ACTIVITIES

For those who have grown weary of beach-bumming, this large jungle island has many natural features to explore, including mountains, waterfalls and spectacular beaches.

WATERFALLS

There are many **waterfalls** throughout the island's interior, four of which gush throughout the year. **Nam Tok Than Sadet** features boulders carved with the royal insignia of Rama V, Rama VII and Rama IX. King Rama V enjoyed this hidden spot so much that he returned over a dozen times between 1888 and 1909. The river waters of Khlong Than Sadet are now considered sacred and used in royal ceremonies. Also near the eastern coast, **Nam Tok Than Prawet** is a series of chutes that snake inland for approximately 2km.

DIVING & SNORKELLING

With Ko Tao, the high-energy diving behemoth, just a few kilometres away, Ko Pha-Ngan enjoys a much quieter, more laid-back diving scene focused on fun diving rather than certifications. Prices are about 2000B to 2500B cheaper on Ko Tao for an Open Water certificate, but group sizes can be smaller on Ko Pha-Ngan since there are less divers in general.

A major perk of diving from Ko Pha-Ngan is the proximity to **Sail Rock** (Hin Bai), perhaps the best dive site in the Gulf of Thailand. An abundance of corals and large tropical fish can be seen at depths of 10m to 30m, and there's a rocky vertical swim-through called 'The Chimney'.

The following local dive operators are recommended:

Haad Yao Divers (☎ 08 6279 3085; www .haadyaodivers.com) Established in 1997, this dive operator has garnered a strong reputation by maintaining high standards of safety and customer service.

Lotus Diving (☎ 0 7737 4142; www.lotus diving.net) This well-reputed dive centre has top-notch instructors, and owns not one, but two beautiful boats (that's two

GULF COAST

SURAT THANI PROVINCE

Ko Pha-Ngan

PAUL DYMOND

more vessels than most of the other operations on Ko Pha-Ngan).

Sail Rock Divers (☎ 0 7737 4321; www.sail rockdiversresort.com) The responsible and friendly staff at Sail Rock satisfy customers at their purpose-built facility, featuring air-con classrooms and a small wading pool.

YOGA

The Ananda Yoga Resort on Hat Chaophao, run by **Agama Yoga** (☎ 08 1397 6280, 08 9233 0217; www.agamayoga.com; Hin Kong, r 500B, bungalows 1200B, four night minimum), gets rave reviews from our readers for its holistic approach to the study of tantric yoga. The centre is often closed from September to December while its instructors travel to other locations around the world spreading the cosmic *ohm*. On the east coast, the Sanctuary (p268) is another popular retreat for yoga enthusiasts.

OTHER ACTIVITIES

The exceedingly popular **Eco Nature Tour** (☎ 08 4850 6273) offers a 'best of' island trip, which includes elephant trekking, snorkelling and a visit to the Chinese temple, a stunning viewpoint and Phang waterfall. The day trip, which costs 1500B, departs at 9am and returns around 3pm.

SLEEPING
HAT RIN

The thin peninsula of Hat Rin features three separate beaches. Hat Rin Nok (Sunrise Beach) is the epicentre of Full Moon tomfoolery, Hat Rin Nai (Sunset Beach) is the less impressive stretch of sand on the far side of the tiny promontory, and Hat Seekantang (also known as Hat Leela), just south of Hat Rin Nai, is a smaller, more private beach. The three beaches are linked by Ban Hat Rin (Hat Rin Town), a small inland collection of restaurants and bars.

Seaside Bungalow (☎ 08 6940 3410, 08 7266 7567; Hat Rin Nai; bungalows 300-600B; ❄) Seaside sees loads of loyal customers who return for the mellow atmosphere, cheap drinks, free pool table and comfy wooden bungalows staggered along Sunset Beach.

Lighthouse Bungalow (☎ 0 7737 5075; Hat Seekantang; bungalows 350-800B) Hidden at the far end of Hat Rin, this low-key collection of humble huts gathers along a sloping terrain punctuated by towering palms.

Sea Breeze Bungalow (☎ 0 7737 5162; bungalows 500-8000B; 🕱) Sea Breeze gets a good report card from our readers, and we agree; the labyrinth of secluded hillside cottages is an ideal hammocked retreat for any type of traveller.

our pick **Sarikantang** (☎ 0 7737 5055, 08 1444 1322; www.sarikantang.com; Hat Seekantang; bungalows 500-3500B; 🕱 🕱) Cream-coloured cabins, framed with teak posts and lintels, are sprinkled amongst swaying palms and crumbling winged statuettes. Inside, the rooms look like the set of a photo shoot for an interior-design magazine.

WEST COAST BEACHES

The atmosphere is a pleasant mix between the east coast's quiet seclusion and Hat Rin sociable vibe, although the beaches along the western shores aren't as picturesque as the other parts of the island.

HAT CHAOPHAO

Like Hat Yao up the coast, this rounded beach is lined with a variety of bungalow operations.

Sunset Cove (☎ 0 7734 9211; www.thai sunsetcove.com; bungalows 1500-3350B; 🕱 🖳 🕱) The beachside abodes are particularly elegant, sporting slatted rectangular windows and barrel-basined bathtubs.

HAT YAO & HAT SON

One of the busier beaches along the west coast, Hat Yao sports a swimmable beach, numerous resorts and a few extra conveniences like ATMs and convenience stores.

Tantawan Bungalow (☎ 0 7734 9108; www.tantawanbungalow.com; bungalows 450-550B; 🕱) Little Tantawan sits high up in the jungle like a tree house, boasting soaring sea views from the sprinkle of rugged bungalows. Guests can take a dip in the trapezoidal swimming pool or enjoy the sunrise on their small bamboo porch.

High Life (☎ 0 7734 9114; www.highlife bungalow.com; bungalows 500-2000B; 🕱 🕱) True to its moniker, the 25 bungalows, of various shapes and sizes, sit on a palmed outcropping of granite soaring high above the cerulean sea. Advance bookings will set you back an extra 200B.

Haad Yao Bay View (☎ 0 7734 9193; www .haadyao-bayviewresort.com; r & bungalows 2000-5000B; 🕱 🖳 🕱) Sparkling after a recent facelift, this conglomeration of bungalows and hotel-style accommodation looks like a tropical mirage on Hat Yao's northern headland.

HAT SALAD

One of the best beaches on the island, Hat Salad has a string of quality accommodation along the sand.

Cookies Salad (☎ 0 7734 9125, 08 3181 7125; www.cookies-phangan.com; bungalows 1500-3000B) The resort with a tasty name has delicious Balinese-style bungalows orbiting a two-tiered lap pool tiled in various shades of blue.

AO MAE HAT

The northwest tip of the island has excellent ocean vistas, and little Ko Ma is connected to Pha-Ngan by a stunning sand bar.

Royal Orchid (☎ 0 7737 4182; royal _orchid_maehaad@hotmail.com; bungalows 300-800B; 🕱 🖳) Handsome backpacker bungalows are arranged like a zipper along a slender garden path – most have fleeting views of the serene beach and idyllic

Morning market, Ko Samui (p254)

AUSTIN BUSH

sand bar that extends to scenic Ko Ma offshore.

Pha-Ngan Utopia Resort (☎ 0 7737 4093; www.phanganutopia.com; bungalows 1500-3000B; 🖼 🖵 🌊) It's pretty audacious to name one's resort 'Utopia', but the owners have done an excellent job of creating an idyllic jungle retreat perched high above the sea.

NORTHERN BEACHES

Stretching from Chalok Lam to Thong Nai Pan, the dramatic northern coast is a wild jungle with several stunning and secluded beaches – it's the most scenic coast on the island.

HAT KHUAT (BOTTLE BEACH)

This isolated dune has garnered a reputation as a low-key getaway, and has thus become quite popular. During high season, places can fill up fast so it's best to try and arrive early. Grab a long-tail taxi boat from Chalok Lam for 50B to 120B (depending on the boat's occupancy).

Bottle Beach II (☎ 0 7744 5156; bungalows 350-400B) At the far eastern corner of the beach, this is the spot where penny pinchers can live out their castaway fantasies.

Smile (☎ 08 1956 3133; smilebeach@hotmail.com; bungalows 400-700B) At the far west corner of the beach, Smile features an assortment of wooden huts that climb up a forested hill. The two-storey bungalows (700B) are our favourite.

Haad Khuad Resort (☎ 0 7744 5153; www.geocities.com/haadkhuad_resort; r 1800-2200B; 🖼) Although significantly more expensive than the other sleeping spots on Bottle Beach, this small hotel is worth the splurge. The rooms are fastidiously clean and they all feature floor-to-ceiling windows that face the cerulean bay.

THONG NAI PAN

The pair of rounded bays at Thong Nai Pan looks a bit like buttocks; Ao Thong Nai Pan Yai (*yai* means 'big') is the northern half, and Ao Thong Nai Pan Noi (*noi* means 'little') curves just below.

our pick **Dolphin** (bungalows 500-1300B; ❄️) This hidden retreat gives yuppie travellers a chance to rough it in style, while granola types will soak up every inch of the laid-back charm. Lodging is only available on a first-come basis.

EAST COAST BEACHES

The east coast is the ultimate hermit hang-out. For the most part, you'll have to hire a boat to get to these beaches, but water taxis are available in Thong Sala and Hat Rin.

THAN SADET & THONG RENG

Accessible by 4WD vehicles and colourful taxi boats, quiet Than Sadet and Thong Reng are the island's best-kept secrets for seclusion seekers.

Treehouse (treehouse.kp@googlemail.com; bungalows from 200B) Ko Chang (the big Ko Chang)'s legendary backpacker hang-out has recently set up shop along the secluded waters of Thong Reng.

Plaa's (☎ 0 7744 5191; bungalows 600B; 🖥️) Plaa's colourful village of bungalows sits on the northern headland of Than Sadet overlooking the bay below.

HAT THIAN

Geographically, Hat Thian is quite close to Hat Rin; however, there are no roads and the crude hiking trail is lengthy and confusing. Ferry taxis are available from Hat Rin for around 150B.

Beam Bungalows (☎ 0 7927 2854, 08 6947 3205; bungalows 300-500B) Beam is set back from the beach and tucked behind a coconut palm grove. Charming wooden huts have dangling hammocks out front, and big bay windows face the ocean through the swaying palms.

Sanctuary (☎ 08 1271 3614; www.the sanctuarythailand.com; dm 120B, bungalows 400-3800B) A friendly enclave promoting re-laxation, this inviting haven offers luxury lodging and also functions as a holistic re-treat offering everything from yoga classes to detox sessions. Accommodation, in various manifestations of twigs, is scat-tered around the resort, married to the natural surroundings.

EATING

Ko Pha-Ngan is no culinary capital, espe-cially since most visitors quickly absorb the lazy lifestyle and wind up eating at their accommodation. Those with an adventurous appetite should check out Thong Sala and the island's southern coast.

HAT RIN

This bustling 'burb has the largest con-glomeration of restaurants and bars on the island, yet most of them are pretty lousy. The infamous Chicken Corner is a popular intersection stocked with several poultry peddlers promising to cure the munchies, be it noon or midnight.

Mr K (☎ 0 7737 5470; dishes 50-80B; ☺ 24hr) Our favourite joint at Chicken Corner, Mr K offers local eats all night long. Cheesy Thai soap-operas blare on the TV, and there's dirt-cheap beer to wash down your meal.

SOUTHERN BEACHES
THONG SALA

our pick **Night Market** (dishes 25-180B; ☺ 6.30-10.30pm) A heady mix of steam and snacking locals, Thong Sala's night market is a must for those looking for a dose of culture while nibbling on a low-priced snack. The best place to grab some cheap grub is the stall in the far right corner with a large white banner. Hit up the vender next door for tasty seafood platters, like red snapper served over a bed of thick noodles. Banana pancakes

Ko Pha-Ngan

ANDERS BLOMQVIST

and fruit smoothies abound for dessert (of course).

BAN TAI & BAN KHAI

Like in Thong Sala nearby, the small villages of Ban Tai and Ban Khai have some solid dining options as well.

Somtum Inter (☎ 0 7737 7334; dishes 40-80B ⏲ breakfast, lunch & dinner) Housed in a breezy open-air pavilion next door to Boat Ahoy (owned by the same family; see below), Somtum announces its speciality in the restaurant's name: spicy papaya salad (*sôm·đam*).

ourpick **Boat Ahoy** (☎ 0 7723 8759, 0 7737 7334; dishes 100-180B ⏲ breakfast, lunch & dinner) A compound of open-air pavilions encased in slats of mahogany wood, Boat Ahoy offers a night's worth of fun.

WEST COAST BEACHES

Tantawan (☎ 0 7734 9108; Hat Son; dishes 60-200B; ⏲ lunch & dinner) This charming teak hut, nestled amongst jungle fronds, drips with clinking chandeliers made from peach coral and khaki-coloured seashells.

DRINKING

Every month, on the night of the full moon, pilgrims pay tribute to the party gods with trance-like dancing, wild screaming and glow-in-the-dark body paint. The throngs of bucket-sippers and fire twirlers gather on the infamous Sunrise Beach (Hat Rin Nok) and party until the sun replaces the moon in the sky.

A few other noteworthy spots can be found around the island for those seeking something a bit mellower.

HAT RIN

Hat Rin is the beating heart of the legendary Full Moon fun, and the area can get pretty wound up even without the influence of lunar phases. The following party venues flank Hat Rin's infamous Sunrise Beach from south to north:

Club Paradise (☎ 0 7737 5244) Paradise basks in its celebrity status as the genesis of the lunar *loco*-motion.

Tommy (☎ 0 7737 5215) One of Hat Rin's largest venues lures the masses with black lights and trance music blaring on the sound system. Drinks are dispensed from a large ark-like bar.

Mellow Mountain (☎ 0 7737 5347) Also called 'Mushy Mountain' (you'll know why when you get there), this trippy hang-out sits at the northern edge of Hat Rin Nok delivering stellar views of the shenanigans below.

This haunt is located elsewhere in Hat Rin:

Coral Bungalows Bar (☎ 0 7737 5023) Back on Hat Rin Nai (Sunset Beach), Coral's pool-centric powwows are so raucous, they might just eclipse the Full Moon parties.

OTHER BEACHES

Eagle Pub (☎ 08 4839 7143; Hat Yao) Located at the southern end of Hat Yao, this drink-dealing shack, built right into the rock face, is tattooed with the neon graffiti of virtually every person that's passed out on the lime-green patio furniture after too many *caiparinhas*.

Pirates Bar (☎ 08 4728 6064; Hat Chaophao) This popular and wacky drinkery is a replica of a pirate ship built into the cliffs.

THE 10 COMMANDMENTS OF FULL MOON FUN

Today, thousands of bodies converge monthly on the powdery sand of Hat Rin Nok to bump, grind, sweat and drink their way through a lunar-lit night filled with thumping DJed beats.

Some critics claim that the party is starting to lose its carefree flavour, especially since the island's government is trying to charge a 100B entrance fee to partygoers. Despite the disheartening schemes hatched by money-hungry locals, the night of the Full Moon is still the ultimate partying experience, so long as one follows the unofficial 10 Commandments of Full Moon fun, as listed here:

- Thou shalt arrive in Hat Rin at least three days early to nail down accommodation during the pre–Full Moon rush of backpackers (see p265 for information about sleeping in Hat Rin).
- Thou shalt double-check the party dates as sometimes they coincide with Buddhist holidays and are rescheduled.
- Thou shalt secure all valuables, especially when staying in budget bungalows.
- Thou shalt savour some fried fare in Chicken Corner (p268) before the revelry begins.
- Thou shalt wear protective shoes during the sandy celebration, unless ye want a tetanus shot.
- Thou shalt cover thyself with swirling patterns of neon body paint.
- Thou shalt visit Magic Mountain or The Rock for killer views of the heathens below.
- Thou shalt not sample the drug buffet, nor shalt thou swim in the ocean under the influence of alcohol.
- Thou shalt stay in a group of two or more people, especially women, and especially when returning home at the end of the evening.
- Thou shalt party until the sun comes up and have a great time.

Reveller at Full Moon party

KRISTIN PILJAY

When you're sitting on the deck and the tide is high (and you've had a couple of drinks), you can almost believe you're out at sea.

GETTING THERE & AWAY
BANGKOK, HUA HIN & CHUMPHON
Lomprayah (www.lomprayah.com) and **Seatran Discovery** (www.seatrandiscovery .com) have bus-boat combination packages departing from Bangkok and passing through Chumphon. It is also quite hassle-free to take the train from Bangkok to Chumphon and switch to a ferry service (it works out to be about the same price). For detailed information about travelling through Chumphon see p254 and p276.

KO SAMUI
There are almost 10 daily departures between Ko Pha-Ngan and Ko Samui (200B to 350B). All leave from either Thong Sala or Hat Rin on Ko Pha-Ngan and arrive either in Na Thon, Mae Nam or the Bang Rak pier on Ko Samui.

KO TAO
Ko Tao–bound Lomprayah and Seatran Discovery ferries depart Ko Pha-Ngan at 8.30am and 1pm and arrive at 9.45am and 2.15pm. Songserm leaves Ko Pha-Ngan at noon and arrives at 1.45pm.

SURAT THANI & THE ANDAMAN COAST
Most travellers will pass through Surat Thani as they swap coasts. There are approximately six daily departures between Ko Pha-Ngan and Surat Thani (220B to 350B, 2½ hours) on the Raja Car Ferry, Songserm or Seatran.

Every night, depending on the weather, a night boat runs from Surat, departing at 11pm.

GETTING AROUND
You can rent motorcycles all over the island for 150B to 250B per day. Car rentals are around 1000B a day.

Sŏrng·tăa·ou chug along the island's major roads and the riding rates double after sunset. The trip from Thong Sala to

Hat Rin is 50B; further beaches will set you back around 100B.

Long-tail boats depart from Thong Sala, Chalok Lam and Hat Rin, heading to a variety of far-flung destinations like Hat Khuat (Bottle Beach) and Ao Thong Nai Pan. Expect to pay anywhere from 50B, for a short trip, to 300B for a lengthier journey.

KO TAO
เกาะเต่า
pop 5000

Diving enthusiasts cavort with sharks and rays in a playground of tangled neon coral. Hikers and hermits can re-enact an episode from 'Lost' in the dripping coastal jungles.

Ko Tao has many years to go before corporate resort owners bulldoze rustic cottages, and visitors start discussing stockholdings rather than sea creatures spotted on their latest dive.

ACTIVITIES
DIVING

Ko Tao is *the* place to lose your scuba virginity. The island issues more scuba certifications than in any other place around the world, which means that prices are low and quality is high as dozens of dive shops vie for your baht. The shallow bays that scallop the island are the perfect spot for newbie divers to take their first stab at scuba.

A **PADI** (www.padi.com) Open Water course costs 9800B; an **SSI** (www.ssithailand .com) Open Water course is slightly less at 9000B, because you do not have to pay for instructional materials. An Advanced certificate will set you back 8500B, a rescue course is 9500B and the Divemaster program costs a cool 25,000B. Fun divers should expect to pay 1000B per dive, or 7000B for a 10-dive package. These rates include gear, boat, instructor and snacks.

The dive schools listed here are among some of the best operators on the island, and all support the Save Koh Tao initiative.

Big Blue Diving (☎ 0 7745 6415; 0 7745 6772; www.bigbluediving.com; Hat Sai Ri) If Goldilocks were picking a dive school, she'd probably pick Big Blue – this midsize operation (not too big, not too small) gets props for fostering a sociable vibe while maintaining a high standard of service.

Crystal Dive (☎ 0 7745 6107; www.crystal dive.com; Mae Hat) It's one of the largest schools on the island (and around the world), although high-quality instructors and intimate classes keep the school feeling quite personal.

New Heaven (☎ 0 7745 6587; www.new heavendiveschool.com; Chalok Ban Kao) The owners of this small diving operation dedicate a lot of their time to preserving the natural beauty of Ko Tao's underwater sites by conducting regular reef checks and contributing to reef restoration efforts.

New Way Diving (☎ 0 7745 6527, 08 6044 0822; www.newwaydiving.com, www.scubadiving kohtao.com; Hat Sai Ri) This tiny school has built its good reputation on offering small diving groups in a professional atmosphere.

SNORKELLING

Orchestrating your own snorkelling adventure is simple, since the bays on the east coast have small bungalow operations offering equipment for between 100B and 200B.

Almost every dive operation offers snorkelling day trips tailored to the customers' desires.

OTHER ACTIVITIES

Although most activities on Ko Tao revolve around the sea, the friendly crew at **Goodtime Adventures** (☎ 08 7275 3604; www.gtadventures.com; Sairee Beach; ⏰ noon-midnight) offers a wide variety of land-based activities to get the blood pumping. Hike through the island's jungly interior, swing from rock to rock during a climbing and abseiling session, or unleash your inner daredevil during an afternoon of cliff jumping.

SLEEPING

If you are planning to dive while visiting Ko Tao, your scuba operator will probably offer you discounted accommodation to sweeten the deal.

SAIREE BEACH (HAT SAI RI)

Giant Sairee Beach is the longest and most developed strip on the island, with a string of dive operations, bungalows, travel agencies, superettes and internet cafes. The narrow 'yellow brick road' stretches the entire length of beach (watch out for motorcycles).

Sairee Cottage (☎ 0 7745 6126, 0 7745 6374; saireecottage@hotmail.com; bungalows 400-1500B; ⚡) Low prices means low vacancy – so arrive early to score one of the brick huts facing out onto a grassy knoll.

Sunset Buri Resort (☎ 0 7745 6266; bungalows 700-2500B; ⚡ 🖥 ⚡) A long beach-bound path is studded with beautiful white bungalows featuring enormous windows and flamboyant temple-like roofing. The kidney-shaped pool is a big hit, as are the large beach recliners sprinkled around the resort.

Ko Tao Cabana (☎ 0 7745 6250; www .kohtaocabana.com; bungalows 3000-6300B; ⚡) This prime piece of beachside property offers timber-framed villas and crinkled white adobe huts dotted along the boulder-strewn.

EAST COAST BEACHES

The serene eastern coast is, without a doubt, one of the best places in the region

Chalok Ban Kao, Ko Tao

RICHARD NEBESKY

to live out your island-paradise fantasies. The views are stunning, beaches are silent, yet all of your creature comforts are 10 minutes away. Accommodation along this coast is organised from north to south.

HIN WONG

A sandy beach has been swapped for a boulder-strewn coast, but the water is crystal clear. The road to Hin Wong is paved in parts, but sudden sand pits and steep hills can toss you off your motorbike.

Hin Wong Bungalows (☎ 0 7745 6006, 08 1229 4810; bungalows from 300B) Pleasant wooden huts are scattered across vast expanses of untamed tropical terrain – it all feels a bit like *Gilligan's Island* (minus the millionaire castaways). A rickety dock, jutting out just beyond the breezy restaurant, is the perfect place to dangle your legs and watch schools of black sardines slide through the cerulean water.

View Rock (☎ 0 7745 6548/9; viewrock@hotmail.com; bungalows 300-400B) When coming down the dirt road into Hin Wong, follow the signs as they lead you north of Hin Wong Bungalows. View Rock is precisely that: views and rocks. The hodgepodge of wooden huts, which looks like a secluded fishing village, is built into the steep crags, offering stunning views of the bay.

LAEM THIAN

Laem Thian is a scenic cape with a small patch of sand.

Laem Thian (☎ 0 7745 6477; r & bungalows 400-1500B; 🏊) Nestled far from civilisation on a lush stretch of jungle, this small boulder-filled resort is the only operation on Laem Thian. The modern rooms tend to be better than the bungalows, so long as you don't mind the ugly facades. The road here is very rough; call for a pick-up.

TANOTE BAY (AO TANOT)

Tanote Bay is slightly more populated than some of the other eastern coves, but it's still quiet and picturesque. It is the only bay on the east coast that is accessible by paved road. Discounted taxis

Village street, Ko Tao

JOHN BORTHWICK

(80B to 100B) bounce back and forth between Tanote Bay and Mae Hat; ask at your resort for a timetable and price details.

Black Tip Dive Resort (☎ 0 7745 6488; www.blacktip-kohtao.com; bungalows 600-2800B; ▣ ▢) Part dive shop and water-sports centre, Black Tip also has a handful of lovely wooden bungalows with thatched roofing.

AO LEUK & AO THIAN OK

The dirt roads to Ao Leuk and Ao Thian Ok are steep, rough and rutty, especially towards the end; don't attempt it on a motorcycle unless you're an expert. Both bays are stunning and serene.

Ao Leuk Bungalows (☎ 0 7745 6692; bungalows 400-1500B) Lodging at Ao Leuk comes in several shapes and sizes ranging from backpacker shacks to modern family-friendly options. Flickering torches and ambient cackles of curious cicadas accent the jet-black evenings.

NORTH COAST

This isolated rocky bay has one sleeping option in a dramatic setting of tangled jungle vines and rocky hills.

Mango Bay Grand Resort (☎ 0 7745 6097; www.mangobaygrandresortkohtaothailand .com; bungalows 1400-3000B; ▣) Spacious mahogany bungalows are perched high on stilts above the ashen boulders lining the bay. A thin necklace of mosaic-lined paths winds through the tropical shrubbery, connecting the secluded villas.

EATING

SAIREE BEACH (HAT SAI RI)

Keep an eye out for rickety food carts scattered around the village serving tasty tea and treats. Stop by the 7-Eleven beside Big Blue Resort to check out Ally the Pancake Man as he dances around, like an Italian

chef making pizza, while cooking your tasty dessert.

White House Food Stalls (dishes 30-70B; ☺ lunch & dinner) Plunked in front of a humble white house amid the bustling action in Sairee, these clinking metallic food stalls sling awesome *sôm-đam* and barbecue treats to crowds of hungry locals.

Blue Wind Bakery (☎ 0 7745 6116; mains 50-120B; ☺ breakfast, lunch & dinner) This beachside shanty dishes out Thai favourites, Western confections and freshly blended fruit juices. Enjoy your thick fruit smoothie and flaky pastry while reclining on tattered triangular pillows.

our pick ZanziBar (☎ 0 7745 6452; sandwiches 90-140B; ☺ breakfast, lunch & dinner) The island's outpost of sandwich yuppie-dom slathers a mix of unpronounceable condiments betwixt two slices of whole-grain bread.

MAE HAT (HAT AO MAE)

our pick Whitening (☎ 0 7745 6199; dishes 90-160B; ☺ dinner) Although menu is multicultural, diners should stick to the phenomenal assortment of Thai dishes like the garlic prawns or the slow-stewed red curry with duck.

Greasy Spoon (☎ 08 6272 1499; English breakfast 120B; ☺ 7am-6pm) Although completely devoid of character, breakfast lovers will be sated by Greasy Spoon's hearty morning repast – eggs, sausage, chips and cooked veggies that'll bring a tear to any Brit's eye.

Café del Sol (☎ 0 7745 6578; dishes 70-250B; ☺ breakfast, lunch & dinner) Even the pickiest eater will be satisfied with the menu's expansive selection of 'world cuisine'. The focus is namely European (French and Italian) with specialties like homemade pâté, bruschetta and tender steaks imported from New Zealand. Free wi-fi available.

CHALOK BAN KAO

New Heaven Restaurant (☎ 0 7745 6462; **dishes 60-350B**; ☒ **lunch & dinner**) The best part about New Heaven Restaurant is the awe-inducing view of Shark Bay (Ao Thian Ok) under the lazy afternoon moon.

DRINKING

After diving, Ko Tao's favourite pastime is drinking, and there's definitely no shortage of places to get tanked. Fliers detailing upcoming parties are posted on various trees and walls along the west coast (check the two 7-Elevens in Sairee). Also keep an eye out for posters touting 'jungle parties' held on nondescript patches of scrubby jungle in the centre of the island.

SAIREE BEACH (HAT SAI RI)

Vibe Sairee's top spot for a sundowner drinks, Vibe has the largest (and best) playlist out of any drinking spot on the island.

MAE HAT (AO HAT MAE)

Safety Stop Pub (☎ 0 7745 6209) A haven for homesick Brits, this pier-side pub feels like a tropical beer garden. Stop by on Sunday to stuff your face with an endless supply of barbecued goodness. Wi-fi is available.

GETTING THERE & AWAY
BANGKOK, HUA HIN & CHUMPHON

The train is a more comfortable option than the bus, and tourists can plan their own journey by taking a boat to Chumphon and the train up to Bangkok (or any town along the upper southern gulf); likewise in the opposite direction.

From Ko Tao, the high-speed catamaran departs for Chumphon at 10.15am and 2.45pm (550B, 1½ hours), the Seatran leaves the island at 4pm (550B, two hours),

and a Songserm fast boat makes the same journey at 2.30pm (450B, three hours).

There's also a midnight boat from Chumphon (600B) arriving early in the morning. It returns from Ko Tao at 11pm.

KO PHA-NGAN

The Lomprayah catamaran offers twice-daily service, leaving Ko Tao at 9.30am and 3pm and arriving on Ko Pha-Ngan around 10.50am and 4.10pm. The Seatran Discovery ferry offers an identical service. The Songserm Express Boat departs daily at 10am and arrives on Samui at 11.30am.

KO SAMUI

The Lomprayah catamaran offers twice-daily service, leaving Ko Tao at 9.30am and 3pm, and arriving on Samui around 11.30am and 4.40pm. The Seatran Discovery ferry offers an identical service. The **Songserm Express Boat** (www.songserm-expressboat.com) departs daily at 10am and arrives on Samui at 12.45pm. Hotel pick-ups are included in the price.

GETTING AROUND

Sŏrng·tăa·ou crowd around the pier in Mae Hat as passengers alight. If you're a solo traveller, you will pay 100B to get to Sai Ri and Chalok Ban Kao. Groups of two or more will pay 50B each. Rides from Sai Ri to Chalok Ban Kao cost 80B per person, or 150B for solo tourists. If taxis are empty, you will be asked to pay for the entire cab (300B to 500B). If you know where you intend to stay, call ahead for a pick-up.

SURAT THANI

อ.เมือง จสุราษฎร์ธานี

pop 111,900

Travellers rarely linger here as they make their way to the deservedly popular islands of Ko Samui, Ko Pha-Ngan and Ko Tao.

Kayakers, Ang Thong Marine National Park

AUSTIN BUSH

⬊ ANG THONG MARINE NATIONAL PARK

อุทยานแห่งชาติหมู่เกาะอ่างทอง

The 40-some jagged jungle islands of **Ang Thong Marine National Park** stretch across the cerulean sea like a shattered emerald necklace – each one piece a virgin realm featuring sheer limestone cliffs, hidden lagoons and perfect peach-coloured sands. These dream-inducing islets inspired Alex Garland's cult classic *The Beach* about dope-dabbling backpackers.

February, March and April are the best months to visit this ethereal preserve of greens and blues; crashing monsoon waves means that the park is almost always closed during November and December.

The best way to reach the park is to catch a private day-tour from Ko Samui or Ko Pha-Ngan (located 28km and 32km away, respectively). The islands sit between Samui and the main pier at Don Sak; however, there are no ferries that stop off along the way. The park officially has an admission fee (adult/child 400/200B), although it should be included in the price of every tour. Private boat charters are also another possibility, although high gas prices will make the trip quite expensive.

GETTING THERE & AWAY

In general, if you are departing Bangkok or Hua Hin for Ko Samui, Ko Pha-Ngan or Ko Tao, consider taking a boat-bus package that goes through Chumphon rather than Surat.

Travellers can also take a train south to Chumphon and then connect to a catamaran service.

AIR

There are two daily shuttles to Bangkok on **Thai Airways International** (☎ 0 7727 2610; 3/27-28 Th Karunarat) for around 3000B (70 minutes).

BOAT

In the high season there are usually bus-boat services to Ko Samui and Ko Pha-Ngan directly from the train station. These services don't cost any more than those booked in Surat Thani and can save you a lot of waiting around. There are also several ferry and speedboat operators that connect Surat Thani to Ko Tao, Ko Pha-Ngan and Ko Samui. See the transport section of your desired destination for exact details.

From Surat there are nightly ferries to Ko Tao (500B, eight hours), Ko Pha-Ngan (200B, seven hours) and Ko Samui (150B, six hours). All leave from the town's central night ferry pier at 11pm. These are cargo ships, not luxury boats, so bring food and water and watch your bags. If Thai passengers are occupying your assigned berth, it's best to grab a different one nearby rather than asking them to move.

BUS & MINIVAN
Most long-distance public buses run from the Talat Kaset 1 and 2 bus terminals. Aircon minivans leave from Talat Kaset 2 and tend to have more frequent departures than buses, although they're usually more expensive.

TRAIN
When arriving by train you'll actually pull into Phun Phin, a cruddy town approximately 14km west of Surat.

From Bangkok, fan/air-con fares cost 297/397B in 3rd class, 438/578B in 2nd-class seat, 498/758B for an upper 2nd-class sleeper and 548/848B for a lower 2nd-class sleeper. First-class sleepers cost 1279B. If you take an early evening train from Bangkok, you'll arrive in the morning.

GETTING AROUND
All boat services to Samui depart from Don Sak (except the night ferry) and ticket prices include the price of the bus transfer.

To travel around town, *sŏrng·tăa·ou* cost 10B to 30B, while *săhm·lór* (three-wheeled vehicles) charge between 30B and 40B.

Orange buses run from Phun Phin train station to Surat Thani every 10 minutes (15B, 25 minutes). For this ride, taxis charge 150B.

Ang Thong Marine National Park (p277)

AUSTIN BUSH

AUSTIN BUSH

Elephant rides, Phuket (p295)

ANDAMAN COAST

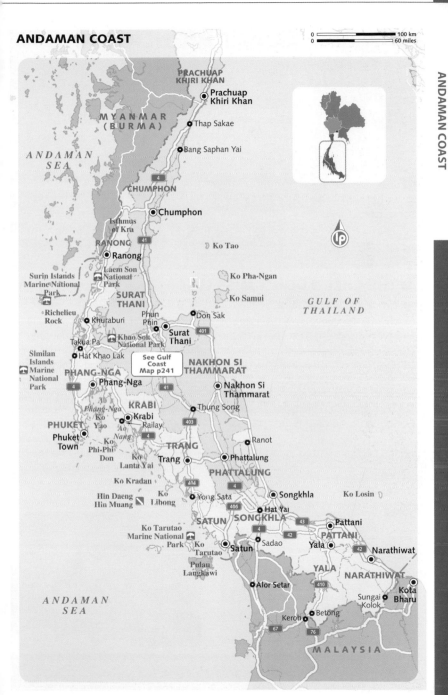

ANDAMAN COAST

0 — 100 km
0 — 60 miles

PRACHUAP
KHIRI KHAN

◉ Prachuap
Khiri Khan

MYANMAR
(BURMA)

◉ Thap Sakae

◉ Bang Saphan Yai

ANDAMAN
SEA

CHUMPHON

◉ Chumphon

◉ Ko Tao

RANONG

◉ Ranong

Laem Son
National
Park

Surin Islands
Marine National
Park

◉ Ko Pha-Ngan

SURAT
THANI

◉ Ko Samui

GULF OF
THAILAND

Richelieu
Rock

Phun
Phin

◉ Don Sak

◉ Khuraburi

Takua Pa

Khao Sok
National Park

◉ Surat
Thani

Similan
Islands
Marine
National
Park

◉ Hat Khao Lak

See Gulf
Coast
Map p241

NAKHON SI
THAMMARAT

PHANG-NGA

◉ Phang-Nga

Ao
Phang-Nga
Ko
Yao

◉ Nakhon Si
Thammarat

KRABI

◉ Krabi
Railay

◉ Thung Song

PHUKET

Ao
Nang

Ko
Phi-Phi
Don

Ko
Lanta Yai

TRANG

◉ Ranot

Phuket
Town

◉ Trang

◉ Phattalung

Ko Kradan

PHATTALUNG

Hin Daeng
Hin Muang

Ko
Libong

◉ Yong Sata

◉ Songkhla

Ko Losin

SATUN

Hat Yai

SONGKHLA

◉ Pattani

Ko Tarutao
Marine National
Park

Ko
Tarutao

◉ Satun

Sadao

PATTANI

◉ Yala

◉ Narathiwat

Pulau
Langkawi

YALA

NARATHIWAT

◉ Alor Setar

Sungai
Kolok

◉ Kota
Bharu

ANDAMAN
SEA

Keroh ◉ Betong

MALAYSIA

ANDAMAN COAST HIGHLIGHTS

1   PHUKET

BY TUMMANOON PUNCHUN, EXECUTIVE CHEF & COOKING COURSE INSTRUCTOR, MOM TRI'S BOATHOUSE

Though many people come for the beaches, Phuket has many restaurants serving different kinds of dishes and all of them are good. Due to the location of Phuket island we have many fresh fish and seafood dishes. Also tourists can learn how to make fresh and tasty Thai food (with a view of the ocean).

↘ THE CHEF'S DON'T MISS LIST

❶ PHUKET'S BEACHES

My favourite beach is Kata. I see it every day at work and like to watch the changing sea. Also I like Nai Harn Beach because it is very quiet and clean. I like to go there by myself and swim in the sea, read a book and relax. A little walking on the beach is the kind of exercise I enjoy most, nothing too strenuous.

❷ DINE LIKE A CHEF

A local restaurant that I really like is **Thammachat** (Natural Restaurant; ☎ 0 7622 4287; 62/5 Soi Phutorn, Th Bangkok, Phuket Town). It serves original Thai food with many special items and the price is reasonable. I go there with my friends and family a lot. My favourite Western restaurant is the **Ninth Floor** (p305); it's French-Swiss style. I know the owner from Switzerland and besides the food I like to watch the panoramic view over Patong.

Clockwise from top: Preparing spring rolls; Street-stall serving noodles; Seafood dish; Chef cooking pàt tai; Boats, Phuket (p295)

❸ GAANG SOM & PÀT TAI

A popular Phuket dish is *gaang sôm ƀlah*. It is a local fish curry prepared southern style with a curry paste that is a bit spicier than most curries; it is cooked without coconut milk. The taste is a little more sweet/sour/salty. In general Phuket food is quite spicy but it doesn't stay on the tongue for a long time. Another favourite is the local *pàt tai* (stir-fried noodles) made with a special curry paste that includes tamarind, sugar, chilli and shrimp paste. It's delicious!

❹ COOKING COURSES

My **cooking classes** (p300), which I started at Mom Tri's in 1999, are hands-on workshops. I explain Thai herbs and spices and let the students taste the ingredients. It makes it easier to understand Thai flavours. I demonstrate and explain the cooking and then the students have a chance to do it themselves. Learning from doing, learning from experience is always a much better way.

↘ THINGS YOU NEED TO KNOW

Avoid Don't toss out the dried chilli seeds when making a curry paste; you need them in order to get a thick consistency **Top Tip** When eating Thai food do as the Thais and order a variety of appetisers and mains so you can enjoy many tastes

ANDAMAN COAST HIGHLIGHTS

2 | KRABI

**BY SUHAI (HEN) HAMMAN, PADDLE GUIDE &
OPERATIONS MANAGER, SEA CANOE THAILAND**

There are more than 30 islands off the coast of Krabi and the
optimal way to get close to nature is aboard a small kayak.
You can explore the off-shore destinations by long-tail boat
but that is only suitable for sightseeing. I'm a Krabi native
and have been leading tours for 10 years; I love showing
tourists the beauty of the coastline.

↘ HEN'S DON'T MISS LIST

❶ MANGROVE SWAMP

Near Krabi, Ao Talen is a strange environment: first we paddle through the
limestone canyon with a fast-moving
current and then we slide through the
mangrove swamp, underneath trees
and past the chatter of insects and
birds. In a kayak you can hear how
loud the mangroves are and can spot
monkeys, water monitors, sea eagles
and Bramany kites.

❷ CAVES & COVES

Ao Phang Nga (p298) and its karst
caves are accessible from Krabi. We
paddle deep into the caves (or *hôrng*,
which in Thai means 'room') without
causing a lot of pollution. Around the
northern part of Ao Phang Nga, in the
Bor Tor area, the geology is amazing and there are prehistoric cave
drawings.

Clockwise from top: Rock climbers (p312), Railay; Swift nests on sheer cliffs, Ko Phi-Phi (p313); Tham Phra Nang
(p312), Krabi Province; Snorkeller; Floating store, Krabi (p309)

CLOCKWISE FROM TOP: CHRISTOPHER GROENHOUT; DALLAS STRIBLEY; PAUL BEINSSEN; DENNIS JOHNSON; WOODS WHEATCROFT

❸ SNORKELLING

There are many smaller islands off the coast of **Krabi** (p309) that are good for snorkelling because they have small, undisturbed coral reefs. These are my favourite because they are so beautiful. They are uninhabited and might have one small beach where you're the only one there. We also paddle into the caves to find hidden lagoons and due to the tides, only kayaks can get into some of these places.

❹ BIRDS' NEST HARVESTING

An old and well-paying job on the Andaman Coast is collecting the nests of cave swifts. On the uninhabited islands off the coast of Krabi, locals shimmy up bamboo poles to the birds' cliffside roosts. The nests are consid-ered a delicacy in China and are the main ingredient in bird's nest soup.

❺ ROCK-CLIMBING

I'm a kayaker so I spend my time in a boat. But many people come to Krabi to go rock climbing. Climbers get a good alternative view of the coastline to the view that you can get in a boat.

⬎ THINGS YOU NEED TO KNOW

Recommended outings Sea Canoe Thailand (p299) has a variety of kayak tours to the area **Top Survival Tip** When you go out paddling in an open kayak, remember to use sunscreen on the tops of your feet

ANDAMAN COAST HIGHLIGHTS

3

⭢ FUN FOR ALL ON PHUKET

There is heaps to do on **Phuket** (p295), Thailand's biggest and most developed resort island. The famous west coast beaches are some of the country's widest and longest, and the tourist scene ranges from seedy to swanky. Bangkok money has brought an added dimension of sophistication along with fusion restaurants, and day trips whisk tourists away from the 'big city' to remote island outings.

4

⭢ SEE MORE SEA

Wake up at dawn on a liveaboard dive trip and slide directly into the sea without having to commute overland. Boats depart from **Khao Lak** (p292) to some of the world's top dive sites. Depending on the duration of the trip, you'll visit the **Similan Islands Marine National Park** (p295) and its underwater geography as well as world-famous Richelieu Rock, where whale sharks congregate.

5 ⬎ SCRAMBLE UP A RAILAY CLIFF

Railay (p312) is a small corner of the Krabi peninsula but it is crowded with peaks onshore and offshore. Rock climbers decided the vertical walls needed some bolts, creating a sporting challenge with fantastic vistas.

6 ⬎ ADORE KO PHI-PHI

Come worship upon the white-sand altar of **Ko Phi-Phi** (p313), one of the most beautiful spots on planet earth. The bearded limestone cliffs, ribbons of emerald and turquoise water, and voluptuous contours of sand are a sensory feast. Soak it all in with early morning strolls, afternoon swims and evening sunsets.

7 ⬎ GET MUDDY IN KHAO SOK

The interior rainforest of **Khao Sok National Park** (p292) is an example of nature at its most primordial. Among the muddy trails and forested karst mountains are monkeys, bugs galore, birds and the rare *Rafflesia kerrii*, a Malay peninsular flower with a fragrance akin to rotten meat.

3 AUSTIN BUSH; 4 JOHN ELK III; 5 JERRY ALEXANDER; 6 DALLAS STRIBLEY; 7 JOE CUMMINGS

3 Swinging around, Phuket (p295); 4 Khao Lak beach (p292), Phang-Nga Province; 5 Rock climbing (p312), Railay; 6 Long-tail boats, Ko Phi-Phi (p313); 7 Khao Sok National Park (p292), Phang-Nga Province

ANDAMAN COAST'S BEST...

⬎ DAY TRIPS

- **Ao Phang-Nga** (p298) A karst mountain–studded bay near Phuket.
- **Ko Phi-Phi Leh** (p316) Ko Phi-Phi's uninhabited sister island decorated with lagoons and technicolour coral.
- **Around Railay** (p312) Lagoons, coral reefs and quiet beaches lie in wait near Railay beach.

⬎ LAID-BACK ISLANDS

- **Ko Lanta** (p316) Scoot around on a motorcycle and enjoy life without a wristwatch.
- **Ko Yao** (p298) Sleepy Muslim fishing village.
- **Trang Islands** (p318) Fewer crowds, just as much sea and sand.

⬎ PLACES TO DIVE & SNORKEL

- **Similan Islands Marine National Park** (p295) Protected park with great visibility and marine life.
- **Surin Islands Marine National Park** (p294) Coral gardens for divers and shallow bays for snorkellers.
- **Ko Lanta** (p316) Undersea pinnacles of Hin Muang and Hin Daeng attract divers and large pelagic fish.

⬎ PLACES FOR A SUNDOWNER

- **White Box** (p305) Phuket's chic and modern setting for romantic cocktails.
- **Carpe Diem** (p316) Ko Phi-Phi's chill zone for cold beers and sandy toes.
- **After Beach Bar** (p307) A cliffside perch in Phuket that is bathed by the setting sun.

LEFT: SEAN CAFFREY; RIGHT: AUSTIN BUSH

Left: Long-tail boat, Ko Phi-Phi Leh (p316); Right: After Beach Bar (p307), Phuket

THINGS YOU NEED TO KNOW

⇲ VITAL STATISTICS

- **Population** 3.91 million
- **Best time to visit** December to April

⇲ ISLANDS & BEACHES IN A NUTSHELL

- **Khao Lak** Mainland departure point for liveaboard dive trips.
- **Phuket** Thailand's number-one beach resort.
- **Railay** Rock-climbing mecca.
- **Ko Phi-Phi** Drop-dead gorgeous island.
- **Ko Lanta** Miss Congeniality with great diving.

⇲ ADVANCE PLANNING

- **One month before** Book accommodation.
- **One week before** Book your dive trip and domestic plane trip.
- **One day before** Book a table at one of Phuket's high-end restaurants.

⇲ RESOURCES

- **Tourism Authority of Thailand** (☎ 0 7621 2213; www.tat.or.th; 73-65 Th Phuket, Phuket Town; ☒ 8.30am-4.30pm)
- **Railay.com** (www.railay.com) Guide to Railay and around.
- **Jamie's Phuket** (www.jamie-monk .blogspot.com) Phuket expat's blog.

⇲ EMERGENCY NUMBERS

- **Fire** (☎ 199)
- **Police/Emergency** (☎ 191)
- **Tourist police** (☎ 1155; ☒ 24hr)

⇲ GETTING AROUND

- **Boat** Everything that floats will take you wherever roads can't; less so during the rainy season (June to October).
- **Bus** Good way to get between mainland towns.
- **Minivan & Share Taxi** Faster but less comfortable than the bus.
- **Motorcycle** Good self-touring option on Phuket and Ko Lanta.
- **Sŏrng·tăa·ou** Small pick-up trucks that act as public buses on the mainland and Phuket.
- **Taxi & Túk-túk** Chartered vehicles that charge a lot on the islands; remember to bargain.

⇲ BE FOREWARNED

- **Dive trips** Book your trip directly with the dive shop not with an agent.
- **Motorcycle travel** Always wear a helmet when riding a motorcycle and don't put valuables in the front basket.
- **Rainy season** Except for Phuket, much of the Andaman closes down between June and October as seas can be too rough for transport and diving.
- **Drownings** Are common on Phuket's west coast beaches.
- **Seashells** Don't buy seashells that have been poached from national parks.

ANDAMAN COAST ITINERARIES

PHUKET IN A NUTSHELL Three Days

The largest of Thailand's islands, **(1) Phuket** (p295) has lovely west-coast beaches that are lined with professional resorts and intimate boutiques, umbrella lounge chairs and warm clear water. Treat yourself to a spa session, a cooking class and a fine meal at Tre or Boathouse Wine & Grill.

Once the sun has set, the night creatures descend on Patong, a rowdy strip of neon lights, ladyboy cabarets, screaming discos and a touch of port-town seediness.

A common day trip from Phuket is to **(2) Ao Phang-Nga Marine National Park** (p298), a protected bay cluttered with more than 40 peaked karst islands. Vast mangrove forests border the bay, providing fertile fishing grounds for local villagers. Tours of the region range from self-negotiated long-tail rides with local boatmen to organised paddling trips.

EXHAUST YOURSELF IN KHAO LAK & KHAO SOK Five Days

If beach resorts make you feel itchy then you need an outdoor adventure. Mountain scrambles, underwater dives, wildlife spotting, nature everywhere…sound better?

Fly into Phuket and catch a bus or minivan to **(1) Khao Lak** (p292), the jumping-off point for multiday liveaboard trips to some of the Andaman's most famous dive sites. Liveaboards depart for two- to five-day trips and afford you full access to the ocean and all of its underwater delights. Due to the weather and park closures, the dive season is from November to May.

Accessible via Khao Lak, the area in and around **(2) Similan Islands Marine National Park** (p295) and **(3) Surin Islands Marine National Park** (p294) boast some of Thailand's best dive sites. Topping the list are Richelieu Rock, a seamount where whale sharks are often spotted; rock reefs at Ko Payu; and dive-throughs at Hin Pousar.

(4) Khao Sok National Park (p292) is a thick rainforest punctuated by craggy karst formations and a scenic lake. The best time of year is the dry season (December to May) when trails aren't as muddy or leech-infested. After the park, you're within striking range of the Gulf coast via Surat Thani.

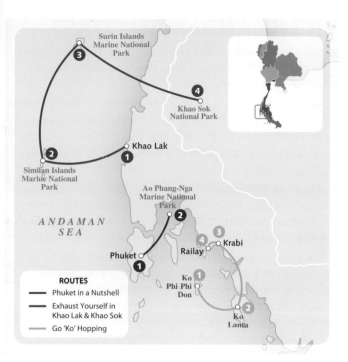

GO 'KO' HOPPING One Week

South of Phuket, small islands and beaches are cradled together and are visited in succession as if they were all cherished family members.

From Phuket, boat down to (1) Ko Phi-Phi Don (p313), the beauty queen of the Thai islands with just the right proportions of mod-cons and back-to-nature.

Then boat to (2) Ko Lanta (p316), which has exceptional dive sites and lots of 'island' personality (but not quite the good looks of Phi-Phi). Rent a motorcycle and cruise the local fishing villages and roadside food shacks to get in touch with Lanta's local population of Muslim and Buddhist Thais as well as *chow lair* (sea gypsies).

Another boat journey will take you to (3) Krabi Town (p309) where you can transfer to a long-tail headed for (4) Railay (p311), a small but scenic peninsula that has developed a thriving rock-climbing scene. You're just a step away from Krabi Town for a quick air return to Bangkok.

DISCOVER THE ANDAMAN COAST

Fortunately, the Andaman Coast is the ultimate land of superlatives: the tall*est* karst formations, the long*est* beaches, the soft*est* sands, the blu*est* water – the list goes on.

Along the coast, boats from Khao Lak idle between the Similan and Surin islands, dropping scuba buffs deep down into the great*est* dive sights around. Further south, Phuket, the bigg*est* island, is the region's hedonistic launching pad, offering a glimmer of what's to come next.

The Andaman's signature pinnacles of jagged jungle-clad slate come to a stunning climax in Krabi. Ko Phi-Phi Don's unimaginable beauty exceeds even the high*est* expectations. At Railay, climbers take in the scenery as they dangle like ornaments on a giant Christmas tree.

Down in Trang, the skyscraping swell of iconic limestone starts to sink back into the deep, but not before punctuating the coastline with a handful of anthropomorphic islets. This quiet getaway, the Andaman's b*est*-kept secret (until now), is the mystical stomping ground of the local sea gypsies, who cast their lines among the fin*est* blooms of snorkel-worthy coral.

PHANG-NGA PROVINCE

KHAO SOK NATIONAL PARK

อุทยานแห่งชาติเขาสก

This dripping, juicy jungle is part of the oldest rainforest in the world, where snakes, monkeys and tigers mingle within the tangle of lazy vines.

Although technically part of Surat Thani Province, **Khao Sok National Park** (☎ 0 7739 5025; www.khaosok.com; admission 400B) is much closer to the Andaman Sea, and possesses the classic Andaman topography: signature ferny cliffs that shoot straight up into the air like crocodile teeth.

SLEEPING & EATING

Khao Sok Rainforest Resort (☎ 0 7739 5006; www.krabidir.com/khaosokrainforest; bun-galows 400-600B) Huts perched high on stilts along the snaking river. In-house conservation programs target low-impact hiking and forest restoration.

Cliff & River Jungle Resort (☎ 08 7271 8787; www.thecliffandriver.com; bungalows 1800B) A beautiful property set just below the jagged silver cliffs. The plunge pool and steam spa are extra perks.

GETTING THERE & AROUND

You can come from the west coast by bus, but you'll have to go to Takua Pa first. Buses from Takua Pa to the park (25B, one hour, nine daily) drop you off on the highway, 1.8km from the visitor centre.

KHAO LAK & AROUND

เขาหลัก/บางเนียง/นางทอง

These days, the big draw is liveaboard diving trips, which explore the stunning Similan and Surin Archipelagos.

SIGHTS & ACTIVITIES

Of Thailand's beach destinations damaged by the 2004 Boxing Day tsunami wave, the area around Khao Lak suffered the most. A **police boat**, slightly north of central Khao Lak, was brought by the tide to its present location (about 2km inland) when the giant wave ploughed through the harbour. The boat remains on the hill – a monument to those lost and a reminder of nature's raw power.

DIVING

Liveaboards range from backpacker-friendly three-day trips priced at 12,000B, to lavish luxury yachts that charge upwards of 25,000B for three days at sea. Snorkellers can hop on selected dive excursions or liveaboards for a discount of around 40%; otherwise, tour agencies all around town offer even cheaper snorkelling trips starting at around 2500B, but these are generally overcrowded and of poor quality.

The following dive schools are highly recommended:

IQ Dive (☎ 0 7648 5614; www.iq-dive.com; Th Phetkasem) A quality operation that focuses on diving and snorkelling day trips.

Sea Dragon Diver Center (☎ 0 7648 5420; www.seadragondivecenter.com; Th Phetkasem) One of the older operations in Khao Lak, Sea Dragon has maintained high standards throughout the years and continues to offer top-notch day trips and liveaboards.

Similan Diving Safaris (☎ 0 7648 5470; www.similan-diving-safaris.com) As far as liveaboards are concerned, this is probably the best bang for your baht.

Wicked Diving (☎ 0 7648 5868; www.wickeddiving.com; Hwy 4) This is a fun and friendly place to do your PADI coursework.

SLEEPING

Khaolak Banana (☎ 0 7648 5889; www.khaolakbanana.com; r 500-1200B) These adorable little bungalows have swirls painted on the cement floors and sun-filled indoor-outdoor bathrooms.

ourpick **Nangthong Bay Resort** (☎ 0 7648 5088; bungalows 2000-3000D; 🛉 🖥 🛋)

POLICE

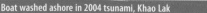
Boat washed ashore in 2004 tsunami, Khao Lak

ANDREW BAIN

JOHN ELK III

Divers, Surin Islands Marine National Park

Nangthong is an excellent place to stay and it's no secret – this place fills up fast.

Similana Resort (☎ 0 7648 7166; www .similanaresort.com; r from 3000B; 🏊 🖳 🖵) Each bungalow is a small work of art, with handcrafted furnishings, dark-wood floors, quilted bedcovers, bay windows and private decks with panoramic views.

EATING & DRINKING

Happy Snapper (☎ 0 7642 3540; Th Phetkasem; dishes 90-290B; 🕙 breakfast, lunch & dinner) Wooden statues lie frozen as patrons bop their heads to the nightly live-music acts. There's a small Thai canteen attached to the bar that serves up tasty usuals.

Pizzeria (☎ 0 7648 5271; dishes 200-300B; 🕙 lunch & dinner) Stuff your face with authentic eats like homemade gnocchi or thin-crust pizzas, and we guarantee you'll be back for seconds.

GETTING THERE & AWAY

Any bus running along Hwy 4 between Takua Pa (50B, 45 minutes) and Phuket (80B, two hours) will stop at Hat Khao Lak if you ask the driver.

SURIN ISLANDS MARINE NATIONAL PARK

อุทยานแห่งชาติหมู่เกาะสุรินทร์

The five gorgeous islands that make up this **national park** (www.dnp.go.th; admission 400B; 🕙 mid-Nov–mid-May) sit about 60km offshore, a measly 5km from the Thai-Myanmar (Burma) marine border. Healthy rainforest, pockets of white-sand beach in sheltered bays and rocky headlands that jut into the ocean characterise these granite-outcrop islands. The clearest of water makes for great marine life, with underwater visibility often up to 35m. The islands' sheltered waters also attract *chow lair* (sea gypsies) who live in a village onshore during the monsoon season from May to November.

Khuraburi is the jumping-off point for the park. The pier is about 9km north of town, as is the mainland **national park office** (☎ 0 7649 1378; 🕙 8am-5pm) with good information, maps and helpful staff.

ACTIVITIES

The best way to explore these all-star dive sites is by joining a multiday liveaboard departing from Khao Lak (p293).

Two-hour snorkelling trips by boat (per person 80B; gear hire per day 150B) leave the island headquarters every day at 9am and 2pm.

SLEEPING & EATING

For park accommodation, book online at www.dnp.go.th or with the mainland **national park office** (☎ 0 7649 1378) in Khuraburi. A park **restaurant** (dishes from 60B) serves authentic Thai food.

GETTING THERE & AWAY

A 'big boat' (return 1200B, 2½ hours one way) leaves the Khuraburi pier at 9am daily, returning at 1pm (though it didn't go when we passed through). Tour operators use speedboats (return 1700B, one hour one way) and will transfer independent travellers on their daily runs.

Several tour operators, all located near the pier, run day/overnight tours (around 2800/3800B) to the park; agencies in Khao Lak (p293) and Phuket (p298) can make bookings for these and other trips.

Three to six daily buses run between Phuket and Khuraburi (160B, 3½ hours) and between Khuraburi and Ranong (60B, 1½ hours).

SIMILAN ISLANDS MARINE NATIONAL PARK

อุทยานแห่งชาติหมู่เกาะสิมิลัน

The fluorescent playground of Khao Lak's booming liveaboard industry, beautiful **Similan Islands Marine National Park** (www.dnp.go.th; admission 400B; ☺ Nov-May) lies 70km offshore, offering some of the finest diving in Thailand, if not the world. Its smooth granite islands are as impressive above water as below, topped with rainforest, edged with white-sand beaches and fringed with coral reef.

The jumping-off point for the park is the pier at Thap Lamu (or Tabla Mu), about 10km south of Khao Lak. The mainland **national park office** (☎ 0 7659 5045; ☺ 8am-4pm) is about 500m before the pier, but there's no information in English available – it's best to head to Khao Lak (p293) to get all the info you need about exploring these nine magical islets and the reefs that surround them.

ACTIVITIES

The Similans offer exceptional diving for all levels of experience, at depths from 2m to 30m. No facilities for divers exist in the national park itself, so you'll need to take a dive tour. Agencies in Khao Lak (p293) and Phuket (p298) book dive trips (three-day liveaboards from around 15,000B).

Snorkelling is good at several points around **Ko Miang**, especially in the main channel; you can hire snorkel gear from the park (per day 100B).

GETTING THERE & AWAY

There's no public transport to the park, and if you book accommodation through the national park you'll have to find your own way there.

PHUKET PROVINCE
PHUKET

ภูเก็ต

pop 83,800

Dubbed the 'pearl of the Andaman' by savvy marketing execs, this is Thailand's original tailor-made fun in the sun.

There's deep-sea diving, high-end dining and soda-white beaches that beckon your book and blanket – whatever your heart desires.

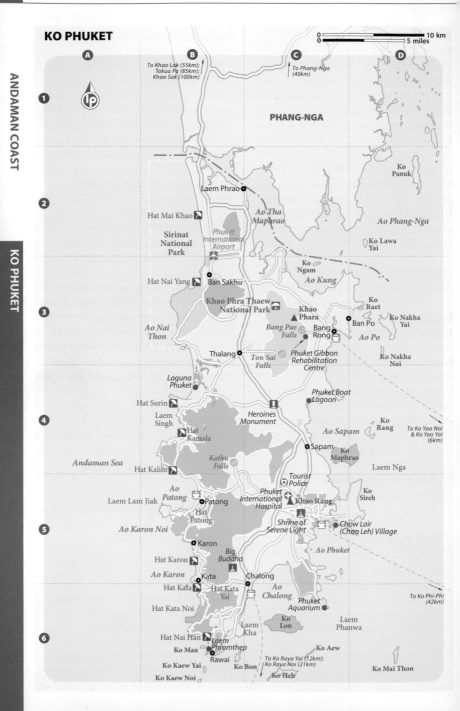

KO PHUKET

0 — 10 km
0 — 5 miles

To Khao Lak (55km);
Takua Pa (85km);
Khao Sok (100km)

To Phang-Nga (40km)

PHANG-NGA

Ko Panuk

Laem Phrao

Hat Mai Khao

Ao Tha Maphrao

Ao Phang-Nga

Sirinat National Park

Phuket International Airport

Ko Lawa Yai

Hat Nai Yang — Ban Sakhu

Ko Ngam

Ao Kung

Khao Phra Thaew National Park

Khao Phara

Ko Raet

Ban Po

Ko Nakha Yai

Ao Nai Thon

Bang Pae Falls

Bang Rong

Ao Po

Thalang

Ton Sai Falls

Phuket Gibbon Rehabilitation Centre

Ko Nakha Noi

Laguna Phuket

Phuket Boat Lagoon

Hat Surin

Heroines Monument

Laem Singh

Ko Rang

To Ko Yao Noi & Ko Yao Yai (6km)

Hat Kamala

Ao Sapam

Sapam

Ko Maphrao

Kathu Falls

Laem Nga

Andaman Sea

Hat Kalim

Tourist Police

Ao Patong

Phuket International Hospital

Khao Rang

Ko Sireh

Laem Lam Jiak

Patong

Shrine of Serene Light

Chow Lair (Chao Leh) Village

Ao Karon Noi

Hat Patong

Ao Phuket

Karon

Big Buddha

Hat Karon

Ao Karon

Kata

Hat Kata Yai

Chalong

Ao Chalong

To Ko Phi-Phi (42km)

Hat Kata

Phuket Aquarium

Hat Kata Noi

Laem Kha

Ko Lon

Laem Phanwa

Hat Nai Han

Ko Man

Laem Phromthep

Ko Aew

Rawai

Ko Kaew Yai

Ko Bon

To Ko Raya Yai (12km); Ko Raya Noi (21km)

Ko Mai Thon

Ko Kaew Noi

Ko Heh

SIGHTS
PHUKET TOWN

Phuket's historic **Sino-Portuguese architecture** is the town's most evocative attraction: stroll along Ths Thalang, Dibuk, Yaowarat, Ranong, Phang-Nga, Rasada and Krabi for a glimpse of some of the best buildings on offer. A handful of Chinese temples inject some added colour into the area. Most are standard issue, but the **Shrine of the Serene Light** (Saan Jao Sang Tham; ☼ 8.30am-noon & 1.30-5.30pm), tucked away at the end of a 50m alley near the Bangkok Bank of Commerce on Th Phang-Nga, is a cut above the rest.

For a bird's-eye view of the city, climb up pretty **Khao Rang** (Phuket Hill), northwest of the town centre.

BIG BUDDHA

Set on a hilltop just northwest of Chalong circle and visible from almost half of the island, the Big Buddha sits at the best viewpoint on Phuket. To get here you'll follow the red signs from the main highway (Hwy 402) and wind up a country road, passing terraced banana groves and tangles of jungle.

LAEM PROMTHEP
แหลมพรหมเทพ

With the exception of the Big Buddha, **Laem Phromthep** (Hwy 4233) is the best place to watch the sunset. Take it from the crowds, most of whom are Thai tourists.

KHAO PHRA THAEW ROYAL WILDLIFE & FOREST RESERVE
อุทยานสัตว์ป่าเขาพระแทว

Khao Phra Thaew National Park (Map p12), in the northern part of the island, is a preserve protecting 23 sq km of virgin rainforest.

The **Phuket Gibbon Rehabilitation Centre** (☎ 0 7626 0492; www.gibbonproject.org; admission by donation; ☼ 9am-4pm), near Bang Pae, is a must-see for park visitors. Funded by donations (1500B will care for a gibbon for one year), the volunteer-run centre adopts gibbons that have been kept in captivity and reintroduces them into the wild after they find a mate.

Phuket Aquarium (p298)

AUSTIN BUSH

ANDAMAN COAST

PHUKET PROVINCE

JOHN ELK III

Ao Phang-Nga

⤵ IF YOU LIKE...

If you like Phuket's scenery and want more, check out these postcard beauties:

- **Ao Phang-Nga** More than 40 humpbacked limestone mountains jut out of this sheltered bay to create a dramatic interplay of land and sea. It also made a cameo appearance as the villain's tropical lair in the James Bond movie *The Man with the Golden Gun*. Protected as a national park, the bay can be explored on day trips from Phuket (opposite).
- **Ko Yao** These two sister islands, Ko Yao Yai (Big Long Island) and Ko Yao Noi (Little Long Island), have an enviable view of Ao Phang-Nga's karst formations. Both are Muslim fishing villages and offer cultural insights along with tropical scenery. **Koh Yao Noi Eco-Tourism Club** (☎ 0 7659 7409, 0 1089 5413; www.koh-yao-noi-eco-tourism-club.com) is a well-respected homestay program. **Lom Lea** (☎ 08 9868 8642; www.lomlae.com; bungalows 2100-5000B) is a delightful retreat along a secluded stretch of beach. From Phuket, the boats depart from Bang Rong pier.

PHUKET AQUARIUM

At the tip of Laem Phanwa, **Phuket Aquarium** (☎ 0 7639 1126; adult/child 100/50B; ⏱ 8.30am-4pm) displays a varied collection of tropical fish and other sea creatures. Follow Rte 4021 south and turn on Rte 4023 outside of Phuket Town.

ACTIVITIES
DIVING

Most operators on Phuket take divers to the nine decent sites orbiting the island, like Ko Raya Noi and Ko Raya Yai (also called Ko Racha Noi and Ko Racha Yai); however, these spots rank lower on the wow-o-meter.

A typical two-dive day trip (including equipment) to nearby sites costs around 3000B to 4000B.

Dive Asia (☎ 0 7633 0598; www.diveasia.com; 24 Th Karon, Kata)

Scuba Cat (☎ 0 7629 3120; www.scubacat .com; 94 Th Thawiwong, Patong)

Sea Bees (☎ 0 7638 1765; www.sea-bees.com; 69 1/3 Moo 9 Viset, Ao Chalong)

Sea Fun Divers (☎ 0 7634 0480; www .seafundivers.com; 29 Soi Karon Nui, Patong) An outstanding and very professional diving operation.

SNORKELLING

Snorkelling is best along Phuket's west coast, particularly at the rocky headlands between beaches.

Recommended snorkel tour operators:

Offspray Leisure (☎ 08 1894 1274; www .offsprayleisure.com; 43/87 Chalong Plaza; trips from 2950B) This dive and snorkelling excursion company specialises in trips to the reefs around Ko Phi-Phi.

Oi's Longtail (☎ 08 1978 5728; 66 Moo 3, Hat Nai Yang; tours 1600B) Oi specialises in two-hour snorkelling tours of the reefs around Ko Waeo.

SURFING

Phuket is a secret surfing paradise. The best waves arrive between June and September, when Hat Kata becomes the island's unofficial surf capital.

Recommended operators:

Blujelly (☎ 08 5880 7954; www.blujelly .com; Bang Thao) Offers kids' lessons and is a good source of info about surfing around Bang Thao.

Saltwater Dreaming (☎ 0 7627 1050; www .saltwater-dreaming.com; Surin) Undoubtedly the island's best surf shop.

KAYAKING & CANOEING

Several companies based on Phuket offer canoe tours of scenic Ao Phang-Nga (opposite).

Operators based in or around Phuket Town:

John Gray's Sea Canoe (☎ 0 7625 4505; www.johngray-seacanoe.com; 124 Soi 1, Th Yaowarat, Phuket Town; trips from 3950B)

Phuket's original kayak outfitter, John Gray and his team of local guides lead ecotours to Ao Phang-Nga's hidden islands, lagoons and *hongs* (caves semi-submerged in the sea), where guests learn about this fragile ecosystem.

Paddle Asia (☎ 0 7624 0952; www .paddleasia.com; 19/3 Th Rasdanusorn, Phuket Town) Groups are small (two to six people) and multiday tours are offered.

Sea Canoe Thailand (☎ 0 7621 2172; www.seacanoe.net; 367/4 Th Yaowarat, Phuket Town) Has a great reputation despite the unoriginal name.

SPAS

Amala Spa (☎ 0 7634 3024; www.bydlofts .com; 5/28 Th Rat Uthit, Patong; treatments from 600B; ⏰ 9am-8pm) Like the rest of the BYD property (p302), this spa offers luxurious

ANDREW WATSON

Temple, Phuket

THE LOW-DOWN ON THE BEST RUB-DOWN

Our three favourite spas:

- The **Banyan Tree Spa** (www .banyantree.com) at the Banyan Tree Phuket (right) is the clear winner.
- The **Six Senses Spa** (www.six senses.com) at the Evason Phuket Resort (p303) is sublimely back-to-nature in setting, yet cutting edge as far as treatments are concerned.
- One of Phuket's first spas, **Hideaway Day Spa** (☎ 0 7627 1549; ☻ 11am-9pm) still enjoys an excellent reputation. More reasonably priced than many hotel counterparts, the Hideaway offers traditional Thai massage, sauna and mud body wraps in a tranquil wooded setting at the edge of a lagoon.

urban design, as well as Thai, oil and reflexology massage, a white-clay body wrap or a detoxifying green-tea body polish.

Atsumi Healing (☎ 08 1272 0571; www .atsumihealing.com; 34/18 Soi Pattana, Rawai; spa treatments from 1000B) Atsumi isn't just a spa, it's an earthy fasting and detox retreat centre.

Spa Royale (☎ 0 7633 3568; www.villaroyale phuket.com; 12 Th Kata Noi; treatments from 1200B; ☻ 9am-8pm) With organic spa products, seaside treatment rooms and highly skilled therapists, this is one of the top spas in southern Phuket.

COURSES

Beach House Cooking School (☎ 08 9651 1064; Hat Surin; class per person 1900B;

☻ 9am-10pm) Peruse the menu, circle the intriguing dishes at this chic beach cafe and you'll learn to make them during your three-hour class run by the owner/ chef. The dining room has live trees rising through the roof, and the student kitchen has ocean views.

Mom Tri's Cooking Class (☎ 0 7633 0015; www.boathousephuket.com; Th Patak West, Kata; 2 classes incl lunch 3200B; ☻ 10am-1pm Sat & Sun) The Boathouse's award-winning executive chef, Tummanoon Punchun, carves a bit of time out of his schedule to teach the basics of Thai cooking. Classes take place just off the Boat-house dining room, so you will cook with a view.

SLEEPING
NORTHERN BEACHES
HAT NAI YANG & HAT MAI KHAO

Both Hat Nai Yang and Hat Mai Khao belong to the supremely serene Sirinat National Park.

Golddigger's Resort (☎ 08 1892 1178; www.airport-phuket.com; r 1200-1500B;) The Swiss-run hotel has just 16 rooms, and its decor, spaciousness and choice furniture take it a step above most beachside sleeping spots in this price bracket.

ourpick Indigo Pearl (☎ 0 7632 7006; www .indigo-pearl.com; r/bungalows 5600-26,000B;) The most unusual and hip of Phuket's high-end resorts takes its design cues from the island's tin-mining history – although it sounds weird, this industrial theme fused with tropical luxe creates a spectacularly beautiful and soothing place to stay. The Sunday brunch (see p304) here is epic.

HAT NAI THON

Improved roads to Hat Nai Thon have brought only a small amount of development to this broad expanse of pristine sand backed by casuarinas and pandanus trees.

Naithon Beach Resort (☎ 0 7620 5379; cottages 1000-1500B; ☼ Nov-May; 🗙) This resort has large, tastefully designed wooden cottages. The resort closes in the rainy season. It is on the opposite side of the access road from the beach.

BANG THAO

If we were forced to pick our favourite beach, it would probably be Bang Thao – an 8km stunner with flaxen dunes that glisten under the tropical sun.

Sheraton Grande Laguna Phuket (☎ 0 7632 4101; www.starwoodhotels.com; r from 4000B; 🗙 ▯ 🎝) A city within a city, the 400-room Sheraton will appeal to families and energetic vacationers.

ourpick **Banyan Tree Phuket** (☎ 0 7632 4374; www.banyantree.com; villas US$550-2500; 🗙 ▯ 🎝) One of Asia's finest hotels, and the first on Phuket to introduce bungalows with their own private pool, the Banyan Tree Phuket (in Laguna Phuket) is an oasis of sedate, understated luxury.

SURIN

Surin is upmarket but completely unpretentious.

Surin Bay Inn (☎ 0 7627 1601; www.surin baylnn.com; r 2000B; 🗙 ▯) Right next to Capri Beach, this is another welcoming midranger.

Benyada Lodge (☎ 0 7627 1261; www .benyadalodge-phuket.com; r 2500-5000B; 🗙 ▯ 🎝) Chic, modern rooms have black louvred closets, terracotta tiles and silk, pastel-coloured throw pillows scattered in the lounging corner.

KAMALA

Sandwiched in between Patong and the tranquil north bays, Hat Kamala is a good spot to call home if you're looking to make naughty and nice.

Orchid House (☎ 0 7638 5445; treepoppanat _kwan@yahoo.com; r 1000-1500B; 🗙) Orchid House is clean and cutesy with patterned tiles and gussied curtains.

Kamala Dreams (☎ 0 7629 1131; www .kamala-beach.net; r 2500-3000B; 🗙) One giant stride from the sea, Kamala Dreams has sparkling surfaces and spotless (though slightly dowdy) rooms with tiled floors and bleached-white walls.

PATONG

Phuket's Costa del Soul-less is a seething beachside city that crams thousands of hotel rooms between its craggy headlands.

AUSTIN BUSH

Bar at Indigo Pearl (p304), Hat Nai Yang

Six Senses Spa (p300)

AUSTIN BUSH

Capricorn Village (☎ 0 7634 0390; 2/29 Th Rat Uthit; bungalows from 700B; 🍴 🖭) Capricorn is a rare cheapie in Patong's inflated sleeping scene. Bright little bungalows with terraces wind back into a quiet garden.

Casa Jip (☎ 0 7634 3019; www.casajip.com; 207/10 Th Rat Uthit; r 1000B; 🍴) Italian-run and great value, this place has very big, luxurious rooms (for the price bracket) with comfy beds and a taste of Thai style.

Baipho & Baithong (☎ 0 7629 2074; www.baipho.com; 205/12 & 205/14 Th Rat Uthit; r incl breakfast 1800-3300B; 🍴 🖳) Zen trimmings mingle with modern urban touches in the dimly lit, nest-like rooms of these twin hotels.

Baramee Resortel (☎ 0 7634 0010; info @barameeresortel.com; 266 Th Phra Barami; r 2700-3300B, ste 5700B; 🍴) Brand-new Baramee is one of the best midrange deals in Patong. Although not located directly on the beach, the hotel has many rooms with ocean views (the others look out onto a parking lot).

BYD Lofts (☎ 0 7634 3024; www.bydlofts .com; 5/28 Th Hat Patong; apt from 5000B; 🍴 🖳 🖭) Style and comfort reign supreme at BYD, whose urban-chic apartments feature loads of white (floors, walls, curtains), which feels angelic when compared to Patong's seedy street scene.

Baan Yin Dee (☎ 0 7629 4104; www .baanyindee.com; 7/5 Th Muean Ngen; r from 6000B; 🍴 🖳 🖭) On a hill overlooking town, this is Patong's premier boutique getaway.

Le Meridien Phuket (☎ 0 7634 0480; www .lemeridien.com; r from 8000B; 🍴 🖳 🖭) Close to the Patong chaos, yet secluded on its own private (and spectacular) beach, Le Meridien offers everything that the international globetrotter could ask for, housed in a bright green compound that reeks of the '70s (in the most charming way possible).

SOUTHERN BEACHES
KARON
Stuck between Patong and Kata, Karon draws a bit of its personality from both,

and that chilled-out-yet-slightly-sleazy vibe can make the beach feel wonderfully peaceful or depressingly backwater, depending on your attitude.

Karon Café (☎ 0 7639 6217; www.karon -phuket-hotels.com; 526/17 Soi Islandia Park Resort; r 800-1000B; ✗) Way less sexy than its neighbours, Karon Café has clean, no-fuss rooms above a friendly eatery.

Karon Living Room (☎ 0 7628 6618; www .karonlivingroom.com; 481 Th Patak; r incl breakfast 900-2000B; ✗ ▢) Karon Living Room provides sparkling clean rooms with air-con set to cryogenic levels.

Casa Brazil (☎ 0 7639 6317; www.phuket homestay.com; 9 Th Luang Pho Chuan; r 1100-1600B; ✗ ▢) There's a whimsically styled and very social cafe on the ground level, and the 20-odd rooms are spacious and tastefully decorated. It's a short walk to both Kata and Karon beaches.

KATA

Kata attracts travellers of all ages with its shopping, surfing and lively beach, and without the seedy hustle endemic to Patong up the coast.

Lucky Guesthouse (☎ 0 7633 0572; lucky guesthousekata@hotmail.com; 110/44 Moo 4 Th Taina; r 450B) Phuket penny-pinchers usually wind up at Lucky, which offers the basic necessities for beach holidays on a shoestring: a bed and a bathroom.

Kata On Sea (☎ 0 7633 0594; bungalows 450-1000B; ✗) 'On Sea'? Hardly. It's a steep 100m climb to this clutch of modest bungalows dotting a quiet green hilltop, but for the price, it's well worth the effort.

Sugar Palm Resort (☎ 0 7628 4404; www .sugarpalmphuket.com; 20/10 Th Kata; r 1800-6000B; ✗ ▢ ✈) It's a 'chic, chill-out world' as this Miami meets Thailand–style resort claims. Sleek rooms mix beachy whisps of colour with the whites and blacks of an old-school photo.

Mom Tri's Boathouse (☎ 0 7633 0015; www.theboathousephuket.com; 2/2 Th Patak West; r 8000-20,000B; ✗ ▢ ✈) For Thai politicos, pop stars, artists and celebrity authors, the intimate boutique Boathouse is still the only place to stay on Phuket. The three on-site restaurants are the best on the island.

Mom Tri's Villa Royale (☎ 0 7633 3568; www.villaroyalephuket.com; ste incl breakfast from 10,000B; ✗ ▢ ✈) Tucked away in a secluded Kata Noi location with the grandest of views, Villa Royale opened in 2006 to nearly instant acclaim.

Also recommended:

Kata Noi Pavilion (☎ 0 7628 4346; www .katanoi-pavilion.com; bungalows 1150-1500B; ✗) Slightly generic, but the rooms are spic and span.

KO HEH & RAWAI

Coral Island (☎ 0 7628 1060; www.coralisland resort.com; bungalows from 2000B; ✗ ✈) For something a bit quieter, grab a long-tail boat to nearby Ko Heh and stay at this secluded spot. A lot of snorkelling day trippers visit the island, but after sunset it's absolutely serene.

Evason Phuket Resort (☎ 0 7638 1010; www.sixsenses.com; 100 Th Viset; r 7500-38,000B; ✗ ▢ ✈) This spa hotel extraordinaire offers copious amounts of luxury. Hip and heavily designed, It is the type of place that appeals to rock stars and moneyed media types. Room prices – opulent villas top the billing – stretch from pricey to impossibly expensive.

PHUKET TOWN

Phuket Town has a healthy assortment of budget lodging options. Although you're nowhere near the beach, foodies will adore the small bundle of kick-ass restaurants tucked between the town's architectural remains of its multicultural past.

Phuket International Youth Hostel (☎ 0 7628 1325; www.phukethostel.com; 73/11 Th Chao Fa, Ao Chalong; dm 250B, r from 600B; 🅿) As a bona fide Hostelling International outfit, this contemporary youth hostel offers comfortable sleeps in typically sterile surrounds. It is located 7km south of Phuket Town.

Crystal Inn (☎ 0 7625 6789; www.phuket crystalinn.com; 2/1-10 Soi Surin, Th Phuket; r from 1000B; 🅿 💻) It may not age well, but for now this is a slick midrange option. With its attractive Rothko-esque murals, it's a stylish alternative to the midrange dreck nearby.

Sino House (☎ 0 7622 1398; www.sino housephuket.com; 1 Th Montri; r 2000-2500B; 🅿 💻) Like a swank Shanghai bordello (in a good way…), Sino House's rooms are massive and dimly lit, and the attached bathrooms feature handmade ceramic basins and quarter moon–shaped bathtubs.

EATING & DRINKING
NORTHERN BEACHES
HAT NAI YANG

our pick **Indigo Pearl** (☎ 0 7632 7006; brunch 1300-1600B; 🍽 breakfast, lunch & dinner) On Sunday, do not pass Go, do not collect $200 (you won't need to – the bill will be way less); head directly to Indigo Pearl for the ultimate in weekend brunching.

BANG THAO

Lotus Restaurant (dishes 50-120B; 🍽 lunch & dinner) An open-walled eatery 500m west of the entrance to Banyan Tree Phuket, this is the first in a row of beachside Thai and seafood restaurants that stretches to the south.

Tawai (☎ 0 7632 5381; Moo 1, Laguna Phuket entrance; dishes from 150B; 🍽 dinner) Set in a lovely old house decorated with traditional art is this gem of a Thai kitchen serving classics like roast-duck curry and pork *lâhp* (minced-pork salad mixed with chilli, mint and coriander), and steamed, grilled and fried seafood.

our pick **Tre** (☎ 0 7632 4374; dishes 550-3000B; 🍽 dinner) This French-Vietnamese fusion masterpiece is located on a silent lagoon in the heart of Banyan Tree Phuket (p301) in Laguna Phuket. If you're feting any special occasion while visiting Phuket, have your celebratory dinner here.

SURIN

Patacharin (☎ 08 1892 8587; dishes from 60B; 🍽 lunch & dinner) This local fish grill is built into the headland at the southernmost end of Hat Surin.

La Plage (☎ 08 1184 7719; dishes from 150B; 🍽 11am-10pm) When two Paris-raised Laotian polyglots (what?) open a fusion restaurant on the sand, you have to swing by to see what it's all about. It serves a fine nicoise salad and a savoury green curry with a kick.

KAMALA

Basilico (☎ 0 7638 5856; 125 Moo 3, Th Hat Kamala; dishes from 180B; 🍽 dinner) Another member of Phuket's ever-growing legion of tasty Italian restaurants. Basilico has

---

TOP SPOTS FOR A SUNDOWNER COCKTAIL

Ask any local expat: sipping sundowner cocktails is an official sport on Phuket. Any west-facing joint will do the trick, but after some serious field research, we've found three seriously special spots to enjoy that 6pm snifter:

- **Rockfish** (p305)
- **White Box** (p305)
- **After Beach Bar** (p307)

Bar at BYD Lofts (p302), Patong

AUSTIN BUSH

good wood-fired pizza, but try the grilled tiger prawns in a parsley-and-garlic marinade, served on a chickpea-and-rosemary mash.

OUR PICK Rockfish (☎ 0 7027 9732; 33/6 Th Hat Kamala; dishes from 240B; ☻ dinner) Kamala's best dining room, a rumoured favourite of pop diva Mariah Carey, is perched above bobbing long-tails offering diners excellent beach, bay and mountain views.

PATONG

OUR PICK Fried Chicken (63/5 Th Phra Barami; dishes from 45B; ☻ 10am-7pm) Three huge fryers are bubbling and splattering with juicy, crispy 'yard bird'. The chicken is served with a tangy hot sauce and sticky rice. It's impossible to overstate this.

Ali Baba (☎ 0 7634 5024; 38 Th Ruamchai; dishes from 70B; ☻ lunch & dinner) A favourite with Patong's resident Indians, Ali Baba serves up delicious subcontinental specialities (the island's best) to diners swathed in hookah smoke.

Takumi (☎ 0 7634 1654; Th Thawiwong; dishes from 160B; ☻ lunch & dinner) This fantastic

find, with a blubbery Ssumo mascot, specialises in *yakiniku* (Japanese barbecue).

Floyd's Brasserie (☎ 0 7637 0000; 18/110 Th Ruamchai; dishes 220-410B; ☻ dinner) Keith Floyd, one of England's favourite celebrity chefs, is the man behind the Burasari resort's popular restaurant.

OUR PICK White Box (☎ 0 7634 6271; 247/5 Th Phra Barami; dishes 280-480B; ☻ lunch & dinner) Who cares if the food at White Box is good or not (although if you are wondering, it is delish); dining at this high-energy supper club is like spending an evening on the starship *Enterprise*.

Ninth Floor (☎ 0 7634 4311; 47 Th Rat Uthit; dishes from 300B; ☻ dinner) This rising star of Phuket's dining scene is the highest open-air restaurant on the island, but its perfectly prepared steaks and chops are what make it a Patong institution

Two Black Sheep (☎ 08 9872 2645; 172 Th Rat Uthit) Owned by a fun Aussie couple, this old-school pub is a great find. It has good grub and live music nightly.

Molly Malone's (☎ 0 7629 2771; Th Thawiwong) Wildly popular with tourists, this pub rocks with Irish gigs every night at 9.45pm.

JP's (☎ 0 7634 3024; 5/28 Th Rat Uthit) This hipster indoor-outdoor lounge at BYD Lofts (p302) definitely brings a touch of style and panache to Patong. There's a low-slung bar, outdoor sofa booths, happy hours (with free tapas) from 10pm and weekly DJ parties.

SOUTHERN BEACHES

KARON

Pad Thai Shop (MTh Patak East; noodles from 40B; ☽ lunch) On the busy main road behind Karon, just north of the tacky Ping Pong Bar, is this glorified food stand that spills from the owners' home onto a dirt lot. It's only open for lunch, when you can find chicken-feet stew, beef-bone soup and the best *pàt tai* on earth.

Mama Noi's (☎ 0 7628 6272; Karon Plaza, 291/1-2 Moo 3, Th Patak East; dishes 50-190B; ☽ breakfast, lunch & dinner) Repeat visitors adore this place, which churns out fantastic Thai and Italian pasta dishes.

KATA

Kwong Shop Seafood (☎ 08 1273 3707; Th Thai Na; dishes 40-130B; ☽ lunch & dinner) Kwong, the friendly owner, utters a big 'OK!' when you order (we're pretty sure it's the only English word he knows), and minutes later out comes tasty Thai treats.

Gueyjah (dishes from 40B; ☽ lunch & dinner) Tucked away on a side road off Rte 4028, Gueyjah is tops for quick and cheap Thai eats, and it's known only to locals.

Ratri Jazztaurant (☎ 0 7633 3538; Th Chalong-Karon; dishes from 140B; ☽ lunch & dinner) If you like jazz, you should wind your way up to this hillside terrace to listen to local and international acts blow like they mean it.

Capannina (dishes 150-350B; ☽ lunch & dinner) Everything here – from the pasta dishes to the sauces – is made fresh. It gets crowded during the high season, so you may want to book ahead.

ourpick **Boathouse Wine & Grill** (☎ 0 7633 0015; Th Patak West; dishes 450-850B; ☽ lunch & dinner) The perfect place to wow a fussy date, the Boathouse has been

Seafood restaurant, Karon

AUSTIN BUSH

PHUKET PROVINCE

the critic's champion for some time. The Mediterranean fusion food is fabulous (think vodka-marinated lobster and foie gras with black-truffle oil), the wine list is endless and the sea views are sublime.

ourpick After Beach Bar (☎ 08 1894 3750; Hwy 4233; ☿ 11am-midnight) It's difficult – make that impossible – to overstate how glorious the view is from this stilted, thatched patio bar hanging off a cliff above Kata.

PHUKET TOWN
Southeast of the centre, on Th Ong Sim Phai, is the town's municipal market where you can buy fresh fruit and vegetables.

ourpick Uptown Restaurant (☎ 0 7621 5359; Th Tilok Uthit; dishes 30-60B; ☿ 10am-9pm) It may not look fancy, but this breezy joint is a favourite spot for the 'hi-so' (high society) folk.

Natural Restaurant (☎ 0 7622 4287; 62/5 Soi Phuthon; dishes 80-200B; ☿ lunch & dinner) Travel round the world in 80 plates at this dazzlingly green Phuket Town eatery.

ourpick Ka Jok See (☎ 0 7621 7903; kajoksee@hotmail.com; 26 Th Takua Pa; dishes 180-480B; ☿ dinner Tue-Sun) Dripping old Phuket charm and creaking under the weight of the owner's fabulous trinket collection, this atmospheric little eatery offers great food, top-notch music and – if you're lucky – some sensationally camp cabaret.

Glastnöst (☎ 08 4058 0288; 14 Soi Rommani) It's about as laid-back and intimate a setting as you could find, and spontaneous jazz jam sessions are the norm.

EAST COAST
Kachang Floating Restaurant (dishes 90-320B; ☿ lunch & dinner) Set adrift in Ao Phuket, rickety Kachang is only a few minutes east of Phuket Town, but it's far off the beaten tourist trail. Enjoy soft-shell

crab in the waning light as the sun dips behind the hills.

Chalong Night Market (Hwy 402 near Chalong Circle; ☿ 6-11pm Wed) One of the most popular night markets on the island, where vendors, farmers and local chefs converge under the gas lamps.

ENTERTAINMENT
PATONG
A walk around Patong at night is an entertaining experience in itself. Th Bangla is the centre of the action, with loud techno music blaring out of exhausted sound systems while go-go girls shake it till they make it (and ladyboys fake it till they make it) on beer-slicked tabletops.

Club Lime (☎ 08 5798 1850; www.clublime .info; ☿ 10pm-2am) A new hot spot gaining steam, this place attracts the beautiful people and a rotating roster of Thai and international DJs.

Seduction (39/1 Th Bangla; admission 500B; ☿ 10pm-4am) Patong's newest and most popular dance hall comes courtesy of a Finnish club impresario. Known for buying up the best clubs in Helsinki, he opened this one in 2006 and has since attracted international party people dancing to well-known global DJs.

GETTING THERE & AWAY
AIR
Phuket International Airport is situated at the northwest end of the island, 30km from Phuket Town.

Thai Airways International (THAI; ☎ 0 7621 1195; www.thaiairways.com; 78/1 Th Ranong, Phuket Town) operates about a dozen daily flights to Bangkok (one way from 2800B); it also has regular flights to/from 11 other cities in Thailand and international destinations including Penang, Langkawi, Kuala Lumpur, Singapore, Hong Kong, Taipei and Tokyo.

Ka Jok See (p307), Phuket

AUSTIN BUSH

Bangkok Airways (☎ 0 7622 5033; www .bangkokair.com; 58/2-3 Th Yaowarat, Phuket Town) has daily flights to Ko Samui (one way 2600B), Bangkok (one way 2800B) and Utapau for Pattaya (one way 3100B).

Nok Air (☎ 1318; www.nokair.co.th; Phuket International Airport) links Phuket with Bangkok, as does **One-Two-Go** (☎ 1141, ext 1126; www.fly12go.com; Phuket International Airport) and web-based **Air Asia** (www .airasia.com), from 2000B one way. Air Asia also flies to Kuala Lumpur (one way from 25,000B) and Singapore (one way 2500B).

Other international airlines with offices in Phuket's Old Town:

Dragonair (☎ 0 7621 5734; Th Phang-Nga)
Malaysia Airlines (☎ 0 7621 6675; 1/8-9 Th Thungkha)

Silk Air (☎ 0 7621 3891; www.silkair.com; 183/103 Th Phang-Nga)

BOAT
Ferries link Phuket Town to Ko Phi-Phi three times per day at 8.30am, 1.30pm and 2.30pm (400B).

MINIVAN
Minivan services (plus a ferry connection) link Phuket to Ko Samui, Ko Pha-Ngan and Ko Tao on the gulf coast.

GETTING AROUND
CAR
There are many petrol stations around the island, but only one in Patong (and it's always very busy).

There are cheap car-hire agencies on Th Rasada in Phuket's Old Town near Pure Car Rent.

Andaman Car Rent (☎ 0 7632 4422; www.andamancarrent.com; Moo 2, Cheangtalay, Thalang)
Budget (☎ 0 7620 5396; www.budget.co.th; Phuket International Airport) Also a branch in Patong.
Phuket New Car Rent (☎ 0 7637 9571; www.phuketnewcarrent.com; 111/85 Moo 8, Th Tharua-Muang mai, Thalang)

SŎRNG·TĂA·OU & TÚK-TÚK
In Phuket Town, large *sŏrng·tăa·ou* run regularly from Th Ranong near the day market to the various Phuket beaches for 40B to 70B per person. They operate from 7am to 5pm; outside these times you have to charter a túk-túk to the beaches, which will set you back 250B to Patong, 280B to Karon and Kata, and 340B for Nai Han and Kamala.

TAXI
Rides generally cost 300B to 500B one way. Motorcycle taxis are much cheaper,

and can cost as little as 30B per ride, but most work exclusively in Phuket's Old Town.

KRABI PROVINCE

KRABI TOWN

กระบี่

pop 27,500

Most travellers just breeze through Krabi's gridiron of travel agencies, optical shops and knick-knack shacks, using the provincial capital as a jumping-off point for wonderful surrounding destinations –

Ko Lanta to the south, Ko Phi-Phi to the southwest and Railay to the west.

SLEEPING

KR Mansion (☎ 0 7561 2761; krmansion @yahoo.com; 52/1 Th Chao Fah; r 300-600B; 🞰 🖳) The rooms in this bright-pink building are quite comfortable.

Chan Cha Lay (☎ 0 7562 0952; 55 Th Utarakit; r 300-650B; 🞰 🖳) The tiled rooms are immaculate and the cafe has dainty trimmings, artistic photos and other bits of art on the walls. The staff are very helpful too.

KRABI TOWN

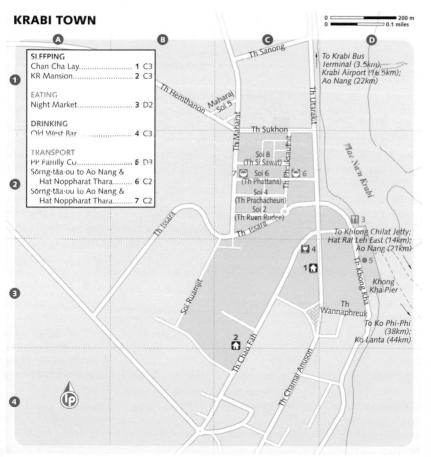

SLEEPING	
Chan Cha Lay.......................... 1	C3
KR Mansion............................. 2	C3
EATING	
Night Market........................... 3	D2
DRINKING	
Old West Bar............................ 4	C3
TRANSPORT	
PP Family Co............................ 5	D3
Sŏrng·tǎa·ou to Ao Nang &	
Hat Nopphrat Thara......... 6	C2
Sŏrng·tǎa·ou to Ao Nang &	
Hat Nopphrat Thara......... 7	C2

To Krabi Bus Terminal (3.5km); Krabi Airport (16.5km); Ao Nang (22km)

Th Sanong

Th Hemthanon

Maharaj Soi 5

Th Maharat

Th Utarakit

Th Sukhon

Th Phruksauthit

Soi 8 (Th Si Sawat)

Soi 6 (Th Phattana)

Soi 4 (Th Prachacheun)

Soi 2 (Th Ruen Rudee)

Th Issara

Mae Nam Krabi

To Khlong Chilat Jetty; Hat Rai Leh East (14km); Ao Nang (21km)

Th Khong Kha

Khong Kha Pier

Th Wannaphreuk

To Ko Phi-Phi (38km); Ko Lanta (44km)

Soi Ruamjit

Th Chao Fah

Th Charnar Anuson

EATING & DRINKING

Night Market (Th Khong Kha; meals 20-50B; ☺ dinner) Found near the Khong Kha pier, this is one of the best places to eat.

Old West Bar (Th Chao Fah; ☺ 1pm-2am) Bamboo and wood inside and out, this Wild West–themed bar booms music nightly and is one popular place for a tipple.

GETTING THERE & AWAY

AIR

Most domestic carriers offer service between Bangkok and Krabi International Airport (one way around 2400B to 3100B, 1¼ hours). **Bangkok Air** (www.bangkokair .com) has daily service to Ko Samui for around the same price.

BOAT

The largest boat operator is **PP Family Co** (☎ 0 7561 2463; Th Khong Kha), which has a ticket office right beside the pier in town. In the high season there are boats to Ko Phi-Phi (450B to 490B, 1½ hours) at 9am, 10.30am and 2.30pm.

From September to May, there are boats to Ko Lanta (450B, 1½ hours) leaving Krabi at 10.30am and 1.30pm.

If you want to get to Railay, head to Ao Nang by taxi (100B) or catch a long-tail boat from Krabi's Khong Kha pier to Hat Rai Leh East from 7.45am to 6pm (200B, 45 minutes); from here it is only a five-minute walk along a paved path to the more appealing Hat Rai Leh West.

BUS

With fewer eager touts and guaranteed departure times, taking a government bus from the **Krabi bus terminal** (☎ 0 7561 1804; cnr Th Utarakit & Hwy 4) in nearby Talat Kao, about 4km from Krabi, is an altogether more relaxing option than taking a private bus.

SŎRNG·TĂA·OU

Useful *sŏrng·tăa·ou* run from the bus station to central Krabi and on to Hat Noppharat Thara (40B), Ao Nang (40B) and the Shell Cemetery at Ao Nam Mao (50B).

GETTING AROUND

Krabi Town is easy to explore on foot, but the bus terminal and airport are both a long way from the centre. Agencies in town can also arrange minivans to the airport for 150B. *Sŏrng·tăa·ou* between the bus terminal and downtown Krabi cost 20B.

AO NANG

อ่าวนาง

pop 12,400

Ao Nang serves as the main jumping-off point for Railay, only a 20-minute long-tail ride away.

Ao Nang is appealing and if you want to partake in the area's popular island-hopping tours or sea-kayaking adventures, most companies are based here. Plus, if having booze with meals is paramount, Ao Nang will do a better job quenching your thirst: many of Railay's resorts are Muslim-owned and don't serve alcohol in their restaurants (although you can buy beer at the local store and take it into restaurants that don't serve alcohol).

ACTIVITIES

At least seven companies offer kayaking tours to mangroves and islands around Ao Nang. **Sea Canoe Thailand** (☎ 0 7569 5387) and **Ao Nang Group** (☎ 0 7563 7660/1) are two recommended companies.

Ao Nang has numerous dive schools offering trips to dive sites at nearby Railay's Laem Phra Nang. It costs about 2200B for two dives. Reliable dive schools include

Tham Phra Nam (p312), Railay

PAOLO CORDELLI

Phra Nang Divers (☎ 0 7563 7064; www.pn divers.com) and **Aqua Vision Dive Center** (☎ 0 7563 7415; www.aqua-vision.net). Dive companies can also arrange snorkelling trips in the area.

EATING
ourpick Sala Bua & Lo Spuntino (☎ 0 7563 7110; dishes 80-520B; ☻ 10am-11pm) Located deep within the bustle of 'Seafood Street', this excellent ocean-facing restaurant serves the best of both worlds – East and West – accompanied by a long list of wines.

Tanta (☎ 0 7563 7118; dishes 180-350B; ☻ lunch & dinner) Tanta offers a great selection of Thai and international dishes. It's a popular modern place with a raised covered terrace and wood accents.

DRINKING & ENTERTAINMENT
Have a drink – there's no shortage of bars in Ao Nang.

Irish Rover Bar & Grill (☎ 0 7563 7607) Sports fans will appreciate the telly broadcasting English footy matches and South African cricket. The place also features live music, tropical cocktails and pool tables.

Encore Café (☻ 4pm-2am in high season) Very popular with holidaying Thais, this live-music club is a fun and modern spot.

GETTING THERE & AROUND
A ferry service to Ko Phi-Phi runs year-round (450B to 490B, two hours) at 9am and includes a ride to/from the pier in nearby Hat Noppharat Thara.

Long-tail boats to the Hat Rai Leh area run daily in good weather and cost 80B (120B after 6pm).

A good way to get around is by *sŏrng·tăa·ou*. Destinations include Krabi (40B), Hat Noppharat Thara (10B) and Ao Nam Mao (20B).

RAILAY
ไร่เล

Krabi's fairytale limestone crags come to a dramatic climax at Railay (also spelled Rai Leh), the ultimate jungle gym for rock-climbing fanatics.

Railay

GLENN VAN DER KNIJFF

◥ IF YOU LIKE...

If you like Railay's craggy karst scenery, explore these other nearby islands on a long-tail or snorkelling tour.

- **Ko Hua Khwan** Excellent snorkelling.
- **Ko Poda** Handsome stretch of white beach.
- **Ko Taloo** Underwater swim-throughs.
- **Tham Phra Nang** Shrine cave.
- **Ko Hong** A hidden lagoon shielded by cliffs.

ACTIVITIES
ROCK CLIMBING

With nearly 700 bolted routes and unparalleled cliff-top vistas, it's no surprise these dramatic rock faces are among the top climbing spots in the world.

The going rate for climbing courses is 800B to 1200B for a half day and 1500B to 2200B for a full day.

Recommended climbing schools:

Hot Rock (☎ 0 7562 1771; www.railay adventure.com; Hat Rai Leh West) Unabashedly the most expensive climbing school in Railay, but the longstanding reputation keeps the operation busy.

Tex Rock Climbing (☎ 0 7563 1509; Rai Leh East) A tiny, venerable school where the owner still climbs and runs the school directly from the shop.

Wee's Climbing School (Hat Ton Sai) A friendly and professional outfit.

WATER SPORTS

Snorkelling trips to Ko Poda and Ko Hua Khwan (Chicken Island) can be arranged through any of the resorts for about 900B by long-tail or 1200B by speedboat.

SLEEPING & EATING
HAT RAILAY WEST

Sand Sea Resort (☎ 0 7562 2170; www.krabi sandsea.com; bungalows 1800-6000B; ✷ ▢ ▨) Solid, well-appointed concrete bungalows with verandahs line a snaking, foliage-laced pathway.

Railay Bay Resort & Spa (☎ 0 7562 2571; www.railaybayresort.com; bungalows 2900-10,000B; ✷ ▨) The campus of charming timber-framed bungalows stretches all the way to Railay East along well manicured grounds.

HAT RAILAY EAST

Often referred to as Sunrise Beach, the 'beach' here is riddled with gnarled mangroves and tends to be quite muddy. It's not the end of the world, as Hat Railay West is just a 10-minute walk away.

Rapala Cabana (☎ 08 6957 8096; bungalows 200B) Superbly located deep in the jungle and high in the hills in a bowl of karst cliff, this uber-rustic, Rasta-run place is the cheapest place to crash in Railay.

Diamond Private Resort (☎ 0 7562 1729; www.diamondprivate-railay.com; r 1800-3500B; ✷ ▨) Although the name sounds a bit like a strip joint, Diamond Private is a family-friendly resort with a swimming pool high on the hilltop with a deck that sports great views of the bay below.

Sunrise Tropical Resort (☎ 0 7562 2599; www.sunrisetropical.com; bungalows 3500-5500B; ✷ ▨) Sunrise has stylish Thai villas with neat decor and very swanky bathrooms.

Rock (dishes 120B; ☼ breakfast, lunch & dinner) The sea views are divine and the large selection of Thai food never gets complaints. Try the refreshing basil smoothies on especially hot days.

HAT TON SAI
The beach isn't spectacular, but there's a welcoming backpacker vibe that'll keep a smile on your face.

Krabi Mountain View Resort (☎ 0 7562 2610; bungalows 1100-1900B; ❄) Cheery and immaculate with mint-green walls, tiled floors and crisp linen – these are Ton Sai's best-value air-con digs.

DRINKING
Although many of the resorts don't serve alcohol, there are a few places on the beaches where you can celebrate the day's climb with a frosty one…or seven…

Chillout Bar (Hat Ton Sai) Climbers like to chill here after a long day on the rocks. The place flies Rasta colours and serves cold beers as fast as you can drink them.

Stone Bar (Rai Leh East) The parties go late and buzz with electronica beats.

GETTING THERE & AROUND
Boats between Krabi and Hat Railay East leave every 1½ hours (or when they have 10 passengers) from 7.45am to 6pm (200B, 45 minutes).

Boats to Hat Railay West or Ton Sai (80B, 15 minutes) leave from the eastern end of the promenade at Ao Nang during daylight hours.

KO PHI-PHI DON
เกาะ พีพีดอน
One glimpse of the island's otherworldly crests and cliffs will turn brutes into poets, and sceptics into believers. Viewpoints reveal soul-altering vistas of the sandy hourglass isthmus that plays host to these legions of visitors and their hedonistic pursuits.

Ko Phi-Phi Don (usually just referred to as Ko Phi-Phi) is part of the Ko Phi-Phi Marine National Park, which also includes uninhabited Ko Phi Phi Leh next door.

DALLAS STRIBLEY

Fishing boat, Ko Phi-Phi Don

GLENN VAN DER KNIJFF

Dive boat, Ko Phi-Phi Leh (p316)

ACTIVITIES

DIVING

Crystal Andaman water and abundant marine life make the perfect recipe for top-notch scuba.

All dive shops in Tonsai Village have standardised their pricing – an Open Water certification course costs 12,400B, while the standard two-dive trips cost 2200B. Trips out to Hin Daeng/Hin Muang will set you back 5500B.

Recommended dive operators:

Adventure Club (☎ 08 1970 0314, 08 1895 1334; www.divingphi.com) Our favourite diving operation on the island runs an excellent assortment of educational, eco-focused diving, hiking and snorkelling tours.

Phi Phi Scuba (☎ 0 7561 2665; www.ppscuba.com) One of the largest operators on the island, churning out dive certifications by the boatload.

SNORKELLING

Snorkelling around Ko Phi-Phi is equally amazing, especially around Ko Phi-Phi Leh. Any travel agency on the island can arrange snorkelling day trips.

If you're going at it on your own, most bungalows and resorts rent out a snorkel, mask and fins for 150B to 200B per day. There is good snorkelling along the eastern coast of **Ko Nok**, near Ao Ton Sai and along the eastern coast of **Ko Nai**.

ROCK CLIMBING

Yes, there are good limestone cliffs to climb on Ko Phi-Phi, and the view from the top is spectacular. **Cat's Climbing Shop** (☎ 08 1787 5101; www.catsclimbingshop.com), in Tonsai Village, is a French-run operation that gets a thumbs up from tourists. **Spider Monkey** (☎ 08 9728 1608) at Hat Hin Khom also gets a good report card.

SLEEPING

TONSAI VILLAGE

The flat, hourglass-shaped land between Ao Ton Sai and Ao Lo Dalam is crowded with loads of lodging options.

Tropical Garden Bungalows (☎ 08 9729 1436; r from 800B;) If you don't mind walking 10 minutes to eat, drink or sunbathe, then you'll love Tropical Garden. At the far end of the main path from Ao Ton Sai, it feels pretty isolated in its fragment of flourishing hillside jungle.

White (☎ 0 7560 1300; www.whitephiphi .com; r 1600-1900B; 🍴 💻) Geared towards the 'flashpacker' crowd, the White has two locations in Tonsai Village with squeaky clean rooms – everything's white (duh).

Phi Phi Banyan Villa (☎ 0 7561 1233; www.phiphi-hotel.com; r 2500-2800B; 🍴 💻) These comfy quarters have all the mod cons and some have a balcony overlooking a garden-lined path. There's a seaside restaurant and the hotel's namesake, a large gnarled banyan tree, sits out front.

Also recommended:

Phi Phi Hotel (☎ 0 7561 1233; www.phiphi -hotel.com; r from 1700B; 🍴 💻) Guests love this hotel, which has amazing views and all the amenities of a posh resort.

HAT HIN KHOM

Between Hat Yao and Tonsai Village, this quieter patch of sand is a great choice if you want to be near the action but also value a quiet night's sleep.

Viking Resort (☎ 0 7581 9399; tak blobk @hotmail.com; bungalows 800-2000B; 💻) Viking Resort has oodles of tiki chic charm on a great beach for swimming and tanning.

HAT YAO

Hat Yao (Long Beach) is a short boat ride (80B) or long sweaty hike (45 minutes) from Ao Ton Sai. The beach here is fantastic and not as crowded as the double bays around Tonsai Village.

Beach Resort (☎ 0 7561 8267; bungalows 3950-5900B; 🍴 💻) An ever-expanding class act with a good pool and chic bar, this resort swarms with package tourists looking for (and finding) comfort.

AO LO BAKAO

Ao Lo Bakao has a beautiful and secluded beach on Phi-Phi's remote northeastern shore. The resort here arranges boat transfers for guests (there's a thin dirt trail for hikers). Long-tails from Ao Ton Sai cost 500B (one way).

Phi Phi Island Village (☎ in Phuket 0 7621 5014, in Bangkok 0 2276 6056; www.ppisland.com; bungalows from 6500B; 🍴 💻) This place really is a village unto itself: its whopping 104 bungalows take up much of the beachfront with only a few lonely palms swaying between them.

HAT LAEM THONG

At the northern end of Ko Nai, Hat Laem Thong features Phi-Phi's who's who of glitzy five star resorts. A long-tail charter from Ao Ton Sai costs 600B.

Holiday Inn Phi Phi Island (☎ 0 7521 1334; www.phiphi-palmbeach.com; bungalows 7500-9000B; 🍴 💻) Amid coconut palm at the southernmost point of the beach, this tastefully decorated resort has large Thai Malay–style bungalows sitting on 2m-high stilts.

EATING

D's Books (☎ 08 4667 7730; coffee 50-110B; 🕐 breakfast, lunch & dinner) In the beating heart of Tonsai Village, this classy cafe has amazing coffee drinks and stacks of cheap reading.

Papaya (dishes 80-180B; 🕐 lunch & dinner) Near Reggae Bar, Papaya is where to go for perfectly cooked Thai standards.

Tonsai (☎ 0 7561 1233; dishes 80-300B; 🕐 lunch & dinner) The best seafood restaurant on Ao Ton Sai serves a mouthwatering assortment of the day's catch.

Ciao Bella (☎ 08 1894 1246; dishes 150-300B; 🕐 breakfast, lunch & dinner) Italian-run Ciao Bella is a long-time expat and traveller fave serving excellent pizzas and seafood in a romantic location by the sea.

DRINKING & ENTERTAINMENT

Reggae Bar (Tonsai Village) The most popular nightspot waves its Rasta flags high. Drinking competitions, *muay thai* boxing and the occasional *gà·teu·i* (ladyboy) cabaret get patrons out of their chairs.

Carpe Diem (☎ 08 4840 1219; Hat Hin Khom) Sit on pillows in the upstairs lounge and watch the sun go down (locals say this is the best spot for sundowners).

Hippies (☎ 08 1970 5483; Hat Hin Khom) Hippies is a good place to end the evening. There are candlelit tables on the beach and chill-out tunes on the sound system. Moon parties are thrown throughout the month.

GETTING THERE & AWAY

Boats link Ko Phi-Phi to Krabi, Phuket, Ao Nang, Ko Lanta, the Trang Islands and Ko Lipe. Most boats moor at Ao Ton Sai, though a few from Phuket use the isolated northern pier at Laem Thong. The Phuket and Krabi boats operate year-round while boats to Ao Nang, Ko Lanta, the Trang Islands and Ko Lipe only run in the November-to-May high season.

GETTING AROUND

There are no roads on Phi-Phi Don so transport is mostly by foot. If you want to visit a remote beach, long-tails can be chartered at Ao Ton Sai for 100B to 500B depending on how far you go.

KO PHI-PHI LEH

เกาะพีพีเล

The smaller and scruffier of the Phi-Phi sisters, the island features rounded soaring cliffs that cut through crystalline waters and gorgeous blooms of coral. Two lovely lagoons hide in the island's interior – **Pilah**

on the east coast and the legendary **Ao Maya** on the west.

At the northeastern tip of the island, **Viking Cave** (Tham Phaya Naak; admission 20B) is a major collection point for swiftlet nests.

There are no places to stay at on Phi-Phi Leh and most people come here on one of the ludicrously popular day trips out of Phi-Phi Don.

KO LANTA

เกาะลันตา

pop 20,000

Long and thin, and covered in bleach-blond tresses, Ko Lanta is Krabi's sexy beach babe.

Ko Lanta is relatively flat compared to the karst formations of its neighbours, so the island can be easily explored by motorbike.

Ko Lanta is technically called Ko Lanta Yai, the largest of 52 islands in an archipelago protected by the Ko Lanta Marine National Park.

SIGHTS

Halfway down the eastern coast, **Ban Lanta** (Old Town) was the island's original port and commercial centre, and provided a safe harbour for Arabic and Chinese trading vessels sailing between the larger ports of Phuket, Penang and Singapore. A few pier restaurants offer up fresh catches of the day and have prime views over the sea. A stop at the **Hammock House** (☎ 0 4847 2012; www.jumbohammock.com; 10am-5pm) is a must. The friendly owners have amassed the largest selection of quality hammocks in Thailand. They are stunning and unique creations woven by indigenous hill tribes.

ACTIVITIES

Vacationers here will be delighted to find that some of Thailand's top spots

ANDAMAN COAST

PAOLO CORDELLI

Sunset, Railay (p311)

KRABI PROVINCE

are within arm's reach. The best diving can be found at the undersea pinnacles called **Hin Muang** and **Hin Daeng**, about 45 minutes away. These world-class dive sites have lone coral outcrops in the middle of the sea, and act as important feeding stations for large pelagic fish such as sharks, tuna and occasionally whale sharks and manta rays.

The best dive operation on the island is **Scubafish** (☎ 0 7566 5095; www.scuba-fish .com), located at Baan Laanta Resort (p318) on Ao Kantiang; there's also a small second office at the Narima resort.

TOURS

Boat tours are a popular way to discover the quieter islands orbiting Ko Lanta. Highly recommended operators:
Freedom Adventures (☎ 08 4910 9132; www.freedom-adventures.net; Hat Khlong Nin) This family-run company focuses on day trips to the Trang Islands.
Scubafish (☎ 0 7566 5095; www.scuba-fish .com; Baan Lanta Resort, Ao Kantiang) This professional and friendly dive operator

offers an interesting array of marine-life classes and site visits through its Aqualogy program.
Sun Island Tours (☎ 08 7891 6619; www .lantalongtail.com; Ban Lanta) Run by an experienced husband-and-wife team, these high-quality tours meander around the Trang Islands or the eastern islands in the Ko Lanta archipelago.

SLEEPING
HAT KHLONG DAO
With perfect white sand stretching for over 2km, it's no wonder this was one of the first beaches to attract tourists and developers.
   Golden Bay Cottages (☎ 0 7568 4161; www.goldenbaylanta.com; bungalows 1200-2800B; ✻ ☒) Bungalows surrounding a leafy courtyard. The air-con rooms offer the best bang for your baht.
   Southern Lanta Resort (☎ 0 7568 4174-7; www.southernlanta.com; bungalows incl breakfast 1800-5000B; ✻ ☒) Loads of shade in the tropical garden and a good-sized beachfront. The resort is family friendly and you

can organise horse riding from here for 600B per hour.

HAT PHRA AE
The beach at Hat Phra Ae (Long Beach) is only mediocre, but the ambience is lively.

Ko Kradan, Trang
FEARGUS COONEY

↘ IF YOU LIKE...
If you like Ko Lanta, there are more subdued islands further south but the journey takes longer.

- **Trang Islands** A collection of limestone-peaked islands clutter the bay off the coast of Trang. Check out **Koh Ngai Resort** (☎ 0 7520 6924; Ko Ngai; bungalows 1500-15,000B; ✷ 🖳 🐾) and **Paradise Lost Resort** (☎ 08 9587 2409/1391; Ko Kradan; www.kokradan.com; bungalows 600-1200B; ✷).

- **Ko Tarutao Marine National Park** (☎ 0 7478 1285; adult/child 400/200B; ☢ Nov-mid-May) Still delightfully under-developed. Accommodation on Ko Tarutao can be booked though the **park's reservation system** (☎ 0 7478 3485; www.dnp.go.th; cabins 600-1200B). Ko Lipe has a mini-tourist scene but still no ATM or 7-Eleven. **Forra Bamboo** (☎ 08 4407 5691; www.forradiving.com; Sunrise Beach; bungalows 700-1200B) provides the quintessential crash pad.

A large travellers' village has set up camp and there are loads of *fa·ràng*-oriented restaurants, beach bars, internet cafes and tour offices.

Sanctuary (☎ 0 1891 3055; bungalows 400-800B) A delightful place to stay. There are artistically designed wood-and-thatch bungalows with lots of grass and a hippyish atmosphere that's low key and friendly. The resort holds yoga classes and has a small art gallery displaying local talent.

HAT KHLONG NIN
Halfway down the island, the tarmac road forks – head inland towards Ban Khlong Nin or continue south along the coast to the marine national park headquarters at Laem Tanod. The first beach here is lovely Hat Khlong Nin, which gets progressively nicer the further south you travel.

Sri Lanta (☎ 0 7569 7288; www.srilanta.com; villas from 4000B; ✷ 🖳 🐾) On the southern (and best) bit of the beach, this sophisticated (but slightly overpriced) resort consists of roomy wooden villas in a hillside garden, set back from the shore.

AO KANTIANG
This bay's tip-top beach has a good sprinkling of sand, and a couple of excellent sleeping options.

Baan Laanta Resort & Spa (☎ 0 7566 5091; www.baanlaanta.com; bungalows 3500-4500B; ✷ 🖳 🐾) Fragrant, green landscaped grounds wind around stylish wooden bungalows and an inviting central pool.

AO KHLONG JAAK
The splendid beach here is named after the inland waterfall.

Andalanta Resort (☎ 0 7566 5018; www.andalanta.com; bungalows 2500-6500B; ✷ 🖳 🐾)

You'll find a large campus of comfortable and modern air-con bungalows (some with a loft), which all face out onto the sea. Overall, Andalanta is one of the top spots for families.

AO MAI PAI

There are only three resorts on this lovely isolated beach, including:

Bamboo Bay Resort (☎ 0 7561 8240; www .bamboobay.net; bungalows 700-1700B) Clinging to the hillside above Ao Mai Pai beach, this place has a variety of brick and concrete bungalows on stilts and a fine restaurant down on the sand.

Baan Phu Lae (☎ 08 1201 1704; www .baanphulae.com; bungalows 900-1200B; 🔀) The restaurant and many of the bungalows sit right on the semi-private beach and have perfect sunset views.

EATING

Ko Lanta's many markets are a great choice for cheap eats.

Bar Kantiang (dishes 50-150B, 😌 dinner) Excellent Thai food comes out of this ramshackle kitchen near Ao Kantiang.

Drunken Sailors (☎ 0 7566 5076; dishes 100-200B; 😌 breakfast, lunch & dinner) This hip, ultra-relaxed, octagonal pad is smothered with beanbags. The coffee drinks are top-notch and go well with interesting bites like the chicken green curry sandwich.

ourpick La Laanta (☎ 0 7566 5066; dishes 100-290B; 😌 breakfast, lunch & dinner) The owners of La Laanta, located at the like-named resort, are from all over Southeast Asia, and their fusion cuisine is a blend of secret family recipes. If you call ahead, they'll pick you up at your hotel free of charge.

GETTING THERE & AWAY
BOAT

There are two piers at Ban Sala Dan. The passenger jetty is about 300m from the main strip of shops; vehicle ferries leave from a second jetty that's several kilometres further east.

Passenger boats between Krabi's Khlong Chilat passenger pier and Ko Lanta run when there are enough passengers and supplies to go through, and take 1½ hours.

Boats between Ko Lanta and Ko Phi-Phi run as long as there are enough passengers, which means that services peter out in the low season.

Two high-speed ferries connect Ko Lanta and Ko Lipe (see opposite; 1800B).

MINIVAN

This is the main way of getting to/from Ko Lanta, and vans run year-round. Daily minivans to Krabi operate between 7am and 8am (350B, 1½ hours). There are also daily air-con vans to Trang (250B, two hours).

GETTING AROUND

Most resorts send vehicles to meet the ferries and you'll get a free ride to your resort. Motorcycles can be rented almost anywhere on the island.

↘ THAILAND IN FOCUS

ARCHITECTURE

Detail of Thai temple

BILL WASSMAN

Thailand's cities are modest in the architectural department. But once you recalibrate your senses and look beyond the bland concrete boxes shielded by huge canvas awnings, you'll see fine examples of old teak shophouses and bombastic heritage-style buildings. Along the country roads, old wooden houses squat confidently beside the rice fields and reflect a successful marriage of form and function.

TRADITIONAL RESIDENTIAL ARCHITECTURE

Traditional Thai homes were adapted to the weather, the family and artistic sensibilities. These antique specimens were humble dwellings consisting of a single-room wooden house raised on stilts. More elaborate homes, for the village chief or minor royalty for instance, might link a series of single rooms by elevated walkways. Since many Thai villages were built near rivers, the elevation provided protection from flooding during the annual monsoon. During the dry season the space beneath the house was used as a hideaway from the heat of the day, an outdoor kitchen or as a barn for farm animals. Later this all-purpose space would shelter bicycles and motorcycles. Once plentiful in Thai forests, teak was always the material of choice for wooden structures and its use typically indicates that a house is at least 50 years old.

Rooflines in central, northern and southern Thailand are steeply pitched and often decorated at the corners or along the gables with motifs related to the *naga*, a mythical water serpent long believed to be a spiritual protector of Tai cultures throughout Asia.

In Thailand's southern provinces it's not unusual to come upon houses of Malay design, using high masonry pediments or foundations rather than wooden stilts. Residents of the south also sometimes use bamboo and palm thatch, which are more plentiful than wood. In the north, the homes of community leaders were often decorated with an ornate horn-shaped motif called *galare,* a decorative element that has become shorthand for old Lanna architecture. Roofs of tile or thatch tend to be less steeply pitched, and rounded gables (a feature inherited from Myanmar) can also be found further north.

MICK ELMORE

Jim Thompson's House (p69)

THE BEST

OLD-FASHIONED THAI HOUSES

- **Jim Thompson's House** (p69)
- **Baan Sao Nak** (p155)
- **Ban Kamthieng** (p76)

TEMPLE ARCHITECTURE

Most striking of Thailand's architectural heritage are the Buddhist temples, which dazzle in the tropical sun with wild colours and soaring rooflines. Thai temples (wat) are compounds of different buildings serving specific religious functions. The most important structures include the *uposatha* (*bòht* in central Thai, *sǐm* in northern and northeastern Thai), which is a consecrated chapel where monastic ordinations are held, and the *wí·hǎhn,* where important Buddha images are housed.

Another classic component of temple architecture is the presence of one or more *chedi* (stupas), a solid mountain-shaped monument that pays tribute to the enduring stability of Buddhism. *Chedi* come in a myriad of styles, from simple inverted bowl-shaped designs imported from Sri Lanka to the more elaborate octagonal shapes found in northern Thailand. Many are believed to contain relics (often pieces of bone) belonging to the historical Buddha. Some *chedi* also house the ashes of important kings and royalty. In northern and northeastern Thailand such stupas are known as *tâht.* A variation of the stupa inherited from the Angkor kingdom is the corn cob–shaped *prang,* a feature in the ancient Thai temples of Sukhothai and Ayuthaya. Dotting the grounds of most temples are smaller squarish *chedi* that contain the ashes of deceased worshippers.

Other structures typically found in temple compounds include one or more *sǎh·lah* (open-sided shelters) that are used for community meetings and *dhamma* (Buddhist philosophy) lectures; a number of *gù·dì* (monastic quarters); a *hǒr đrai* (Tripitaka library), where Buddhist scriptures are stored; plus various ancillary buildings, such as schools and clinics.

TEMPLE SYMBOLS

The architectural symbolism of temple buildings relies heavily on Hindu-Buddhist iconography. *Naga,* the mythical serpent that guarded Buddha during meditation, is depicted in the temple roofline where the green and gold tiles are said to represent the serpent's scales (others say that the tiles represent the land and the king) and the soaring eaves represent its diamond-shaped head. On the tip of the roof is the silhouette of the *chôr fáh:* often bird-shaped decorations the colour of gold. Rooflines are usually tiered into three levels, representing the triple gems of Buddhism: the Buddha, the *dhamma* and the *sangha* (the Buddhist community).

The lotus bud is another sacred motif that is used to decorate the tops of the temple gates and posts, veranda columns and spires of Sukhothai-era *chedi*. Images of the Buddha often depict him meditating in a lotus blossom–shaped pedestal. The lotus bud was extensively used before the introduction of monk-like figures depicting the Buddha. It carries with it a reminder of the tenets of Buddhism. In a practical sense, the lotus plant can create a dramatic flower even in the most rancid pond – a natural phenomenon reminding the faithful of religious perfection. Many Thai markets sell lotus buds, which are used solely for merit-making in Thailand, not as secular decorations.

CONTEMPORARY ARCHITECTURE

Thais began mixing traditional architecture with European forms in the late 19th and early 20th centuries, as exemplified by Bangkok's Vimanmek Teak Mansion and certain buildings of the Grand Palace (p65).

The port cities of Thailand, including Bangkok and Phuket, acquired fine examples of Sino-Portuguese architecture – buildings of stuccoed brick decorated with an ornate facade – a style that followed the sea traders during the colonial era. In Bangkok this style is often referred to as 'old Bangkok' or 'Ratanakosin'.

Buildings of mixed heritage in the north and northeast exhibit French and English influences, while those in the south typically show Portuguese influence. Shophouses *(hôrng tăa·ou)* throughout the country, whether 100 years or 100 days old, share the basic Chinese shophouse design, where the ground floor is reserved for trading purposes while the upper floors contain offices or residences.

SEAN CAFFREY

Grand Palace (p65), Bangkok

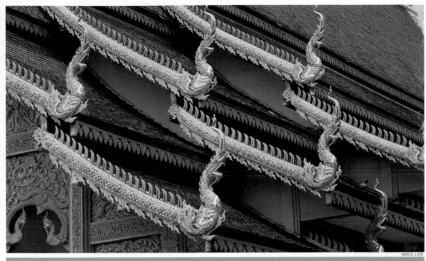
Decorative dragons on temple roof

KRAIG LIEB

MODERNISM & BEYOND

In the 1960s and 1970s the trend in modern Thai architecture, inspired by the European Bauhaus movement, shifted towards a stark functionalism – the average building looked like a giant egg carton turned on its side. When Thai architects began experimenting with form over function during the building boom of the mid-1980s, the result was high-tech designs such as ML Sumet Jumsai's famous Robot Building on Th Sathon Tai in Bangkok. Rangsan Torsuwan, a graduate of the Massachusetts Institute of Technology (MIT), introduced the neoclassic (or neo-Thai) style. A traditional-building specialist, Pinyo Suwankiri designs temples, government buildings and shrines for hospitals and universities in Thailand. His work is ubiquitous and the blueprint for an institutional aesthetic of architecture.

In the new millennium, Duangrit Bunnag has excited the design world with his nearly undressed glass boxes offering a contemporary twist on mid-century modernism. The H1 complex on Soi Thonglor in Bangkok is a series of interconnected geometric cubes with flat cantilevered roofs, glass curtain windows and exposed steel ribs, arranged around a courtyard much like a traditional Thai house. Encore performances include the Pier restaurant on Ko Samui and Costa Lanta on Ko Lanta.

BANGKOK: DECONSTRUCTING DESIGN

Climb aboard Bangkok's Skytrain to get an above-ground view of this tower-filled town. There are skyscrapers that look like elephants, townhouses replicating Italian villas, empty and forgotten construction projects that have been transformed into graffiti murals and big holes in the ground where sandal-clad construction workers assemble the steel ribs of a yet another condo complex.

THAILAND IN FOCUS

ARTS

ARTS

Ramakian mural, Wat Phra Kaew (p65), Bangkok

GREG ELMS

Thais have a refined sense of beauty that is reflected in their rich and varied artistic traditions, ranging from Buddhist sculpture to humble handicrafts. The monarchs were the country's great artistic patrons and, in their honour, ornate temple stupas served as funeral monuments and handicrafts were developed specifically for royal usage. Today religious artwork continues to dominate the artistic imagination but it has been adapted to the modern context with museum multimedia installations and contemporary canvas works.

RELIGIOUS ART

Although most Thais go to temples for religious reasons, tourists go for artistic appreciation. Temples are the country's artistic repositories where you'll find ornate murals depicting Hindu-Buddhist mythology and Buddha sculptures, which define Thailand's most famous contribution to the world of religious art.

Always instructional in intent, temple murals often show depictions of the *jataka* (stories of the Buddha's past life) and the Thai version of the Hindu epic Ramayana. Reading the murals requires both knowledge of these religious tales and an understanding of the mural's spatial relationship and chronology. Most murals are divided into scenes, in which the main theme is depicted in the centre with resulting events taking place above and below the central action. Usually in the corner of a dramatic episode between the story's leading characters are independent scenes of Thai village life: women carrying food in bamboo baskets, men fishing, or a happy communal get-together; all of these simple village folk wear the ubiquitous Thai smile.

Early temple murals were made from natural pigments, a temperamental medium that didn't survive the elements. The study and application of mural painting has been kept alive, and today's practitioners often use improved techniques and paints that hold much longer than the temple murals of old.

Alongside the vivid murals in the sacred temple spaces are revered Buddha images that trace Thailand's sculptural evolution. The country is most famous for its graceful and serene Buddhas that emerged during the Sukhothai era, but originals and reproduction from all the artistic periods are sought after by art collectors and connoisseurs of religious sculpture.

ARTISTIC PERIODS

The development of Thai religious art and architecture is broken into different periods or schools defined by the patronage of the ruling capital. The best examples of a period's characteristics are seen in the depiction of the Buddha's facial features, the top flourish on the head, the dress and the position of the feet in meditation.

Another signature of the artistic periods is the size and shape of the temples' *chedi* (stupas) – tell-tale characteristics are shown in the pedestal and the central bell before it begins to taper into the uppermost tower. For more information on temple architecture, see p323.

DVARAVATI PERIOD (7th–11th CENTURIES)

This period refers to the Mon kingdom that occupied areas of central Thailand. The Buddha sculptures depict a thick body shape, along with large hair curls, arched eyebrows to represent a flying bird, protruding eyes, thick lips and a flat nose.

Lamphun in northern Thailand was an outpost of the Mon kingdom and today contains several temples displaying the needle-like *chedi* spires associated with this period.

KHMER PERIOD (9th–11th CENTURIES)

The great Angkor empire sowed an enduring artistic seed into Thai soil. The image of Buddha meditating under a canopy of the seven-headed *naga* (a mythical serpent-being) and atop a lotus pedestal was a favourite Khmer motif. But the most famous Khmer contribution to temple architecture is the central corn cob–shaped stupa, called a *prang*. Examples can be seen at Sukhothai Historical Park (p171) and Phimai (p203).

GREG ELMS

Detail of mural, Wat Phra Kaew (p65), Bangkok

PLACES TO SEE TEMPLE MURALS

- **Wat Ratburana** (p134)
- **Wat Phra Kaew** (p65)
- **National Museum** (p64)
- **Wat Rong Khun** (p162)

CHIANG SAEN-LANNA PERIOD (11th–13th CENTURIES)

This northern Thai kingdom drew inspiration from its Lao, Shan and Burmese neighbours in depicting Buddha, who appears with a plump figure and round, smiling face, with both pads of the feet facing upward in the meditation position. Instructional poses are often depicted in Buddha figures and the Lanna period favoured the standing pose showing Buddha dispelling fear or giving instruction. Lanna-style temples were typically made of teak and the *chedi* are indented instead of rounded. Examples can be found in the temples and museums of Chiang Mai and at Chiang Saen National Museum (p165).

SUKHOTHAI PERIOD (13th–15th CENTURIES)

Sukhothai set forth the underlying aesthetic of successive generations of Thai artists. This artistic period was heavily influenced by the Khmers but evolved unique imprints on the inherited blueprints. Buddha images were graceful and serene and were often depicted 'walking'. A sense of motion was shown through the flair of the robe or the tilt of the hand but the figures were purposefully devoid of anatomical human detail, an artistic conceit suggesting the Buddha's divine nature. The telltale Sukhothai *chedi* are fairly slim spires topped with a lotus-bud motif. Examples can be seen at Sukhothai Historical Park (p171).

AYUTHAYA PERIOD (14th–18th CENTURIES)

Incorporating elements inherited from the Khmer and Sukhothai kingdoms, Ayuthaya morphed the Buddha image into a king wearing a gem-studded crown and royal regalia instead of an austere monk's robe. The period's bell-shaped *chedi*, with an elongated, tapering spire, can be seen at Ayuthaya (p134).

RICHARD I'ANSON

Art on display

BANGKOK-RATANAKOSIN PERIOD (19th CENTURY–)

The religious artwork of the modern capital is noted for merging traditional Thai styles with Western influences. Wat Phra Kaew and the Grand Palace (p65) are good starting points.

CONTEMPORARY ART

Adapting traditional themes and aesthetics to the secular canvas began around the turn of the 20th century, as Western influence surged in the region. In general, Thai painting favours abstraction over realism and continues to preserve the one-dimensional perspective of traditional mural paintings. There are two major trends in Thai art: the updating of religious themes and tongue-in-cheek social commentary.

Italian artist Corrado Feroci is often credited as the father of modern Thai art. He was first invited to Thailand by Rama VI in 1924 and built Bangkok's Democracy Monument, among other European-style statues. Feroci founded the country's first fine arts institute in 1933, a school that eventually developed into Silpakorn University, Thailand's premier training ground for artists. In gratitude, the Thai government made Feroci a Thai citizen, with the Thai name Silpa Bhirasri.

THE MODERN BUDDHA

In the 1970s, Thai artists began to tackle the modernisation of Buddhist themes through abstract expressionism. Leading works in this genre include the mystical pen-and-ink drawings of Thawan Duchanee. Receiving more exposure overseas than at home, Montien Boonma used the ingredients of Buddhist merit-making, such as gold leaf, bells and candle wax, to create abstract temple spaces within museum galleries.

PROTEST & SATIRE

In Thailand's quickly industrialising society, many artists have watched as the rice fields became factories, the forests became asphalt and the spoils went to the politically connected. During the student activist days of the 1970s, the Art for Life Movement was the banner under which creative discontents – including musicians, intellectuals and painters – rallied against the military dictatorship and embraced certain aspects of communism and workers' rights. Sompote Upa-In and Chang Saetang are two important artists from that period.

During and after the boom times of the 1980s, an anti-authority attitude emerged in the work of the artists known as the Fireball School. Manit Sriwanichpoom is best known for his *Pink Man on Tour* series, in which he depicted artist Sompong Thawee in a pink suit and with a pink shopping cart amid Thailand's most iconic attractions, suggesting that Thailand's culture and natural spaces were for sale. He's since followed up this series with other socially evocative photographs poking fun at ideas of patriotism and nationalism.

FINDING A HOME FOR ART

Being a hierarchical society, artistic innovation is often stifled by the older generation that holds prestige and power. In the 1990s there was a push to move art out of the dead zones of the museums, where the ideas were strictly defined, and into the public spaces beyond the reach of the cultural authoritarians. An artist and art organiser, Navin Rawanchaikul started his 'in-the-streets' collaborations in his hometown of Chiang Mai and then moved his big ideas to Bangkok where he filled the city's taxi cabs with art installations, a show that literally went on the road. His other works have had a way with words, such as the mixed media piece *We Are the Children of Rice (Wine)* in 2002 and his rage against the commercialisation of museums in his epic painting entitled *Super (M)art Bangkok Survivors* (2004), which depicts famous artists, curators and decision-makers in a crowded Paolo Veronese setting. The piece was inspired by the struggles the Thai art community had getting the new contemporary Bangkok art museum to open without becoming a shopping mall in disguise.

POP FUN

True to the Thai nature, some art is just fun. The works of Thaweesak Srithongdee are pure pop. He paints flamboyantly cartoonish human figures woven with elements of traditional Thai handicrafts or imagery. In a similar vein, Jirapat Tasanasomboon pits traditional Thai figures in comic book-style fights or in sensual embraces with Western icons. In *Hanuman is Upset!* the monkey king chews up the geometric lines of Mondrian's famous grid-like painting.

SCULPTURE

Although lacking in commercial attention, Thai sculpture is often considered to be the strongest of the contemporary arts, not surprising considering the country's relationship with Buddha figures. Moving into nonreligious arenas, Khien Yimsiri is the modern master creating elegant human and mythical forms out of bronze. Kamin Lertchaiprasert explores the subject of spirituality and daily life in his sculptural installations, which often include a small army of papier-mâché figures. One of his most recent exhibitions, *Ngern Nang* (Sitting Money), included a series of figures made of discarded paper bills from the national bank embellished with poetic instructions on life and love.

MICK ELMORE

Contemporary Thai sculpture

THEATRE & DANCE

Traditional Thai theatre consists of dance-dramas, in which stories are acted out by masked or costumed actors. There are a variety of classical forms, sharing cultural influences from Chinese operas and stylised Indian dancing. Traditional theatre was reserved for royal or religious events but with the modernisation of the monarchy, the once cloistered art forms have lost their patrons and have gone into decline.

Traditional Thai dance, on the other hand, has survived quite well in the modern era and is still widely taught in the schools and universities. The dances involve precise and synchronised hand and foot motions that are pieced together to tell a story.

KŎHN & LÍ·GAIR

Kŏhn is a masked dance-drama depicting scenes from the Ramakian (the Thai version of India's Ramayana). The central story revolves around Prince Rama's search for his beloved Princess Sita, who has been abducted by the evil 10-headed demon Ravana and taken to the island of Lanka.

Perhaps because it was once limited to royal venues and hence never gained a popular following, the *kŏhn* tradition nearly died out in Thailand.

THAILAND IN FOCUS

ARTS

HANDICRAFTS

Thailand's handicrafts live on for the tourist markets, and some have been updated by chic Bangkok designers.

- **Ceramics** The best-known ceramics are the greenish Thai-style celadon; the red-earth clay of Dan Kwian (p203); and central Thailand's *ben·jà·rong* (five colour), an adaptation of a Chinese style.
- **Lacquerware** Northern Thailand is known for lacquerware inherited from Burma.
- **Textiles** The northeast is famous for *mát·mèe* cloth – a thick cotton or silk fabric woven from tie-dyed threads. Each hill tribe has a tradition of embroidery; Chiang Mai and Chiang Rai are popular handicraft centres.

Villages had their own traditional forms of entertainment that were often less stylised and a little bawdier than those for royalty. In outlying working-class neighbourhoods in Bangkok, the gaudy and raucous *lí·gair* performances present a colourful mixture of folk and classical music, outrageous costumes, melodrama, slapstick comedy, sexual innuendo and up-to-date commentary on Thai politics and society.

PUPPET THEATRE

Puppet theatre *(lá·kon lék)* was once a popular court entertainment. Stories are drawn from Thai tales, particularly Phra Aphaimani, and occasionally from the Ramakian.

The puppets were metre-high marionettes made of paper and wire, dressed in elaborate costumes modelled on those of the *kŏhn* and were manipulated by two to three puppet masters to imitate the dance movements that depicted the great battles.

Shadow-puppet theatre – in which two-dimensional figures are manipulated between a cloth screen and a light source at night-time performances – has been a Southeast Asian tradition for perhaps five centuries. Originally brought to the Malay peninsula by Middle Eastern traders, the technique eventually spread to all parts of mainland and peninsular Southeast Asia; in Thailand it is mostly found in the south. As

THAILAND IN FOCUS

ARTS

THE PUPPET MASTER

Bangkok used to be filled with court musicians, artisans and actors, and Nonthaburi-native Sakorn Yangkhiawsod was born to such an artistic family in the 1920s. After years of stage experience he revived the dying art form of *lá·kon hùn lék* (puppet theatre) using smaller, more agile puppets. Earning the nickname Joe Louis he established a puppet troupe with his children that lives on today and performs at the Aksra Theatre (p89) in Bangkok.

in Malaysia and Indonesia, shadow puppets in Thailand are carved from dried buffalo or cow hides *(năng)*.

Like their Malay-Indonesian counterparts, Thai shadow puppets represent an array of characters from classical and folk drama, principally the Ramakian and Phra Aphaimani in Thailand. A single puppet master manipulates the cut-outs, which are bound to the ends of buffalo-horn handles. Shadow puppets still occasionally appear at temple festivals in the south, mostly in Songkhla and Nakhon Si Thammarat provinces. Performances are also held periodically for tour groups or visiting dignitaries from Bangkok.

CLASSICAL & FOLK DANCE

Inherited from the Khmer, classical dance was a holy offering performed by the earthly version of *apsara* (heavenly maidens blessed with beauty and skilled in dance and depicted in graceful positions in temple murals and bas reliefs). But traditional dancing enjoyed its own expressions in the villages and defined each region. In some cases the dances describe the rice-planting season, while others tell tales of flirtations. During local festivals and street parades, especially in the northeast, troupes of dancers, ranging in age from elementary school to college, will be swathed in

MICK ELMORE

Actors performing kŏhn – a traditional masked dance-drama (p308)

traditional costumes, ornate headdresses and white-powder make up to perform synchronised steps accompanied by a travelling band of musicians.

MUSIC

Classical Thai music features a dazzling array of textures and subtleties, hair-raising tempos and pastoral melodies. The classical orchestra is called the *ɓèe pâht* and can include as few as five players or more than 20. Among the more common instruments is the *ɓèe*, a woodwind instrument that has a reed mouthpiece; it is heard prominently at Thai-boxing matches. The *rá·nâht èhk*, a bamboo-keyed percussion instrument resembling the xylophone, carries the main melodies. The slender *sor*, a bowed instrument with a coconut-shell sound-box, is sometimes played solo by street buskers.

THE BEST

RICHARD CUMMINS

Masks, Patravadi Theatre (p89), Bangkok

PLACES TO SEE TRADITIONAL THEATRE & DANCE

- **Chalermkrung Royal Theatre** (p89)
- **Aksra Theatre** (p89)
- **Street parades & festivals** (p46)

If you take a cab in Bangkok, you're likely to hear Thailand's version of country music: *lôok tûng* (literally 'children of the fields'). Lost love, tragic early death and the plight of the hard-working farmers are popular themes sung plaintively over a melancholy accompaniment. More upbeat is *mŏr lam*, a folk tradition from the rural northeast that has been electrified with a fast-paced beat.

Step into a shopping mall or a Thai disco and you'll hear the bouncy tunes of Thai pop (also dubbed 'T-pop'), a favourite with teens. The ageing hippies from the protest era of the 1970s and 1980s pioneered *pleng pêu·a chee·wít* (songs for life), which feature in the increasingly hard-to-find Thai country bars.

CULTURE & CUSTOMS

Hill-tribe children in traditional dress

FELIX HUG

It is easy to love Thailand: the pace of life is unhurried and the people are friendly and kind-hearted. A smile is a universal key in most social situations, a cheerful disposition will be met in kind, and friendships are spontaneous creations requiring little more than curiosity and humour. Though Thais don't expect foreigners to know much about their small country, they are delighted and grateful if you do. And a rudimentary enquiry into their culture and customs will reveal an ancient heritage that intrigues and confounds Westerners.

THE MONARCHY

Thailand's most striking cultural quirk is the deep reverence the average Thai has for the reigning monarch, King Bhumibol Adulyadej. Life-size billboards of the king and queen line Th Ratchadamnoen Klang, Bangkok's royal avenue. Pictures of the king are enshrined in nearly every household and business. His image, which is printed on money and stamps, is regarded as sacred, resulting in such taboos as not stepping on money (in the case of a dropped bill) or licking stamps.

KING BHUMIBOL

The monarch's relationship to the people is intertwined with the religion; it is deeply spiritual and personal. Though not universal, many view the king as a god, or at least as a father figure (his birthday is recognised as national Father's Day) and as a protector of the good of the country. In times of political crisis, Thais have often looked to this figurehead for guidance, a role King Bhumibol adroitly played through most of his 60-plus year reign. However, the most recent political upheaval (starting with the 2006 coup) indicates a general unease regarding the ailing monarch and the succession of the Crown Prince Vachiralongkorn, who does not enjoy as much adoration as his father.

In June 2006, the king celebrated his 60th year on the throne, an anniversary that has earned him the title of the world's longest reigning monarch. Starting with the celebrations, Thais began wearing yellow shirts embossed with the royal seal to show their support of the king. Yellow is the colour associated with Monday, the day of the week the king was born. Other remnants from the king's Diamond Jubilee are bumper stickers that read in Thai *Rao Rak Nai Luang* (We Love the King), and yellow wrist bands.

> ### THE NAME GAME
>
> Every Thai has a short and plucky nickname that is more commonly used than their formal first and family names. Girls are usually Noi or Lek (both meaning 'small'), animal names such as *Gòp* (frog) or *Gûng* (shrimp) are popular, and increasingly borrowed English words, like Bank and Boat, are word plays on a parent's desire for inanimate possessions.

HISTORIC KINGS

Looking back through history, there have been other monarchs who have crossed into national-hero status, including King Chulalongkorn (Rama V, 1868–1910), whose picture often decorates residences and amulets.

Procession celebrating King Bhumibol Adulyadej's birthday

TOM COCKREM

RAY LASKOWITZ
Schoolgirls celebrating Buddha Day

THE NATIONAL PSYCHE

Thais place a high value on having *sà·nùk* (fun). It is the underlying measure of a worthwhile activity, the guiding principle for most social interactions and the reason why the country ranks so highly as a tourist destination. Thais are always up for a party, be it their own invention or an import. Case in point – Thais celebrate three new years: the eve of the re-setting of the international calendar, the lunar Chinese New Year and Songkran (the Southeast Asian Buddhist new year).

This doesn't mean that Thais are adverse to work. On the contrary, most offices are typically open six, sometimes seven, days a week, and professionals from poor farming families are expected to have side jobs to provide extra income to their parents. But every chore has a social aspect to it that lightens the mood and keeps it from being too 'serious' (a grave insult). Thais labour best as a group to avoid loneliness and ensure an element of playfulness. The back-breaking work of rice farming, the tedium of long-distance bus driving, the dangers of a construction site: Thais often mix their job tasks with a healthy dose of socialising. Watch these workers in action and you'll see them flirting with each other, trading insults or cracking jokes. The famous Thai smile comes from a genuine desire to enjoy life.

Thais in the tourism industry extend this view towards their guests and will often describe the foreign visitors as needing a rest after a year of hard work. This cultural mindset is reflective of the agricultural clock in which a farmer works dawn to dusk during rice planting and harvesting season then rests until the next year's rains. That resting period involves a lot of hanging out, going to festivals and funerals (that are more party than pity) and loading up family and friends into the back of a pick-up truck for a *têe·o* (trip). Thais have been practicing the art of a good time for a long time.

STATUS

Though Thai culture is famously non-confrontational and fun-loving, it isn't a social free-for-all. Thais are very conscious of status and the implicit rights and responsibilities that go along with one's station in life. Buddhism plays a large part in defining the social strata with the heads of the family, religion and monarchy sitting at the top of various tiers. A good indicator of status is the depth of the *wâi* (the traditional prayerlike greeting). In most cases the fingertips will touch between the lips and nose but will migrate above the crown of the head when greeting or showing gratitude to a monk.

Gauging where you as a foreigner fit into this system is a convenient ice breaker. Thais will often ask a laundry list of questions: where are you from, how old are you, are you married, do you have children. They are getting to know you and

DOS & DON'TS

- Do stand politely at the beginning of a movie when the royal anthem is played.
- The national anthem is played at 8am and 6pm; do stand politely during the song's duration.
- Thais have many feet taboos: do take your shoes off before entering a private home or temple building, don't prop your feet on furniture, and do sit in the mermaid position (with your legs tucked beside you) inside a temple.
- Women shouldn't touch monks or their belongings; don't sit next to them on buses or accidentally brush past them.

sizing you up in the social strata. In most cases you'll get the best of both worlds: Thais will care for you as if you are a child and honour you as if you are a *pôo yài* (literally 'big person' or elder). Don't be surprised if a Thai host puts the tastiest piece of fish from a shared meal on your plate.

Thais regard each other as part of an extended family and will use familial prefixes such as *pêe* (elder sibling) and *nórng* (younger sibling) when addressing friends as well as blood relations. This convention is often translated into English by bilingual Thais, leading foreigners to think that their Thai friends have large immediate families. Thais might also use *bâh* (aunt) or *lung* (uncle) to refer to an older person. Rarely do foreigners get embraced in this grand family reunion; we're just *fa·ràng*, the catch-all term for foreigner that is mostly descriptive but can sometimes express cultural frustrations.

SAVING FACE

Interconnected with status is the concept of 'saving face', a common consideration in Asian cultures. In a nutshell, 'face' means that you strive for social harmony by avoiding firm or confrontational opinions and avoiding displays of anger. Thais regard outbursts of emotions and discourteous social interactions as shameful, whereas Westerners might shrug it off as minor embarrassments or a necessary by-product to achieving fairness.

SOCIAL CONVENTIONS & ETIQUETTE

The traditional Thai greeting is with a prayerlike palms-together gesture known as a *wâi*. If someone shows you a *wâi*, you should return the gesture, unless the greeting comes from a child or a service person. Foreigners are continually baffled by when and how to use the *wâi* and such cultural confusion makes great conversation fodder with a Thai who will be delighted for the opportunity to explain it.

The all-purpose greeting is a cheery *sà·wàt·dee kráp* if you're male or *sà·wàt·dee kâ* if you're female. A smile usually accompanies this and goes a long way in diffusing nervousness or shyness that a Thai might have when interacting with a foreigner. Plus Thais are great connoisseurs of beauty and a smile accentuates one's countenance.

In the more traditional parts of the country, it is not proper for members of the opposite sex to touch one another, either as lovers or as friends. Hand-holding is not acceptable behaviour outside of Bangkok. But same-sex touching is quite common and is typically a sign of friendship, not sexual attraction. Older Thai men might grab a younger man's thigh in the same way that buddies slap each other on the back. Thai women are especially affectionate with female friends, often sitting close to one another or linking arms.

VISITING TEMPLES

When visiting a temple, it is very important to dress modestly (covered to the elbows and the ankles) and to take your shoes off when you enter any building that contains a Buddha image. Buddha images are sacred objects, so don't pose in front of them for pictures and definitely do not clamber upon them. When visiting a religious building, act like a worshipper by finding a discreet place to sit (with your feet tucked behind you so that they point away from the Buddha images). Also take the time to observe the worshippers' praying rituals and feel free to attempt it yourself to honour the sacred space. Temples are maintained from the donations received and contributions from visitors are appreciated.

RAY LASKOWITZ

Burning incense

ENVIRONMENT

Sign on Ko Samui

Thailand clings to a southern spur of the Himalayas. It cradles fertile river plains and tapers between warm and shallow seas fringed by coral reefs. The country's shape is often likened to the head of an elephant, with the shaft of the trunk being represented by the Malay peninsula. From north to south, the country spans 1650km and 16 latitudinal degrees, resulting in the most diverse climate of any country in Southeast Asia.

NORTHERN THAILAND

Northern Thailand is fused to Myanmar (Burma), Laos and southern China through the southeast-trending extension of the Himalayan mountain range known as the Dawna-Tenasserim. The tallest peak is Doi Inthanon (measured heights vary from 2565m to 2576m), which is topped by a mixed forest of hill evergreen and swamp species, including a thick carpet of moss. Monsoon forests comprise the lower elevations and are made up of deciduous trees, which are green and lush during the rainy season but dusty and leafless during the dry season. Teak is one of the most highly valued monsoon forest trees but it now exists only in limited quantities and is illegal to harvest.

The cool mountains of northern Thailand are considered to be some of the most accessible and rewarding birding destinations in Asia and are populated by montane species and migrants with clear Himalayan affinities such as flycatchers and thrushes.

CENTRAL THAILAND

In the central region, the topography mellows into a flat rice basket, fed by rivers that are as revered as the national monarchy. Thailand's most exalted river is the Chao Phraya, which is formed by the northern tributaries of the Ping, Wang, Yom and Nan – a lineage as notable as any aristocrat's. The river delta spends most of the year in cultivation – changing with the seasons from fields of emerald-green rice shoots to golden harvests. This region has been heavily sculpted by civilisation: roads, fields, cities and towns have transformed the landscape into a working core.

In the western frontier, bumping into the mountainous border with Myanmar (Burma), is a complex of forest preserves that cover 4.4 million acres, the largest protected area in Southeast Asia and a largely undisturbed habitat for endangered elephants and tigers. These parks have little in the way of tourist infrastructure or commercial development.

NORTHEASTERN THAILAND

The landscape of Thailand's northeastern border is occupied by the arid Khorat Plateau rising some 300m above the central plain. This is a hardscrabble land where the rains are meagre, the soil is anaemic and the red dust stains as stubbornly as the betel nut chewed by the ageing grandmothers. The dominant forest is dry dipterocarp, which consists of deciduous trees that shed their leaves in the dry season to conserve water. The region's largest forest preserve is Khao Yai National Park, which together with nearby parks, has been recognised as a Unesco World Heritage site. The park is mainly arid forests, a favourite for hornbills and over 300 other bird species. There is a small population of wild elephants in the park but development around the perimeter has impacted important wildlife corridors.

THE MEKONG RIVER

Defining the contours of Thailand's border with Laos is the Mekong River, Southeast Asia's artery. The Mekong is a workhorse, having been dammed for hydroelectric power, and a mythmaker, featuring in local people's folktales and festivals. The river winds in and out of the steep mountain ranges to the northeastern plateau where it swells and contracts based on the seasonal rains. In the dry season, riverside farmers plant vegetables in the muddy floodplain, harvesting the crop before the river reclaims its territory.

As the former Indochinese countries have become more open and accessible, scientists have begun to document the regions of the Mekong River and have

THAILAND ENVIRONMENTAL TRIVIA

- Thailand is equivalent to the size of France.
- Bangkok sits at about N14° latitude, level with Madras, Manila, Guatemala and Khartoum.
- The Mekong used to flow through central Thailand, terminating at present day Bangkok; its current route emerged 5000 years ago.
- Thailand's karst formations are made of limestone, a soft sedimentary rock containing quantities of calcium carbonate from shells and coral that populated an ancient sea bed 250 to 300 million years ago.

THAILAND IN FOCUS

ENVIRONMENT

Prepared for city traffic, Bangkok

RAY LASKOWITZ

identified it as having an impressive biodiversity. As many as 1000 previously uniden-
tified species of flora and fauna have been discovered in the last decade in the Mekong
region (which includes Vietnam, Laos and Cambodia).

GULF COAST & ANDAMAN COAST

The kingdom's eastern rivers dump their waters and sediment into the Gulf of Thailand,
a shallow basin off the neighbouring South China Sea. In the joint of the fishhook-
shaped gulf is Bangkok, surrounded by a thick industrial zone that has erased or pol-
luted much of the natural environment. The extremities of the gulf, both to the east
and to the south, are more characteristic of coastal environments: mangrove swamps
form the transition between land and sea and act as the ocean's nursery, spawning
and nurturing fish, bird and amphibian species. Thailand is home to nearly 75 species
of these salt-tolerant trees that are often regarded as wastelands and are vulnerable
to coastal development. Destruction of mangroves is most obvious on the narrow
beaches of Ko Chang.

The long slender 'trunk' of land that runs between the Gulf of Thailand and the
Andaman Sea is often referred to as the Malay peninsula. This region is Thailand's most
tropical: rainfall is plentiful, cultivating thick rainforests that stay green year-round.
Malayan flora and fauna predominate and a scenic range of limestone mountains,
vestiges of an ancient sea bed that was raised up during intercontinental collisions,
meander from land to sea.

On the west coast, the Andaman Sea is an outcropping of the larger Indian Ocean
and has cultivated some astonishing coral reefs that feed and shelter thousands of
varieties of fish and act as breakwaters against tidal surges. Many of the coral-fringed
islands are designated as marine national parks that limit, to some degree, coastal

THAILAND IN FOCUS

ENVIRONMENT

development and boat traffic, both contributors to coral destruction. A 2009 report by Phuket Marine Biological Centre found that between 25% and 50% of the Andaman reefs, especially around Krabi and further south, were in relatively good health, while only 15% to 20% of the Gulf coast coral, especially around the Samui islands, earned the same marks.

NATIONAL PARKS & PROTECTED AREAS

With 15% of the kingdom's land and sea designated as park or sanctuary, Thailand has one of the highest percentages of protected areas of any Asian nation. There are over 100 national parks, plus over 1000 'nonhunting areas', wildlife sanctuaries, forest reserves, botanical gardens and arboretums. Twenty-six of the national parks are marine parks that protect coastal, insular and open-sea areas. Thailand began its conservation efforts in 1960 with the creation of a national system of wildlife sanctuaries under the Wild Animals Reservation and Protection Act, followed by the National Parks Act of 1961. Khao Yai National Park was the first wild area to receive this new status.

↘**THE BEST**

JOHN ELK III

Surin Islands Marine National Park (p272)

NATIONAL PARKS

- Khao Yai National Park (p205)
- Khao Sok National Park (p292)
- Doi Inthanon National Park (p114)
- Similan Islands Marine National Park (p295)
- Surin Islands Marine National Park (p294)

Despite promises, official designation as a national park or sanctuary does not always guarantee protection for habitats and wildlife. Local farmers, well-moneyed developers and other business interests easily win out, either legally or illegally, over environmental protection in Thailand's national parks. Few people adhere to the law and there is little government muscle to enforce regulations. Ko Chang, Ko Samet and Ko Phi-Phi are examples of coastal areas that are facing serious development issues despite being national parks.

FAMILY TRAVEL

VIVIANE PONTI

Mother elephant and her baby

Thais are so family focused that even grumpy taxi drivers want to pinch at your baby's cheeks and play a game of peekaboo (called *já ăir*). On crowded buses, adults will stand so that children can sit, and hotel and restaurant staff willingly set aside chores to be a child's playmate.

SIGHTS & ACTIVITIES

Children will especially enjoy the beaches, as most are in gentle bays good for beginner swimmers. Bo Phut on Ko Samui is a favourite for young families because the village is pedestrian-friendly enough to push a stroller – a tall order in Thailand where the pavements are crowded by food stalls and inexplicable pieces of plumbing. The smaller islands, like Ko Pha-Ngan and Ko Lanta, will also suit families who want to camp by the beach.

Crocodile farms, monkey shows and tiger zoos abound in Thailand, but conditions are often below Western standards. There is a new generation of eco-tour projects that focus on humane conditions and animal conservation. The mahout-training schools and elephant sanctuaries are excellent places to see the revered pachyderm in a dignified setting. For older children, jungle-trekking tours often include elephant rides and bamboo rafting.

In urban areas, kids might feel cooped up, in which case a hotel with a small garden or swimming pool will provide necessary play space. Playgrounds are not widespread or well maintained, though every city has an exercise park where runners and families go in the early evening. Though Bangkok is lean on green, it is still great fun for kids in awe of construction sites, jackhammers and concrete-pouring trucks.

If you're worried about long-distance journeys with a fussy passenger, opt for the train. Kids can walk around the car and visit with the friendly locals; they are assigned the lower sleeping berths which have views of the stations, trotting dogs and dust-kicking motorcycles.

KID-FRIENDLY EATS

In general Thai children don't start eating spicy food until elementary school; before then they seemingly survive on *kôw něe·o* (sticky rice) and junk food. Other kid-friendly meals include chicken in all of its non-spicy permutations – *gài yâhng* (grilled chicken), *gài tôrt* (fried chicken) and *gài pàt mét má·môo·ang* (chicken stir-fried with cashews). Some kids will even branch out to *kôw pàt* (fried rice), though the strong odour of *nám blah* (fish sauce) might be a deal breaker. Helpful restaurant staff will enthusiastically recommend *kài jee·o* (Thai-style omelette), which can be made in a jiffy.

If all else fails, tropical fruits and fruit juices are ubiquitous and delectable and will keep the kids hydrated. Of course, most tourist centres also have Western restaurants catering to homesick eaters of any age.

THE NITTY GRITTY

- **Change Facilities** Non-existent.
- **Cots** By special request at mid-range and top-end hotels.
- **Health** Drink a lot of water; wash hands regularly; warn children against playing with animals.
- **Highchairs** Sometimes available in resort areas.
- **Nappies** (diapers) Minimarkets and 7-Elevens carry small sizes; Tesco Lotus or Tops Market for size 3 or larger.
- **Strollers** Bring a compact umbrella stroller.
- **Transport** Car seats and seat belts are not widely available on public or hired transport.

PAUL BEINSSEN

Young boys in traditional Khmer-era dress

FOOD & DRINK

JERRY ALEXANDER

Selection of curries

One of the country's most famous exports, Thai food is known for expertly balancing the fundamental spicy, sweet, sour and salty flavours into complex and zesty combinations. Ingredients are fresh and vibrant, aromas are intense and the sting of the beloved chilli triggers an adrenaline rush. Thai food is so widespread outside of the country that most visitors arrive already knowing their way around a basic menu. But it isn't until you wake up in Thailand, with its food traditions and rituals, that you can truly appreciate its cuisine.

IN THE MORNING

In the morning, the smell of rice being cooked mingles with the burning joss sticks that adorn the household shrines. And though you might be accustomed to toast and jam at this hour, if a part of you wonders if a stir-fry might be better, then your stomach is in sync with Thais, who make few distinctions between breakfast and lunch.

One classic morning meal in the land of rice is usually just that – a watery rice soup (either *jóhk* or *kôw đôm*) that is the ultimate comfort food, ideal for jet-lagged appetites, tender bellies or as a hangover cure, but it is about as exciting as oatmeal on a cold winter day. More alluring morning options are a thick cup of coffee spiked with sweetened condensed milk accompanied by *bah·tôrng·gŏh* (Chinese-style doughnuts). Forget about Red Bull (a Thai invention by the way), this meal will give you wings.

After breakfast you can go on an eating expedition, watching the street stalls gear up for the lunch rush and chowing down on perfectly sweet-and-sour pineapple, chopped into bite-size pieces before your eyes, before picking another street stall for the next instalment.

NOODLES

Day or night, city or village, you'll find the original Thai fast-food: gŏo·ay đĕe·o (noodle soup), a ubiquitous and highly adaptive dish that demonstrates Thais' peculiar penchant for micro-managing flavours. Gŏo·ay đĕe·o is all about having it your way – you choose the kind of noodle, the kind of meat and you flavour it yourself with a little fish sauce, sugar, vinegar and chillies; don't shy away from the sugar, it works wonders.

There are three basic kinds of rice noodles – sên yài (wide), sên lék (thin) and sên mèe (thinner than thin) – as well as bà·mèe, which is a curly noodle made from wheat flour and egg. Most of these noodles only appear in noodle soups but a few are used in various stir-fries, like pàt tai (thin rice noodles stir-fried with dried or fresh shrimp, tofu and egg). In Bangkok, the noodle cult is especially evolved and Thais take great pains in finding the best broth (the key to a good bowl of noodles).

Head to the morning market for a bowl of kà·nŏm jeen (rice noodles doused in a thin curry). Spicy, fishy, salty, soupy, this dish is all the flavours rolled into one and piled high with strange pickled and fresh vegetables that will make you feel like you've grazed on the savannah and swam through the swamp. Kà·nŏm jeen is usually served at rickety wooden tables shared with working-class ladies dressed in modest market clothes, or students that might giggle at the arrival of a foreigner. Without the hubbub of the market, the dish is not as delicious.

WHAT TO ORDER

If you need to break from the pàt tai rut, try out these popular dishes that can be made by any cook with a wok:

- pàt pàk bûng – morning glory flash-fried with garlic and chilli; typically eaten as a side dish.
- kôw pàt – fried rice.
- gŏo·ay đĕe·o pàt kêe mow – stir-fried noodles with basil, lots of chillies and a choice of meat (usually chicken).
- pàt gá·prow – freshly sliced chillies, holy basil and a choice of chicken or pork stir-fry served over rice.
- pàt pàk ká·náh – stir-fried Chinese kale often matched with mŏo gròrp (crispy fried pork).

CURRIES

The overseas celebrity of Thai cuisine, curry (gaang) enjoys an entirely different position on home turf. It is a humble dish that is usually eaten for breakfast or lunch. At roadside stands, especially in southern Thailand, big metal pots contain various curry concoctions of radioactive colours. When you ask the vendor what they have, they'll lift the lids and name the type of meat in each: gaang gài (curry with chicken), gaang ʙlah (shorthand for sour fish curry). In Bangkok, streetside vendors and small shops will display their curry-in-a-hurry in buffet-style trays. In either case, you point to one and it will be ladled over rice and you use a spoon to scoop it up. Push the lime leaves to the side (they aren't edible).

All curries start with a basic paste that includes ground coriander seed, cumin seed, garlic, lemongrass, kaffir lime, galangal, shrimp paste and chillies (either dried or fresh). Thai cooks used to make these from scratch but these days busy households go to the market and buy it in bulk from large pyramid-shaped displays. The curry paste recipe varies from region to region: *gaang mát·sà·màn* (Muslim curry) uses star anise, a spice associated with southern Thai-Muslim cooking, and the northern Thai curries have Burmese influences. Most visitors know their curries by their colour, mainly red (from dried red chillies) and green (from fresh green chillies). Green curry is a classic central Thai dish.

A true Thai curry will be a fairly thin soup containing curry paste, some meat and pea-sized aubergines; depending on the type of curry it may or may not have coconut milk. A garnish of basil leaves might be added at the end of cooking. The four flavours (salty, sweet, spicy and sour) should be at play but to cater to foreigners, some curries will be excessively sweet and thick from too much coconut milk and sugar. Another foreigner concession is the addition of carrots and broccoli (which overpower the delicate flavour balance).

SOUPS

When Thais go out to restaurants in the evening they usually order a soup, sometimes a curry but more often *đôm yam,* (a spicy and sour broth often served with shrimp) or the milder *đôm kàh gài* (chicken soup with galangal and coconut milk). These simple but zesty dishes are enhanced through the attendant serving ritual. The soups are served in an elevated bowl with a small Sterno flame underneath and the process of ladling the soup into the diner's individual bowl is a quintessential experience of eating Thai-style. To kick off the meal, the server will do the honours but subsequent

JOE CUMMINGS

Cooking pàt tai

refills will typically be done by the junior member of the party. An expert ladler will avoid the inedible bits of galangal. Keep in mind that all Thai soups and curries are meant to be taken with rice, not sipped alone.

REGIONAL CUISINES

In the past 20 years there has been so much economic migration within Thailand that many of the once region-specific dishes have been adopted throughout the country as part of its national cuisine.

NORTHEASTERN THAI

In Bangkok and in the resort beaches of the south, the labourers, housekeepers and taxi drivers are typically Isan folks who never leave home without their triumvirate dishes: *sôm·đam* (green papaya salad), *kôw něe·o* (sticky rice) and *gài yâhng* (grilled chicken). Once considered low-class and foreign, *sôm·đam* has been adopted by adventurous Bangkokians who have brought it into the fusion kitchens where it is mixed with expensive ingredients like cashew nuts.

Interacting with the cuisine in its home provinces is a powerful food memory. In the morning, the barbecue carnage begins with large, open-coal grills loaded up with marinated chicken that send up big plumes of smoke that waft across the city as free advertising. Alongside the grill is a large mortar and pestle in which the *sôm·đam* is prepared. In go strips of green papaya, sugar, chillies, fish sauce, green beans, tomatoes, dried shrimps and a few special requests: peanuts to make it *sôm·đam Thai*; or field crabs and *ɓlah ráh* (fermented fish sauce) to make it *sôm·đam Lao* (referring both to the country and to the ethnic Lao who live in Isan).

The vendor pounds the ingredients together with the pestle to make a musical 'pow-pow-pow' sound that is sometimes used as an onomatopoetic nickname. Isan girls are often told that they'll make good wives if they are adept at handling the pestle when making *sôm·đam* – the obvious sexual connotations are intended.

NORTHERN THAI

True to its Lanna character, northern Thai cuisine is more laid-back, the flavours are mellow and the influences have migrated over mountains from Myanmar (Burma) and China. The curry and noodle dishes here are heartier, imparting more fuel to keep warm during chilly mornings. Thanks

⬎**THE BEST**

CAROL WILEY

Food stall at a night market

CURRY & NOODLE SHOPS

- Kow Soy Siri Soy, Chiang Mai (p116)
- Paa Suk, Chiang Rai (p160)
- Ban Mai, Phitsanulok (p170)
- Mae Si Bua, Mae Hong Son (p183)
- Bang Po Seafood, Ko Samui (p261)
- Pad Thai Shop, Phuket (p306)
- Kalapapruek, Bangkok (p84)

to the travelling Chinese caravans and settlers, northern cuisine is enamoured with pork, which features in almost every dish including *sâi òo·a* (local-style sausages), *kâap mǒo* (fried crackling snacks) and the popular street food of *mǒo ʉîng* (grilled pork skewers). The Burmese influence has imparted the use of turmeric and ginger (though some could argue that northern Burmese was influenced by Chinese) into the curry pastes used in *gaang hang·lair* (rich pork stew). Northern flavours favour sour notes. Pickled vegetables are loaded on top of the signature noodle dishes of *kôw soy* (wheat-and-egg noodles with a thick coconut red curry) and *kà·nǒm jeen nám ngée·o* (rice noodles served with thin curry broth made with pork and tomatoes); shallots and lime wedges are common seasoning garnishes. Northern Thailand shares Isan's love of *kôw něe·o,* which is often served in rounded wicker baskets and accompany such standard dishes as *nám prík òrng* (a chilli paste made with ground pork and tomato).

> ## TIPS ON TIPPLES
>
> - Thai beers, such as Singha (pronounced 'sing'), are hoppy lagers, and often mixed with ice to keep them cool.
> - Fruit shakes are refreshing on a hot day and are served with pinch of salt to help regulate body temperature.
> - Sweet iced coffee and tea are popular street stall drinks, served in handy plastic bags.
> - Thais get their drink on with rice whisky, mixed with ice, soda water and a splash of Coke.

SOUTHERN THAI

Along the narrow Malay peninsula of southern Thailand, a whole different flavour constellation awaits. Southern Thai food draws from the traditions of seafaring traders, many of whom were Muslims from India, or ethnic Malays, who are now referred to as Thai-Muslims. Indian-style flat bread (known as *rotii*) often competes with rice as a curry companion or is drizzled with sugar and sweetened condensed milk as a market dessert. Turmeric imparts its tell-tale yellow hue to *kôw mòk gài* (chicken biryani) and southern-style fried chicken. The curries here are flamboyant, with dry-roasted spice bases prepared in the Indian fashion and lots of locally produced coconut milk. Shaved, milked, strained and fresh – the coconut is a kitchen mainstay. Before tourism transformed the islands into global getaways, coconuts were the cash crop and the favoured son or daughter inherited the interior land where the plantations thrived. The coastal land was less desirable and fell into the hands of the humble fishermen, a paradigm overturned by tourism. Seafood is plentiful and fresh in southern cuisine. Plump squids are grilled and served on a stick with an accompanying sweet-and-spicy sauce. Whole fish are often stuffed with lemongrass and limes and barbecued over a coconut husk fire.

HISTORY

Detail of statues, Wat Mahathat (p172), Sukhothai

Thai history has all the dramatic elements that inspire the imagination: palace intrigue, wars waged with spears and elephants, popular protest movements and a penchant for 'smooth-as-silk' coups.

FROM THE BEGINNING

Though there is evidence of prehistoric peoples, most scholars start the story of Thai nationhood at the arrival of the Tai people during the first millennium AD. The Tai people migrated from southern China and spoke Tai-Kadai, a family of tonal languages said to be the most significant ethno-linguistic group in Southeast Asia. The language group branched off into Laos (the Lao people) and Myanmar (the Shan). Most of these new arrivals were farmers, hunters and close-distance traders who lived in loosely organised villages, usually near a river source, with no central government or organised military.

The indigenous Mon people are often credited with assembling an early confederation in central and northeastern Thailand from the 6th to 9th centuries. Little is known

4000–2500 BC	6th–11th centuries	10th century
Prehistoric inhabitants of northeastern Thailand develop pottery, rice cultivation and bronze metallurgy.	City-states influenced by the Mon-Dvaravati thrive in central Thailand, especially Nakhon Pathom and Lopburi.	Tai people from Yunnan region in China begin migrating south into modern-day Thailand.

about this period, but scholars believe that the Mon named their kingdom Dvaravati and that Nakhon Pathom, outside of Bangkok, was the administrative centre, with outposts in Lamphun and Lopburi.

However the great Khmer empire, based in Cambodia, expanded across the western frontier into present-day northeastern and central Thailand starting in the 11th century, supplanting the Mon-Dvaravati. Lopburi (then known as Lavo), Sukhothai and Phimai were regional Khmer administrative centres that were connected by roads with way-station temples that made travel easier and were visible symbols of imperial power. The Khmer monuments started out as Hindu but were later converted into Buddhist temples after the regime converted. Though their power would eventually decline, the Khmer imparted the evolving Thai nation with an artistic, bureaucratic and even monarchical legacy.

The history of Thailand is usually told from the perspective of the central region, where the current capital Bangkok resides. But the southern region has a separate historical narrative that didn't merge until the modern era. Between the 8th and 13th centuries, southern Thailand was controlled by the maritime empire of Srivijaya (based in southern Sumatra, Indonesia), that controlled trade between the Straits of Malacca.

THE RISE OF THAI KINGDOMS

With the regional empires beginning to decline in the 12th to 16th centuries, Tai peoples in the hinterlands established new states that would eventually unite the country.

LANNA KINGDOM

In the northern region, the Lanna kingdom, founded by King Mengrai, built Chiang Mai (meaning 'new city') in 1292 and proceeded to unify the northern communities into one cultural identity. In the second half of the 14th century, the Sinhalese sect (from Sri Lanka) of Theravada Buddhism spread across Burma and northern Thailand and was adopted by the Lanna kingdom. For a time, Chiang Mai was something of a religious centre for the region. However Lanna was plagued by dynastic intrigues, fell to the Burmese in 1556 and was later eclipsed by Sukhothai and Ayuthaya as the progenitor of the modern Thai state.

SUKHOTHAI KINGDOM

Then just a frontier town on the westernmost edge of the ailing Khmer empire, Sukhothai expelled the distant power in the mid-13th century and crowned the local chief Bang Klang Hao as King Sri Indraditya, the first king of Sukhothai. But it was his son Ramkhamhaeng that led the city-state to become a regional power

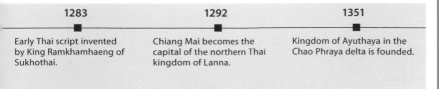

1283	1292	1351
Early Thai script invented by King Ramkhamhaeng of Sukhothai.	Chiang Mai becomes the capital of the northern Thai kingdom of Lanna.	Kingdom of Ayuthaya in the Chao Phraya delta is founded.

THAILAND IN FOCUS

HISTORY

↘ THE BEST

JOHN ELK III

Wat Si Sawai (p173), Sukhothai Historical Park

HISTORICAL SIGHTS

- **Sukhothai Historical Park** (p171)
- **Ayuthaya** (p134)
- **Phimai Historical Park** (p203)

with dependencies in modern-day Laos and southern Thailand. The city-state's local dialect (known as Siamese Tai) became the language of the ruling elite and the king is credited for further defining Thai identity by inventing an early version of script that is still used today. Sukhothai replaced Chiang Mai as a centre of Theravada Buddhism on mainland Southeast Asia and created many monuments that helped define a distinctive Thai-style architecture that is often referred to as the golden age of Thai artistic achievement. After his death, however, Ramkhamhaeng's empire disintegrated. In 1378 Sukhothai became a tributary of Ayuthaya.

AYUTHAYA KINGDOM

Closer to the Gulf of Thailand, a new city-state called Ayuthaya grew rich and powerful from the international sea trade. The legendary founder was King U Thong, one of 36 kings and five dynasties that steered Ayuthaya through a 416-year lifespan.

Ayuthaya presided over an age of commerce in Southeast Asia. It was both the royal city and the major port, connected by a river system to the Gulf of Thailand and beyond. Ayuthaya's main exports were rice and forest products, and many commercial and diplomatic foreign missions set up their main headquarters outside the royal city.

Ayuthaya adopted Khmer court customs, honorific language and ideas of kingship. The monarch styled himself as a Khmer *devaraja* (divine king) instead of the Sukhothai ideal of *dhammaraja* (righteous king). Ayuthaya paid tribute to the Chinese emperor, who rewarded this ritualistic submission with generous gifts and commercial privileges.

Ayuthaya's reign was constantly under threat by the expansionist Burmese. The city was occupied in 1569 but was later liberated under the leadership of King Naresuan. In 1767, Burmese troops successfully sacked the capital and dispersed the Thai leadership into the hinterlands. The destruction of Ayuthaya remains a vivid historical event in the nation and the tales of court life are as evocative as the stories of King Arthur.

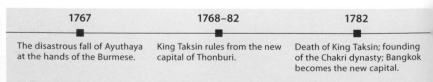

1767	1768–82	1782
The disastrous fall of Ayuthaya at the hands of the Burmese.	King Taksin rules from the new capital of Thonburi.	Death of King Taksin; founding of the Chakri dynasty; Bangkok becomes the new capital.

THAILAND IN FOCUS

HISTORY

Wat Phra Kaew (p65), Bangkok

THE BANGKOK ERA
THE REVIVAL

With Ayuthaya in ruins and the dynasty destroyed, a former general named Taksin filled the power vacuum and established a new capital in 1768 in Thonburi, across the river from modern day Bangkok. King Taksin, the son of a Chinese immigrant father and Thai mother, strongly promoted trade with China, but he was deposed and executed in 1782 by subordinate generals. One of the leaders of the coup, Chao Phraya Chakri, was crowned King Yot Fa (Rama I), the founder of the current Chakri dynasty. He moved the capital across the river to the Ko Ratanakosin district of present-day Bangkok.

The new kingdom was viewed as a revival of Ayuthaya and its leaders attempted to replicate the former kingdom's laws, government practises and cultural contributions. They also built a powerful military that avenged Burmese aggression, kicking them out of Chiang Mai, and charged into Laos and Cambodia. The Bangkok rulers continued courting Chinese commercial trade and cultural exchange. Unlike the Ayuthayan rulers who identified with the Hindu god Vishnu, the Chakri kings positioned themselves as defenders of Buddhism.

1851–68	1868–1910	1874
Reign of King Mongkut (Rama IV); waning Chinese influence; increasing Western influence.	Reign of King Chulalongkorn (Rama V); modernisation; European imperialism.	The edict of abolishing slavery is issued in an effort to modernise Thailand.

THAILAND IN FOCUS

HISTORY

THE REFORM ERA

The Siamese elite had long admired China but by the 1800s, the West soon dominated international trade and geopolitics.

Often credited with modernising the kingdom, King Mongkut (Rama IV) spent 27 years prior to assuming the crown as a monk in the Thammayut sect, a reform movement he founded to restore scholarship to the faith. He was known as a student of ancient Asian and Western languages and sciences. During his reign, the country was integrated into the prevailing market system that broke up royal monopolies and granted more rights to foreign powers.

Mongkut's son, King Chulalongkorn (Rama V) was to take much greater steps in replacing the old political order. He abolished slavery and introduced the creation of a salaried bureaucracy, a police force and a standing army. His reforms brought uniformity to the legal code, law courts and revenue offices. Schools were established along European models. Universal conscription and poll taxes made all men the king's men. Many of the king's advisors were British, who ushered in a remodelling of the old Ayuthaya-based system.

Distant subregions were brought under central command and railways were built to link them to population centres. Pressured by French and British colonies on all sides, the modern boundaries of Siam came into shape, partly out of ceding territory.

Successive kings continued to adopt European procedures and models to better survive in the new world order.

> ### NAME CHANGES
> The country known today as Thailand has had several monikers:
> - The Khmers are credited for naming this area Siam.
> - Bangkok is known in Thai as Krungthep (the City of Angels), a shortened form of a much longer formal name.
> - By 1902, the country was renamed Prathet Thai (meaning 'the country of the Thai').
> - In 1939 the English name of the country was changed from Siam to Thailand.

DEMOCRACY VS DICTATORSHIP
THE 1932 REVOLUTION

During a period of growing independence movements in the region, a group of foreign-educated military officers and bureaucrats led a successful (and bloodless) coup against absolute monarchy in 1932. But democracy did not (and still doesn't) have a smooth road ahead.

The pro-democracy party soon splintered into factions and by 1938, General Phibul Songkhram, one of the original democracy supporters, seized control of the country

1909	1916	1932
Siam's boundaries are defined through a treaty with the British.	The first Thai university, Chulalongkorn University, is established in Bangkok.	Bloodless revolution by young military and civilian officers ends the absolute monarchy.

MICK ELMORE

Wat Phra Kaew (p65), Bangkok

THAILAND IN FOCUS

HISTORY

as Japanese aggression during WWII changed the regional political landscape. Phibul (pronounced 'pee-boon') was staunchly anti-royalist, strongly nationalistic and pro-Japanese, allowing that country to occupy Thailand as a base for assaults on British colonies in Southeast Asia. Near the end of the war, with Japan in retreat, Phibul was forced to resign by his former democracy rival, Pridi Phanomyong, whose subsequent government passed the 1946 constitution that created a fully elective legislature. But democracy lasted only one year until the military felt that the government was moving too far left, resulting in the return of Phibul, who instituted a new era of anti-communist policies and a cooperative relationship with the USA.

THE COLD WAR

Through the middle of the 20th century, Thailand was ruled primarily by the military, with brief hiccups of elected civilian governments that operated with the consent and support of the military. The military leaders seized power from one another through bloodless coups, totalling 19 attempts by the 1990s. During the Cold War and the US conflict in Vietnam, the military leaders of Thailand gained legitimacy and economic support from the USA in exchange for the use of military installations in Thailand.

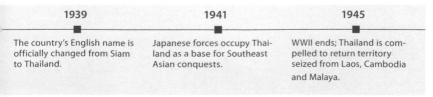

1939	1941	1945
The country's English name is officially changed from Siam to Thailand.	Japanese forces occupy Thailand as a base for Southeast Asian conquests.	WWII ends; Thailand is compelled to return territory seized from Laos, Cambodia and Malaya.

By the 1970s a new era of political consciousness bubbled up from the universities marking a period of cultural turmoil in the country. In 1973, more than half a million people – intellectuals, students, peasants and workers – demonstrated in Bangkok and in major provincial towns, demanding a constitution from the military government. The bloody dispersal of the Bangkok demonstration on 14 October led to the collapse of the regime and the ushering in of an elected constitutional government. This lasted for three years until another bloody massacre occurred on 6 October 1976 during a student-led demonstration inside Thammasat University in Bangkok that was viewed as a threat to civil order and the military seized control of the government.

By the 1980s, in response to the student movements, home-grown problems with communism and US withdrawal from Vietnam, the military made steps towards more democratic participation by working with an elected parliament. The 'political soldier' General Prem Tinsulanonda is credited with fashioning a period of political and economic stability that led to the 1988 elections of a civilian government. Prem is still involved in politics today as the president of the palace's privy council, a powerful position that joins the interests of the monarchy with the military.

THE BUSINESS ERA

The new civilian government was composed of former business executives, many of whom were closely allied to provincial commercial interests, instead of Bangkok-based military officials, signalling a shift in the country's political dynamics. Though the country was doing well economically, the government was accused of corruption and vote buying and the military moved to protect its privileged position in the state with the 1991 coup, Thailand's second ouster of an elected government.

Throughout Thailand's most recent political history, the populace has not always sided unilaterally with democracy. In the case of the 1991 coup, the Bangkok business community and the educated class supported the military, reflecting class divisions between urban and rural interests. The modern era of business versus the military is an ongoing power struggle and the elite often discuss the shortcomings of democracy in their country.

Elected leadership was restored shortly after the 1991 coup and the Democrat Party, with the support of the business and urban middle class, dominated the parliament and functioned within the old paradigm of compromise between bureaucrats and politicians. The 1997 Asian currency crisis derailed the surging economy and the government was criticised for mismanagement and ineffectiveness. That same year, the parliament passed the watershed 'people's constitution' that enshrined human rights, freedom of expression and granted more power to a civil society to counter corruption.

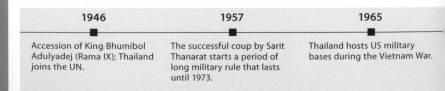

1946	1957	1965
Accession of King Bhumibol Adulyadej (Rama IX); Thailand joins the UN.	The successful coup by Sarit Thanarat starts a period of long military rule that lasts until 1973.	Thailand hosts US military bases during the Vietnam War.

JOHN ELK III

Three Kings Monument, Chiang Mai City Arts & Cultural Centre (p107)

THE RISE OF THAKSIN

By the turn of the millennium, the economy had recovered and business interests had succeeded the military as the dominant force in politics. The telecommunications billionaire and former police officer, Thaksin Shinawatra, embodied this new spirit and ushered in the era of the elected CEO. He was a capitalist with a populist message and garnered support from the rural and urban poor. From 2001 to 2005, Thaksin and his Thai Rak Thai party transformed national politics into one-party rule.

THE FALL OF THAKSIN

Though Thaksin enjoyed massive popular support from the working class, his regime was viewed by urban intellectuals as a cleptocracy, with the most egregious example of corruption being the tax-free sale of his family's Shin Corporation stock to the Singaporean government in 2006, with a windfall of 73 billion baht (US$1.88 billion) that was engineered by special legislation. This enraged the upper and middle classes and led to large street protests in Bangkok. Meanwhile behind the scenes, Thaksin had been working to replace key military figures with his loyalists, strategic moves that would cut the military out of its traditional power positions.

On 19 September 2006, the military staged a bloodless coup (the first in 15 years) that brought an end to the country's longest stretch of democratic rule. The military

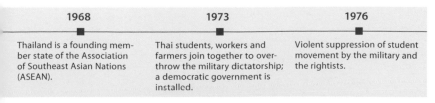

1968	1973	1976
Thailand is a founding member state of the Association of Southeast Asian Nations (ASEAN).	Thai students, workers and farmers join together to overthrow the military dictatorship; a democratic government is installed.	Violent suppression of student movement by the military and the rightists.

HISTORICAL TRIVIA

- King Mongkut (Rama IV) and his son King Chula (Rama V) were the first Thai monarchs to allow themselves to be seen in public by commoners. Chula especially liked posing for photographs. His image was also reproduced on coins, stamps and sculptures.
- During WWII, Thailand officially declared war on the Allieds but the Thai ambassador in Washington (a member of the opposition party) refused to deliver the declaration, sparing Thailand from the serious consequences of defeated-nation status.

dissolved the so-called people's constitution that had sought to ensure a civil government and introduced a new constitution that limited the resurgence of one-party rule by interests unsympathetic to the military and the elites.

THE ONGOING CRISIS

Since the coup, political stability has yet to be achieved. Reinstatement of elections restored Thaksin's political friends to power, an unacceptable victory for Bangkok's aristocracy who, with the implicit support of the military, staged huge protests that closed down Bangkok's two airports for a week in 2008. Their demands for the removal of Thaksin's political allies from their elected and appointed positions were met, and Thailand limped into the global recession with a tarnished reputation.

In 2008, parliamentary negotiations and coalition-building placed Democrat Abhisit Vejjajiva as Thailand's 27th prime minister and the third person to hold the position. The country remains deeply divided, with anti-government protesters often staging rallies that beam in satellite addresses from an exiled Thaksin, who promises his return to power with such lofty goals as poverty eradication. If Thai history is any guide, Thaksin will be back.

THE MODERN MONARCHY

The country's last absolute monarch was King Prajathipok (Rama VII) who accepted the 1932 constitution, abdicated the throne and went into exile. By 1935 the new democratic government reinstated the monarchy, appointing the abdicated king's 10-year-old nephew, Ananda Mahidol (Rama VIII), who was living in Europe at the time. In 1946, after the king came of age, he was shot dead under mysterious circumstances. His younger brother was crowned King Bhumibol (Rama IX) and remains the current monarch today.

At the beginning of his reign, King Bhumibol was primarily a figurehead promoted by various factions to appeal to the public's imagination of national unity and to provide legitimacy. The military dictator, General Sarit, who controlled the government from

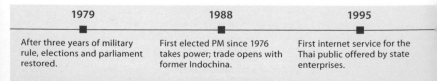

1979	1988	1995
After three years of military rule, elections and parliament restored.	First elected PM since 1976 takes power; trade opens with former Indochina.	First internet service for the Thai public offered by state enterprises.

1958 to 1963, supported the expansion of the king's role as a symbol of modern Thailand. The attractive royal couple, King Bhumibol and Queen Sirikit, made state visits abroad, met Elvis and were portrayed in photographs in much the same way as the US president John F Kennedy and his wife, young and fashionable models of the postwar generation.

THE PEOPLE'S CARETAKER

Through rural development projects, the king was known as the champion of the poor. The Royal Project Foundation was founded in 1969 and is credited with helping eradicate opium cultivation among the northern hill tribes. During the violence of the 1970s protest movements, the king came to be regarded as a mediating voice in tumultuous political times and called for the resignation of the

MORE THAN FASHION

Through the contentious political battles resulting from the 2006 coup, the warring factions have adopted coloured T-shirts to identify themselves. Thaksin opponents wear yellow, the colour traditionally associated with the monarchy. Thaksin supporters wear red, which has been dubbed the colour of democracy. The average Thai who wants to avoid political confrontations has to be careful when getting dressed in the morning.

Crowd gathered at Royal Plaza, Dusit Palace Park (p69), Bangkok

MICK ELMORE

1997	2001	2004
Thailand reels under impact of Asian economic crisis; passage of 'people's constitution'.	Telecommunications tycoon, Thaksin Shinawatra, is elected prime minister.	Tsunami hits Andaman Coast, killing 5000 people and damaging tourism and fishing.

THAILAND IN FOCUS

HISTORY

military leaders. He also gave his consent to the reinstatement of military rule three years later, a symbolic gesture that helped ensure civil order. During another political crisis in 1992, the king summoned the leaders of the warring factions to the palace in an effort to quell street protests. His annual birthday speech (5 December) is often regarded as something akin to the State of the Union address and indicates palace sentiments towards rival factions.

The king is in his eighth decade now and his health has been failing while the country's political future remains uncertain. Since the late 1950s, the palace and the military have been closely aligned, a relationship that is currently cemented by General Prem Tinsulanonda, a retired military commander, former prime minister and current high-ranking palace advisor who is believed to have instigated the 2006 coup. In previous political confrontations, the king has appeared above the bickering, but the palace's role in the ouster of the popular prime minister and the ensuing street protests between anti-Thaksin groups, who wear the royal colours and proclaim to be protecting the king, and the pro-Thaksin groups, who see themselves as the inheritors of the 1932 revolution, indicate a destabilisation of the monarch as a unifying figure. Though King Bhumibol has carved out a unique niche for the post-modern monarch, it is uncertain if this role will survive the current political crisis and be inherited by his son Crown Prince Vachiralongkorn.

GREG ELMS

Billboard of the Thai king, Bangkok

2006	2007	2008
King's 60th year on the throne; military ousts Thaksin government.	Democratic elections return civilian rule to Thailand in December. Samak is announced as prime minister the following month.	Bangkok's airports are closed by anti-government protestors; global economic recession affects Thai economy.

⬊ RELIGION

Golden Buddha, Wat Phra That Doi Suthep (p112), Chiang Mai

Religion is alive and well in Thailand and colourful examples of daily worship can be found on nearly every corner. Walk the streets early in the morning and you'll see the solemn progression of the Buddhist monks, with shaved heads and orange-coloured robes, engaged in *bin·dá·bàht*, the daily house-to-house alms food gathering. Small household shrines decorate the humblest abodes and headscarved women are predominate in the Muslim south.

BUDDHISM

Approximately 95% of Thai people are Theravada Buddhists, often called the Southern School because it travelled from the Indian subcontinent to Southeast Asia. Mahayana, the other branch of Buddhism, followed a northern migration through Nepal, Tibet, China and the rest of East Asia. These two forms differ in doctrine, canonical texts and monastic practices.

RELIGIOUS PRINCIPLES

Buddhism was born in India in the 6th century. A prince named Siddhartha Gautama left his life of privilege, seeking religious fulfilment. According to the Hindu practices of the time, he became an ascetic and subjected himself to many years of severe austerity before he realised that this was not the way to reach the end of suffering. He became known as Buddha, 'the enlightened' or 'the awakened' and spoke of four noble truths that had the power to liberate any human being who could realise them.

The four noble truths deal with the nature and origin of suffering and the path to the cessation of suffering. Loosely explained this includes *dukkha* (all forms of existence are subject to suffering, disease, imperfection), *samudaya* (the origin of suffering is desire), *nirodha* (cessation of suffering is the giving up of desire), *magga* (the path to cessation of suffering is the eightfold path).

The eightfold path is often described as the middle path: a route between extreme asceticism and indulgence. Following the path will lead to *nibbana* ('nirvana' in Sanskrit), which literally means the 'blowing out' or extinction of all grasping and thus of all suffering. Effectively, *nibbana* is also an end to the cycle of rebirths (both moment-to-moment and life-to-life) that is existence.

RELIGIOUS PRACTICE

In reality, most Thai Buddhists aim for rebirth in a 'better' existence rather than the supramundane goal of *nibbana*. By feeding monks, giving donations to temples and performing regular worship at the local temple they hope to improve their lot, acquiring enough merit (*bun* in Thai) to prevent or at least reduce their number of rebirths. The concept of rebirth is almost universally accepted in Thailand, even by non-Buddhists.

Thai Buddhists look to the Triple Gems for guidance in their faith: the Buddha, the *dhamma* and the *sangha*. The Buddha, in a myriad of sculptural forms, is usually the centrepiece of devotional activity inside a temple and many of the most famous Thai Buddha images have supernatural tales associated with them. The *dhamma* is chanted morning and evening in every temple and taught to every Thai citizen in primary school. There are two *sangha* sects in Thailand: the Mahanikai and Thammayut. The former places more emphasis on scholarship, while the later prefers proficiency in meditation.

HINDUISM & ANIMISM

There are many enduring legacies of Hinduism and animism in Thai culture and in the practice of Thai Buddhism today. Hinduism was the religious parent of Buddhism, imparting lasting components of mythology, cosmology and symbolism. Thais recognise the contributions of Hinduism and treat its deities with reverence. Bangkok is especially rich in Hindu shrines, where Thai Buddhists worship devoutly. Many of the royally associated ceremonies stem from Brahmanism.

Spirit worship and Buddhism have co-mingled to the point that it is difficult to filter the two. Monks often perform obviously animistic rituals and Thais believe that making merit benefits deceased relatives. In fact much of the religious rituals of Thai Buddhists, apart from meditation, appear to be deeply rooted in the spirit world. Household shrines and spirit houses are erected to shelter and placate the guardian spirits of the land. Trees are wrapped in sacred cloth to honour the spirits of the natural world. Altars are erected on the dashboards of taxis to ensure immunity from traffic laws and accidents. Thais often wear amulets embossed with a Buddha figure or containing sacred soil from a revered temple to protect the wearer from misfortune.

MONKS & MONASTERIES

Every Thai male is expected to become a monk (*prá* or *prá pík·sù* in Thai) for a short period in his life, optimally between the time he finishes school and the time he starts a career or marries. A family earns great merit when one of its sons 'takes robe and bowl' and many young men enter the monastery to make merit for a deceased patriarch or matriarch. Traditionally, Buddhist Lent *(pan·săh)*, which begins in July and coincides with the three-month period of the rainy season, is when most temporary monks enter the monastery. Nowadays, however, men may spend as little as a week.

Historically the temple provided a necessary social safety net for families in need. The monastery functioned in some ways like an orphanage, caring for and educating children whose parents couldn't provide for them. In rural areas, older men would retire to the monastery after a lifetime of work. Though these charitable roles are not as sought after today, the temples still give refuge and sanctuary to all living creatures. This might mean that they help feed families in need, adopt orphaned or injured animals and give shelter to overnight travellers (usually impoverished Thai university students).

DIVERSE BUDDHISM

Throughout its history Thailand has embraced many forms of Buddhism. An Indian form of Theravada existed during the Dvaravati kingdom (6th to 11th centuries), while Mahayana Buddhism was known in pockets of the northeast under Khmer control in the 10th and 11th centuries. But the most enduring form is the Sinhalese Theravada version, which arrived in the 13th century. Thailand and Sri Lanka have long shared religious traditions, often exchanging monks for religious instruction.

THAILAND IN FOCUS

RELIGION

TOM COCKREM

Thai Buddhist monks

THAILAND IN FOCUS

In Thai Buddhism, women who seek a monastic life are given a minor role in the temple that is not equal to full monkhood. A Buddhist nun is known as *mâa chee* (mother priest) and lives as an *atthasila* (eight-precept) nun, a position traditionally occupied by women who had no other place in society. Thai nuns shave their heads, wear white robes and take care of temple chores. Generally speaking, *mâa chee* aren't considered as prestigious as monks and don't have a function in the laypeople's merit-making rituals.

Over the years there have been some rebels who have sought equal ordination status as monks. One of the most prominent was Voramai Kabilsingh, who went to Taiwan to receive full ordination as a *bhikkhuni* (the female version of a *bhikku*, or male monk) through the Mahayana tradition. Her daughter, Chatsumarn Kabilsingh, has continued the tradition by seeking a Theravada ordination in Sri Lanka in 2003.

TEMPLE VISITS

Thai Buddhism has no particular Sabbath day when the faithful are supposed to make temple visits. Instead, Thai Buddhists visit whenever they feel like it, most often on *wan prá* (holy days), which occur every seventh or eighth day depending on phases of the moon.

A temple visit is usually a social affair involving groups of friends, families or office workers. Thais will also make special pilgrimages to famous temples in other regions as sightseeing and merit-making outings. For the older generation this is the time to show off their most beautiful Thai silk dresses, which follow a standard pattern style of

Reclining Buddha, Wat Phra That Hariphunchai (p154), Lamphun

JERRY ALEXANDER

RICHARD I'ANSON

Offerings of incense

a tailored shirt and ankle-length skirt. The younger generation regards these dresses as old-fashioned.

Most merit-makers visit the *wí·hăhn* (the central sanctuary), which houses the primary Buddha figure. Worshippers will offer lotus buds (a symbol of enlightenment) or flower garlands, light three joss sticks and raise their hands to their forehead in a prayerlike gesture. In some cases, Thai Buddhists will consult with monks in order to pick an auspicious time to get married or start a business. Funeral rites are also held at the temple.

Other merit-making activities include offering food to the temple *sangha* (community), meditating (individually or in groups), listening to monks chanting *suttas* (Buddhist discourse) and attending a *têht* or *dhamma* (teachings) talk by the abbot or some other respected teacher.

See Culture & Customs (p337) for tips on temple etiquette.

ISLAM & OTHER RELIGIONS

Although Thailand country is predominantly Buddhist, the minority religions often practice alongside one another. The green-hued onion domes of a mosque marks a neighbourhood as Muslim, while large, rounded doorways flanked by red paper lanterns mark the location of a *săhn jôw,* a Chinese temple dedicated to the worship of Buddhist, Taoist and Confucian deities.

About 4.6 % of the population are followers of Islam. The remainder are Christian, including missionised hill tribes and Vietnamese immigrants, as well as Confucianists, Taoists, Mahayana Buddhists and Hindus.

The majority of Muslims in Thailand live in the southern provinces, though there are pockets in Bangkok, and central and northern Thailand. In the southernmost provinces the Muslims are ethnic Malays, while northern Thailand's Muslims are Yunnanese descendents. The form of Islam found in southern Thailand is mixed with elements of Malay culture and animism, creating a more culturally relaxed religion than that of Arab nations. Thai Muslim women function in the society as actively as their Buddhist sisters: working outside the home, getting a mainstream education and being equal partners with their spouses. There is a degree of separation of the sexes in the classrooms and at the mosques. Headscarves are prevalent but not mandatory: in some case we've often only figured out that someone is a Muslim after they've declined an offering of pork at the dinner table.

Devout Thai Muslims often encounter spiritual incompatibilities with their identities as Thai citizens, which is largely defined by the Buddhist majority. The popular view of the Thai monarch as a god or at least as god-like is a heresy for a monotheistic religion like Islam, though many Thai Muslims respect and even love the king and do not voice open criticism of his veneration. Muslims also avoid alcohol and gambling (in varying degrees) – two pursuits that define much of rural life for Buddhist Thais. In this way, religious precepts keep the two cultures distinct and slightly distrustful of each other.

MUSLIM FISHERFOLK

Many of the islands of the Andaman coast are populated by Thai-Muslim fishing families. The men set their nets around noon with the changing of the tide and retrieve the catch before sunset. Coffee is a local obsession and caged song birds often decorate storefronts. Bird singing competitions and buffalo fights are common rural entertainment. Close to the Malaysian border, Thai-Muslims speak Yawi, an ancient Malay language, but elsewhere in the region, most speak the southern Thai dialect, known for its rapid cadence.

THE DEEP SOUTH

The southernmost provinces of Yala, Pattani and Narathiwat contain the country's largest Muslim majority and have long been geographically isolated and culturally alien to the mainstream society. Historically, parts of these provinces were independent sultanates that were conquered by the Bangkok-based kings. During the ultranationalist era in the 1940s, this region responded with separatist resistance, later becoming a sanctuary for communist and insurgent activities in the 1980s. During the Thaksin administration, the security situation dissolved into a low-scale war that persists today. There have been coordinated bombings in the provincial capitals, assassinations and beheadings of symbols of the state, ethnic cleansing of mixed Buddhist-Muslim villages, human rights abuses by the Thai military, arson attacks on schools and most recently armed militia groups with little oversight. Most analysts view the conflict as an ethno-national struggle and not part of the global Islamic terror campaign but it is still uncertain what the demands are and who is organising the violence.

⬂ DIRECTORY & TRANSPORT

DIRECTORY

ACCOMMODATION

Thailand offers a wide variety of accommodation, from cheap and basic to pricey and luxurious. Accommodation rates listed in this book are high-season prices for either single or double rooms. Icons are included to indicate where internet access, swimming pools or air-con are available; otherwise, assume that there's a fan.

A two-tiered pricing system has been used in this book to determine budget category (budget, midrange, top end). In big cities and beach resorts, rates under 1000B are budget, under 3000B are midrange, with top end over 3000B. For small towns, rates under 600B are budget, under 1500B are midrange and top end over 1500B.

GUESTHOUSES

Guesthouses are generally the cheapest accommodation in Thailand, and can be found all along the backpacker trail. In areas like the northeast and parts of the southeast, guesthouses (as well as tourists) are not as widespread.

Most guesthouses cultivate a travellers' ambience with friendly, knowledgeable

> ### ↘ BOOK YOUR STAY ONLINE
>
> For more accommodation reviews and recommendations by Lonely Planet authors, check out the online booking service at www.lonelyplanet.com. You'll find the true, insider lowdown on the best places to stay. Reviews are thorough and independent. Best of all, you can book online.

staff and minor amenities such as tourist information and a book exchange.

Increasingly guesthouses can handle advance reservations, but due to inconsistent cleanliness and quality it is advisable to always look at a room in person before committing. In tourist centres, if your preferred place is full, there are usually a dozen alternatives nearby. Guesthouses typically accept cash-only payments.

HOTELS

In provincial capitals and small towns, the options are often only older Thai-Chinese hotels, once the standard in all of Thailand. Most cater to Thai guests, and English is usually limited.

These hotels are multi-storey buildings and might offer a range of rooms from midrange options such as private bathrooms, air-con and TV, to cheaper ones with shared bathroom facilities and a fan. In some of the older hotels, the toilets are squats and the 'shower' is a *klong* jar (a large terracotta basin from which you scoop out water for bathing). Although the Thai-Chinese hotels have got tons of accidental retro charm, unless the establishment has been recently refurbished, we've found that they are too old and worn to represent good value compared to guesthouses.

In major tourist towns, new 'flashpacker' hotels have dressed up the utilitarian options of the past with stylish decor and creature comforts.

International chain hotels can be found in Bangkok, Chiang Mai, Phuket and other high-end beach resorts.

Most top-end hotels and some midrange hotels add a 7% government tax (VAT) and an additional 10% service charge. The additional charges are often referred to as 'plus plus'. A buffet breakfast will often be included in the room rate. If the hotel offers Western breakfast, it is usually referred to as 'ABF', a strange shorthand meaning American breakfast.

Midrange and chain hotels, especially in major tourist destinations, can be booked in advance and some offer internet discounts through their websites or online agents. They also accept most credit cards, but only a few deluxe places accept American Express.

NATIONAL PARKS ACCOMMODATION

Most national parks have bungalows or campsites available for overnight stays. Bungalows typically sleep as many as 10 people and rates range from 800B to 2000B, depending on the park and the size of the bungalow.

Camping is available at many parks for 60B per night. Some parks rent tents (300B a night) and other sleeping gear, but the condition of the equipment can be poor.

The National Parks' department (www .dnp.go.th/parkreserve) now has a comprehensive, if slightly clunky, online booking system for all parks. Note that reservations for campsites and bungalows are handled on different pages within the website.

ACTIVITIES
DIVING & SNORKELLING

Thailand's two coastlines and countless islands are popular with divers for their warm, calm waters and colourful marine life.

Reef dives along the Andaman Coast are particularly rewarding, with hundreds of hard corals and reef fish catalogued in this fertile marine zone. The most spectacular diving is in the marine parks of the Similan Islands (p295) and Surin Islands (p294). Most dive operators run liveaboard trips out of Phuket and Khao Lak.

Diving on the Gulf Coast is available just about anywhere foreigners rest their luggage. Ko Tao (p272) has the reputation of providing the cheapest dive training but

SAFETY GUIDELINES FOR DIVING

Before embarking on a scuba diving, skin diving or snorkelling trip, carefully consider the following points to ensure a safe and enjoyable experience:

- Possess a current diving-certification card from a recognised scuba diving instructional agency.
- Obtain reliable information about physical and environmental conditions at the dive site (eg from a reputable local dive operation).
- Be aware of local laws, regulations and etiquette about marine life and the environment.
- Dive only at sites within your realm of experience; if available, engage the services of a competent, professionally trained dive instructor or dive master.
- Be aware that underwater conditions vary significantly from one region, or even site, to another. Seasonal changes can significantly alter any site and dive conditions.
- Ask about the environmental characteristics that can affect your diving and how trained local divers deal with these considerations.

most courses feel like factories instead of classrooms.

Most islands have easily accessible snorkelling amid offshore reefs that are covered by water no deeper than 2m. If you're particular about the quality and condition of the equipment you use, bring your own mask and snorkel – some of the stuff for rent is second rate.

KAYAKING

The most dramatic scenery for kayaking is along the Andaman Coast. It's littered with bearded limestone mountains and semi-submerged caves. Many of the sea-kayaking tours take visitors to scenic Ao Phang-Nga (p298). At Krabi (p309), the one-stop beach destination for sporty types, sea-kayaking tours explore emerald lagoons and sea caves. Kayaking trips through the Ang Thong Marine National Park (p277), off the coast of Ko Samui, is the Gulf's premier paddling spot.

ROCK CLIMBING

Railay (p312) is Thailand's climbing mecca. The huge headland and tiny islands nearby offer high-quality limestone with steep pocketed walls, overhangs and the occasional hanging stalactite. But what makes climbing here so popular are the views.

TREKKING

Wilderness walking or trekking is one of northern Thailand's biggest draws. Many routes feature daily walks through forested mountain areas coupled with overnight stays in hill-tribe villages and elephant rides to satisfy both ethno- and ecotourism urges. Chiang Mai and Chiang Rai are the primary base points for these tours. Other trekking areas in the north include Mae Hong Son, Pai, Chiang Dao, Tha Ton, Nan and Um Phang. In southwestern Thailand, Kanchanaburi has become an outdoor trekking destination with easier access to Bangkok.

It is difficult to recommend a particular trekking company as guides often float between companies and the participants will vary each trip. Officially all guides should be licensed by the Tourism Authority of Thailand (TAT). This means they have received at least regional and survival training, and they are registered, which is useful if there are problems later. The guide should be able to show you their licence and certificate. In general, tour companies are safer and better regulated now than years past but you should still talk to fellow travellers for recommendations.

If an organised trek doesn't appeal to you, consider travelling to Mae Salong, an interesting highland town where you can arrange independent trekking trips.

The best time to trek is during the cool season (roughly November to February) when the weather is refreshing, the landscape is still green, the waterfalls are full from the monsoon rains, and the wildflowers are in bloom. Between March and May the hills are dry and the weather is hot. The second-best time is early in the rainy season, between June and July, before the dirt roads become too saturated.

BUSINESS HOURS

Most government offices are open from 8.30am to 4.30pm weekdays. Some government offices close from noon to 1pm for lunch, while others follow Saturday hours (9am to 3pm). Banking hours are typically 9.30am to 3.30pm Monday to Friday. ATMs are usually accessible 24 hours a day and bank branches with extended hours can be found at the big department stores such as Tesco Lotus and Big C.

Privately owned stores usually operate between 10am and 5pm daily. Most local restaurants are open 10am until 10pm, with an hour's variation on either side. Some restaurants specialising in morning meals close by 3pm.

Note that all government offices and banks are closed on public holidays (see p378). For typical hours, see p372.

CHILDREN

To smooth out the usual road bumps of dragging children from place to place, check out Lonely Planet's *Travel with Children,* which contains useful advice on how to cope with kids on the road, with a focus on travel in developing countries.

See also p343 for further information on travelling with children.

CLIMATE CHARTS

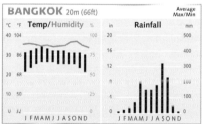

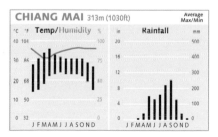

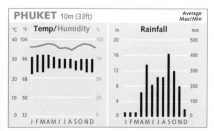

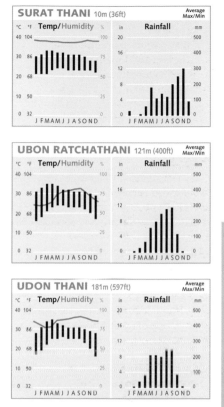

See p44 for further information on choosing the best time of year for your visit to Thailand.

COURSES
COOKING

Cooking courses pop up wherever there are tourists willing to dice shallots. Bangkok's courses (p72) are more formal, with dedicated kitchen facilities and individual work stations, but Chiang Mai is the undisputed cooking-course capital (p113).

MEDITATION

Unique to Buddhism, particularly Theravada and to a lesser extent Tibetan Buddhism, is a system of meditation

TYPICAL OPENING HOURS

- Bars – 6pm-midnight or 1am (times vary depending on local enforcement of national curfew laws)
- Department stores – 10am-8pm or 9pm Monday to Sunday
- Discos – 8pm-2am
- Live-music venues – 6pm-1am
- Restaurants – 10am-10pm
- Local shops – 10am-6pm Monday to Saturday, some open Sunday

known as *vipassana* (*wí·bàt·sà·nah* in Thai), a Pali word that roughly translates as 'insight'. Foreigners who come to Thailand to study *vipassana* can choose from dozens of temples and meditation centres specialising in these teachings. Thai language is usually the medium of instruction but several places also provide instruction in English.

Some places require that you wear white clothes when staying overnight. For even a brief visit, wear clean and neat clothing (ie long trousers or skirt, and sleeves that cover the shoulders).

CUSTOMS REGULATIONS

Thailand prohibits the import of firearms and ammunition (unless registered in advance with the police department), illegal drugs and pornographic media. A reasonable amount of clothing, toiletries and professional instruments are allowed in duty free. Up to 200 cigarettes and 1L of wine or spirits can be brought into the country duty free. The customs department (www.customs.go.th) maintains a helpful website with more specific information.

When leaving Thailand, you must obtain an export licence for any antiques or objects of art, including newly cast Buddha images. Export licence applications can be made by submitting two front-view photos of the object(s), a photocopy of your passport, along with the purchase receipt and the object(s) in question, to the **Department of Fine Arts** (**DFA**; ☎ 0 2628 5032). Allow three to five days for the application and inspection process to be completed.

DANGERS & ANNOYANCES

In reality, you are more likely to be ripped off or have a personal possession surreptitiously stolen than you are to be physically harmed.

ASSAULT

Assault of travellers is rare in Thailand, but it does happen. We've received letters detailing fights between travellers and Thai guesthouse workers or other Thai youths. While both parties are probably to blame (and alcohol is often a factor), do be aware that causing a Thai to 'lose face' (feel public embarrassment or humiliation) might elicit an inexplicably strong and violent reaction.

There is a surprising amount of assaults in Ko Samui and Ko Pha-Ngan considering their idyllic settings. Oftentimes alcohol is the number one contributor to bad choices and worse outcomes. Ko Pha-Ngan's Full Moon party is becoming increasingly violent and dangerous. There are often reports of fights, rapes and robbings.

Women, especially solo travellers in Samui or Pha-Ngan, need to be smart and somewhat sober when interacting with the opposite sex, be they Thai or *fa·ràng* (Westerners).

BORDER ISSUES

Thailand enjoys much better relations with its neighbours than it did a decade ago and many land borders are now functional and safe passages for goods and people. The ongoing violence in the Deep South has made the once-popular crossing at Sungai Kolok a potentially dangerous proposition.

The long-contested border temple of Khao Phra Wihan (known as 'Preah Vihear' in Cambodia), in the far northeast of the country, resulted in a military build-up and violent clashes between Thai and Cambodian forces in 2007. Although tensions have relaxed since, the temple is still closed to visitors.

DRUGGINGS & DRUG POSSESSION

It is illegal to buy, sell or possess opium, heroin, amphetamines, hallucinogenic mushrooms and marijuana in Thailand. A new era of vigilance against drug use and possession was ushered in by former Prime Minister Thaksin Shinawatra's 2003 war on drugs; during the height of the campaign police searched partygoers in Bangkok nightclubs and effectively scared many of the recreational drug users into abstinence for a time. Things have relaxed somewhat since the 2006 coup but the country is no longer a chemical free-for-all.

Possession of drugs can result in at least one year of prison time. Drug smuggling – defined as attempting to cross a border with drugs in your possession – carries considerably higher penalties, including execution.

During citywide festivals such as Bangkok's New Year's Eve and Ko Pha-Ngan's Full Moon parties, police set up road blocks and inspection stations in an attempt to apprehend drug suppliers and

their contraband. In some cases, enforcement of the drug laws is merely leverage for exacting massive bribes. Ko Pha-Ngan's police are notorious for bribable 'sting' operations in which a drug dealer makes an exchange with a customer, followed shortly by a police bust and an on-site demand of 70,000B to avoid arrest.

Pai, another party town, has seen a recent revival of the Thaksin-era urine drug tests on bar patrons by police. As of writing, the strong-arm gift of freedom in such cases is 10,000B.

SCAMS

Bangkok is especially good at elaborate frauds that dupe travellers into thinking that they've made a friend and are getting a bargain.

Most scams begin in the same way: a friendly and well-dressed Thai, or sometimes even a foreigner, approaches you and strikes up a conversation. Invariably your destination is closed or being cleaned, but your new friend offers several alternative activities, such as sightseeing at smaller temples or shopping at authentic markets. After you've come to trust the person, you are next invited to a gem and jewellery shop because your new-found friend is picking up some merchandise for himself. Somewhere along the way he usually claims to have a connection, often a relative, in your home country (what a coincidence!) with whom he has a regular gem export-import business. One way or another, you are convinced that you can turn a profit by arranging a gem purchase and reselling the merchandise at home.

There are seemingly infinite numbers of variations on the scam described above, almost all of which end up with you making a purchase of small, low-quality gems and posting them to your home country. Once you return home, of course, the cheap jewels turn out to be worth much less than you paid for them (perhaps one tenth to one half).

The Thai police are usually no help, believing that merchants are entitled to whatever price they can get.

Card games are another way to separate travellers from their money.

Other minor scams involve túk-túk drivers, hotel employees and bar girls who take new arrivals on city tours; these almost always end up in high-pressure sales situations at silk, jewellery or handicraft shops. In this case the victim's greed isn't the ruling motivation – it's simply a matter of weak sales resistance.

Follow TAT's number-one suggestion to tourists: *Disregard all offers of free shopping or sightseeing help from strangers*. These invariably take a commission from your purchases.

Contact the **tourist police** (☎ 1155) if you have any problems with consumer fraud.

THEFT & FRAUD

Exercise diligence when it comes to your personal belongings. Ensure that your room is securely locked and carry your most important effects (passport, money, credit cards) on your person. Take care when leaving valuables in a hotel safe.

Follow the same practice when you're travelling. A locked bag will not prevent theft on a long-haul bus when you're snoozing and the practised thief has hours alone with your luggage. This is a common occurrence on the tourist buses from Khao San Rd to the southern beaches or north to Chiang Mai.

When using a credit card, don't let vendors take your credit card out of your sight to run it through the machine. Unscrupulous merchants have been known to rub off three or four or more receipts with one purchase.

To avoid losing all of your travel money in an instant, always use a credit card that is not directly linked to your bank account back home so that the operator doesn't have access to immediate funds.

TOUTS

Touting is a long-time tradition in Asia, and while Thailand doesn't have as many touts as, say, India, it has its share.

In popular tourist spots you'll be approached, sometimes surrounded, by guesthouse touts who get a commission for bringing in potential guests. While it is annoying for the traveller, it's an acceptable form of advertising among small-scale businesses. Travel agencies are notorious for talking newly arrived tourists into staying at badly located, over-priced hotels.

Travel agencies often masquerade as TAT, the government-funded tourist information office. They might put up agents wearing fake TAT badges or have signs that read TAT in big letters to entice travellers into their offices where they can sell them overpriced bus and train tickets. Be aware that the official TAT offices do not make hotel or transport bookings.

When making transport arrangements, talk to several travel agencies to look for the best price, as the commission percentage varies greatly between agents. Also resist any high-sales tactics from an agent trying to sign you up for everything: plane tickets, hotel, tours etc. The most honest Thais are typically very low-key and often sub-par salespeople.

EMBASSIES & CONSULATES

Foreign embassies are located in Bangkok; some nations also have consulates in Chiang Mai.

Australia (Map pp80-1; ☎ 0 2344 6300; www
.austembassy.or.th; 37 Th Sathon Tai, Bangkok)

Canada Bangkok (Map pp80-1; ☎ 0 2636
0540; www.dfait-maeci.gc.ca/bangkok; 15th fl,
Abdulrahim Bldg, 990 Th Phra Ram IV); Chiang
Mai (off Map pp98-9; ☎ 0 5385-0147; 151 Superhighway, Tambon Tahsala) Consulate only
at Chiang Mai.

France Bangkok (Embassy Map pp80-1;
☎ 0 2657 5100; www.ambafrance-th.org; 35 Soi
36, Th Charoen Krung; Consular Section Map
pp80-1; ☎ 0 2627 2150; 29 Th Sathon Tai); Chiang Mai (Map pp108-9; ☎ 0 5328 1466; 138 Th
Charoen Prathet) Consulates only in Chiang
Mai, Phuket and Surat Thani.

Germany (Map pp80-1; ☎ 0 2287 9000;
www.german-embassy.or.th; 9 Th Sathon Tai,
Bangkok)

Ireland (Map pp80-1; ☎ 0 2677 7500; www
.irelandinthailand.com; 28th fl, Q House, Th Sathon
Tai, Bangkok) Consulate only; the nearest
Irish embassy is in Kuala Lumpur.

Japan Bangkok (Map pp80-1; ☎ 0 2207 8500;
www.th.emb-japan.go.jp; 177 Th Withayu); Chiang Mai (Map pp98-9; ☎ 0 5320 3367; 104-107
Airport Business Park, Th Mahidon) Consulate
only in Chiang Mai.

Malaysia (Map pp80-1; ☎ 0 2679 2190-9; 35
Th Sathon Tai, Bangkok) There's also a consulate in Songkhla.

New Zealand (Map pp80-1; ☎ 0 2254 2530;
www.nzembassy.com; 14th fl, M Thai Tower, All
Seasons Pl, 87 Th Withayu, Bangkok)

Singapore (Map pp80-1; ☎ 0 2286 2111;
www.mfa.gov.sg/bangkok; 129 Th Sathon Tai,
Bangkok)

UK Bangkok (Map p68; ☎ 0 2305 8333; www
.britishembassy.gov.uk; 14 Th Withayu); Chiang
Mai (Map pp108-9; ☎ 0 5326 2015; British Council, 198 Th Bamrungrat) Consulate only in
Chiang Mai.

USA Bangkok (Map pp80-1; ☎ 0 2205 4000;
http://bangkok.usembassy.gov; 95 Th Withayu);
Chiang Mai (Map pp108-9; ☎ 0 5310 7700; 387
Th Wichayanon) Consulate in Chiang Mai.

FESTIVALS & EVENTS
Thai festivals tend to be linked to the
agricultural seasons or to Buddhist holi-
days. The general word for festival in
Thai is *ngahn têt·sà·gahn*. See the Events
Calendar (p46) for more information.

FOOD
Most restaurants in Thailand are inexpensive by international standards and food
prices tend to hold steady throughout
the year.

A typical meal at a street stall should
cost 25B to 40B; a meal at a typical mum-
and-dad Thai restaurant for one should
be about 80B to 150B. Guesthouses and
restaurants catering to foreigners tend
to charge more than local restaurants.
See p345 for descriptions of the cuisine
and the kinds of restaurants you'll find in
Thailand.

GAY & LESBIAN TRAVELLERS
Thai culture is relatively tolerant of both
male and female homosexuality. There is
a fairly prominent gay and lesbian scene
in Bangkok, Pattaya and Phuket. With
regard to dress or mannerism, lesbians
and gays are generally accepted without
comment. However, public displays of af-
fection – whether heterosexual or homosexual – are frowned upon. Utopia (www
.utopia-asia.com) posts lots of Thailand
information for gay and lesbian visitors
and publishes a guidebook to the kingdom for homosexuals.

HEALTH
Travellers tend to worry most about contracting exotic infectious diseases when
visiting the tropics, but such infections are
a far less common cause of serious illness
or death in travellers than pre-existing
medical conditions such as heart disease

DIRECTORY

FESTIVALS & EVENTS

DIRECTORY

HEALTH

and accidental injury (especially as a result of a traffic accident).

Becoming ill in some way is common, however. Respiratory infections, diarrhoea and dengue fever are particular hazards in Thailand.

Fortunately most common illnesses can either be prevented with some common-sense behaviour or are easily treated with a well-stocked traveller's medical kit.

VACCINATIONS

Ideally you should visit a doctor six to eight weeks before departure, but it is never too late. Ask your doctor for an International Certificate of Vaccination (otherwise known as the yellow booklet), which will list all the vaccinations you've received.

The following vaccinations are those recommended by the World Health Organization (WHO) for travellers to Thailand: adult diphtheria, tetanus and pertussis; hepatitis A and B; measles, mumps and rubella; polio, typhoid and varicella.

MEDICAL CHECKLIST

Recommended items for a personal medical kit include:

- antibacterial cream, eg Muciprocin
- antibiotic for skin infections, eg Amoxicillin/Clavulanate or Cephalexin
- antibiotics for diarrhoea, eg Norfloxacin, Ciprofloxacin or Azithromycin for bacterial diarrhoea; Tinidazole for giardiasis or amoebic dysentery
- antifungal cream, eg Clotrimazole
- antihistamine – there are many options, eg Cetrizine for daytime and Promethazine for night
- antiseptic, eg Betadine
- antispasmodic for stomach cramps, eg Buscopan
- contraceptives
- decongestant
- DEET-based insect repellent
- first-aid items such as scissors, Elastoplasts, bandages, gauze, thermometer (but not mercury), sterile needles and syringes, safety pins and tweezers
- hand gel (alcohol based) or alcohol-based hand wipes
- ibuprofen or another anti-inflammatory
- indigestion medication, eg Quick Eze or Mylanta
- laxative, eg Coloxyl
- migraine medication – take along your personal medicine
- oral rehydration solution for diarrhoea (eg Gastrolyte), diarrhoea 'stopper' (eg Loperamide) and antinausea medication (eg Prochlorperazine)
- paracetamol
- Permethrin to impregnate clothing and mosquito nets if at high risk
- steroid cream for allergic/itchy rashes, eg 1% to 2% hydrocortisone
- sunscreen, hat and sunglasses
- throat lozenges
- thrush (vaginal yeast infection) treatment, eg Clotrimazole pessaries or Diflucan tablet
- Ural or equivalent if you are prone to urine infections

AVAILABILITY & COST OF HEALTH CARE

Bangkok is considered the nearest centre of medical excellence for many countries in Southeast Asia (such as Cambodia, Laos and Vietnam) and there are a number of excellent hospitals in the city.

In rural areas, however, it remains difficult to find reliable medical care. Your embassy and insurance company can be good contacts.

Buying medication over the counter is not recommended, because fake medications and poorly stored or out-of-date drugs are common.

TRAVELLER'S DIARRHOEA

Traveller's diarrhoea is by far the most common problem affecting travellers – between 30% and 50% of people will suffer from it within two weeks of starting their trip. In over 80% of cases, traveller's diarrhoea is caused by a bacteria (there are numerous potential culprits), and therefore responds promptly to treatment with antibiotics.

Traveller's diarrhoea is defined as the passage of more than three watery bowel movements within 24 hours, plus at least one other symptom such as vomiting, fever, cramps, nausea or feeling generally unwell.

Treatment consists of staying well hydrated; rehydration solutions such as Gastrolyte are the best for this.

DIRECTORY

HEALTH

DISEASES

Dengue Fever

This mosquito-borne disease is becoming increasingly problematic throughout Southeast Asia, especially in the cities. As there is no vaccine available it can only be prevented by avoiding mosquito bites. The mosquito that carries dengue is a daytime biter, so use insect-avoidance measures at all times. Symptoms include high fever, severe headache (especially behind the eyes), nausea and body aches (dengue was previously known as 'breakbone fever'). Some people develop a rash (which can be very itchy) and experience diarrhoea.

The southern islands of Thailand are particularly high risk. There is no specific treatment, just rest and paracetamol – do not take aspirin or ibuprofen as they increase the risk of haemorrhaging. See a doctor to be diagnosed and monitored. Dengue can progress to the more severe and life-threatening dengue haemorrhagic fever, however this is very uncommon in tourists. The risk of this increases substantially if you have previously been infected with dengue and are then infected with a different serotype.

Malaria

Most parts of Thailand visited by tourists, particularly city and resort areas, have minimal to no risk of malaria, and the risk of side effects from taking anti-malarial tablets is likely to outweigh the risk of getting the disease itself. For some rural areas, however, the risk of contracting the disease outweighs the risk of any tablet side effects. Remember that malaria can be fatal. Before you travel, seek proper medical advice on the right medication and dosage for you.

Malaria is caused by a parasite transmitted by the bite of an infected mosquito. The most important symptom of malaria is fever, but general symptoms such as headache, diarrhoea, cough or chills may also occur – the same symptoms as many other infections.

HOLIDAYS

Government offices and banks close on the following days.

January 1 New Year's Day

April 6 Chakri Day, commemorating the founder of the Chakri dynasty, Rama I

May 5 Coronation Day, commemorating the 1946 coronation of HM the King and HM the Queen

July (date varies) *Kôw pan·săh*, the beginning of Buddhist Lent

August 12 Queen's Birthday

October 23 Chulalongkorn Day

October/November (date varies) *Òrk pan·săh*, the end of Buddhist Lent

December 5 King's Birthday

December 10 Constitution Day

INSURANCE

A travel-insurance policy to cover theft, loss and medical problems is a good idea. Policies offer differing medical-expense options. Be sure that the policy covers ambulances or an emergency flight home.

Some policies specifically exclude 'dangerous activities', which can include scuba diving, motorcycling or even trekking.

Worldwide travel insurance is available at lonelyplanet.com/bookings. You can buy, extend and claim online anytime – even if you're already on the road.

INTERNET ACCESS

You'll find plenty of internet cafes in most towns and cities, and in many guesthouses and hotels as well. The going rate is anywhere from 40B to 120B an hour, depending on how much competition there is. Connections tend to be pretty fast and have been sped up with the proliferation of wireless access, which is fairly widespread throughout the country, including the rural northeast.

LEGAL MATTERS

In general, Thai police don't hassle foreigners, especially tourists. One major exception is drugs, which most Thai police view as either a social scourge against which it's their duty to enforce the letter of the law, or an opportunity to make untaxed income via bribes.

If you are arrested for any offence, the police will allow you the opportunity to make a phone call to your embassy or consulate in Thailand (if you have one), or to a friend or relative if not.

Thai law does not presume an indicted detainee to be either 'guilty' or 'innocent' but rather a 'suspect', whose guilt or innocence will be decided in court. Trials are usually speedy.

The **tourist police** (☎ 1155) can be very helpful in cases of arrest. Although they typically have no jurisdiction over the kinds of cases handled by the regular police, they may be able to help with translations or with contacting your embassy.

MONEY

The basic unit of Thai currency is the baht. There are 100 satang in one baht; coins include 25-satang and 50-satang pieces and baht in 1B, 2B, 5B and 10B coins. Older coins have Thai numerals only, while newer coins have Thai and Arabic numerals. The 2B coin was introduced in 2007 and is confusingly similar in size and design to the 1B coin. The two satang coins are typically only issued at supermarkets where prices aren't rounded up to the nearest baht, which is the convention elsewhere.

Paper currency is issued in the following denominations: 20B (green), 50B (blue), 100B (red), 500B (purple) and 1000B (beige). In the 1990s, the 10B bills were phased out in favour of the 10B coin but occasionally you might encounter a paper survivor.

ATMS & CREDIT/DEBIT CARDS

Debit and ATM cards issued by a bank in your own country can be used at ATM machines around Thailand to withdraw cash (in Thai baht only) directly from your account back home. ATMs are widespread throughout the country and can be relied on for the bulk of your spending cash. You can also use ATMs to buy baht at foreign-exchange booths at some banks.

Credit cards as well as debit cards can be used for purchases at many shops, hotels and restaurants. The most commonly accepted cards are Visa and MasterCard. American Express is typically only accepted at top-end hotels and restaurants.

To report a lost or stolen credit/debit card, call the following hotlines in Bangkok.

American Express (☎ 0 2273 5544)
Diners Club (☎ 0 2238 3660)
MasterCard (☎ 001 800 11887 0663)
Visa (☎ 001 800 441 3485)

CHANGING MONEY

Banks and the rarer, private money-changers offer the best foreign-exchange rates. When buying baht, US dollars are the most accepted currency, followed by British pounds then euros. Most banks charge a commission and duty for each travellers cheque cashed.

FOREIGN EXCHANGE

There is no limit to the amount of Thai or foreign currency you may bring into the country.

There are certain monetary requirements for foreigners entering Thailand; demonstrations of adequate funds varies per visa type but typically does not exceed a traveller's estimated trip budget. Rarely will you be asked to produce such financial evidence, but be aware that such laws do exist. For specific amounts for each visa type, visit the website of the Ministry of Foreign Affairs (www.mfa .go.th).

Upon leaving Thailand, you're permitted to take out a maximum of 50,000B per person without special authorisation; export of foreign currencies is unrestricted.

TIPPING

Tipping is not generally expected in Thailand. The exception is loose change from a large restaurant bill; if a meal costs 488B and you pay with a 500B note, some Thais will leave the 12B change. It's not so much a tip as a way of saying 'I'm not so money grubbing as to grab every last baht'. Apart from this, it is not customary to leave behind the change if it is less than 10B.

At many hotel restaurants or other up-market eateries, a 10% service charge will be added to your bill. Bangkok has adopted some tipping standards, especially in restaurants frequented by foreigners.

PHOTOGRAPHY

Thais are gadget fans and most have made the transition to digital. Memory cards for digital cameras are generally widely available in the more popular formats and available in the electronic sections of most shopping malls. In tourist areas, many internet shops have CD-burning software if you want to offload your pictures. Alternatively, most places have sophisticated enough connections that you can quickly upload digital photos to a remote storage site.

Be considerate when taking photographs of the locals. Learn how to ask politely in Thai and wait for an embarrassed nod. In some of the regularly visited hill-tribe areas be prepared for the photographed subject to ask for money in exchange for a picture. Other hill tribes will not allow you to point a camera at them.

POST

Thailand has a very efficient postal service and local postage is inexpensive. Typical provincial post offices are open 8.30am to 4.30pm weekdays and 9am to noon on Saturday. Larger main post offices in provincial capitals may also be open for a half-day on Sunday.

Most provincial post offices sell do-it-yourself packing boxes, and some will pack your parcels for a small fee. Don't send cash or other valuables through the mail.

SHOPPING

Many bargains await you in Thailand but don't go shopping in the company of touts, tour guides or friendly strangers as they will inevitably take a commission on anything you buy, thus driving prices up beyond an acceptable value and creating a nuisance for future visitors.

ANTIQUES

Real antiques cannot be taken out of Thailand without a permit. No Buddha image, new or old, may be exported without the permission of the Department of Fine Arts; see p372 for information.

Real Thai antiques are increasingly rare. Today most dealers sell antique reproductions or items from Myanmar (Burma). Bangkok and Chiang Mai are the two centres for the antique and reproduction trade.

BARGAINING

If there isn't a sign stating the price for an item then the price is negotiable. Bargaining for non-food items is common in street markets and some family-run shops. Prices in department stores, minimarts, 7-Elevens etc are fixed.

Thais respect a good haggler. Always let the vendor make the first offer then ask 'Can you lower the price?'. Now it's your turn to make a counter-offer; always start low but don't bargain at all unless you're serious about buying.

It helps immeasurably to keep the negotiations relaxed and friendly, and always remember to smile.

CLOTHING

Larger-sized clothes are available in metropolitan malls, such as Bangkok's MBK and Central Department Store, as well tourist-oriented shops throughout the country. Markets sell cheap, everyday items and are handy for picking up something when everything else is dirty. For chic clothes, Bangkok and Ko Samui lead the country with design-minded fashions. The custom of returns is not widely accepted in Thailand, so be sure everything fits before you leave the store.

Thailand has a long sartorial tradition, practised mainly by Thai-Indian Sikh families. You're more likely to get a good fit from a custom-made piece by a tailor, but this industry is filled with cut-rate operators and commission-paying scams.

FAKES

In Bangkok, Chiang Mai and other tourist centres there's a thriving black-market street-trade in fake designer goods. Technically it is illegal for these items to be produced and sold, and Thailand has often been pressured by intellectual- property enforcement agencies to close down the trade.

GEMS & JEWELLERY

Although there are a lot of gem and jewellery stores in Thailand, it has become so difficult to dodge the scammers that the country no longer represents a safe and enjoyable place to buy these goods. See p373 for a detailed warning on gem fraud.

TELEPHONE

The telephone system in Thailand has been deregulated and the once state-owned entities have been privatised.

The telephone country code for Thailand is ☎ 66 and is used when calling the country from abroad. You must also dial an international exchange prefix (for Australia it is ☎ 0011, for the UK ☎ 00 and for the US ☎ 001) before the country code.

Thailand no longer uses separate area codes for the provinces, so all phone numbers in the country use eight digits (preceded by a '0' if you're dialling domestically). To accommodate the growth in mobile (cell) phone usage, Thailand has introduced an '8' prefix to all mobile numbers; ie ☎ 01 234 5678 is now ☎ 081 234 5678. If you're calling a mobile phone from overseas you would omit the initial '0' for both mobile and landline numbers.

INTERNATIONAL CALLS

If you want to call an international number from a telephone in Thailand, you must first dial an international access code before dialling the country code followed by the subscriber number.

In Thailand, there are varying international access codes charging different rates per minute. The standard direct-dial prefix is ☎ 001; it is operated by CAT and is considered to have the best sound quality. It connects to the largest number of countries but is the most expensive. The next best is ☎ 007, a prefix operated by TOT with reliable quality and slightly cheaper rates. Economy rates are available with ☎ 008 and ☎ 009, both of which use Voice over Internet Protocol (VoIP), with varying but adequate sound quality.

There are also a variety of international phonecards available through CAT (www.cthai.com) offering promotional rates as low as 1B per minute.

Dial ☎ 100 for operator-assisted international calls. To make a reverse-charges (or collect) call, use this prefix. Alternatively contact your long-distance carrier for their overseas operator number, a toll-free call, or try ☎ 001 9991 2001 from a CAT phone and ☎ 1 800 000 120 from a TOT phone.

PHONES

Calling overseas through phones in most hotel rooms usually incurs additional surcharges (sometimes as much as 50% over and above the CAT rate); however sometimes local calls are free or at standard rates. Some guesthouses will have a mobile phone or landline that customers can use for a per-minute fee for overseas calls.

There is also a variety of public payphones that use prepaid phonecards for calls (both international and domestic) and coin-operated pay phones for local calls. Using the public phones can be a bit of a pain: they are typically placed beside a main thoroughfare, where you're cooked by the sun and the conversation is drowned out by traffic noise.

The red and blue public phones are for local calls and are coin-operated; it typically costs 5B to initiate a call. Then there are the phonecard phone booths that accept only certain kinds of cards. The green phones take domestic TOT phonecards. The yellow phones (labelled either domestic or international) take the respective Lenso phonecards. These phonecards can be bought from 7-Elevens in 300B and 500B denominations and rates vary between 7B and 10B per call.

MOBILE PHONES

Thailand is on a GSM network. Mobile (cell) phone operators in Thailand include AIS, DTAC and True Move (formerly Orange). You have two hand-phone options: you can either buy a mobile phone in Thailand at one of the shopping malls (such as Bangkok's MBK), or you can use an imported phone that isn't SIM-locked. Most mobile users in Thailand use the prepaid services of a particular carrier (AIS and DTAC are the most popular). To get started, buy a SIM card, which includes an assigned telephone number. Once your phone is SIM-enabled you can buy minutes with prepaid phonecards. SIM cards and refill cards can be bought from 7-Elevens throughout the country. There are various promotions but rates typically hover around 2B to 3B per minute anywhere in Thailand and between 5B and 7B for international calls. SMS is usually 5B per message, making it the cheapest 'talk' option for baht-strapped mobile users.

TIME

Thailand's time zone is seven hours ahead of GMT/UTC (London). At government offices and local cinemas, times are often expressed according to the 24-hour clock, eg 11pm is written '2300'.

The official year in Thailand is reckoned from 543 BC, the beginning of the Buddhist Era, so that AD 2009 is BE 2552, AD 2010 is BE 2553 etc.

TOILETS

As in many other Asian countries, the 'squat' toilet is the norm except in hotels and guesthouses geared towards tourists and international business travellers. Squat toilets sit flush with the surface of the floor, with two footpads on either side. For travellers who have never used a squat toilet, it takes a bit of getting used to.

Toilet users scoop water from an adjacent bucket or tank with a plastic bowl and use it to clean their nether regions while still squatting over the toilet. A few extra scoops of water must be poured into the toilet basin to flush waste into the septic system.

Even in places where sit-down toilets are installed, the septic system may not be designed to take toilet paper. In such cases the usual washing bucket will be standing nearby or there will be a waste basket where you place used toilet paper.

TOURIST INFORMATION

The government-operated tourist information and promotion service, **Tourism Authority of Thailand** (TAT; www.tourism thailand.org), was founded in 1960 and produces excellent pamphlets on sightseeing, accommodation and transport.

The following are a few of TAT's overseas information offices; check its website for contact information in Hong Kong, Taipei, Seoul, Tokyo, Osaka, Fukuoka, Stockholm and Rome.

Australia (☎ 02 9247 7549; www.thailand .net.au; Level 20, 75 Pitt St, Sydney, NSW 2000)
Singapore (☎ 65 6235 7901; tatsin@signet .com.sg; c/o Royal Thai Embassy, 370 Orchard Rd, 238870)

UK (☎ 020 7925 2511; www.tourismthailand .co.uk; 3rd fl, Brook House, 98-99 Jermyn St, London SW1Y 6EE)

USA New York (☎ 212 432 0433; tatny@tat .or.th; 61 Broadway, Ste 2810, New York, NY 10006); Los Angeles (☎ 323 461 9814; tatla@ ix.netcom.com; 1st fl, 611 North Larchmont Blvd, Los Angeles, CA 90004)

TRAVELLERS WITH DISABILITIES

Thailand presents one large, ongoing obstacle course for the mobility impaired. With its high curbs, uneven footpaths and nonstop traffic, Bangkok can be particularly difficult. Many streets must be crossed via pedestrian bridges flanked with steep stairways, while buses and boats don't stop long enough even for the fully abled. Rarely are there any ramps or other access points for wheelchairs.

Counter to the prevailing trends, Worldwide Dive & Sail (www.worldwide diveandsail.com) offers liveaboard diving programs for the deaf and hard of hearing.

VISAS

The Ministry of Foreign Affairs (www.mfa .go.th) oversees immigration and visa issues. Check the website or the nearest Thai embassy or consulate for application procedures and costs. In the past five years there have been some shifting rules on visas and visa extensions; Thaivisa (www.thaivisa.com) stays abreast of any changes and developments.

TOURIST VISAS & EXEMPTIONS

The Thai government allows tourist-visa exemptions for 41 different nationalities, including those from Australia, New Zealand, the USA and most of Europe, to enter the country without a pre-arranged visa. Do note that in 2008, the length of stay

for citizens from exempted countries was slightly altered from years past. For those arriving in the kingdom by air, a 30-day visa is issued without a fee. For those arriving via a land border, the arrival visa has been shortened to 15 days (no fee is charged).

Without proof of an onward ticket and sufficient funds for one's projected stay any visitor can be denied entry, but in practise your ticket and funds are rarely checked if you're dressed neatly for the immigration check.

If you plan to stay in Thailand longer than 30 days (or 15 days for land arrivals), you should apply for the 60-day tourist visa from a Thai consulate or embassy before your trip. Obtaining a tourist visa is a good idea for overland travellers who need more time in Thailand than the land-arrival visa allows. Alternatively you can extend your visa in Thailand (see below), but it will be cheaper and you'll get more time if you arrange for a tourist visa before your arrival. Contact the nearest Thai embassy or consulate to obtain application procedures and fees for tourist visas.

NON-IMMIGRANT VISAS

The Non-Immigrant Visa is good for 90 days and is intended for foreigners entering the country for business, study, retirement or extended family visits. There are multiple-entry visas available in this visa class; you're more likely to be granted multiple entries if you apply at a Thai consulate in Europe, the US or Australia than elsewhere. If you plan to apply for a Thai work permit, you'll need to possess a Non-Immigrant Visa first.

VISA EXTENSIONS & RENEWALS

You can apply at any immigration office in Thailand for visa extensions. Most foreigners use the **Bangkok immigration** office (☎ 0 2287 3101; Soi Suan Phlu, Th Sathon Tai; ⊙ 9am-noon & 1-4.30pm Mon-Fri, 9am-noon Sat) or the Chiang Mai immigration office (☎ 0 5320 1755-6; Th Mahidon; ⊙ 8.30am-4.30pm Mon-Fri) for extensions of most types of visa. The usual fee for a visa extension is 1900B.

Those issued with a standard stay of 15 or 30 days can extend their stay for seven to 10 days (depending on the immigration office) if the extension is handled before the visa expires. The 60-day tourist visa can be extended by up to 30 days at the discretion of Thai immigration authorities.

If you overstay your visa, the usual penalty is a fine of 500B per day, with a 20,000B limit. Fines can be paid at the airport or in advance at an immigration office. If you've overstayed only one day, you don't have to pay. Children under 14 travelling with a parent do not have to pay the penalty.

WOMEN TRAVELLERS

In the provincial towns, it is advisable that women travellers dress conservatively, covering shoulders, belly buttons and thighs. Outside of Bangkok, most Thai women cover up in the sun to avoid unnecessary exposure since lighter skin is considered more beautiful.

Attacks and rapes are not common in Thailand, but incidents do occur, especially when an attacker observes a vulnerable target: a drunk or solo woman. The regular Full Moon party at Ko Pha-Ngan is a common trouble spot.

TRANSPORT

GETTING THERE & AWAY

ENTERING THE COUNTRY

Entry procedures for Thailand, by air or by land, are straightforward: you'll have to show your passport (see p383 for information about visa requirements); and you'll need to present completed arrival and departure cards.

Flights, tours and rail tickets can be booked online at lonelyplanet.com/bookings.

AIR

AIRPORTS

The Suvarnabhumi Airport opened in September 2006 and has replaced the airport at Don Muang for all international flights and some domestic flights. It is located in the Nong Ngu Hao area of Samut Prakan – 30km east of Bangkok and 60km from Pattaya. The airport code for Suvarnabhumi is BKK.

⬎ CLIMATE CHANGE & TRAVEL

Travel – especially air travel – is a significant contributor to global climate change. At Lonely Planet, we believe that all who travel have a responsibility to limit their personal impact. As a result, we have teamed with Rough Guides and other concerned industry partners to support Climate Care, which allows people to offset the greenhouse gases they are responsible for with contributions to energy-saving projects and other climate-friendly initiatives in the developing world. Lonely Planet offsets all staff and author travel.

For more information, turn to the responsible travel pages on www.lonelyplanet.com. For details on offsetting your carbon emissions and a carbon calculator, go to www.climatecare.org.

The country's second-busiest airport for passenger service is Phuket International Airport.

Other airports with limited connections to Asian capitals can be found in Chiang Mai (with services to Taipei, Singapore, Kuala Lumpur, Luang Prabang and Vientiane), Udon Thani (with services to Luang Prabang), Ko Samui (with services to Singapore and Hong Kong) and Hat Yai (with services to Kuala Lumpur).

AIRLINES TRAVELLING TO/FROM THAILAND

The following airlines fly to and from Thailand:

Air Canada (Map pp80-1; ☎ 0 2670 0400; www.aircanada.com; Ste 1708, River Wing West, Empire Tower, 195 Th Sathon Tai)

Air France (Map pp80-1; ☎ 0 2635 1191; www.airfrance.fr; 20th fl, Vorawat Bldg, 849 Th Silom)

Air New Zealand (Map pp80-1; ☎ 0 2235 8280; www.airnewzealand.com; 11th fl, 140/17 ITF Tower, Th Silom)

Bangkok Airways (☎ 1771; www.bangkokair.com; Suvarnabhumi International Airport)

British Airways (Map pp80-1; ☎ 0 2627 1701; www.britishairways.com; 21st fl, Charn Issara Tower, 942/160-163 Th Phra Ram IV)

Cathay Pacific Airways (Map p68; ☎ 0 2263 0606; www.cathaypacific.com; 11th fl, Ploenchit Tower, 898 Th Ploenchit)

China Airlines (Map p68; ☎ 0 2250 9898; www.china-airlines.com; 4th fl, Peninsula Plaza, 153 Th Ratchadamri)

Emirates (Map pp74-5; ☎ 0 2664 1040; www.emirates.com; 2nd fl, BB Bldg, 54 Soi 21/Asoke, Th Sukhumvit)

Eva Air (Map pp74-5; ☎ 0 2269 6288; www.evaair.com; 2nd fl, Green Tower, 3656/4-5 Th Phra Ram IV)

Japan Airlines (Map p68; ☎ 0 2649 9520; www.jal.co.jp; 1st fl, Nantawan Bldg, 161 Th Ratchadamri)

Jetstar Airways (☎ 0 2267 5125; www.jetstar.com; Suvarnabhumi International Airport)

KLM-Royal Dutch Airlines (Map pp80-1; ☎ 0 2635 2300; www.klm.com; 20th fl, Vorawat Bldg, 849 Th Silom)

Korean Air (Map pp80-1; ☎ 0 2635 0465; www.koreanair.com; 1st fl, Kongboonma Bldg, 699 Th Silom)

Lufthansa Airlines (Map pp74-5; ☎ 0 2264 2484, reservations 0 2264 2400; www.lufthansa.com; 18th fl, Q House, Soi 21/Asoke, Th Sukhumvit)

Northwest Airlines (Map p68; ☎ 0 2660 6999; www.nwa.com; 4th fl, Peninsula Plaza, 153 Th Ratchadamri)

Philippine Airlines (Map pp74-5; ☎ 0 2633 5713; Manorom Bldg, 3354/47 Th Phra Ram IV)

Qantas Airways (Map pp80-1; ☎ 0 2236 2800; www.qantas.com.au; Tour East, 21st fl, Charn Issara Tower, 942/160-163 Th Phra Ram IV)

Singapore Airlines (Map pp80-1; ☎ 0 2353 6000; www.singaporeair.com; 12th fl, Silom Center Bldg, 2 Th Silom)

Thai Airways International (www.thaiair.com) Banglamphu (Map pp80-1; ☎ 0 2356 1111; 6 Th Lan Luang); Silom (Map p66; ☎ 0 2232 8000; 1st fl, Bangkok Union Insurance Bldg, 175-177 Soi Anuman Rajchathon, Th Surawong)

United Airlines (Map pp80-1; ☎ 0 2353 3900; www.ual.com; 6th fl, TMB Bank Silom Bldg, 393 Th Silom)

TICKETS

Booking flights in and out of Bangkok during the high season (from December to March) can be difficult and expensive. For air travel during these months you should make your bookings as far in advance as you possibly can.

GETTING AROUND
AIR

Hopping around the country by air is becoming more and more affordable thanks to airline deregulation. Most

THAI AIR FARES & RAIL LINES

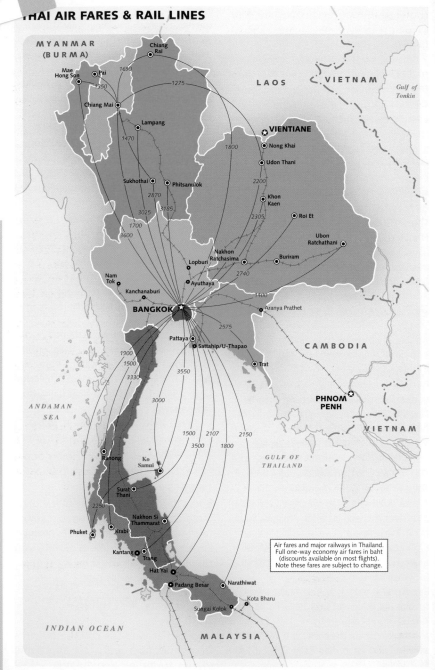

Air fares and major railways in Thailand.
Full one-way economy air fares in baht
(discounts available on most flights).
Note these fares are subject to change.

routes originate from Bangkok, but Chiang Mai, Ko Samui and Phuket all have routes to other Thai towns.

THAI operates many domestic air routes from Bangkok to provincial capitals. Bangkok Air is another established domestic carrier. One-Two-Go, Nok Air and Air Asia all tend to be cheaper than the older carriers.

BICYCLE

For travelling just about anywhere outside Bangkok, bicycles are an ideal form of local transport – cheap, non-polluting and slow moving enough to allow travellers to see everything.

Bicycles can be hired in many locations, especially guesthouses, for as little as 50B per day.

BOAT

The true Thai river transport is the *reu·a hǎhng yow* (long-tail boat), so-called because the propeller is mounted at the end of a long drive shaft extending from the engine.

Between the mainland and islands in the Gulf of Thailand and the Andaman Sea, the standard craft is an 8m to 10m wooden boat with an inboard engine, a wheelhouse and a simple roof to shelter passengers and cargo. Faster, more expensive hovercraft or jetfoils are sometimes available in tourist areas.

BUS

The bus network in Thailand is prolific and reliable, and is a great way to see the countryside and sit among the locals. The Thai government subsidises the **Transport Company** (bò·rí·sàt kŏn sòng; ☎ 0 2936 2841; www.transport.co.th), usually abbreviated to Baw Khaw Saw (BKS). Every city and town in Thailand linked by bus has a BKS station, even if it's just a patch of dirt by the side of the road.

SAFETY

The most reputable bus companies depart from the public BKS bus terminals. Private buses and minivans that pick up customers from tourist centres such as Th Khao San in Bangkok experience a higher incidence of reported theft, lateness and unreliability.

Keep all valuables on your person, not stored in your luggage because even locked bags can be tampered with and you might not realise anything is missing until days later.

RESERVATIONS

You can book air-con BKS buses at any BKS terminal. Privately run buses can be booked through most hotels or any travel agency, but it's best to book directly through a bus office to be sure that you get what you pay for.

SAMPLE BUS FARES TO BANGKOK

DESTINATION	DISTANCE FROM BANGKOK	VIP (B)	1ST CLASS (B)	2ND CLASS (B)
Chiang Mai	685km	695	596	(n/a)
Kanchanaburi	130km	(n/a)	139	112
Krabi	817km	1100	700	(n/a)
Hat Yai	993km	1075	740	(n/a)
Trat	313km	(n/a)	260	223

CAR & MOTORCYCLE

DRIVING LICENCE

Short-term visitors who wish to drive vehicles (including motorcycles) in Thailand need an International Driving Permit.

FUEL & SPARE PARTS

Modern petrol (gasoline) stations are in plentiful supply all over Thailand wherever there are paved roads. In more remote, off-road areas *ben·sin/nám·man rót yon* (petrol containing benzene) is usually available at small roadside or village stands.

HIRE & PURCHASE

Cars, 4WDs and vans can be rented in most major cities and airports from local companies as well as international chains. Check the tyre treads and general upkeep of the vehicle before committing.

Motorcycles can be rented in major towns and many smaller tourist centres from guesthouses and small, local businesses. For daily rentals, most businesses will ask that you leave your passport as a deposit. Before renting a motorcycle, check the vehicle's condition and ask for a helmet (which is required by law).

Many tourists are injured riding motorcycles in Thailand because they don't know how to handle the vehicle and are unfamiliar with road rules and conditions. Drive sensibly to avoid damage to yourself and to the vehicle, and be sure to have adequate health insurance. If you've never driven a motorcycle before, stick to the smaller 100cc step-through bikes with automatic clutches. Remember to distribute weight as evenly as possible across the frame of the bike to improve handling.

INSURANCE

Thailand requires a minimum of liability insurance for all registered vehicles on the road. The better hire companies include comprehensive coverage for their vehicles. Always verify that a vehicle is insured for liability before signing a rental contract; you should also ask to see the dated insurance documents. If you have an accident while driving an uninsured vehicle, you're in for some major hassles.

ROAD RULES & HAZARDS

Thais drive on the left-hand side of the road (most of the time!). Other than that, just about anything goes, in spite of road signs and speed limits.

The main rule to be aware of is that right of way goes to the bigger vehicle; this is not what it says in the Thai traffic law, but it's the reality. Maximum speed limits are 50km/h on urban roads and 80km/h to 100km/h on most highways – but on any given stretch of highway you'll see various vehicles travelling as slowly as 30km/h and as fast as 150km/h.

Indicators are often used to warn passing drivers about oncoming traffic. A flashing left indicator means it's OK to pass, while a right indicator means that someone's approaching from the other direction. Horns are used to tell other vehicles that the driver plans to pass. When drivers flash their lights, they're telling you not to pass.

LOCAL TRANSPORT

CITY BUS & SŎRNG·TĂA·OU

Bangkok has the largest city-bus system in the country. Elsewhere, public transport is typically supplied by *sŏrng·tăa·ou* (literally 'two rows' – small pick-up trucks with two rows of bench seats down both sides of the truck bed) that run established routes, although Udon Thani and a few other provincial capitals have city buses.

The etiquette for riding public transport is to hail the vehicle by waving your hand palm-side downward. You typically pay the fare once you've taken a seat or when you disembark.

Sŏrng·tăa·ou sometimes operate on fixed routes, just like buses, but they may also run a share-taxi service where they pick-up passengers going in the same general direction. In tourist centres, *sŏrng·tăa·ou* can be chartered individually just like a regular taxi, but you'll need to negotiate the fare beforehand.

MASS TRANSIT

Bangkok is the only city in Thailand to have either an above-ground or underground light-rail public transport system.

MOTORCYCLE TAXI

Many cities in Thailand also have *mor·đeu·sai ráp jâhng* (100cc to 125cc motorcycles) that can be hired, with a driver, for short distances.

In most cities, you'll find motorcycle taxis clustered near street intersections rather than cruising the streets looking for fares. Usually they wear numbered jerseys. Fares tend to run from 10B to 50B, depending on the distance.

SĂHM·LÓR & TÚK-TÚK

Sătum·lór means 'three wheels' and that's just what they are – three-wheeled vehicles.

You'll find motorised sătum·lór (better known as túk-túk) throughout the country. They're small utility vehicles, powered by horrendously noisy engines (usually LPG-powered); if the noise and vibration don't get you, the fumes will.

The non-motorised sătum·lór (ie the bicycle rickshaw or pedicab) is similar to what you may see in other parts of Asia. With either form of sătum·lór, the fare must be established by bargaining before departure.

TAXI

Bangkok has the most formal system of metered taxis. In other cities, a taxi can be a private vehicle with negotiable rates. You can also travel between cities by taxi but you'll need to negotiate a price as few taxi drivers will run a meter for intercity travel.

TOURS

Long-running, reliable tour wholesalers in Thailand include the following:

Asian Trails (Map p68; ☎ 0 2626 2000; www .asiantrails.net; 9th fl, SG Tower, 161/1 Soi Mahatlek Leung 3, Th Ratchadamri, Bangkok)

Diethelm Travel (Map pp80-1; ☎ 0 2660 7000; www.diethelmtravel.com; 12th fl, Kian Gwan Bldg II, 140/1 Th Withayu, Bangkok)

World Travel Service (Map pp80-1; ☎ 0 2233 5900; www.wts-thailand.com; 1053 Th Charoen Krung, Bangkok)

OVERSEAS COMPANIES

The better overseas tour companies build their own Thailand itineraries from scratch and choose their local suppliers based on which best serve these itineraries.

Asia Transpacific Journeys (☎ 800 642 2742; www.southeastasia.com; 2995 Center Green Dr, Boulder, CO 80301, USA) Small-group highlight tours and speciality trips.

Club Adventure (☎ 514 527 0999; www .clubaventure.com; 757 ave du Mont-Royal Est, Montreal, QUE H2J 1W8, Canada) Canadian French-language tour operators.

Exodus (☎ 800 843 4272; www.exodustravels .co.uk; 1311 63rd St, Ste 200, Emeryville, CA 94608, USA) Award-winning agency, known for its environmentally responsible tours.

TRANSPORT

GETTING AROUND

Hands Up Holidays (☎ 0 800 783 3554; www.handsupholidays.com; 5 Kendal Pl, London SW15 2QZ, UK) Volunteer and sightseeing programs for comfort travellers.

Intrepid Travel (www.intrepidtravel.com) Specialises in small-group travel geared toward young people; visit the website for country-specific contact details.

I-to-I (☎ 800 985 4852; www.i-to-i.com) Volunteer and sightseeing tours.

Starfish Ventures (☎ 44 800 1974817; www.starfishvolunteers.com) Organises a gap-year volunteer and sightseeing package, among other programs.

Tours with Kasma Loha-Unchit (☎ 510 655 8900; www.thaifoodandtravel.com; PO Box 21165, Oakland, CA 94620, USA) This Thai cookbook author offers personalised 'cultural immersion' tours of Thailand.

TRAIN

The government rail network, operated by the **State Railway of Thailand** (SRT; ☎ 1690; www.railway.co.th), covers four main lines: the northern, southern, northeastern and eastern lines (see Map p386 for major routes).

The train is most convenient as an alternative to buses for the long journey north to Chiang Mai or south to Surat Thani. The train is also ideal for trips to Ayuthaya and Lopburi from Bangkok.

CLASSES

The SRT operates passenger trains in three classes – 1st, 2nd and 3rd – but each class varies considerably depending on whether you're on an ordinary, rapid or express train.

THIRD CLASS

A typical 3rd-class carriage consists of two rows of bench seats divided into facing pairs. Express trains do not carry 3rd-class carriages at all. Commuter trains in the Bangkok area are all 3rd class.

SECOND CLASS

The seating arrangements in a 2nd-class, non-sleeper carriage are similar to those on a bus, with pairs of padded seats, usually recliners, all facing toward the front of the train.

On 2nd-class sleeper cars, pairs of seats face one another and convert into two fold-down berths, one over the other. Curtains provide a modicum of privacy and the berths are fairly comfortable, with fresh linen for every trip. The lower berth has more headroom than the upper berth and this is reflected in a higher fare. Children are always assigned a lower berth.

Second-class carriages are found only on rapid and express trains. Air-con 2nd class is more common nowadays than ordinary (fan) 2nd class (with the latter available only on rapid lines).

FIRST CLASS

Each private cabin in a 1st-class carriage has individually controlled air-con (older trains also have an electric fan), a washbasin and mirror, a small table and long bench seats that convert into beds. First-class carriages are available only on rapid, express and special-express trains.

RESERVATIONS

Advance bookings can be made from one to 60 days before your intended date of departure. It is advisable to make advanced bookings for long-distance sleeper trains between Bangkok and Chiang Mai or from Bangkok to Surat Thani during holidays – especially around Songkran in April, Chinese New Year and during the peak tourist-season months of December and January.

You can make bookings from any train station. Train tickets can also be purchased at travel agencies, which usually add a service charge to the ticket price.

If you are planning long-distance train travel from outside the country, you should email the State Railway of Thailand (passenger-ser@railway.co.th) at least two weeks before your journey. You will receive an email confirming the booking. Pick up and pay for tickets an hour before leaving at the scheduled departure train station.

For short-distance trips you should purchase your ticket at least a day in advance for seats (rather than sleepers).

TRANSPORT

GETTING AROUND

⬎ GLOSSARY

This glossary includes Thai, Pali (P) and Sanskrit (S) words and terms frequently used in this book.

baht – *(bàat)* the Thai unit of currency

BKS – Baw Khaw Saw (Thai acronym for the Transport Company)

BTS – Bangkok Transit System (Skytrain); Thai: *rót fai fáḥ*

CAT – CAT Telecom Public Company Limited (formerly Communications Authority of Thailand)

chedi – see *stupa*

hàht – beach; spelt 'Hat' in proper names

hŏr ḍrai – a Tripitaka (Buddhist scripture) hall

hôrng – *(hong)* room; in southern Thailand this refers to semi-submerged island caves

Isan – *(ee·săhn)* general term used for northeastern Thailand

jataka (P) – *(chah·dòk)* stories of the Buddha's previous lives

klorng – canal; spelt 'Khlong' in proper nouns

kŏhn – masked dance-drama based on stories from the Ramakian

kŏw – hill or mountain; spelt 'Khao' in proper names

kôw – rice

lék – little, small (in size); see also *noi*

Mahanikai – the larger of the two sects of Theravada Buddhism in Thailand

mahathat – *(má·hăh tâht)* common name for temples containing Buddha relics; from the Sanskrit-Pali term *mahadhatu*

masjid – *(mát·sà·yít)* mosque

meu·ang – city or principality

mon·dòp – small square, spired building in a wát; from Sanskrit *mandapa*

naga (P/S) – *(nâhk)* a mythical serpent-like being with magical powers

ná·kon – city; from the Sanskrit-Pali *nagara;* spelt 'Nakhon' in proper nouns

nám ḍòk – waterfall; spelt 'Nam Tok' in proper nouns

ngahn têt·sà·gahn – festival

nibbana (P/S) – nirvana; in Buddhist teachings, the state of enlightenment; escape from the realm of rebirth; Thai: *níp·pahn*

noi – *(nóy)* little, small (amount); see also *lék*

ow – bay or gulf; spelt 'Ao' in proper nouns

pík·sù – a Buddhist monk; from the Sanskrit *bhikshu,* Pali *bhikkhu*

prá – an honorific term used for monks, nobility and Buddha images; spelt 'Phra' in proper names

prang – *('brahng)* Khmer-style tower on temples

prasada – blessed food offered to Hindu or Sikh temple attendees

prasat – *('brah·sàht)* small ornate building, used for religious purposes, with a cruciform ground plan and needlelike spire, located on temple grounds; any of a number of different kinds of halls or residences with religious or royal significance

rót aa – blue-and-white air-con bus
rót 'bràp ah·gàht – air-con bus
rót fai fáh – Bangkok's Skytrain system
rót fai đâi din – Bangkok's subway system
rót norn – sleeper bus
rót tam·má·dah – ordinary (non air-con) bus or train
rót too·a – tour or air-con bus

sǎhm·lór – three-wheeled pedicab
samsara (P) – in Buddhist teachings, the realm of rebirth and delusion
sangha – (P) the Buddhist community
satang – *(sà·đahng)* a Thai unit of currency; 100 satang equals 1 baht
soi – lane or small street
Songkran – Thai New Year, held in mid-April
sǒrng·tǎa·ou – (literally 'two rows') common name for small pick-up trucks with two benches in the back, used as buses/taxis; also spelt *'sǎwngthǎew'*
stupa – conical-shaped Buddhist monument used to inter sacred Buddhist objects

tâh – pier, boat landing; spelt 'Tha' in proper nouns
tâht – four-sided, curvilinear Buddha reliquary, common in Northeastern Thailand; spelt 'That' in proper nouns

tâm – cave; spelt 'Tham' in proper nouns
TAT – Tourism Authority of Thailand
Thammayut – one of the two sects of Theravada Buddhism in Thailand; founded by King Rama IV while he was still a monk
thanǒn – *(tà·nǒn)* street; spelt 'Thanon' in proper noun and shortened to 'Th'
trimurti (S) – collocation of the three principal Hindu deities, Brahma, Shiva and Vishnu
Tripitaka (S) – Theravada Buddhist scriptures; (Pali: *Tipitaka*)
tú·dong – a series of 13 ascetic practices (for example eating one meal a day, living at the foot of a tree) undertaken by Buddhist monks; a monk who undertakes such practices; a period of wandering on foot from place to place undertaken by monks
túk-túk – *(đúk-đúk)* motorised sǎhm·lór

vipassana (P) – *(wí·bàt·sà·nah)* Buddhist insight meditation

wâi – palms-together Thai greeting
wan prá – Buddhist holy days, falling on the days of the main phases of the moon (full, new and half) each month
wat – temple-monastery; from the Pali term *avasa* meaning 'monk's dwelling'; spelt 'Wat' in proper nouns

↘ BEHIND THE SCENES

THE AUTHORS
CHINA WILLIAMS

Coordinating Author, This Is Thailand, Thailand's Top 25 Experiences, Thailand's Top Itineraries, Planning Your Trip, Chiang Mai, Northern Thailand, Thailand In Focus, Directory & Transport

China has been a Thailand observer for more than a decade. Her relationship with the country began in the rural northeastern town of Surin as an English teacher just as the Asian currency crisis in 1997 toppled the Thai economy. For the past seven years she's been hopping across the Pacific Ocean from her home in the US to work on various Lonely Planet guidebooks to the kingdom. During that time she's seen the middle class swell, Thaksin rise and fall, and democracy come and go. On her most recent trips to Thailand, she's taken along her toddler-aged son who wowed the Thai crowds with his ear-to-ear grin. For the rest of the time she lives outside of Baltimore, Maryland (USA) with her husband, Matt, and son, Felix.

Author thanks Thanks to Nong and Ruengsang, my great email pals. Also thanks to the interview subjects who shared their time and insights. (A little trivia here: June was my student at Rajabhat Surin.) Equal gratitude to Tashi Wheeler, who thinks of me for assignments long before I feel the need to pester. And more nods to the Lonely Planet production team, including Dave Connolly.

MARK BEALES   Central Thailand

Mark moved to Thailand in 2004, leaving behind life as a journalist in England. Various jobs including English teacher, TV presenter and freelance writer have given him a chance to explore almost every part of the country. During his trips, Mark has swum with whale sharks, been bitten by leeches and watched gibbons threaten to invade his log cabin. When Mark isn't on the road he teaches English near Bangkok and attempts to improve his Thai with help from his ever-patient wife, Bui.

LONELY PLANET AUTHORS

Why is our travel information the best in the world? It's simple: our authors are passionate, dedicated travellers. They don't take freebies in exchange for positive coverage so you can be sure the advice you're given is impartial. They travel widely to all the popular spots, and off the beaten track. They don't research using just the internet or phone. They discover new places not included in any other guidebook. They personally visit thousands of hotels, restaurants, palaces, trails, galleries, temples and more. They speak with dozens of locals every day to make sure you get the kind of insider knowledge only a local could tell you. They take pride in getting all the details right, and in telling it how it is. Think you can do it? Find out how at lonelyplanet.com.

TIM BEWER — Northeastern Thailand

While growing up, Tim didn't travel much except for the obligatory pilgrimage to Disney World and an annual summer week at the lake. He's spent most of his adult life making up for this, and has since visited over 50 countries, including most in Southeast Asia. After university he worked briefly as a legislative assistant before quitting Capitol life in 1994 to backpack around West Africa. It was during this trip that the idea of becoming a freelance travel writer and photographer was hatched, and he's been at it ever since. This is his 12th book for Lonely Planet. The half of the year he isn't shouldering a backpack somewhere for work or pleasure he lives in Khon Kaen, Northeastern Thailand.

CATHERINE BODRY — Southeastern Thailand, Gulf Coast

Catherine grew up in the Pacific Northwest and moved to Alaska in her early 20s, so it's no surprise that frequent, extended tropical vacations were often in order. She first visited Thailand in 2004 as part of a round-the-world trip (which included only countries where the temperature stayed firmly above 30°C) and returned a year later to perfect her bargaining skills and eat as much curry as possible. This research trip marked Catherine's third visit to the country, and she's probably still sweating curry from it. When Catherine isn't flagging down 2nd-class buses and learning local slang on Lonely Planet research trips, she's usually tromping around the mountains near her home in Seward, Alaska.

AUSTIN BUSH — Bangkok, Northern Thailand, Food & Drink section

After graduating from the University of Oregon in 1999 with a degree in linguistics, Austin received a scholarship to study Thai at Chiang Mai University and has remained in Thailand ever since. After working several years at a stable job, he made the questionable decision to pursue a career as a freelance writer and photographer, endeavours that have taken him as far as Pakistan's Karakoram Highway and as near as Bangkok's Or Tor Kor Market. Austin enjoys writing about and taking photos of food most of all because it's a great way to connect with people. Samples of his work can be seen at www.austinbushphotography.com.

BRANDON PRESSER — Gulf Coast, Andaman Coast

Growing up in a land where bear hugs are taken literally, this wanderlust-y Canadian always craved swaying palms and golden sand. A trek across Southeast Asia as a teenager was the clincher – he was hooked, returning year after year to scuba dive, suntan and savour spoonfuls of spicy *sôm·dam* (papaya salad). Brandon was primed to research Thailand's top holiday destinations, but it wasn't all fun and games – there were beaches to be judged, curries to be sampled and kiteboards to be test-ridden. Brandon spends most of the year writing his way around the world and has co-authored several other Lonely Planet guides to Southeast Asia, including *Thailand's Islands & Beaches* and *Malaysia, Singapore & Brunei*.

CONTRIBUTING AUTHORS

Dr Trish Batchelor is a general practitioner and travel medicine specialist who currently works in Canberra and is Medical Advisor to the Travel Doctor New Zealand clinics. She has just returned from working in Vietnam and has previously worked in

Nepal and India. Trish teaches travel medicine through the University of Otago, New Zealand, and is interested in underwater and high-altitude medicine, and the impact of tourism on host countries. She has travelled extensively through Southeast and East Asia. She wrote the Health section for this edition.

David Lukas is a naturalist who lives on the edge of Yosemite National Park. He has contributed chapters on the environment and wildlife for nearly 30 Lonely Planet guides, including *Vietnam, Cambodia, Laos & the Greater Mekong*; *Thailand's Islands & Beaches*; *Bangkok*; *Thailand*. He wrote the Environment section for this edition.

Bhawan Ruangsilp wrote the History section. She is a native of Bangkok and a published historian of the Ayuthaya period at Chulalongkorn University. She finds 17th-century Western travel literature on Siam fascinating.

THIS BOOK

This 1st edition of *Discover Thailand* was coordinated by China Williams, and researched and written by Mark Beales, Tim Bewer, Catherine Bodry, Austin Bush and Brandon Presser. This guidebook was commissioned in Lonely Planet's Melbourne office, and produced by the following:

Commissioning Editor Tashi Wheeler
Coordinating Editor Dianne Schallmeiner
Coordinating Cartographer Corey Hutchison
Coordinating Layout Designer Jim Hsu
Managing Editor Liz Heynes
Managing Cartographer David Connolly
Managing Layout Designer Sally Darmody
Assisting Editor Rowan McKinnon
Assisting Cartographer Alex Leung
Cover Naomi Parker, lonelyplanetimages.com
Internal image research Sabrina Dalbesio, lonelyplanetimages.com
Project Manager Chris Girdler
Language Content Annelies Mertens

Thanks to Sasha Baskett, Glenn Beanland, Yvonne Bischofberger, Stefanie Di Trocchio, Eoin Dunlevy, Bruce Evans, Ryan Evans, Suki Gear, Joshua Geoghegan, Mark Germanchis, Michelle Glynn, Brice Gosnell, Imogen Hall, Jane Hart, Steve Henderson, Lauren Hunt, Laura Jane, Chris Lee Ack, Nic Lehman, Alison Lyall, James Hardy, John Mazzocchi, Jennifer Mullins, Wayne Murphy, Darren O'Connell, Naomi Parker, Piers Pickard, Howard Ralley, Lachlan Ross, Julie Sheridan, Jason Shugg, Caroline Sieg, Naomi Stephens, Geoff Stringer, Jane Thompson, Sam Trafford, Clifton Wilkinson, Juan Winata, Emily K Wolman, Nick Wood

Internal photographs p4 Coral rock cod, Michael Aw; p10 Monks on morning alms round, Austin Bush; p12 Phra Mahathat Naphamethanidon, Felix Hug; p31 Bananas, Damnoen Saduak Floating Market, Viviane Ponti; p39 Ko Muk, Trang, Frank Carter;

p3, p50 Shopper, Chinatown, Bangkok, Greg Elms; p3, p97 Wat Phra That Doi Suthep, Felix Hug; p3, p123 Ayuthaya, James Marshall; p3, p143 Hill-tribe girls, Antony Giblin; p3, p191 Trishaw detail, Phimai, Tom Cockrem; p3, p217 Timber jetty, Ko Samet, Frank Carter; p3, p239 Spa at Anantara, Ko Samui, Austin Bush; p3, p279 Wooden boat bow, Maya Bay, Felix Hug; p320 Buddhist monks, Yi Peng Sansai Kathina Ceremony, Felix Hug; p367 Market stall, Bangkok, John Hay

All images are copyright of the photographer unless otherwise indicated. Many of the images in this guide are available for licensing from Lonely Planet Images: www .lonelyplanetimages.com.

BEHIND THE SCENES

THIS BOOK

SEND US YOUR FEEDBACK

We love to hear from travellers – your comments keep us on our toes and help make our books better. Our well-travelled team reads every word on what you loved or loathed about this book. Although we cannot reply individually to postal submissions, we always guarantee that your feedback goes straight to the appropriate authors, in time for the next edition. Each person who sends us information is thanked in the next edition and the most useful submissions are rewarded with a free book.

To send us your updates – and find out about Lonely Planet events, newsletters and travel news – visit our award-winning website: lonelyplanet.com/contact.

Note: we may edit, reproduce and incorporate your comments in Lonely Planet products such as guidebooks, websites and digital products, so let us know if you don't want your comments reproduced or your name acknowledged. For a copy of our privacy policy visit lonelyplanet.com/privacy.

NOTES

NOTES

↘INDEX

INDEX

C–E

000 Map pages
000 Photograph pages

000 Map pages
000 Photograph pages

INDEX

P–S

MAP LEGEND

ROUTES

Tollway	One-Way Street
Freeway	Mall/Steps
Primary	Tunnel
Secondary	Pedestrian Overpass
Tertiary	Walking Tour
Lane	Walking Tour Detour
Under Construction	Walking Path
Unsealed Road	Track

TRANSPORT

Ferry	Rail/Underground
Metro	Tram
Monorail	Cable Car, Funicular

HYDROGRAPHY

River, Creek	Canal
Intermittent River	Water
Swamp/Mangrove	Dry Lake/Salt Lake
Reef	Glacier

BOUNDARIES

International	Regional, Suburb
State, Provincial	Marine Park
Disputed	Cliff/Ancient Wall

AREA FEATURES

Area of Interest	Forest
Beach, Desert	Mall/Market
Building/Urban Area	Park
Cemetery, Christian	Restricted Area
Cemetery, Other	Sports

POPULATION

✪ **CAPITAL (NATIONAL)**	◉ **CAPITAL (STATE)**
● **LARGE CITY**	● **Medium City**
● Small City	● Town, Village

SYMBOLS

Sights/Activities

Buddhist	
Canoeing, Kayaking	
Castle, Fortress	
Christian	
Confucian	
Diving	
Hindu	
Islamic	
Jain	
Jewish	
Monument	
Museum, Gallery	
Point of Interest	
Pool	
Ruin	
Sento (Public Hot Baths)	
Shinto	
Sikh	
Skiing	
Surfing, Surf Beach	
Taoist	
Trail Head	
Winery, Vineyard	
Zoo, Bird Sanctuary	

Information

Bank, ATM	
Embassy/Consulate	
Hospital, Medical	
Information	
Internet Facilities	
Police Station	
Post Office, GPO	
Telephone	
Toilets	
Wheelchair Access	

Eating
Eating

Drinking
Cafe
Drinking

Entertainment
Entertainment

Shopping
Shopping

Sleeping
Camping
Sleeping

Transport

Airport, Airfield	
Border Crossing	
Bus Station	
Bicycle Path/Cycling	
FFCC (Barcelona)	
Metro (Barcelona)	
Parking Area	
Petrol Station	
S-Bahn	
Taxi Rank	
Tube Station	
U-Bahn	

Geographic

Beach	
Lighthouse	
Lookout	
Mountain, Volcano	
National Park	
Pass, Canyon	
Picnic Area	
River Flow	
Shelter, Hut	
Waterfall	

LONELY PLANET OFFICES

Australia

Head Office
Locked Bag 1, Footscray, Victoria 3011
☎ 03 8379 8000, fax 03 8379 8111
talk2us@lonelyplanet.com.au

USA

150 Linden St, Oakland, CA 94607
☎ 510 250 6400, toll free 800 275 8555,
fax 510 893 8572
info@lonelyplanet.com

UK

2nd fl, 186 City Rd,
London EC1V 2NT
☎ 020 7106 2100, fax 020 7106 2101
go@lonelyplanet.co.uk

Published by Lonely Planet
ABN 36 005 607 983

Printed by Hang Tai Printing Company, Hong Kong
Printed in China